NEW YORK REVIEW COMICS

FATHER AND SON

E.O. PLAUEN was the pseudonym of Erich Ohser (1903–1944). In the 1920s, he studied art in Leipzig and began a career as a cartoonist and illustrator. He moved to Berlin in 1927, and began collaborating with his friend, the writer Erich Kästner, including drawing illustrations for Kästner's first book of poetry (which would later be burned by the Nazis). Ohser's caricatures of high-ranking Nazis such as Goebbels and Hitler led to his being banned from publishing after they took power. Unable to use his own name, he paired his initials, "E.O.," with "Plauen," the town he grew up in, and using this pseudonym created *Vater und Sohn* in 1934; it appeared in the *Berliner Illustrirte Zeitung*, to great acclaim, until 1937. Though he was allowed to return to regular magazine work in 1940—his caricatures of Stalin were especially popular—he was arrested four years later by the Gestapo for disparaging the regime. The day before his trial, he committed suicide in his cell.

JOEL ROTENBERG was trained as a linguist and now translates from German and French. He lives in New York.

NOV   2017

THIS IS A NEW YORK REVIEW COMIC
PUBLISHED BY THE NEW YORK REVIEW OF BOOKS
435 Hudson Street, New York, NY 10014
www.nyrb.com

© Graphic design by WARUM—Wandrille, 2015

"A Note on the Text" adapted from the text of the WARUM edition of *Pere et Fils* by Marc Lizano, Sylvain Farge, and Dominique Herody

Biographical afterword copyright © 2015 Philipp Reclam jun. GmbH & Co. KG, Stuttgart

A catalog record for this book is available from the Library of Congress

ISBN 978-1-68137-120-7
Available as an electronic book; ISBN 978-1-68137-121-4

Printed in the United States of America
10 9 8 7 6 5 4 3 2 1

FATHER AND SON

E.O. PLAUEN

Translated by
JOEL ROTENBERG

Lettering by
JEREMY SORESE

Biographical afterword by
ELKE SCHULZE

NEW YORK REVIEW COMICS · *New York*

A note on the preparation of this book

A foreign edition of any book is an interpretation—even if the book is mostly wordless, as in this case. This note explains the decisions we have made.

Our aim in this complete edition was to create the most accessible edition possible, while respecting the original intent of E. O. Plauen. Plauen's original drawings were lost in a studio fire; most of the strips were scanned from contemporaneous published compilations drawn from the *Berliner Illustrirte Zeitung*. These documents, not all of which were in the best condition, were reproduced unchanged in most subsequent collections.

Some of the drawings were damaged, some details lost, some lines weakened. Where the artist's intention was clear, the drawings have been completed, the lines strengthened, and the frames cleaned up, in order to provide the smoothest possible reading.

For the hand-lettered text within the comics, cartoonist Jeremy Sorese drew new lettering that recreates the look and feel of Plauen's original lettering.

In their original publication, the comics' panels were numbered to assist readers unaccustomed to reading comic strips. These numbers have been removed in this edition.

Western comic strips in our era have long had the characters move from left to right, so that the reader would turn the pages to follow the action. Plauen didn't always adhere to the formula, so much of the action in the strips—running, fleeing, movement out of frame—proceed from right to left. A mirror-image reversal would have been simple, but the drawings were meant to be read the other way and would have lost some of their impact. Action panels have therefore been left unchanged.

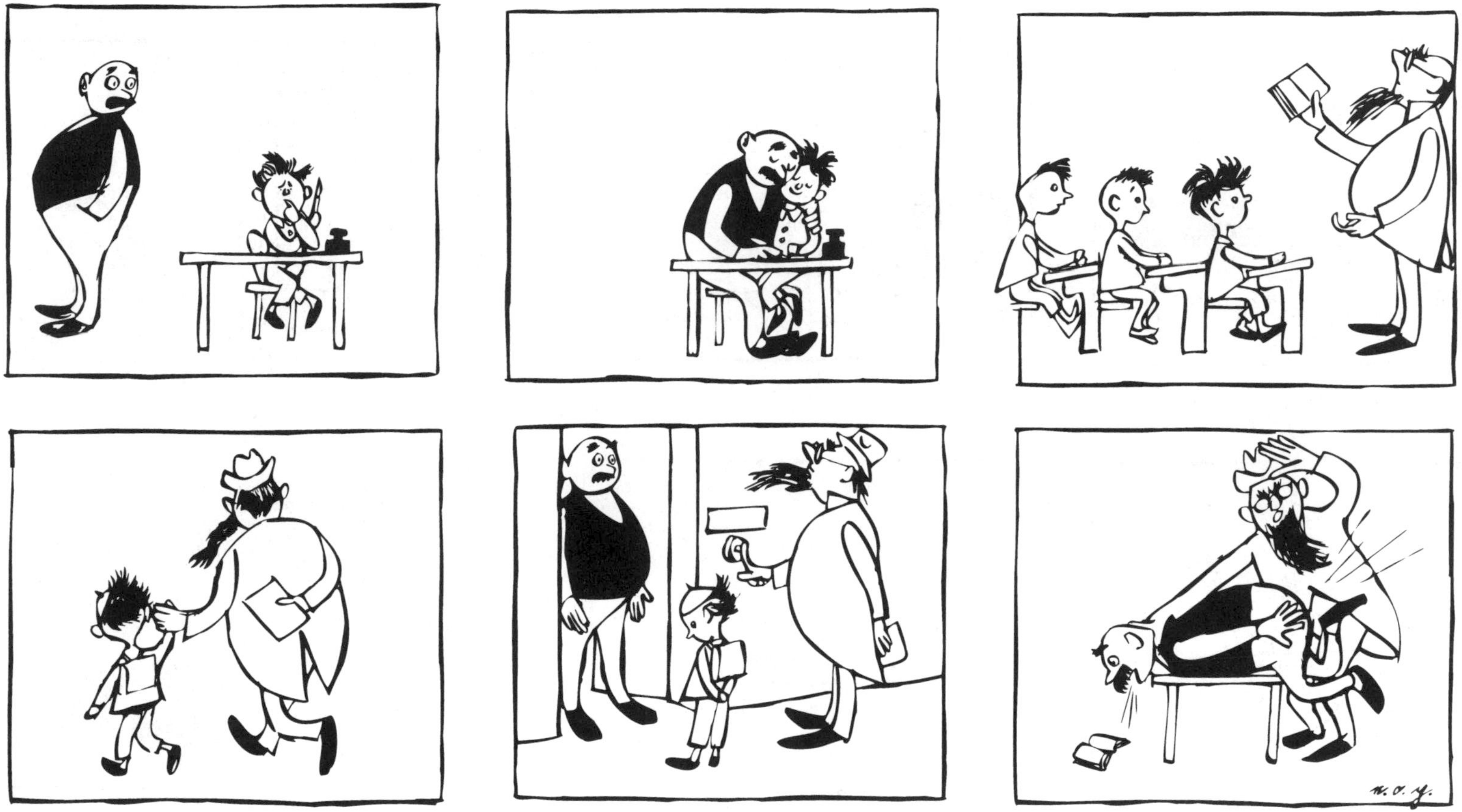

Some help from father

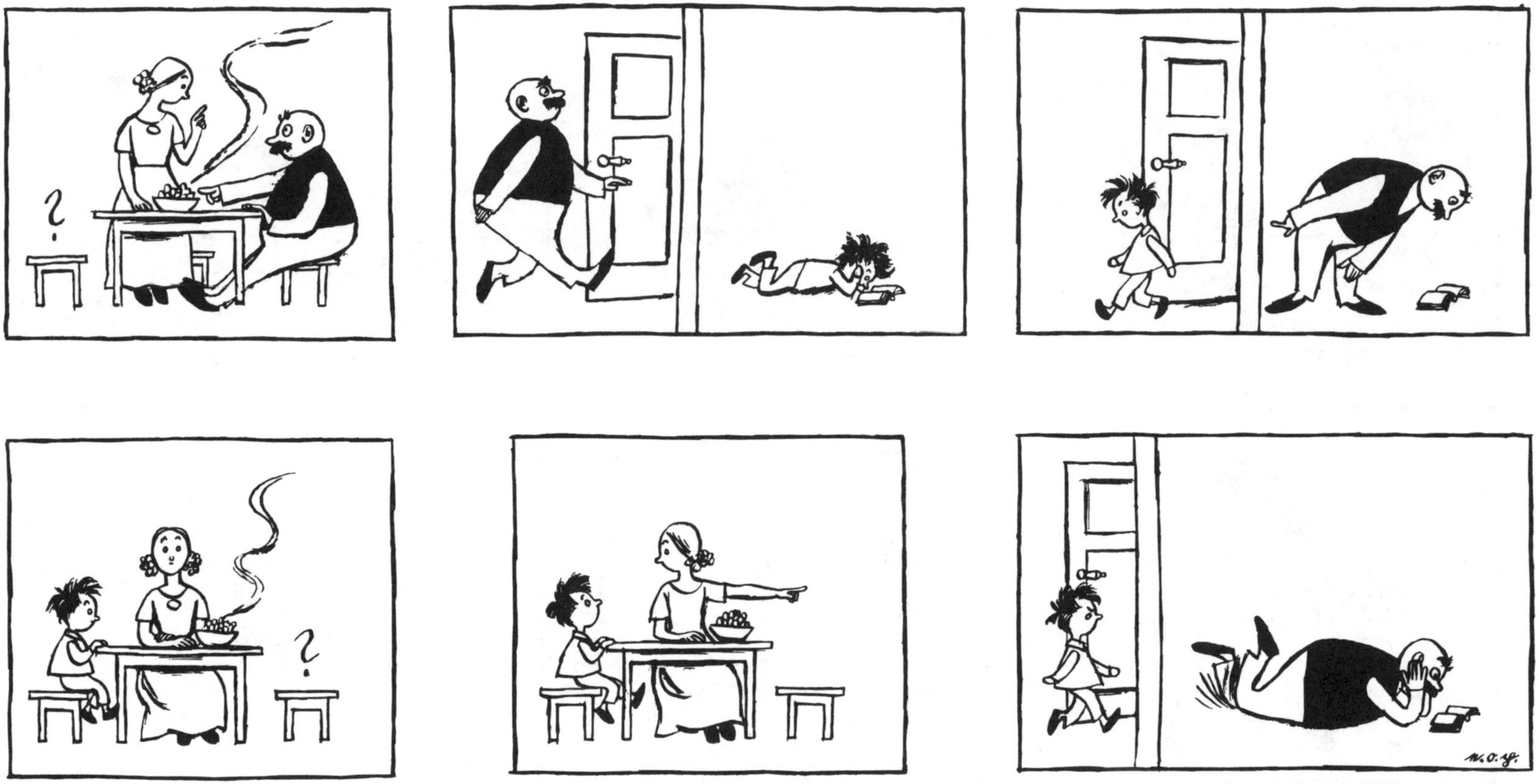

The page-turner

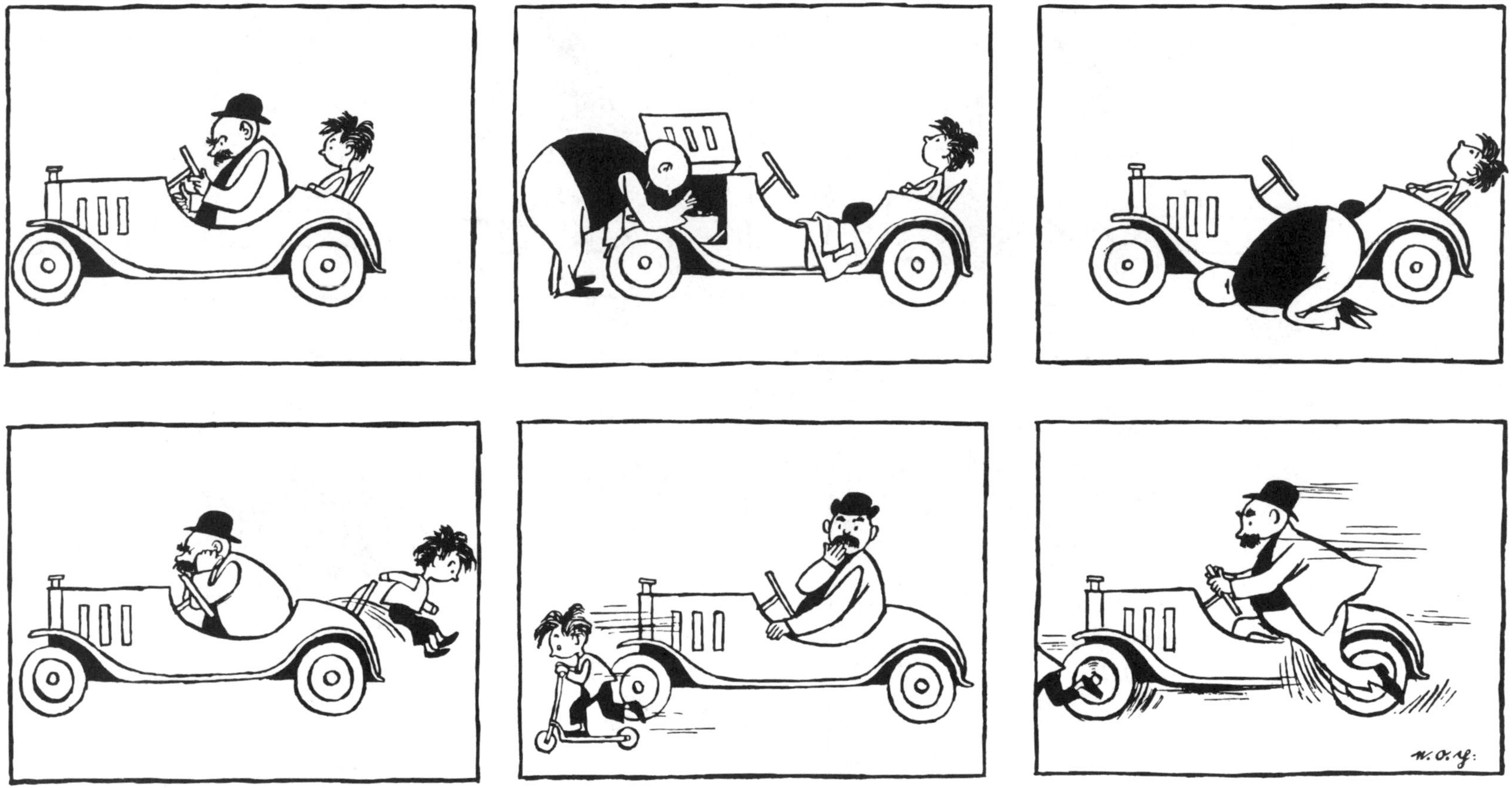

Little scooter, big scooter

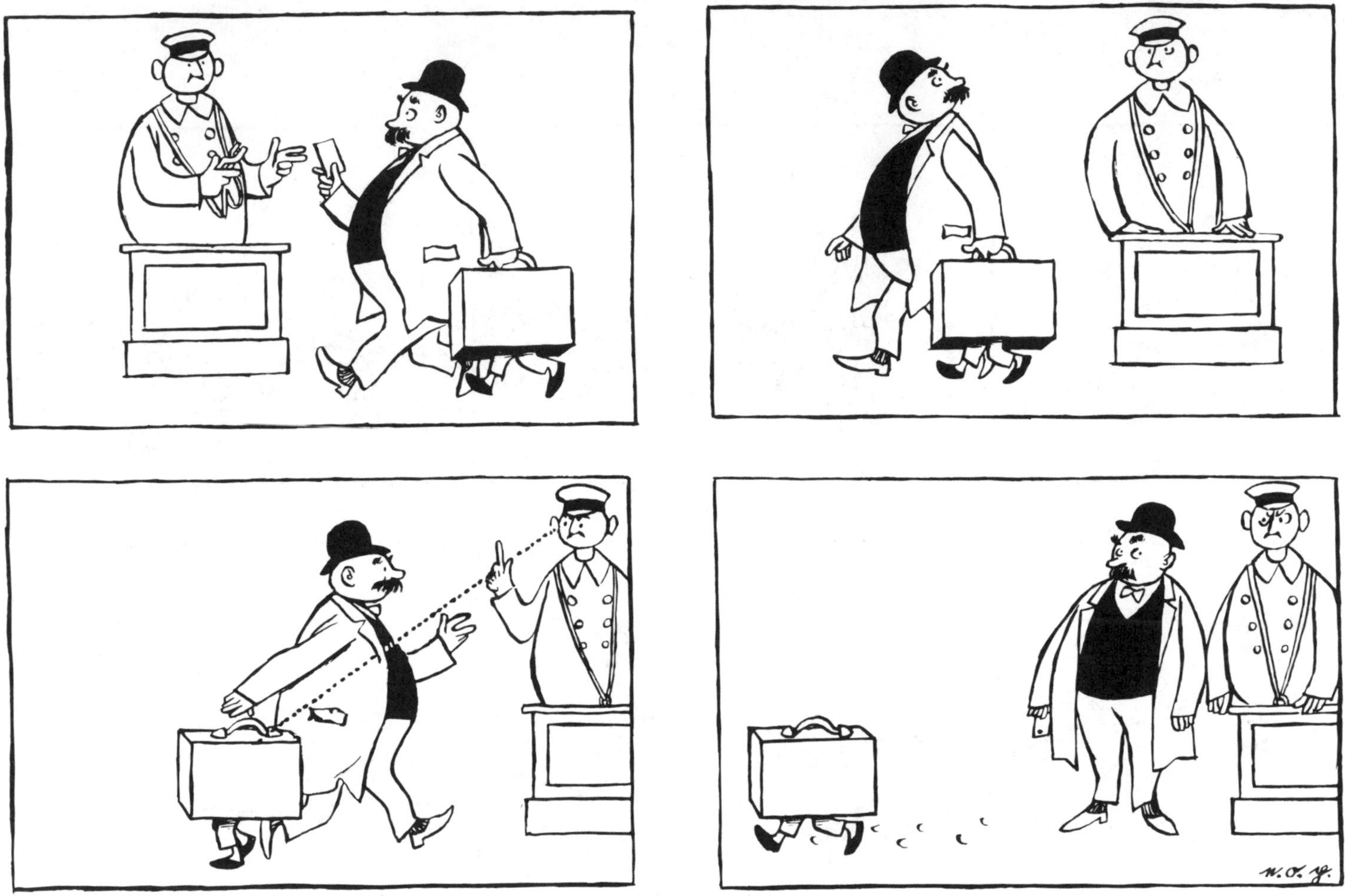

The fugitive suitcase

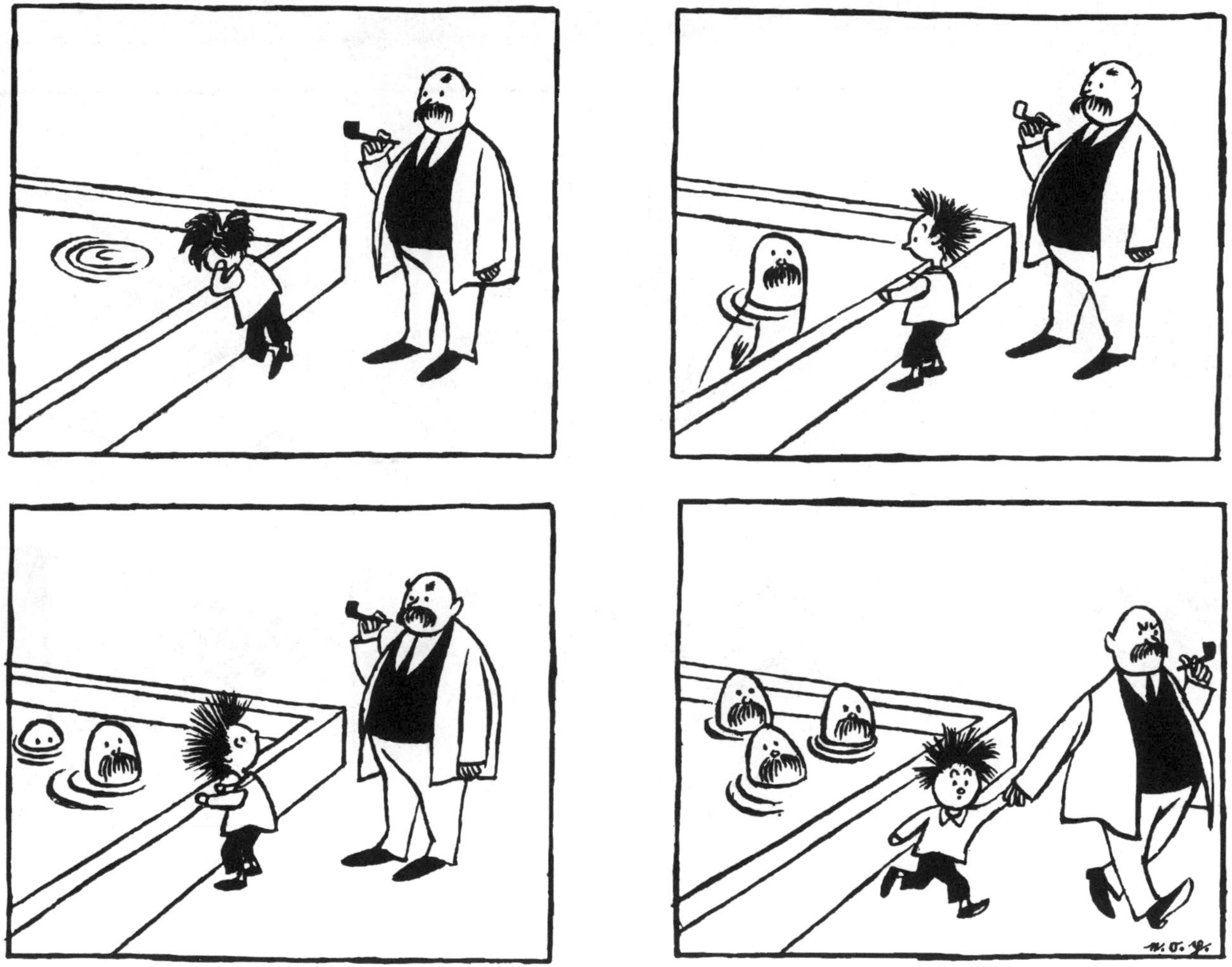

Resemblance

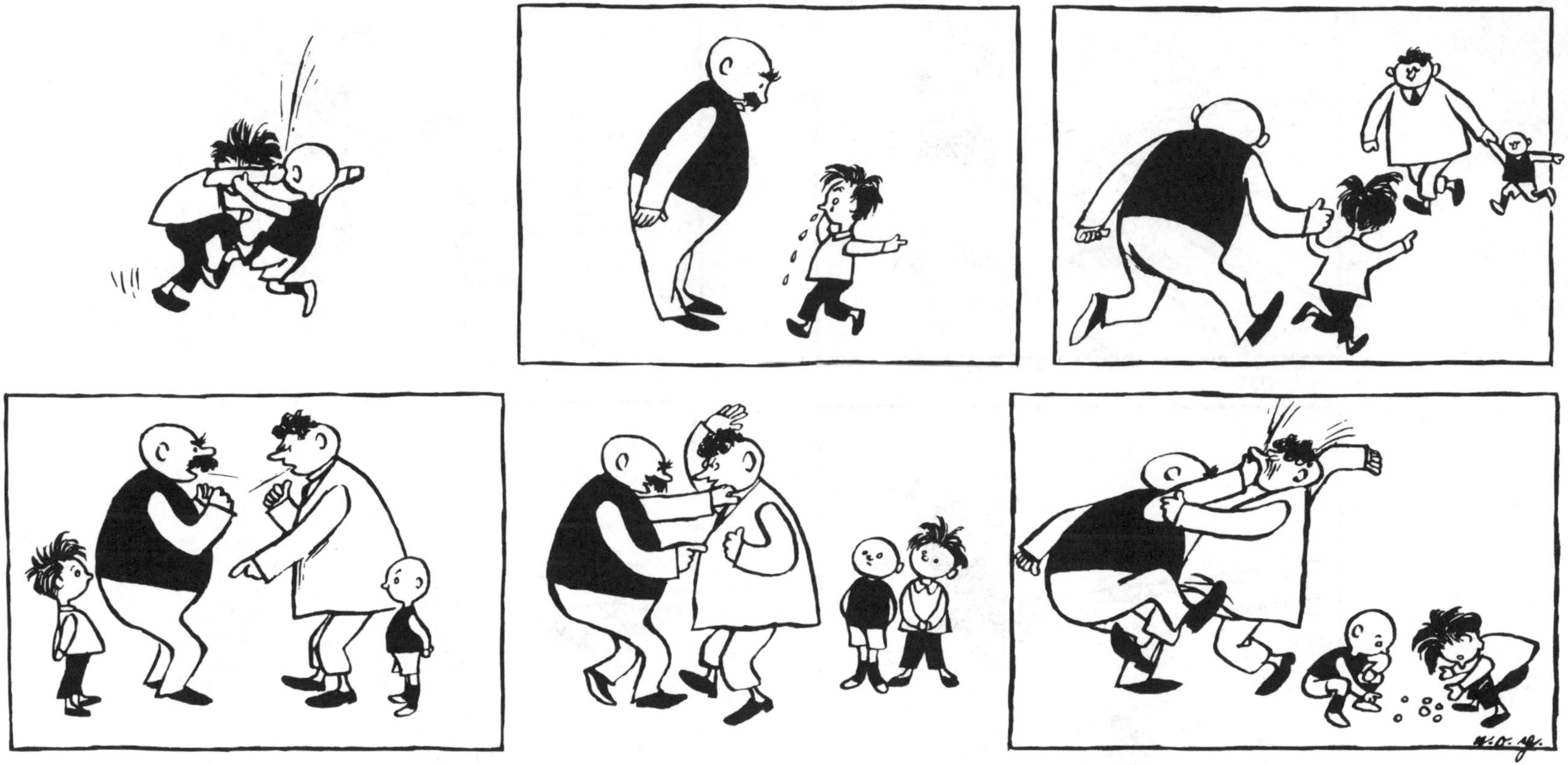

Like father, like son

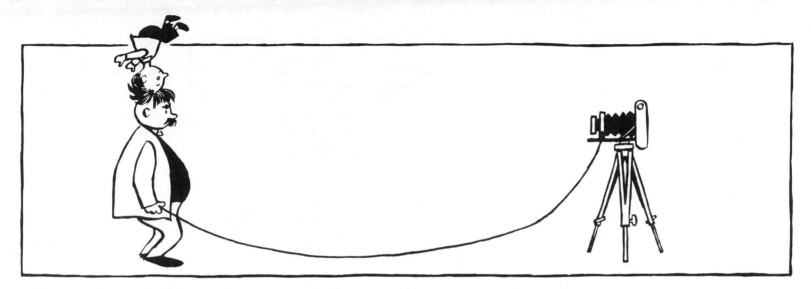

Nicely cropped

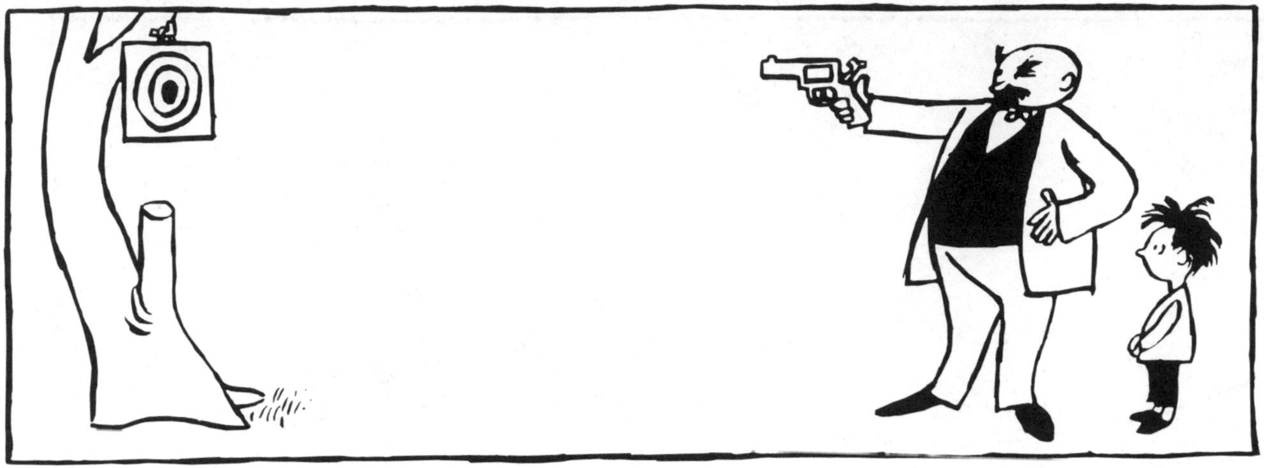
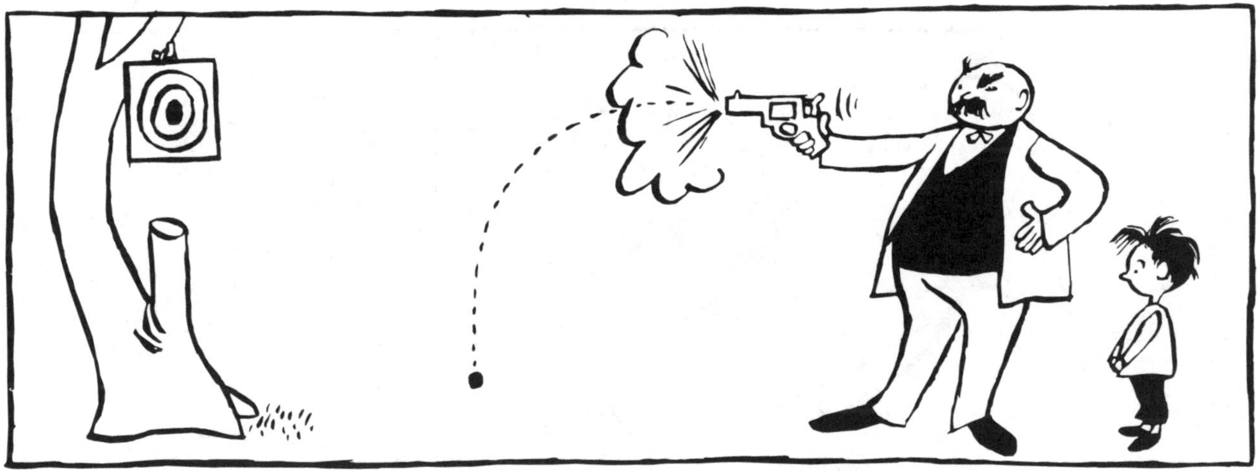

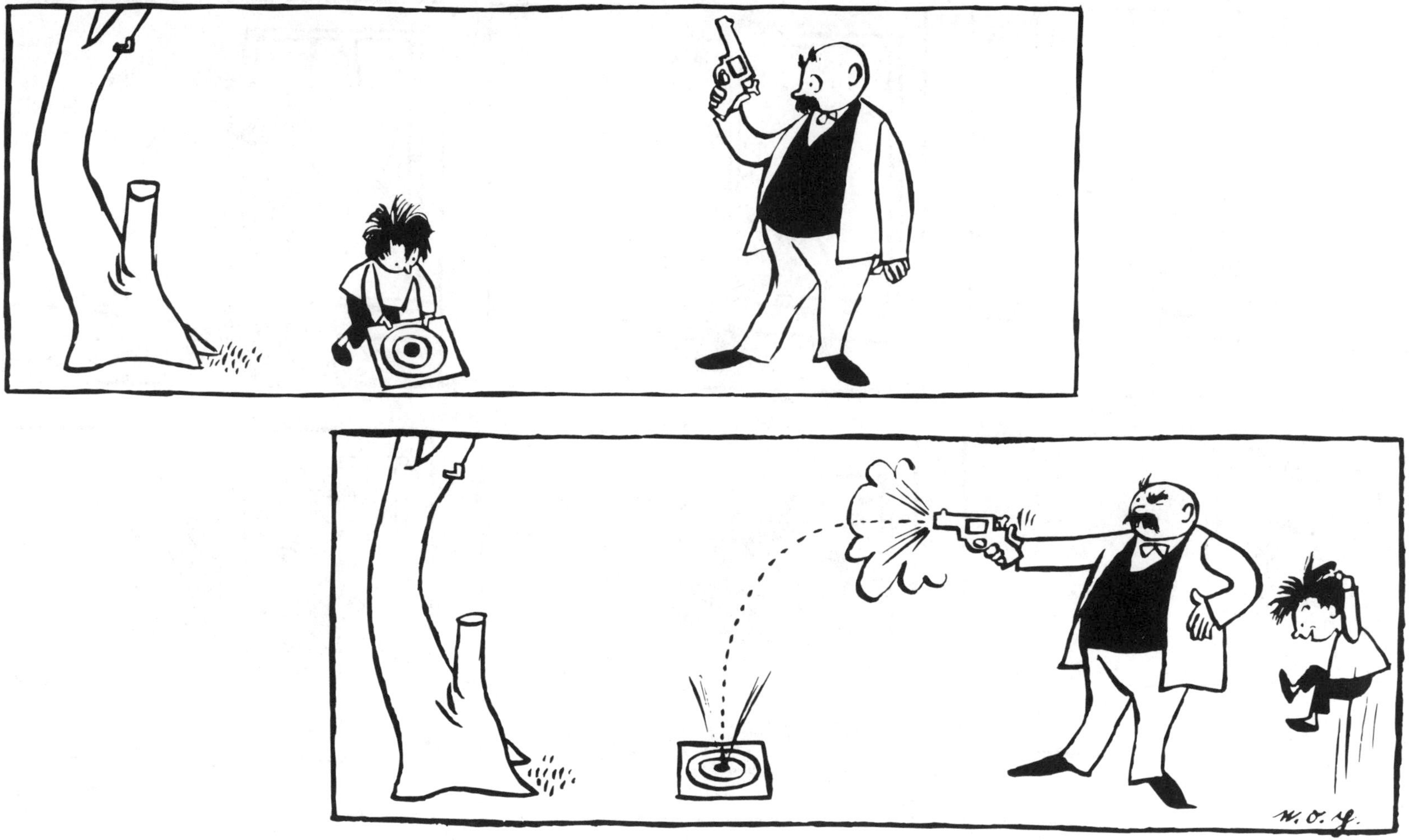

Target practice

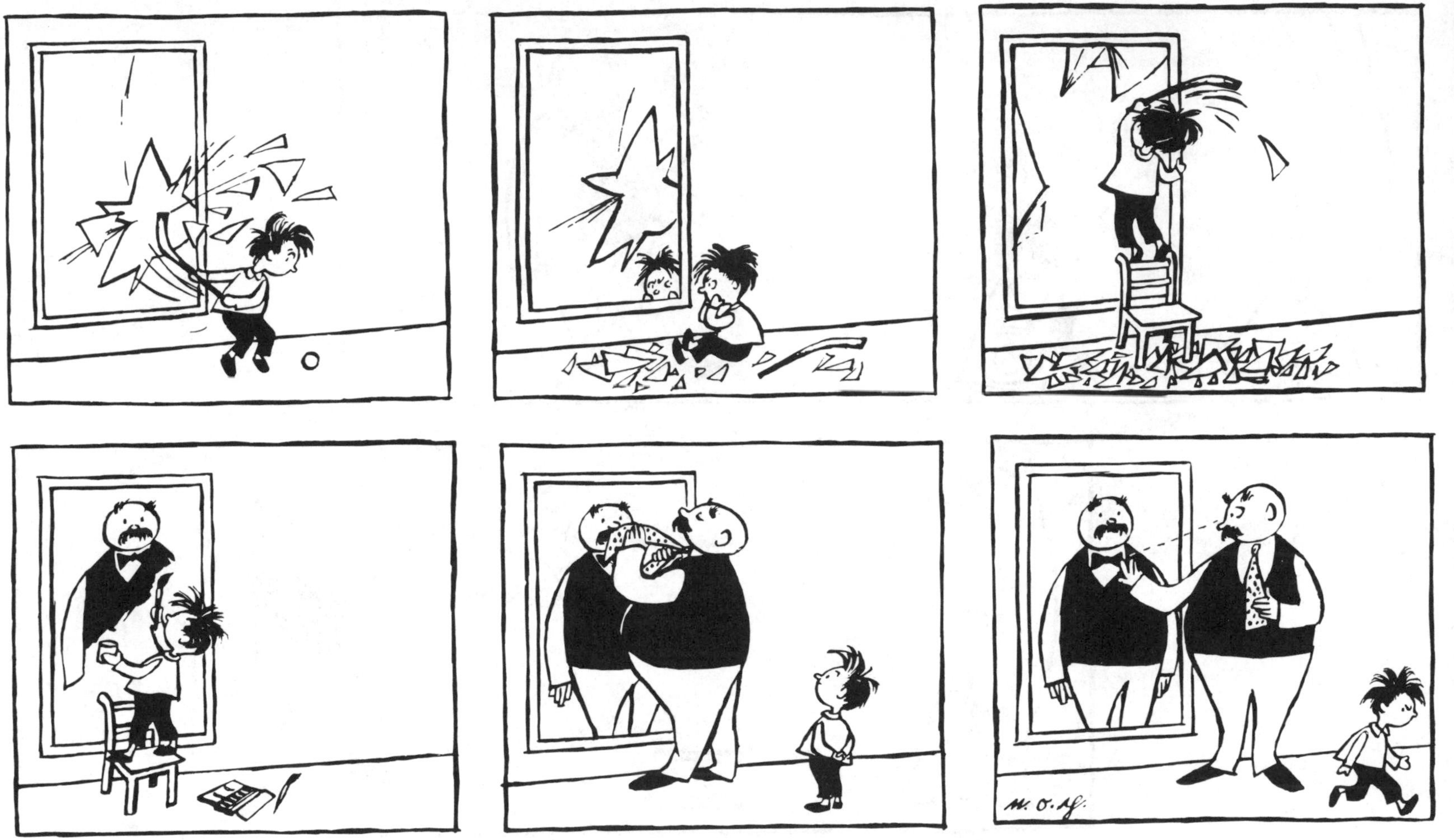

The limits of art

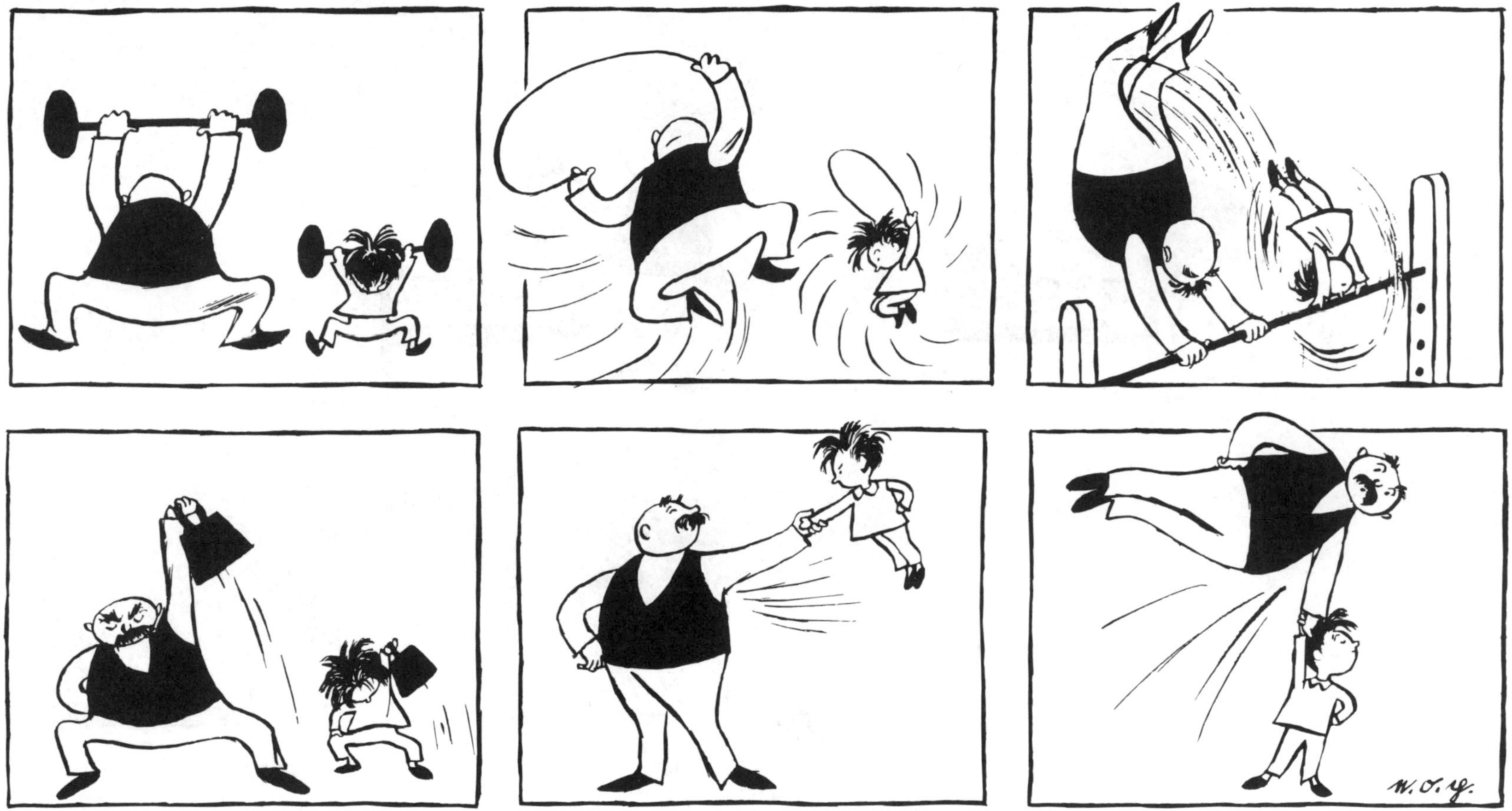

Practice makes perfect

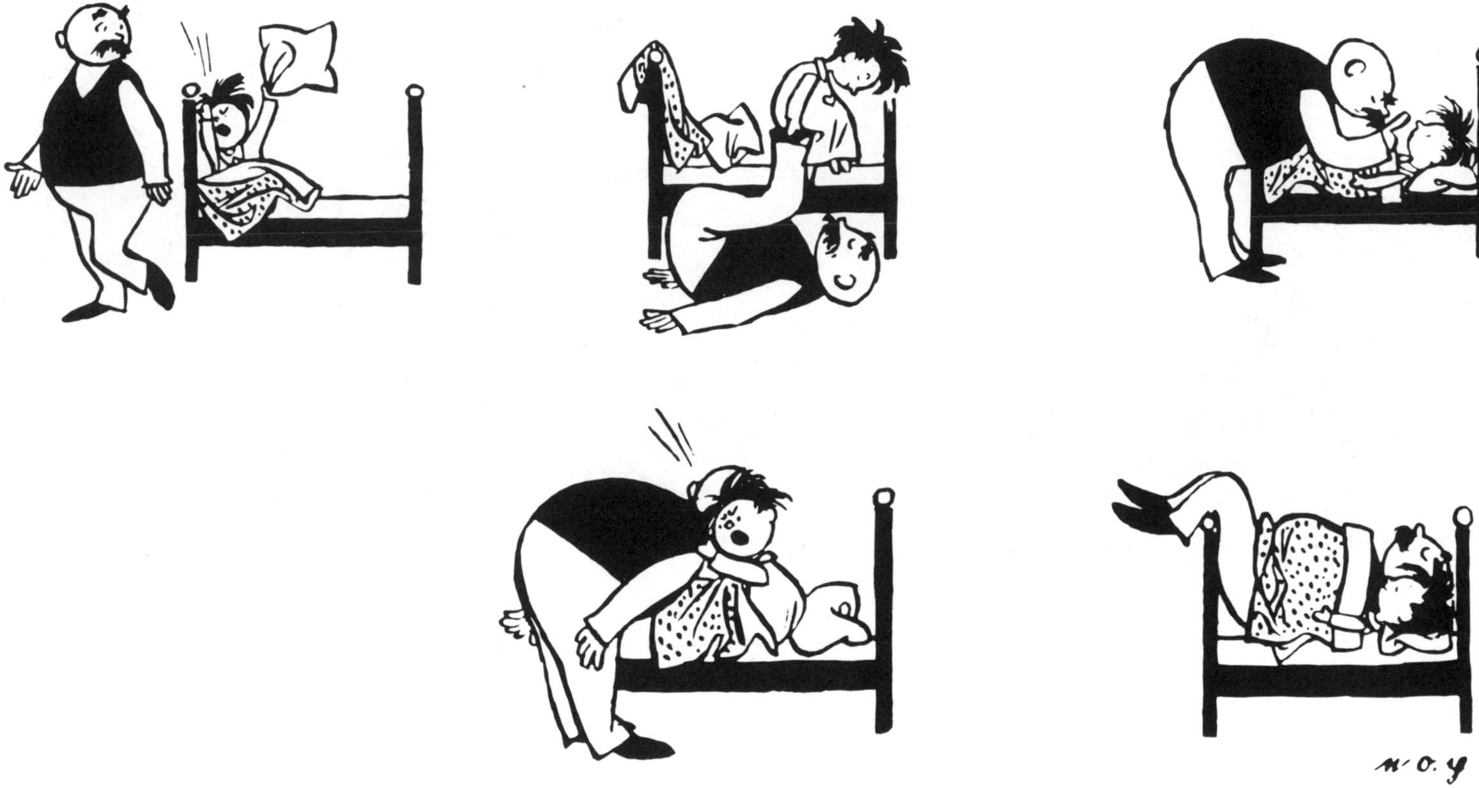

Bedtime

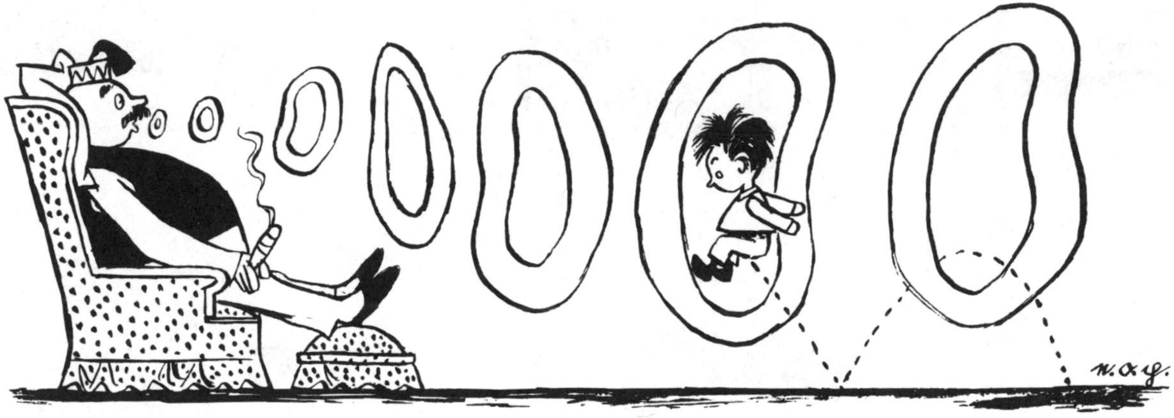
w.a.g.

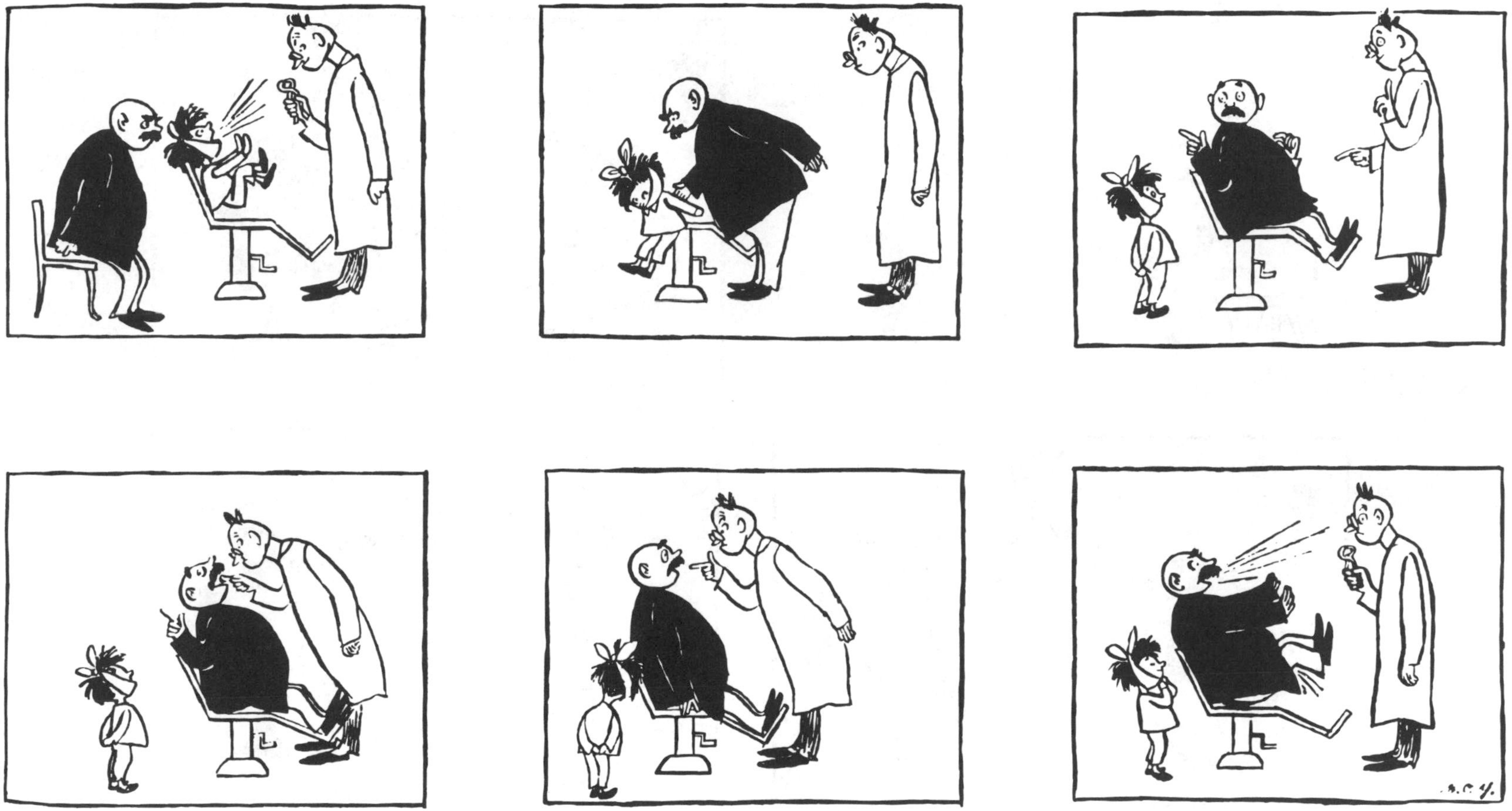

The good example

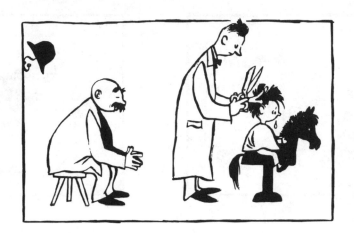

"Long in front, short in back!"

RAISINS

RAISINS

RAISINS

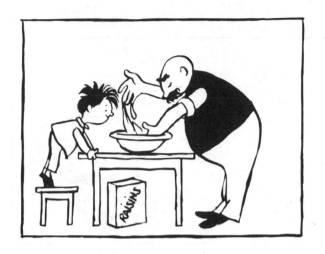

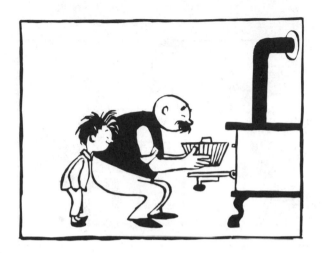

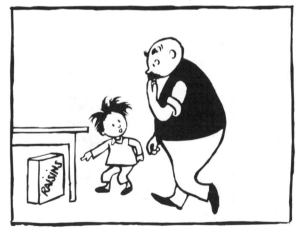

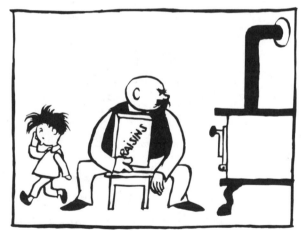

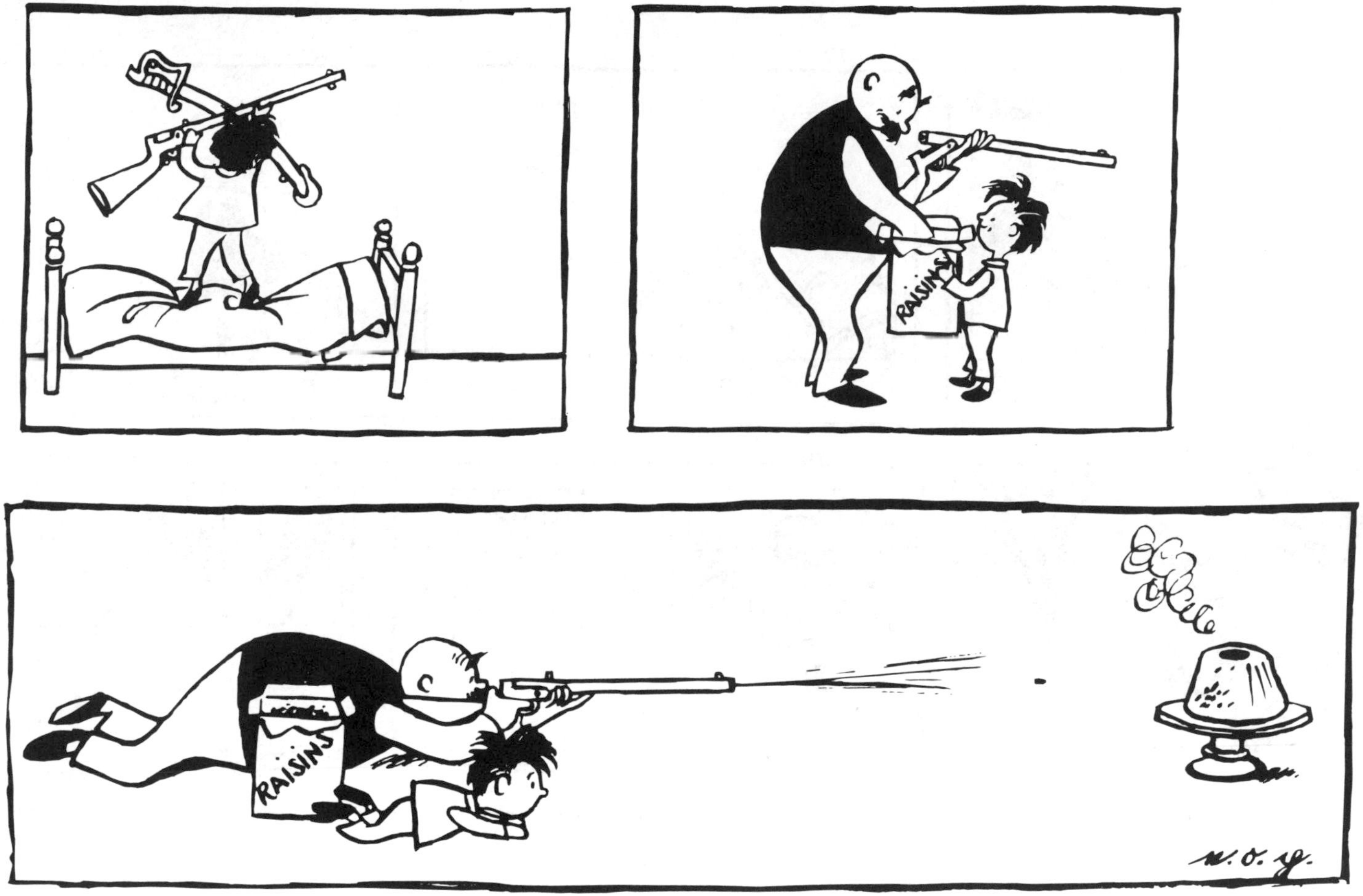
RAISINS
RAISINS

The forgotten raisins

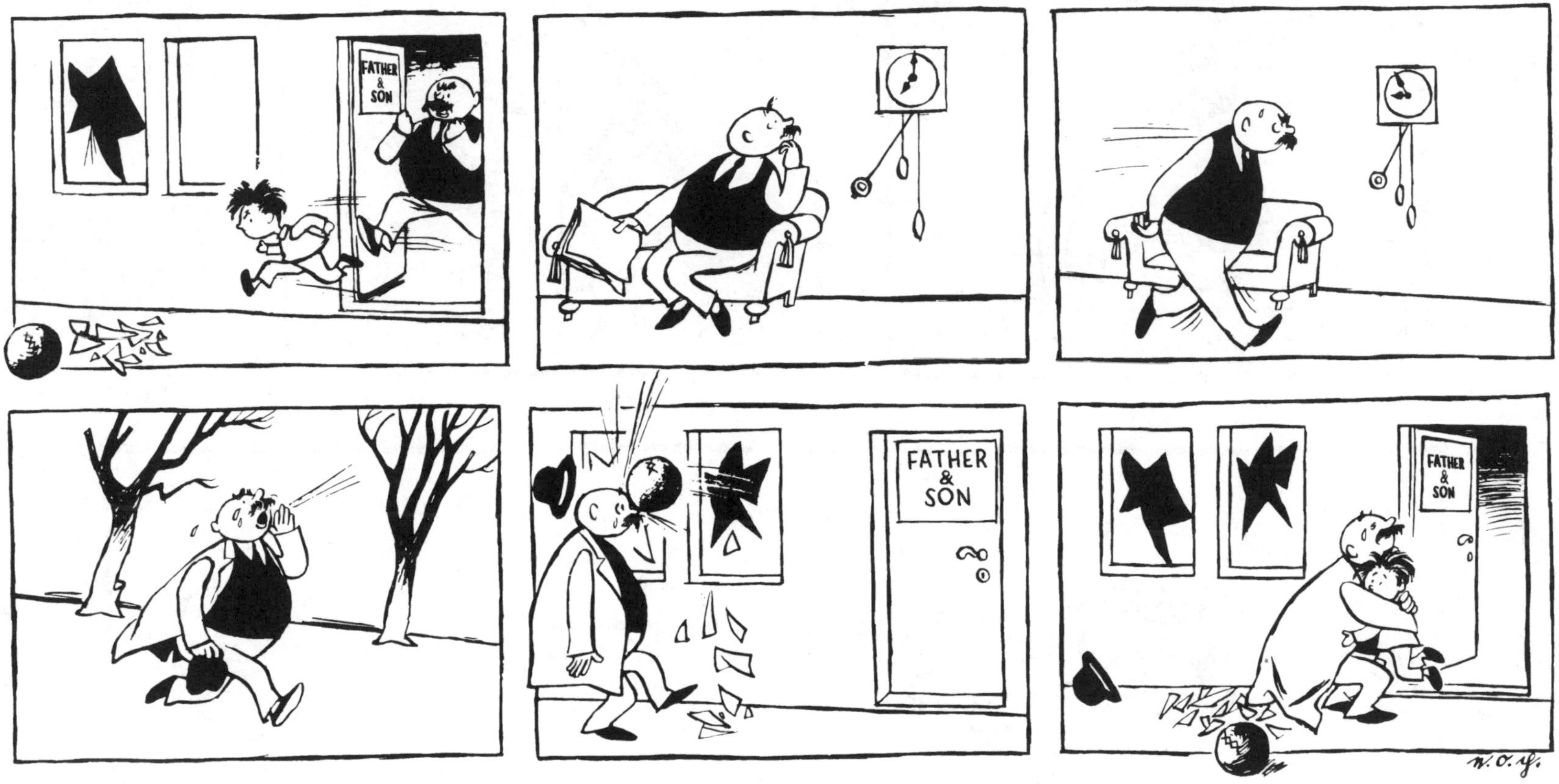
FATHER & SON
FATHER & SON
FATHER & SON

The prodigal son

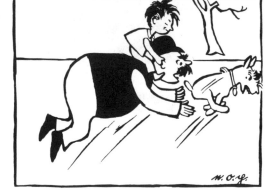

Horse and rider

27

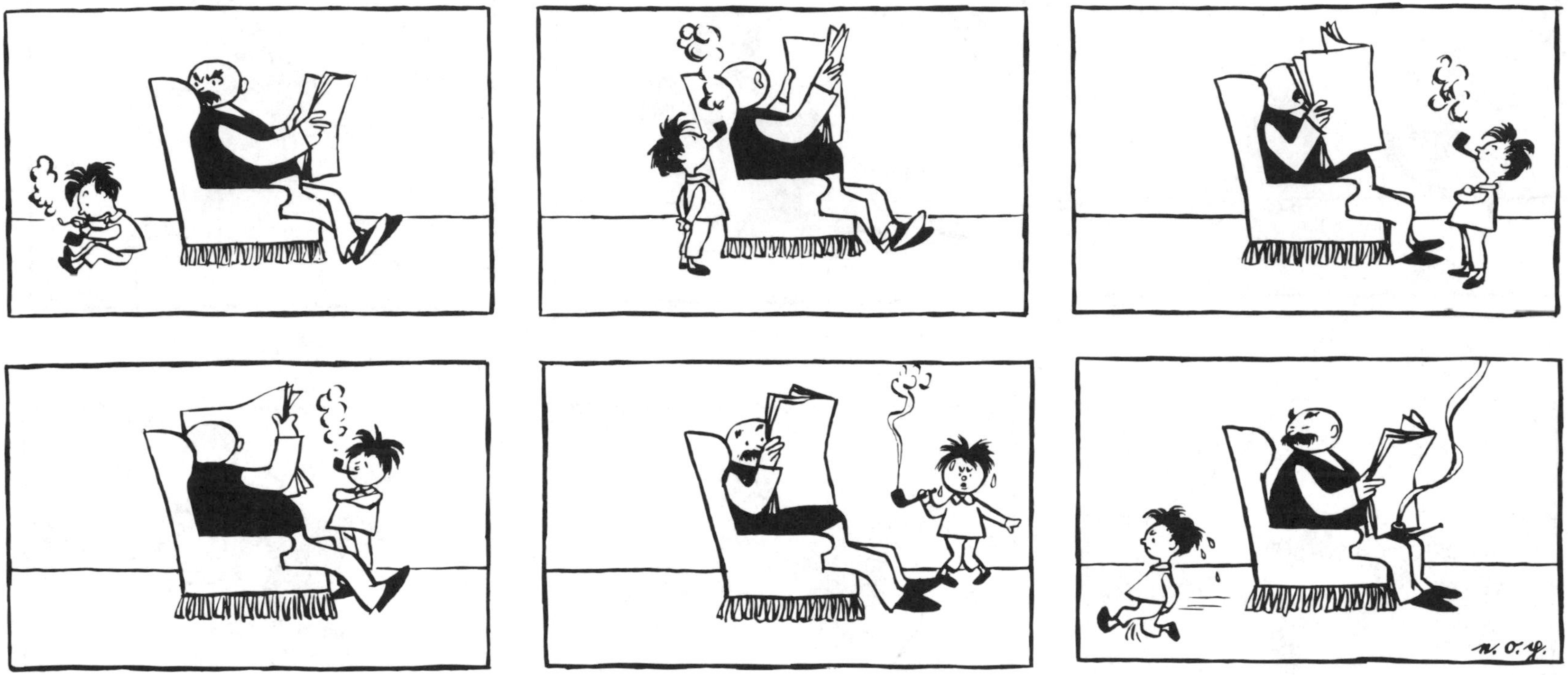

Unsuccessful provocation

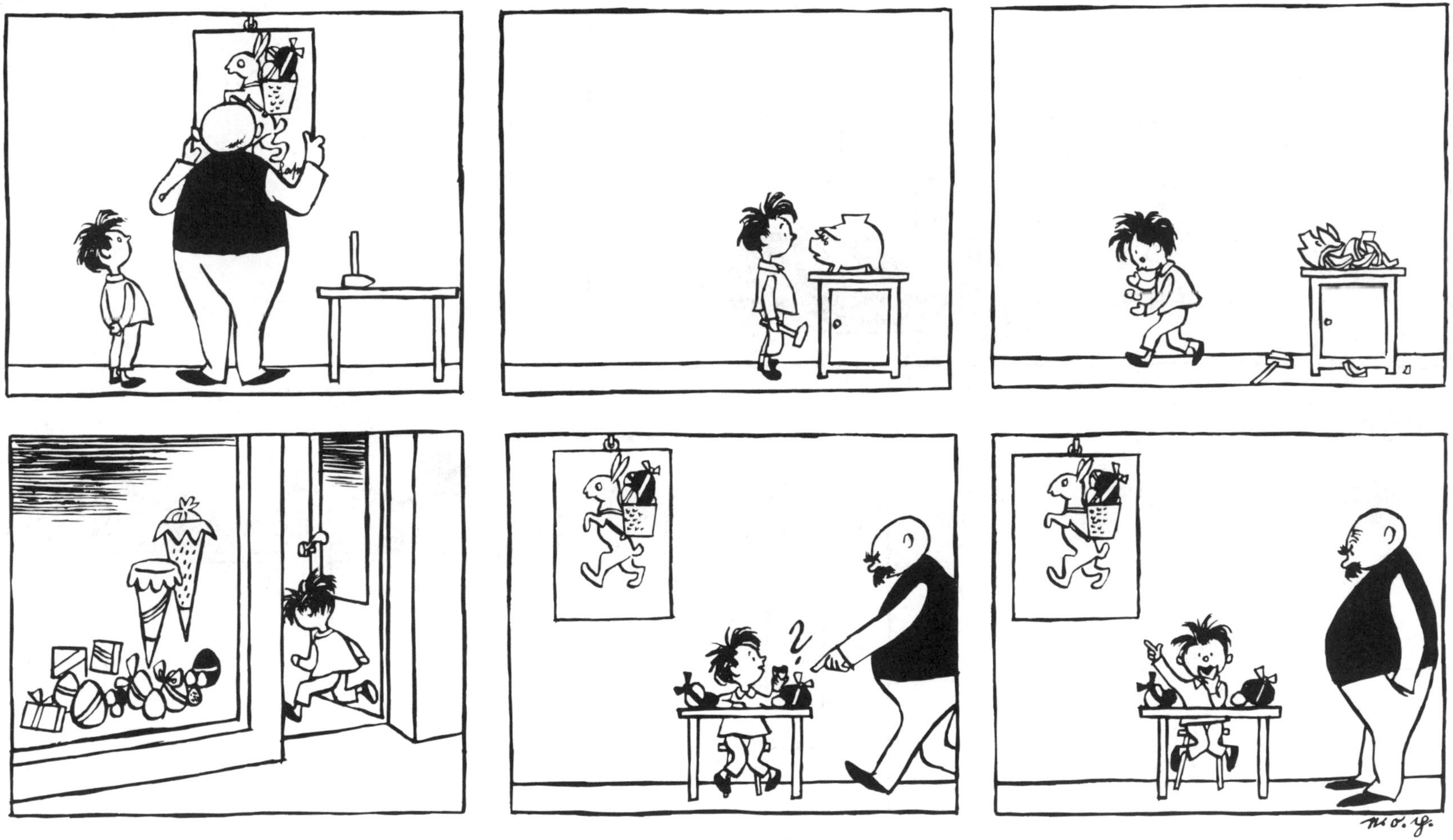

Easter eggs come from the Easter bunny

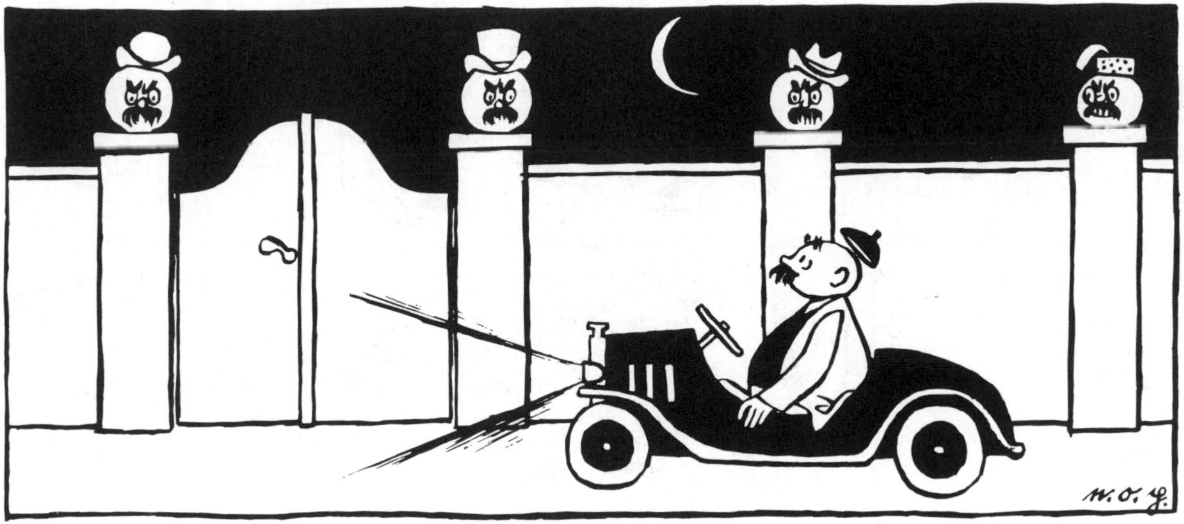

w. o. g.

The revenge of the stay-at-home

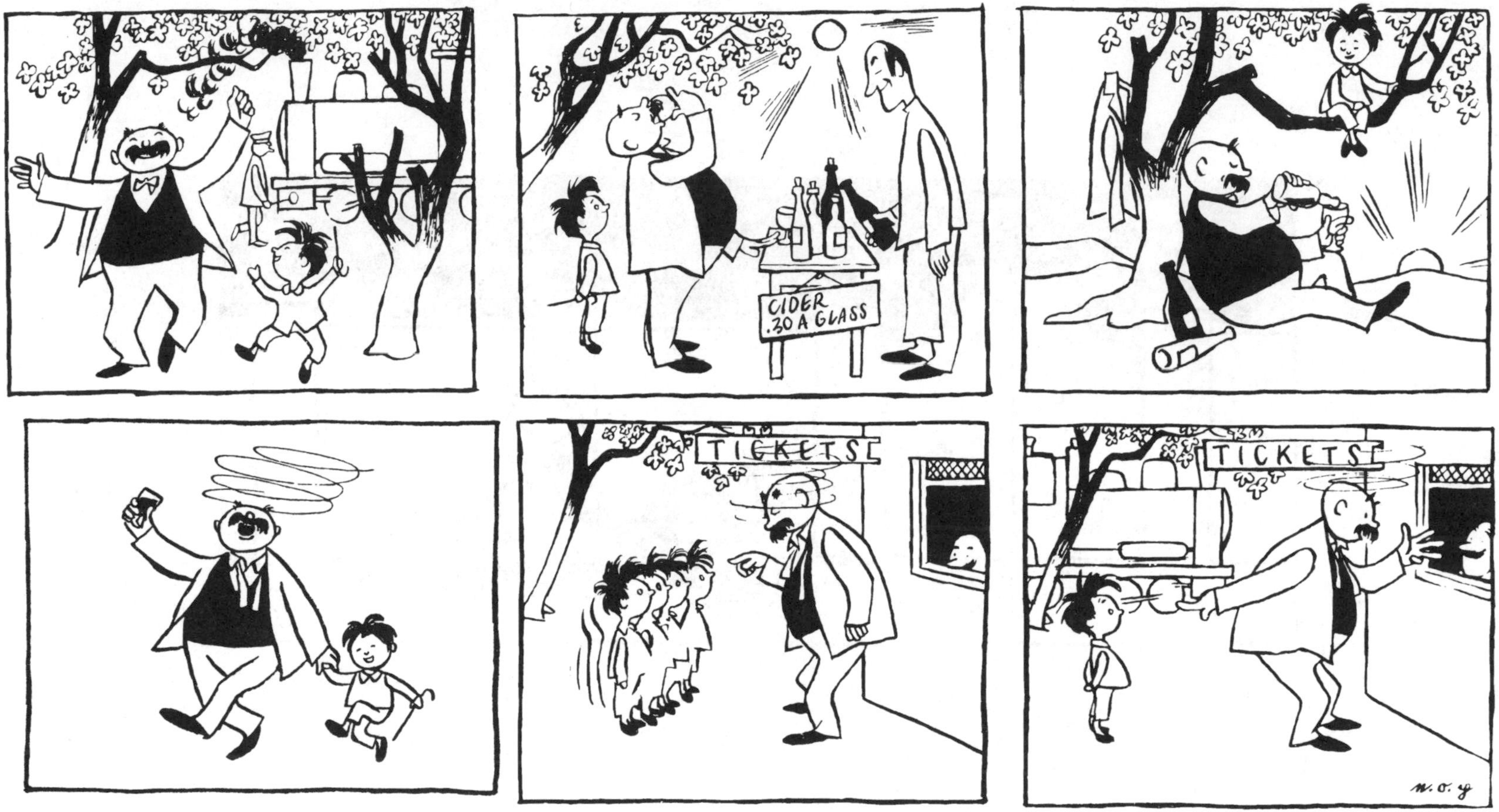
CIDER
.30 A GLASS
TICKETS
TICKETS

"Four child's fares, please!"

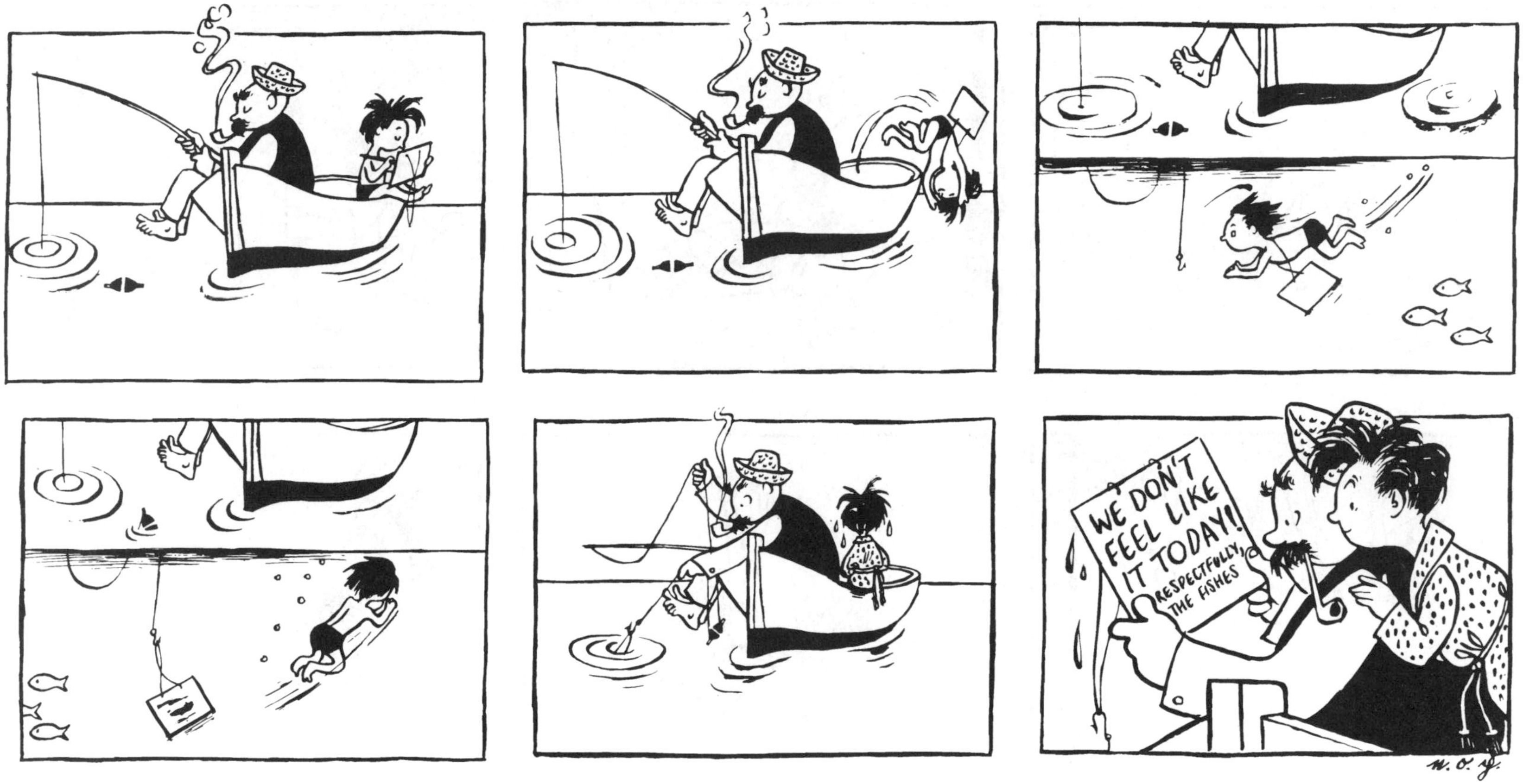
WE DON'T FEEL LIKE IT TODAY!
RESPECTFULLY, THE FISHES

A letter from the fishes

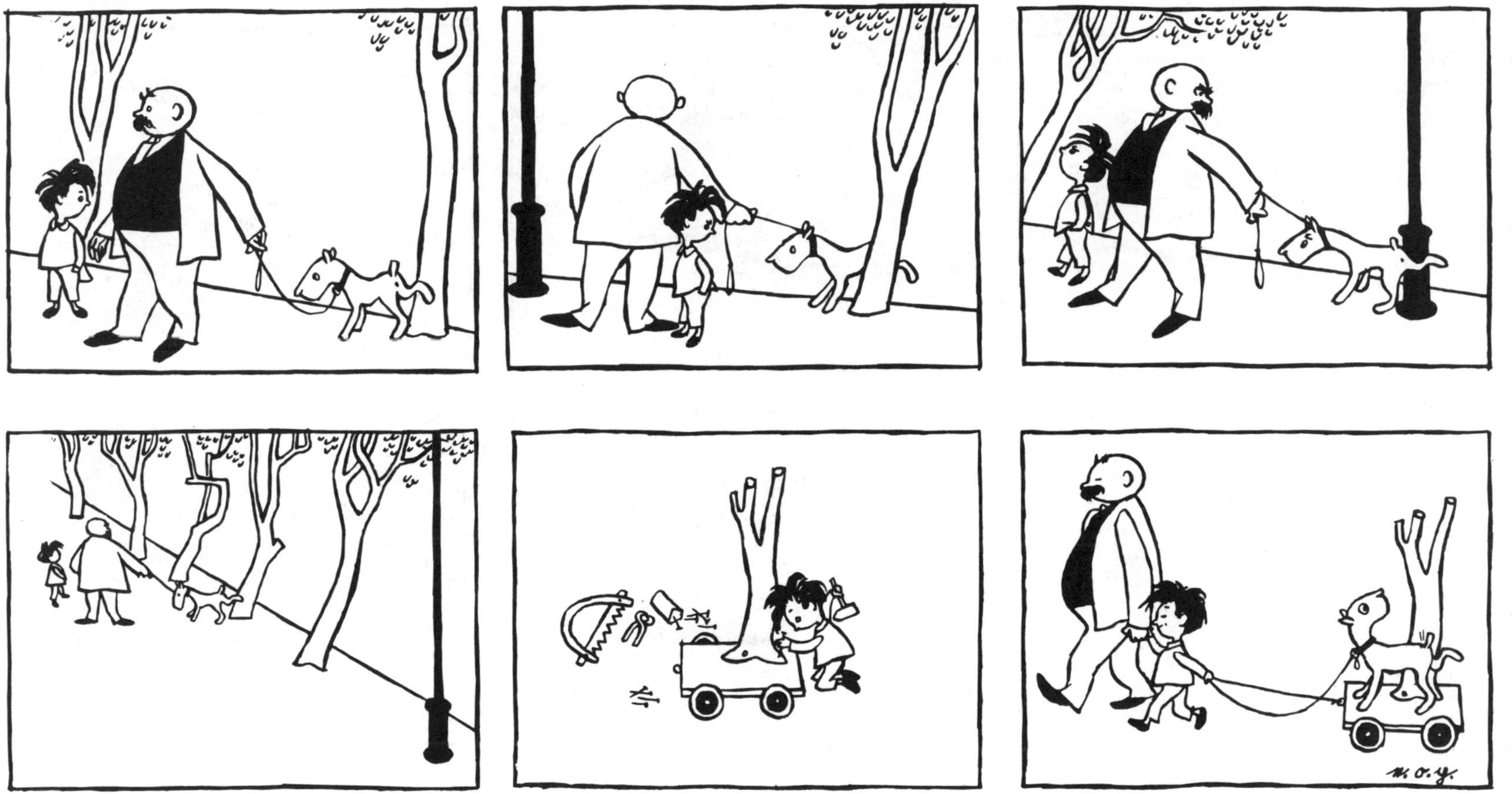
M. O. Y.

The invention

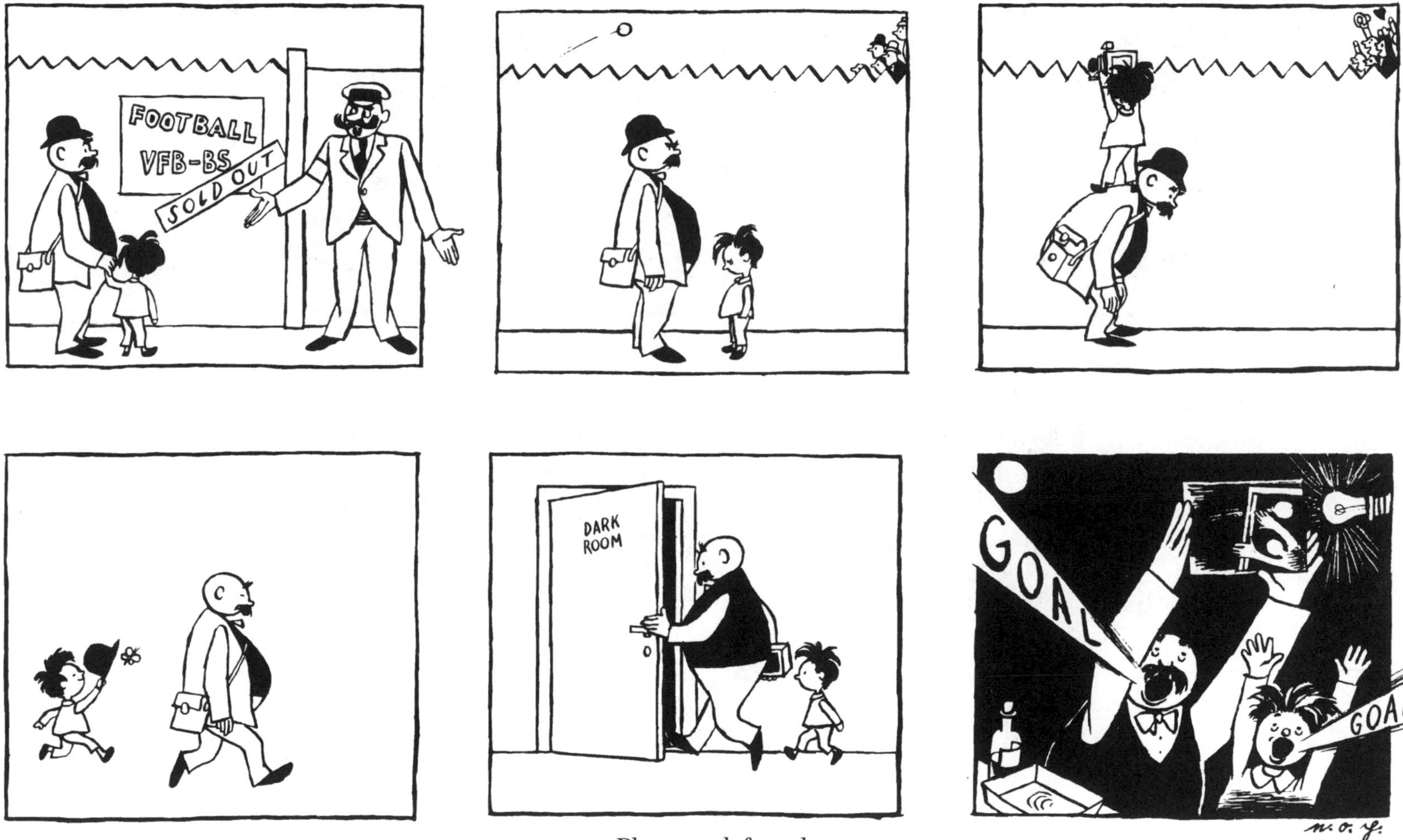
FOOTBALL
VFB-BS
SOLD OUT
DARK ROOM
GOAL
GOAL!

Pleasure deferred

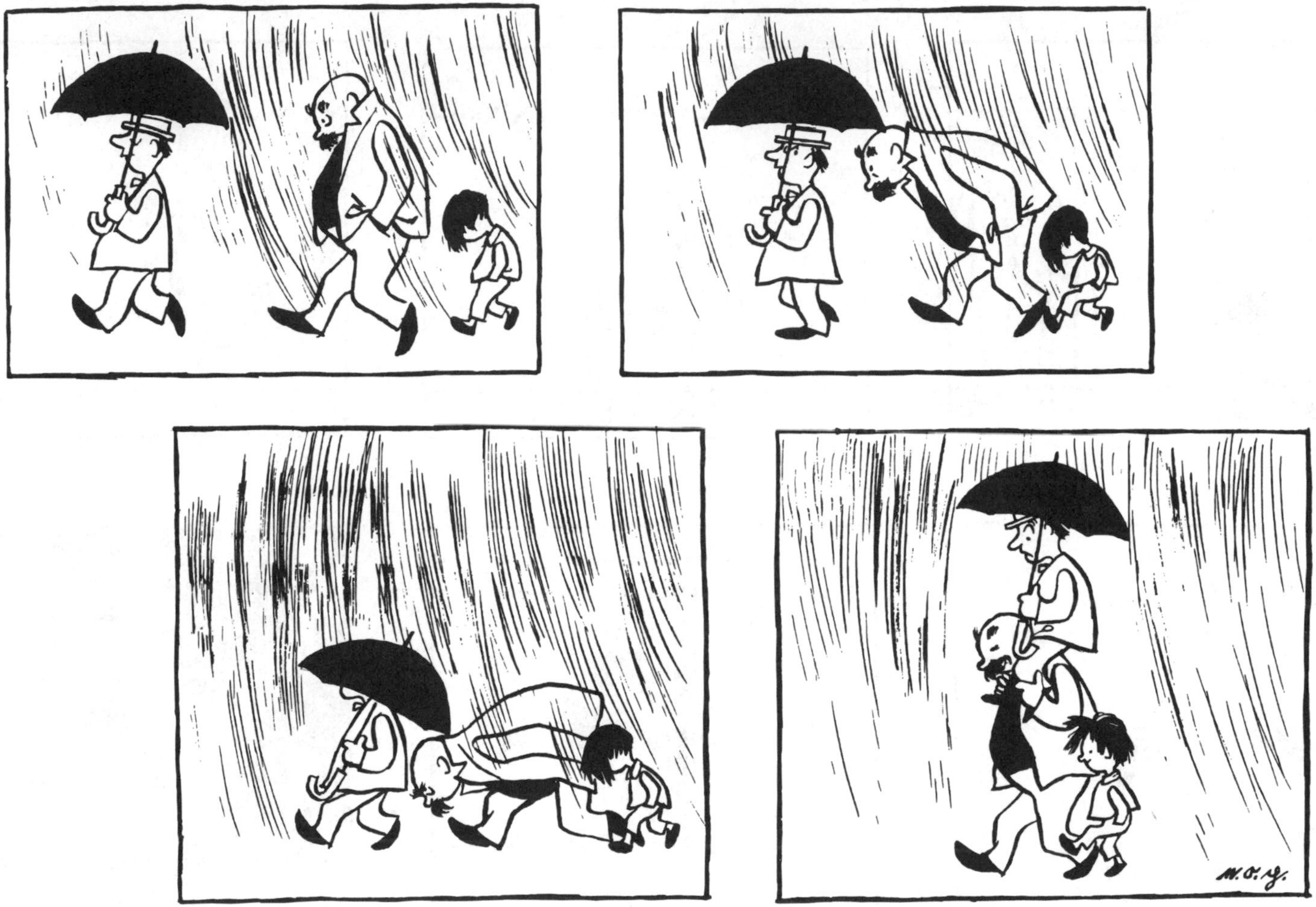

Taking him for a ride

One year later

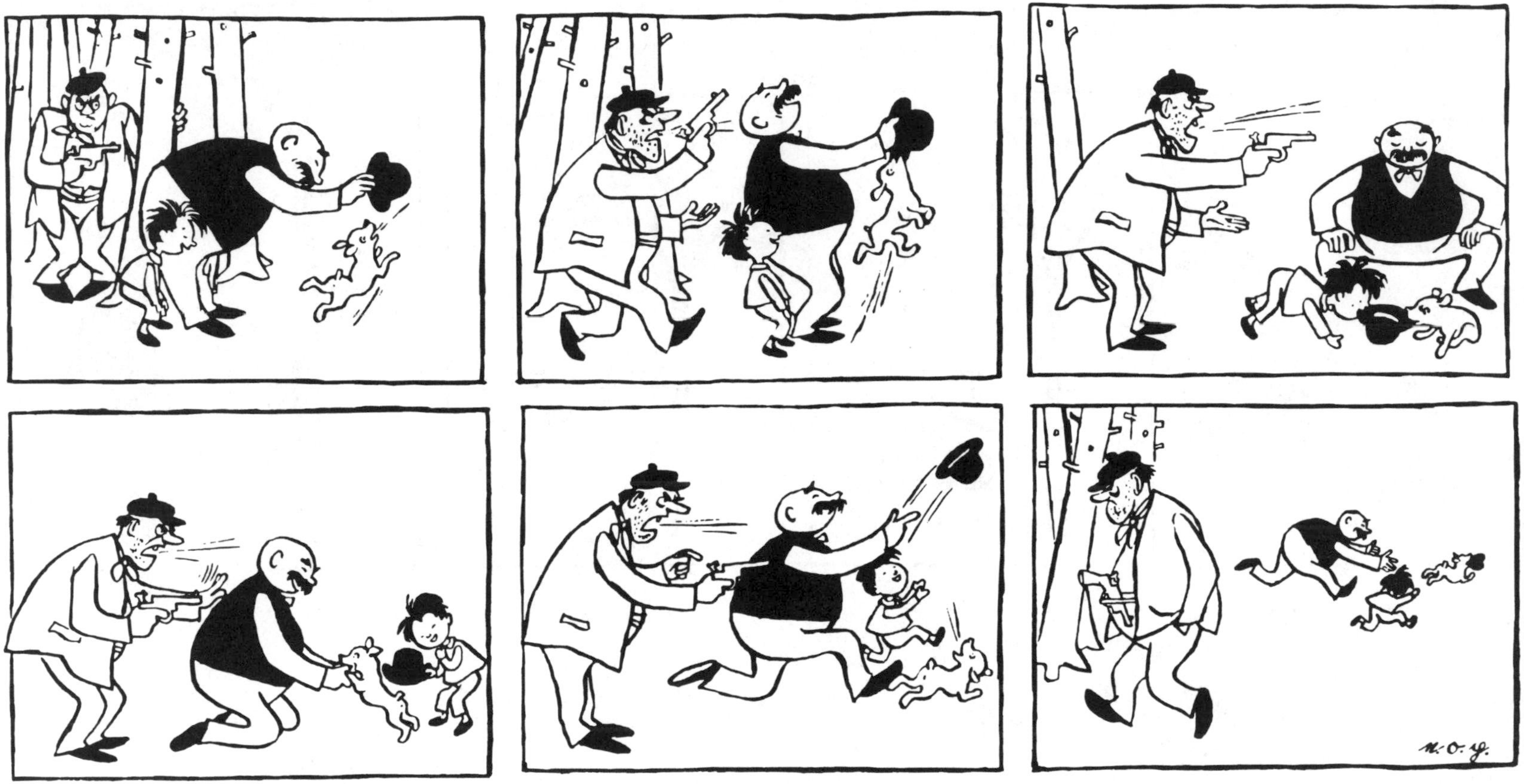

Unnoticed stickup

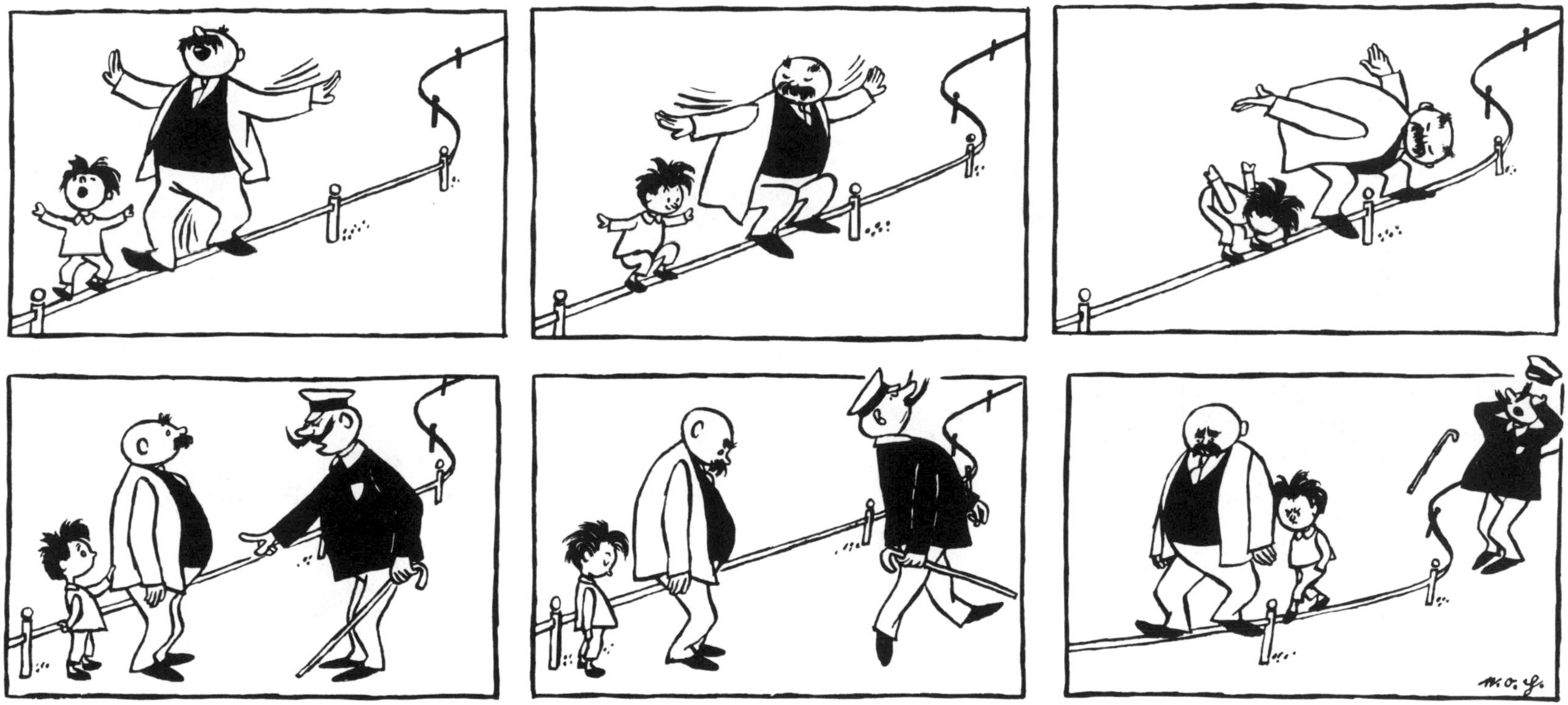

Hopeless case

The birthday surprise

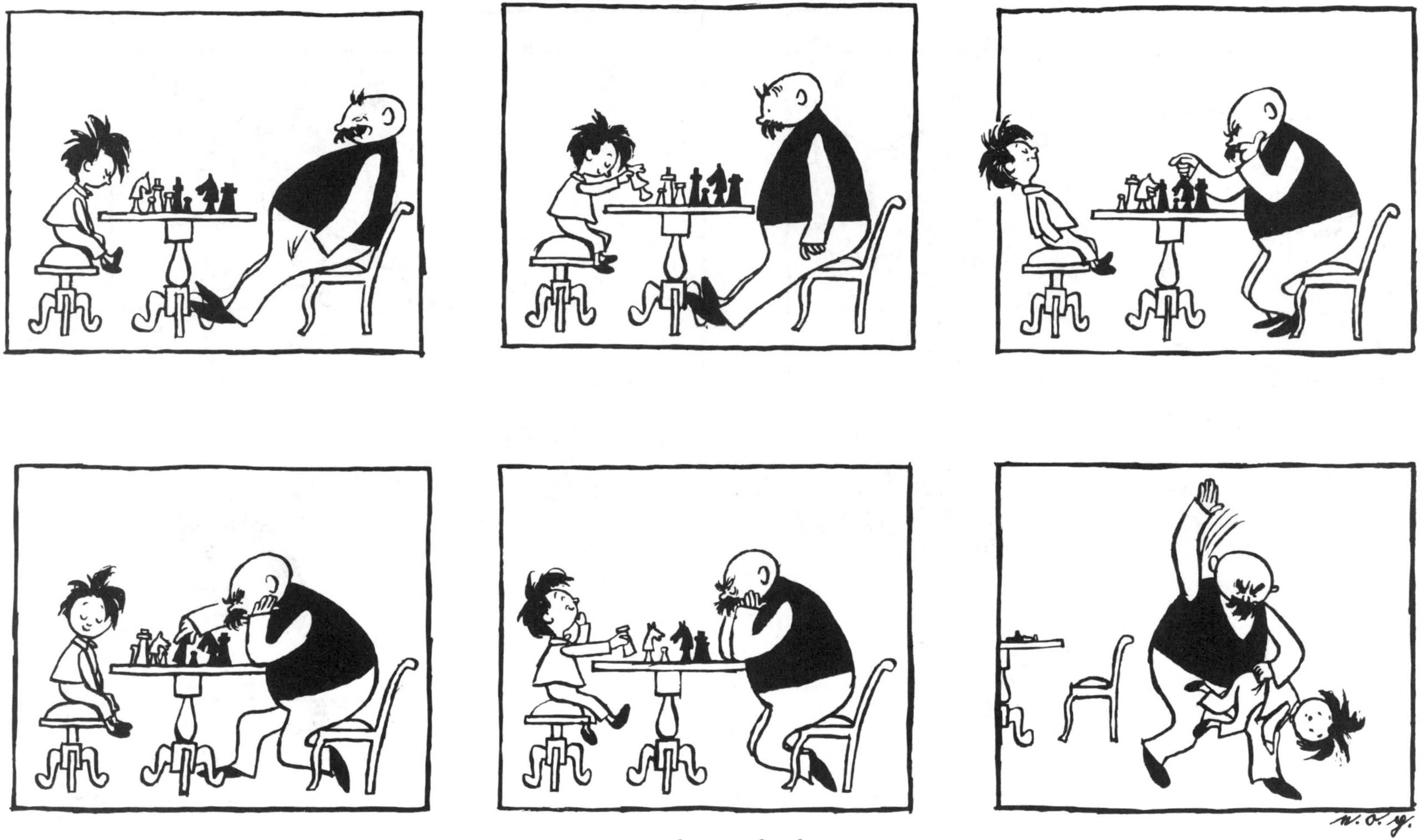

Father in check

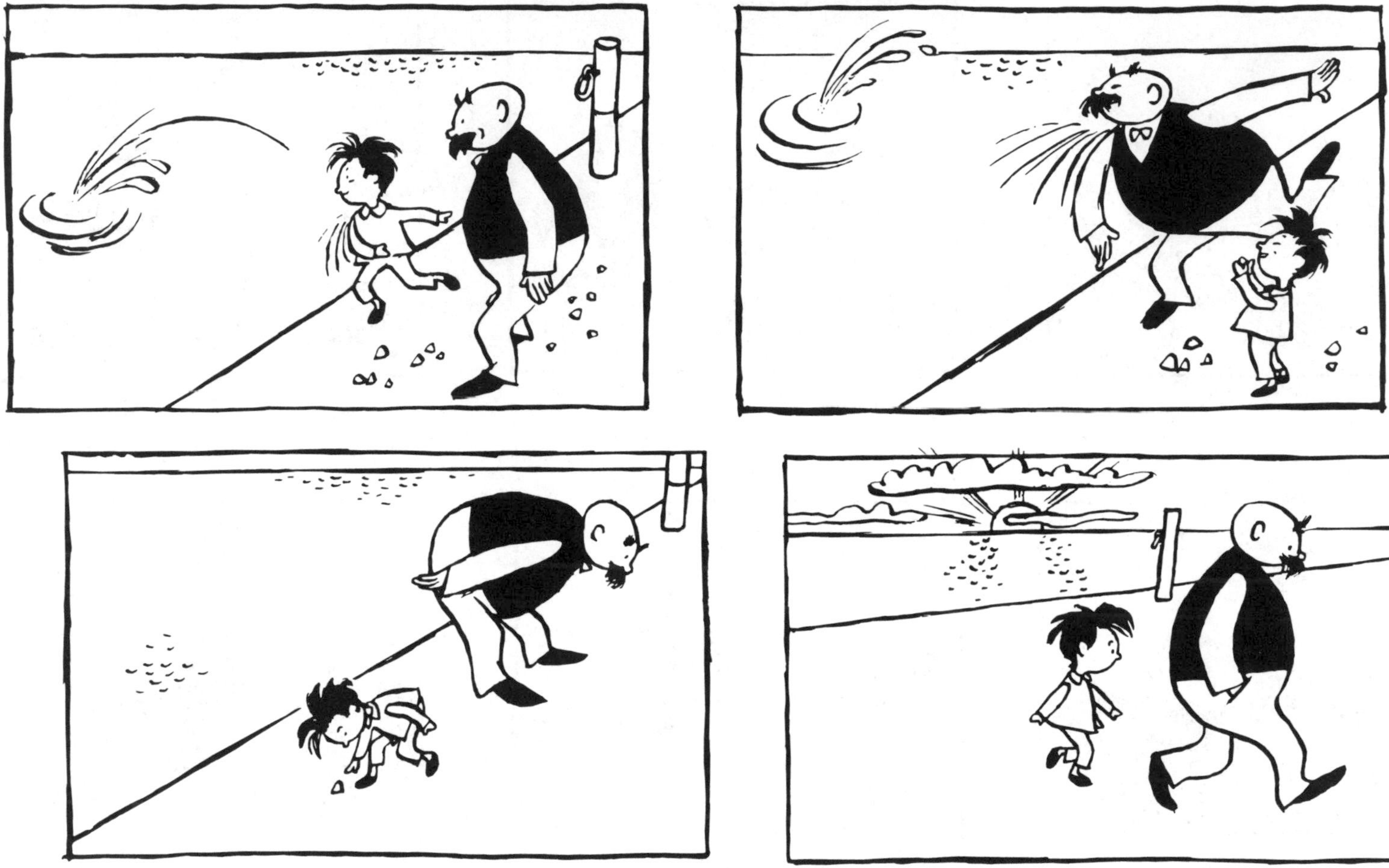

What a good fellow!

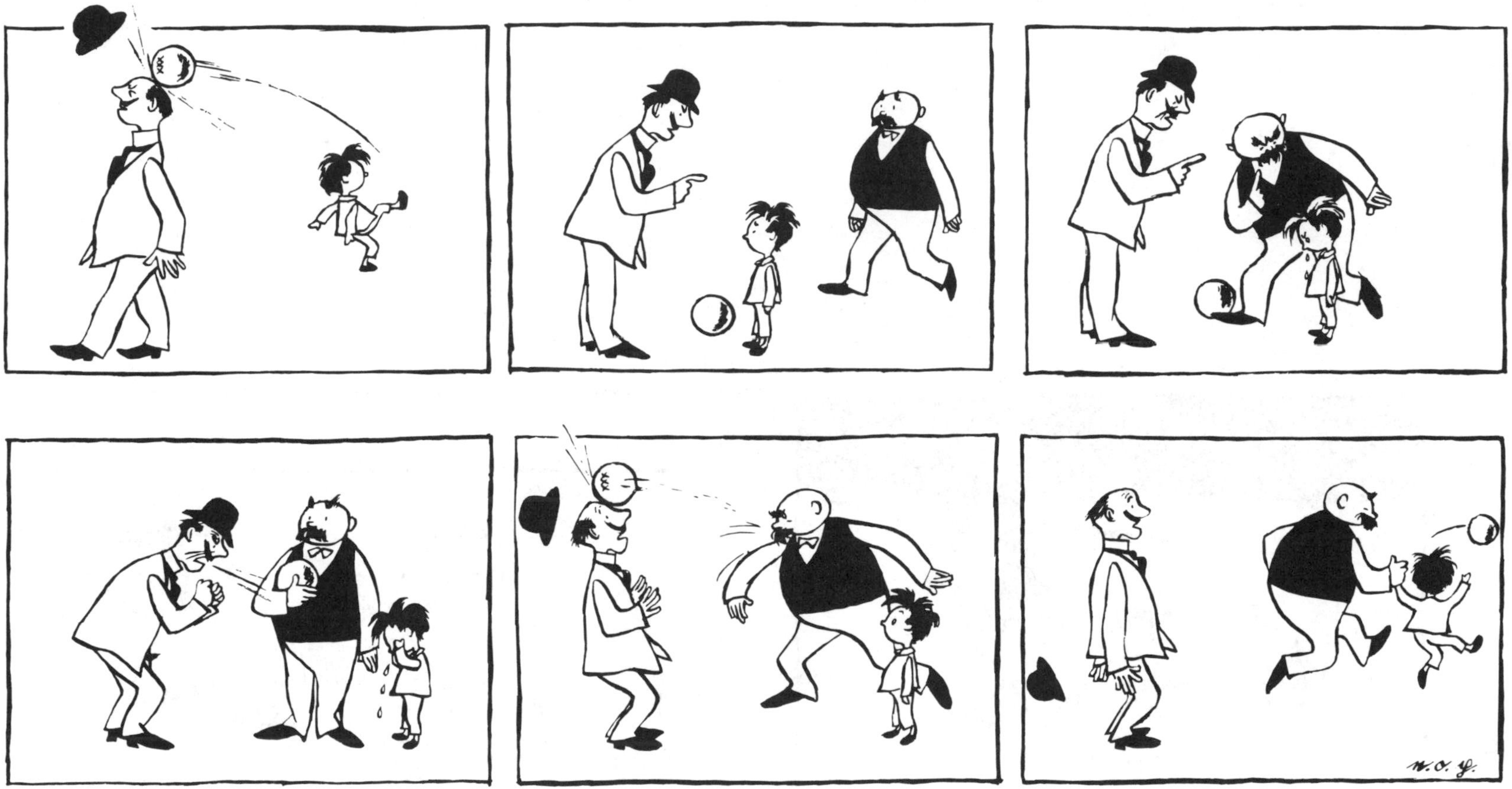

That's going too far

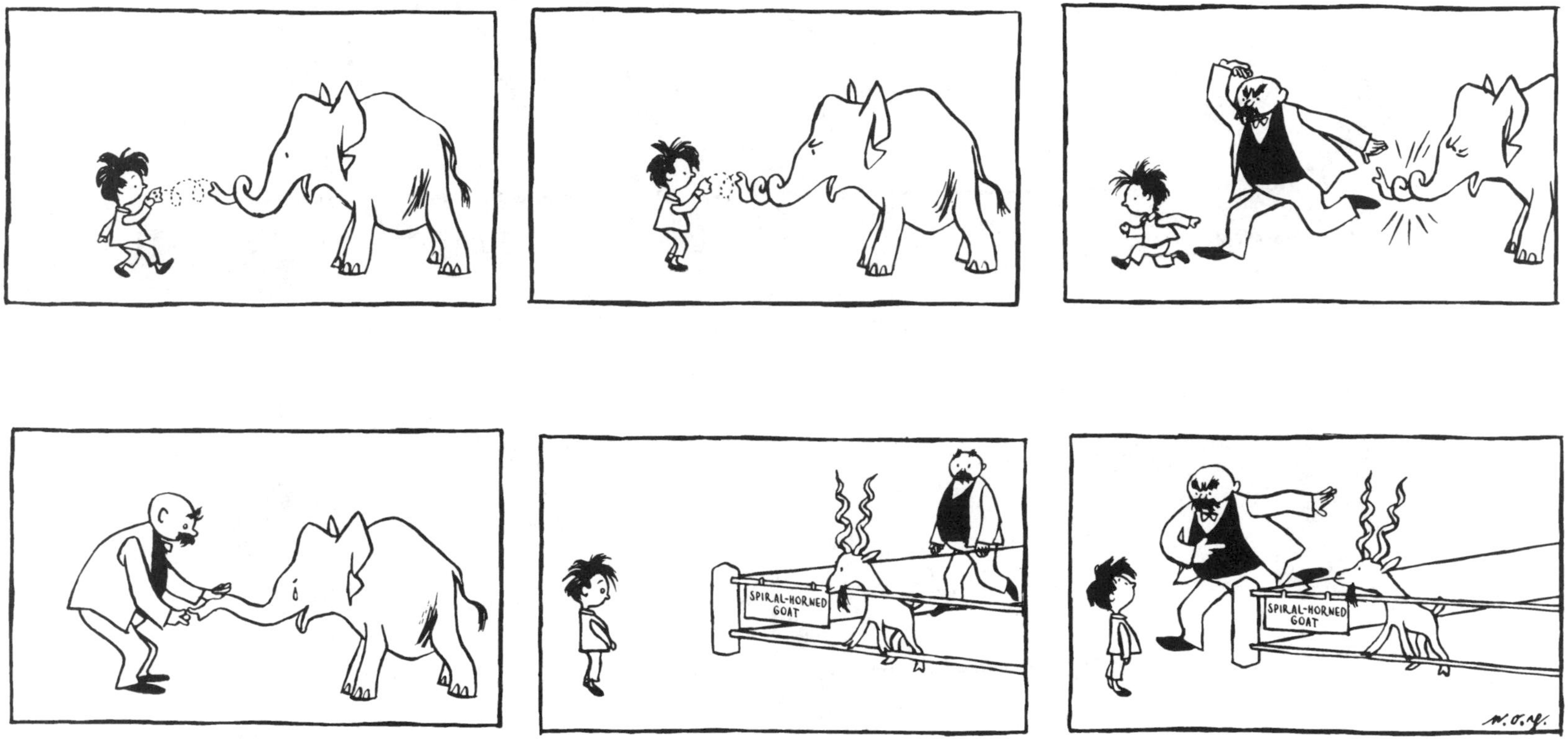
SPIRAL-HORNED GOAT
SPIRAL-HORNED GOAT

Suspicious corkscrews

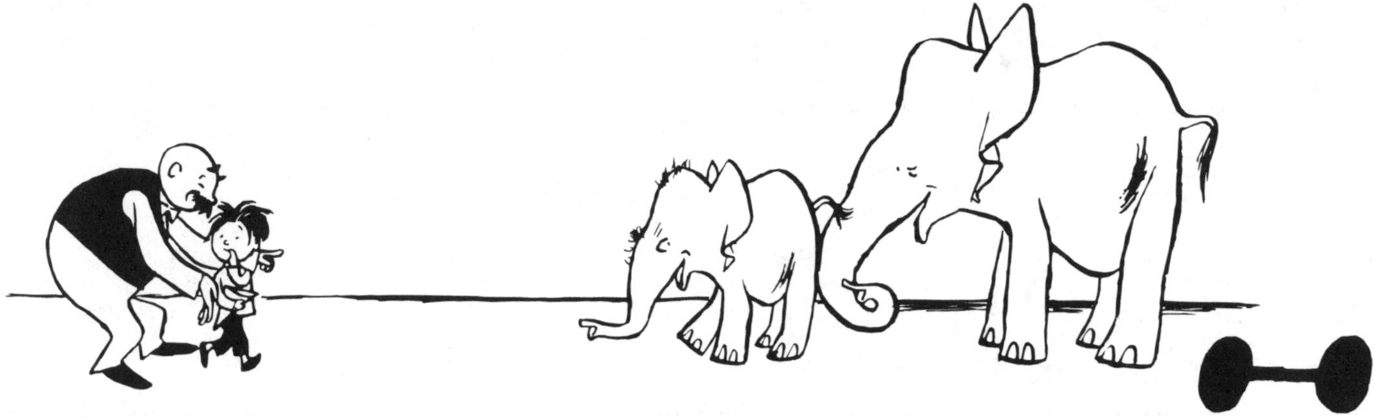

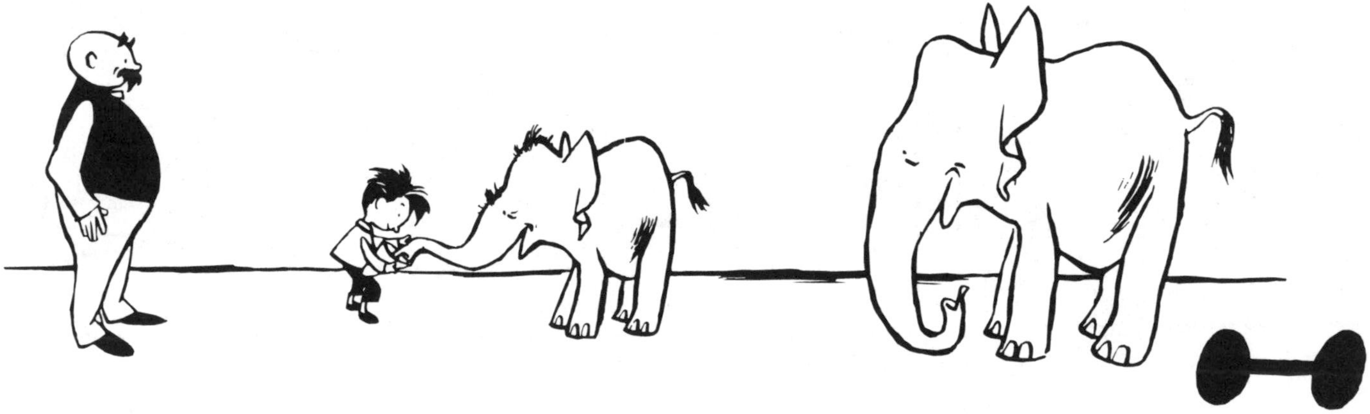

Fathers and sons

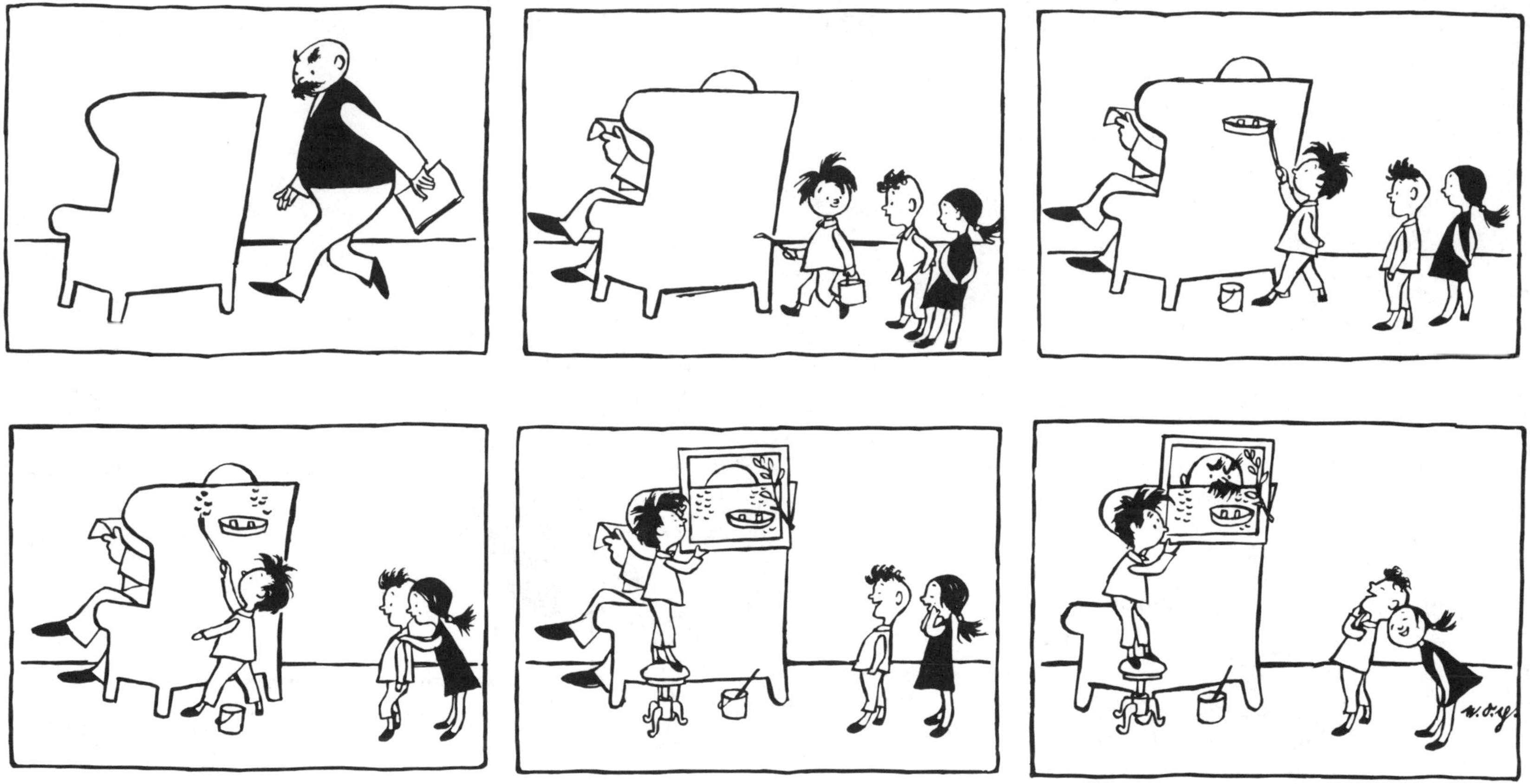

The sunset

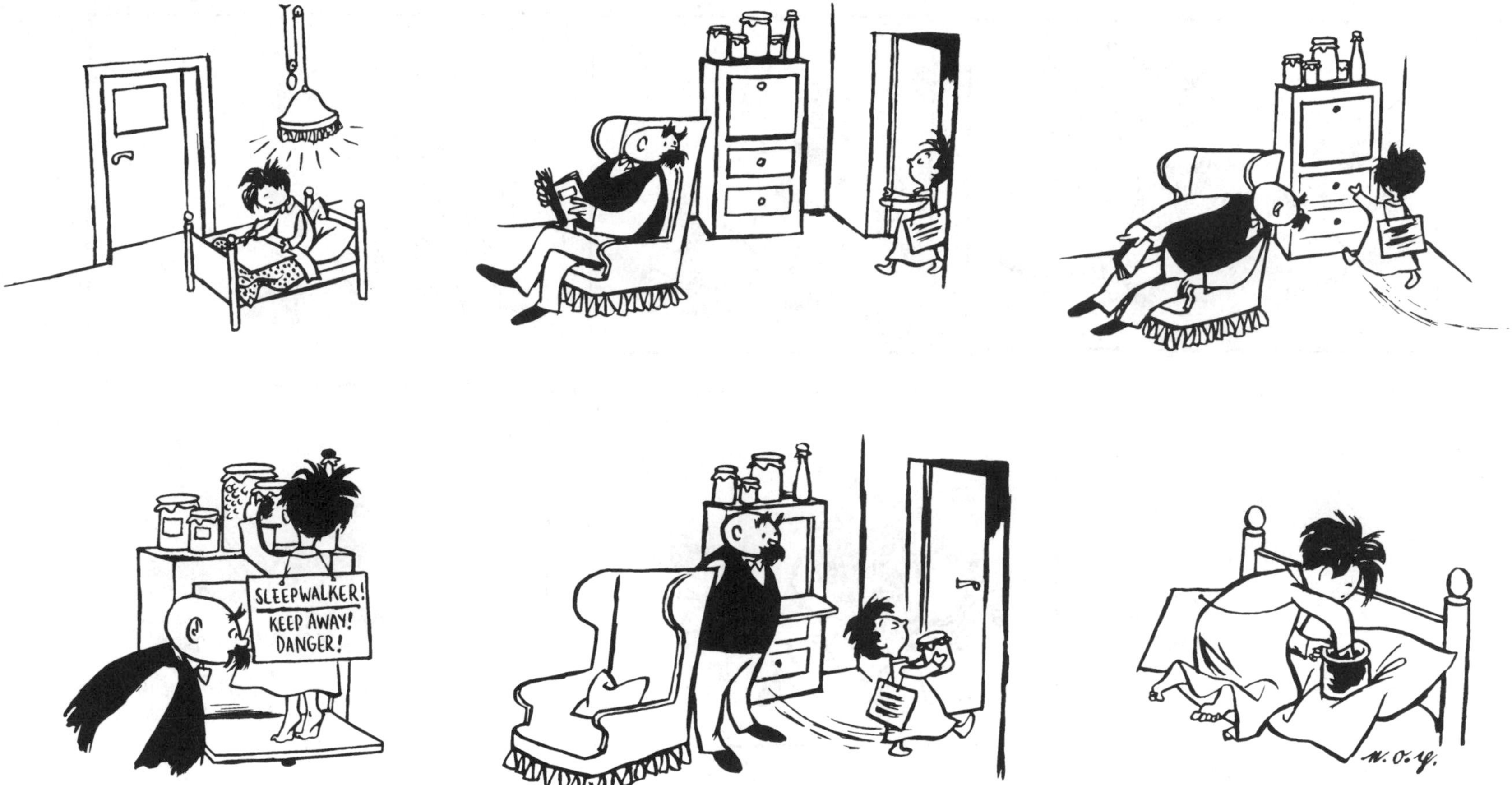
SLEEPWALKER!
KEEP AWAY!
DANGER!

The sleepwalker

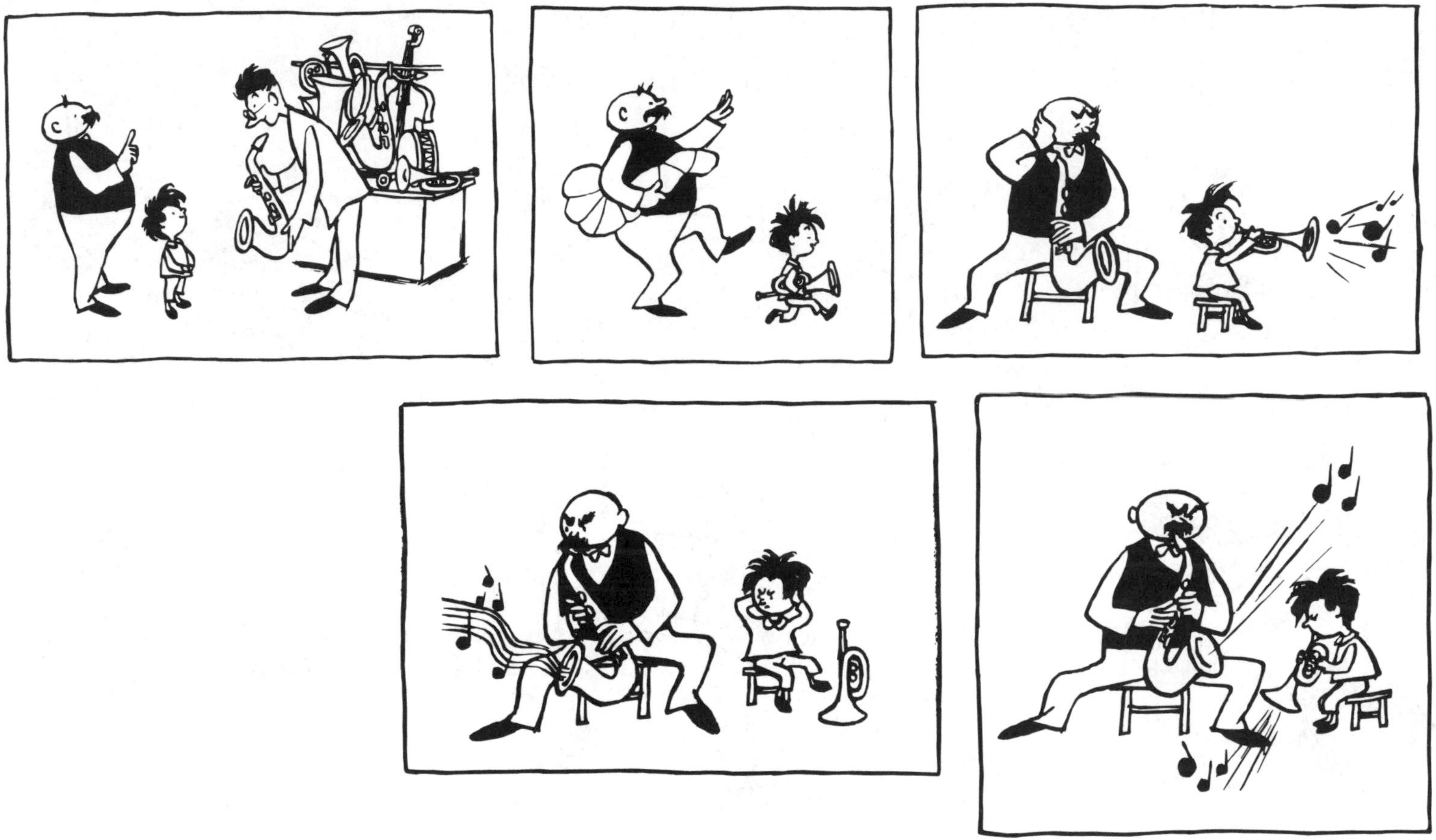

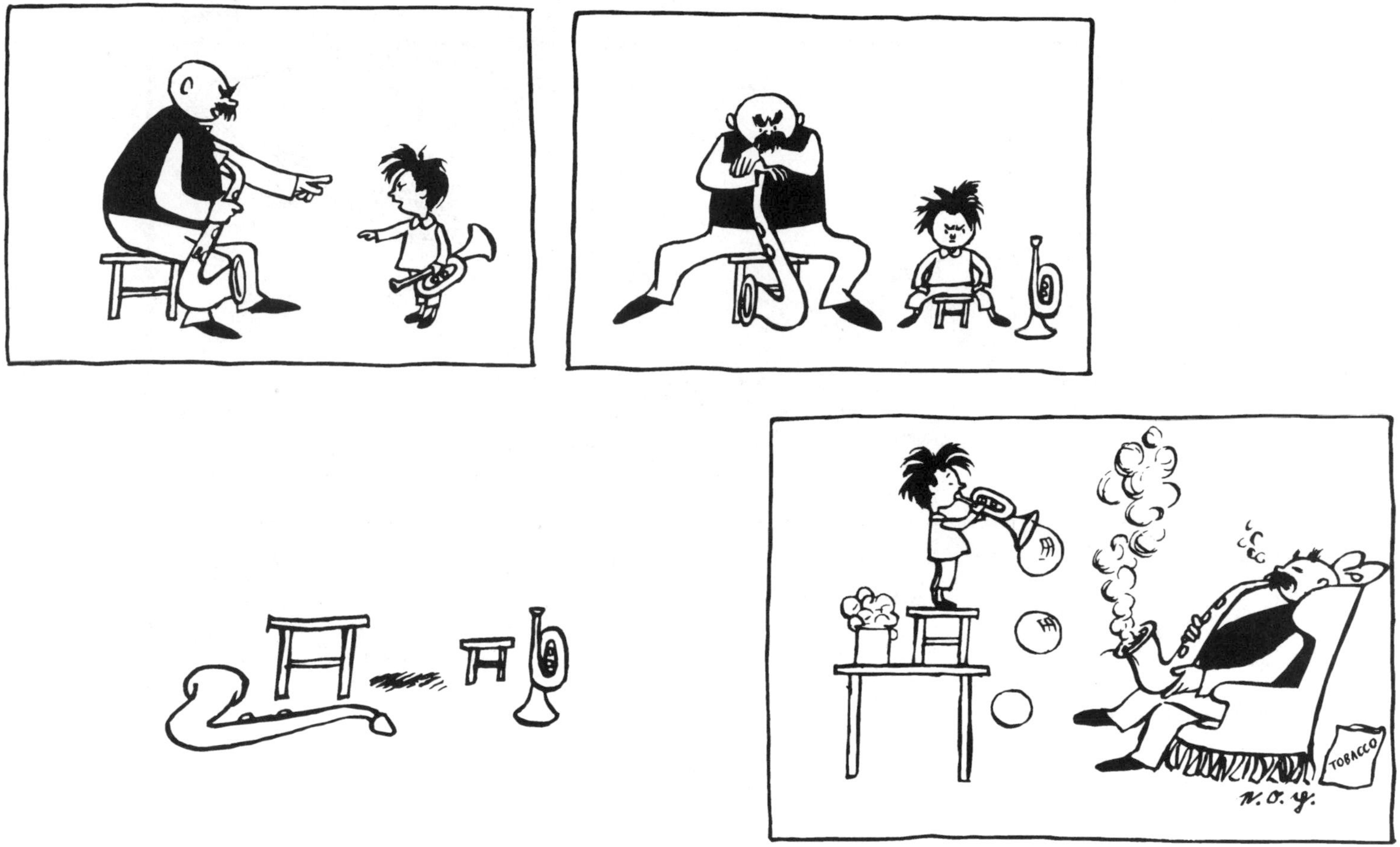
TOBACCO
N.O.Y.

Blow-out

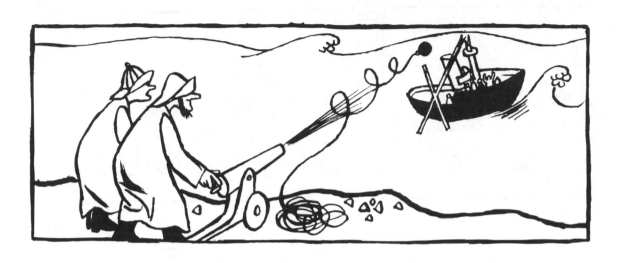

"That was great, let's do it again!"

Playing ball

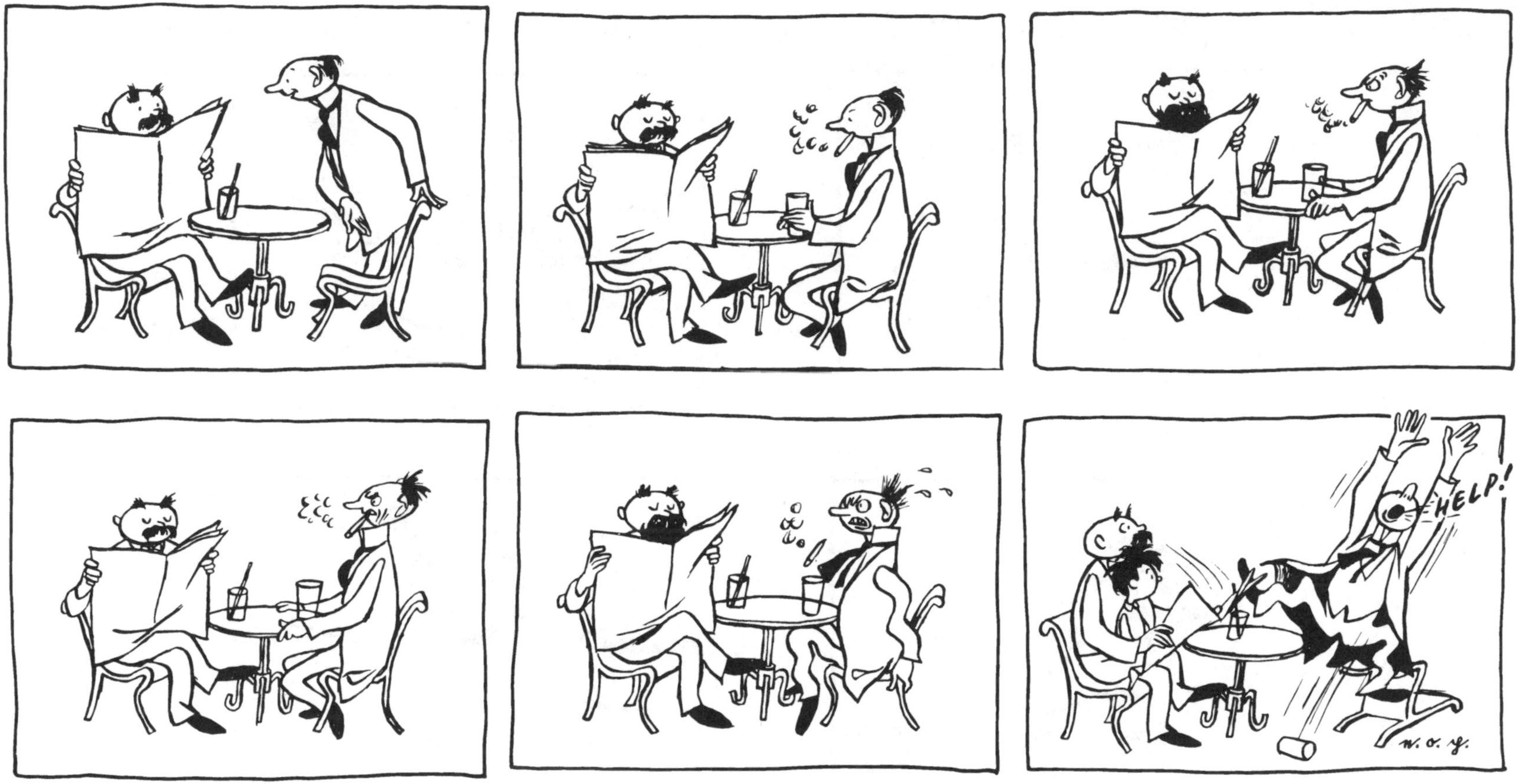
HELP!

The peculiar tablemate

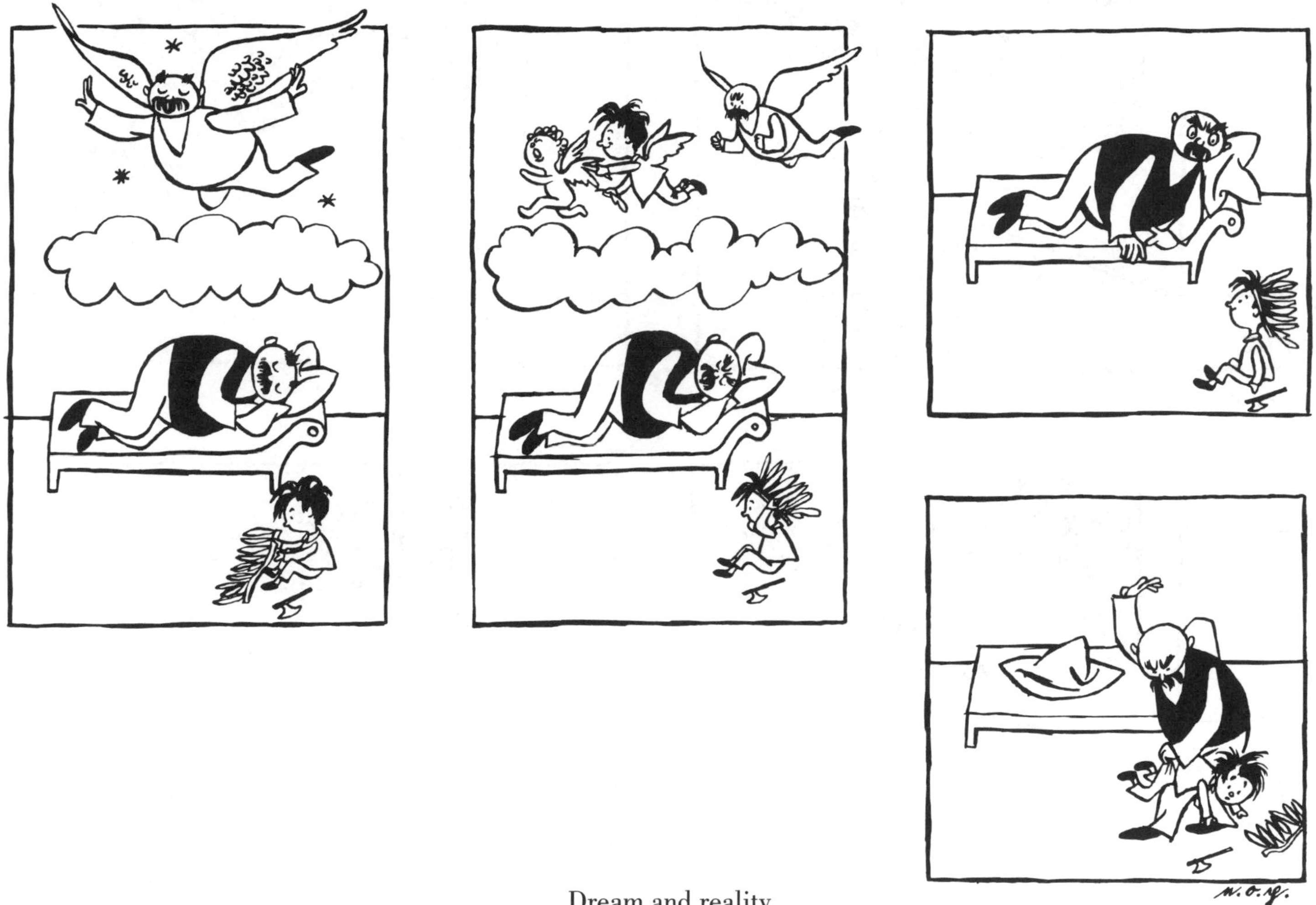

Dream and reality

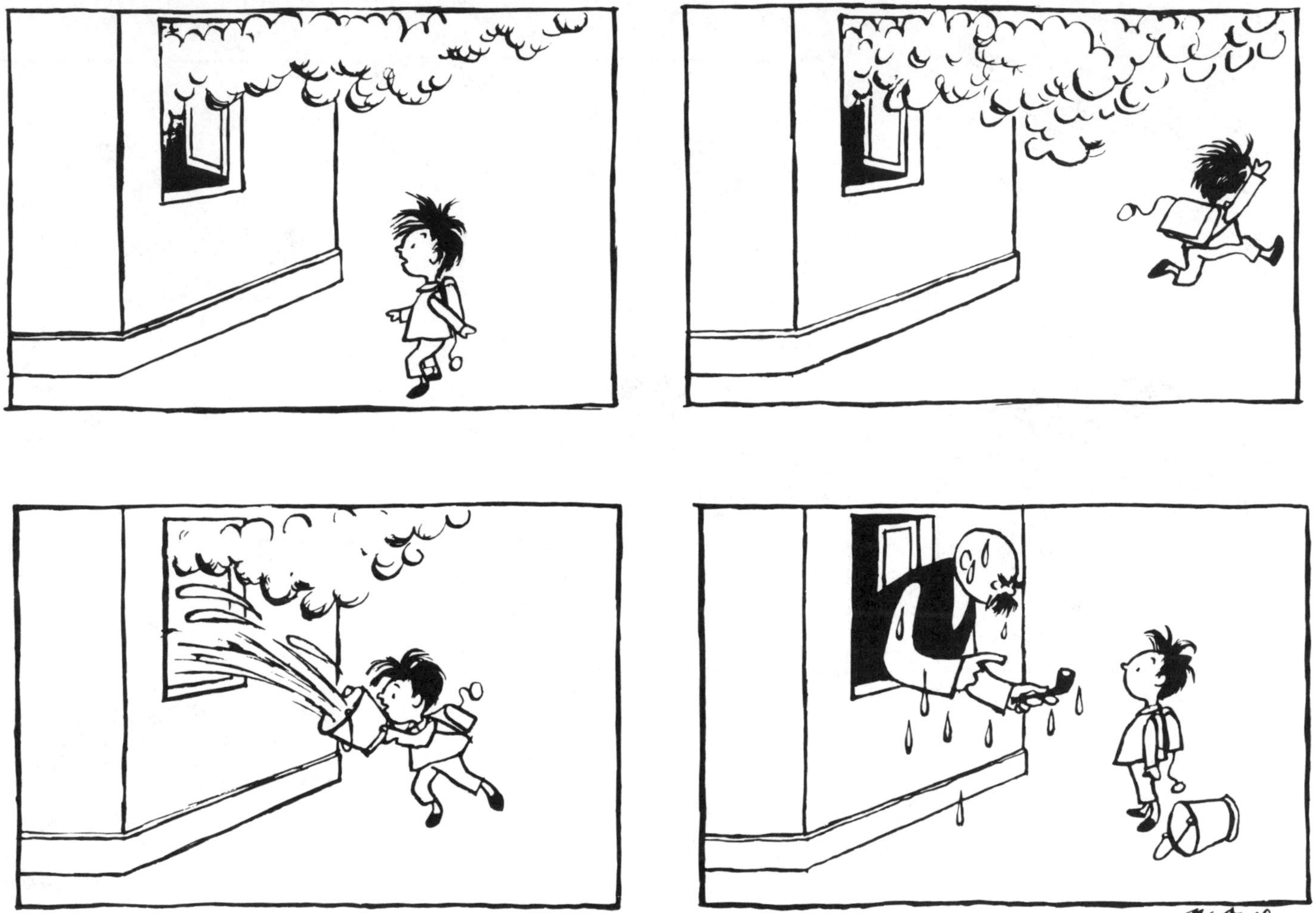

Father is extinguished

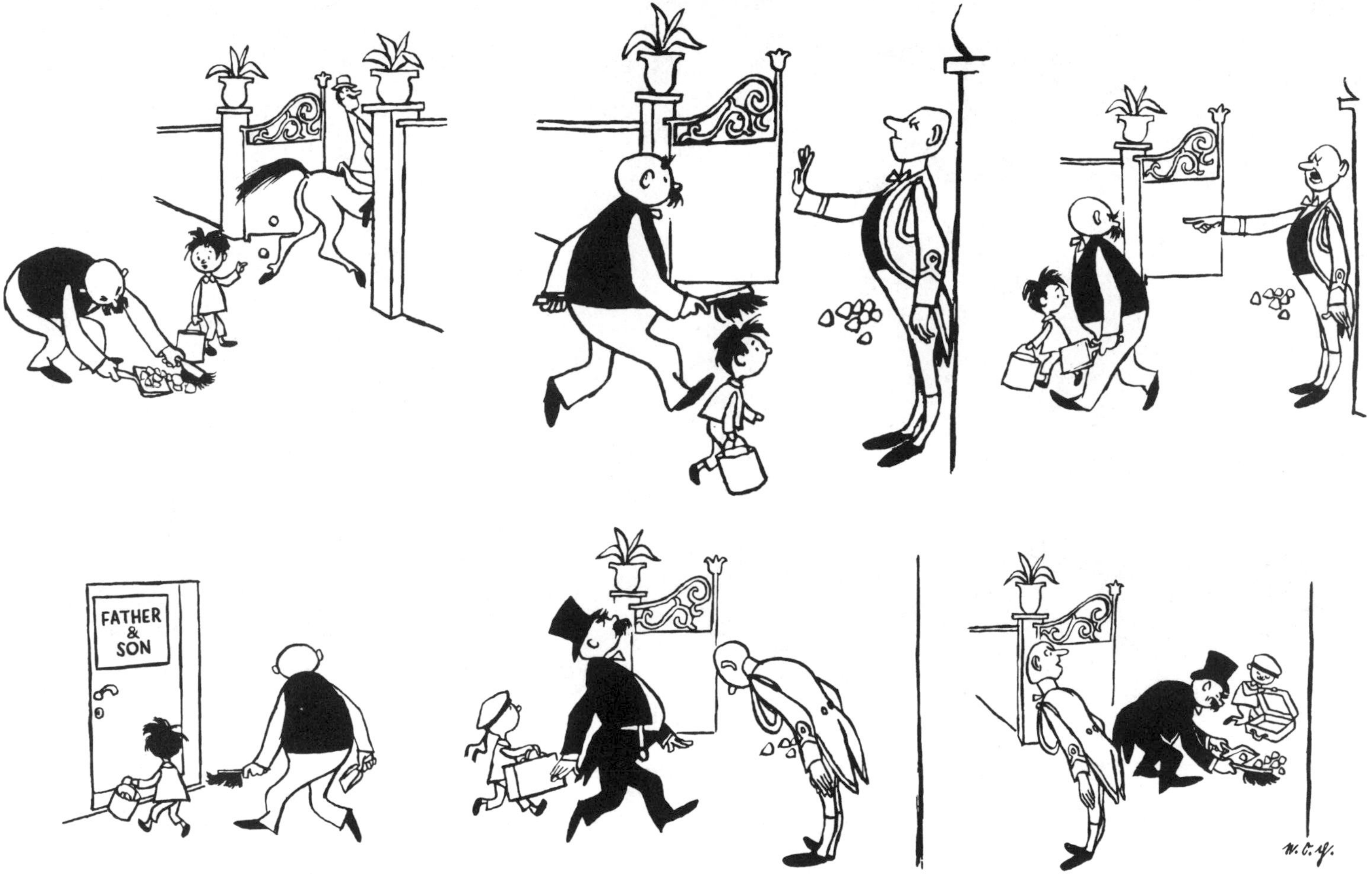
FATHER
&
SON

Clothes make the man

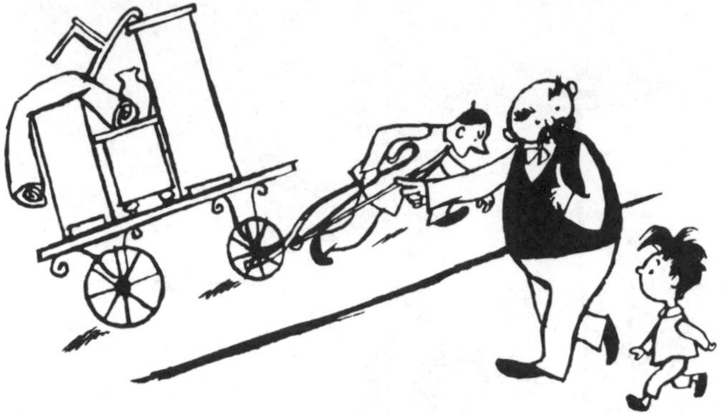
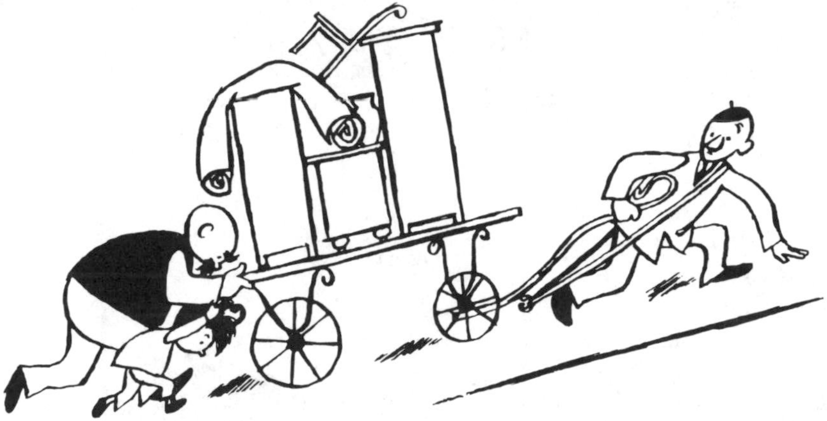
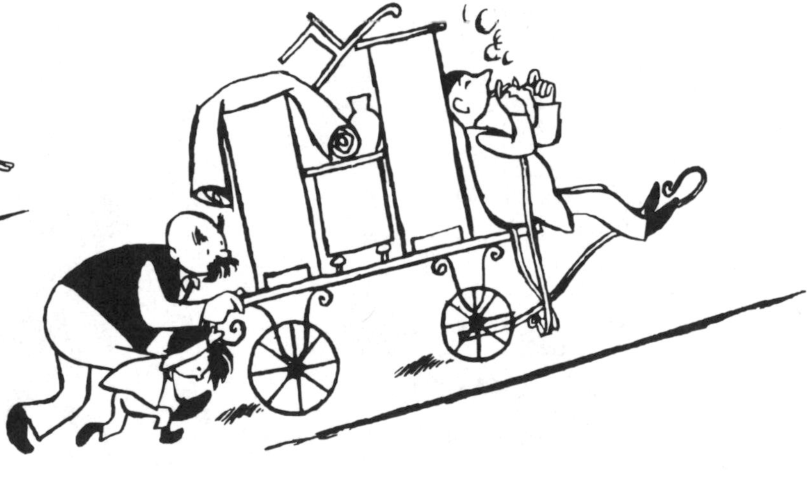

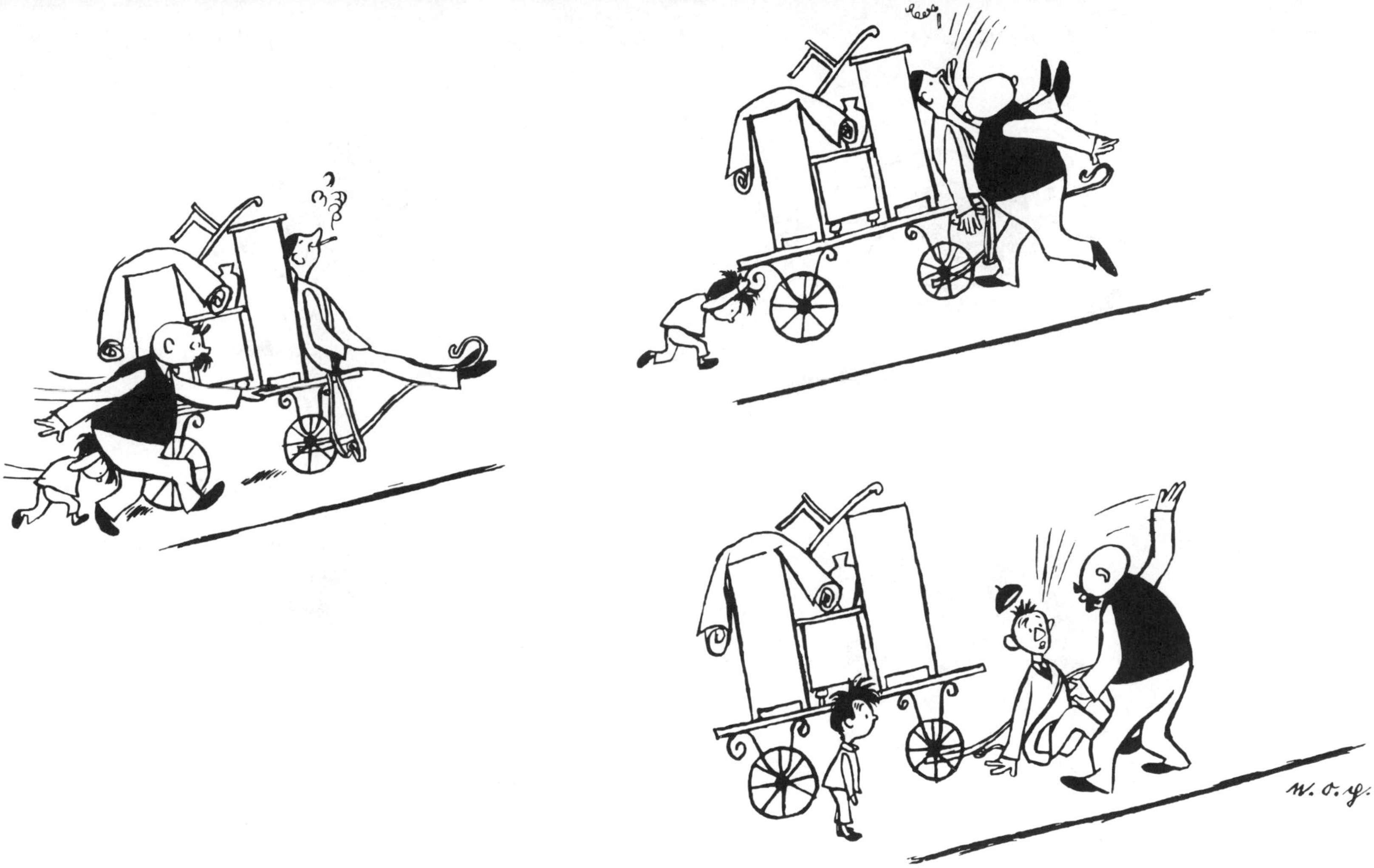

A lesson on lending a hand

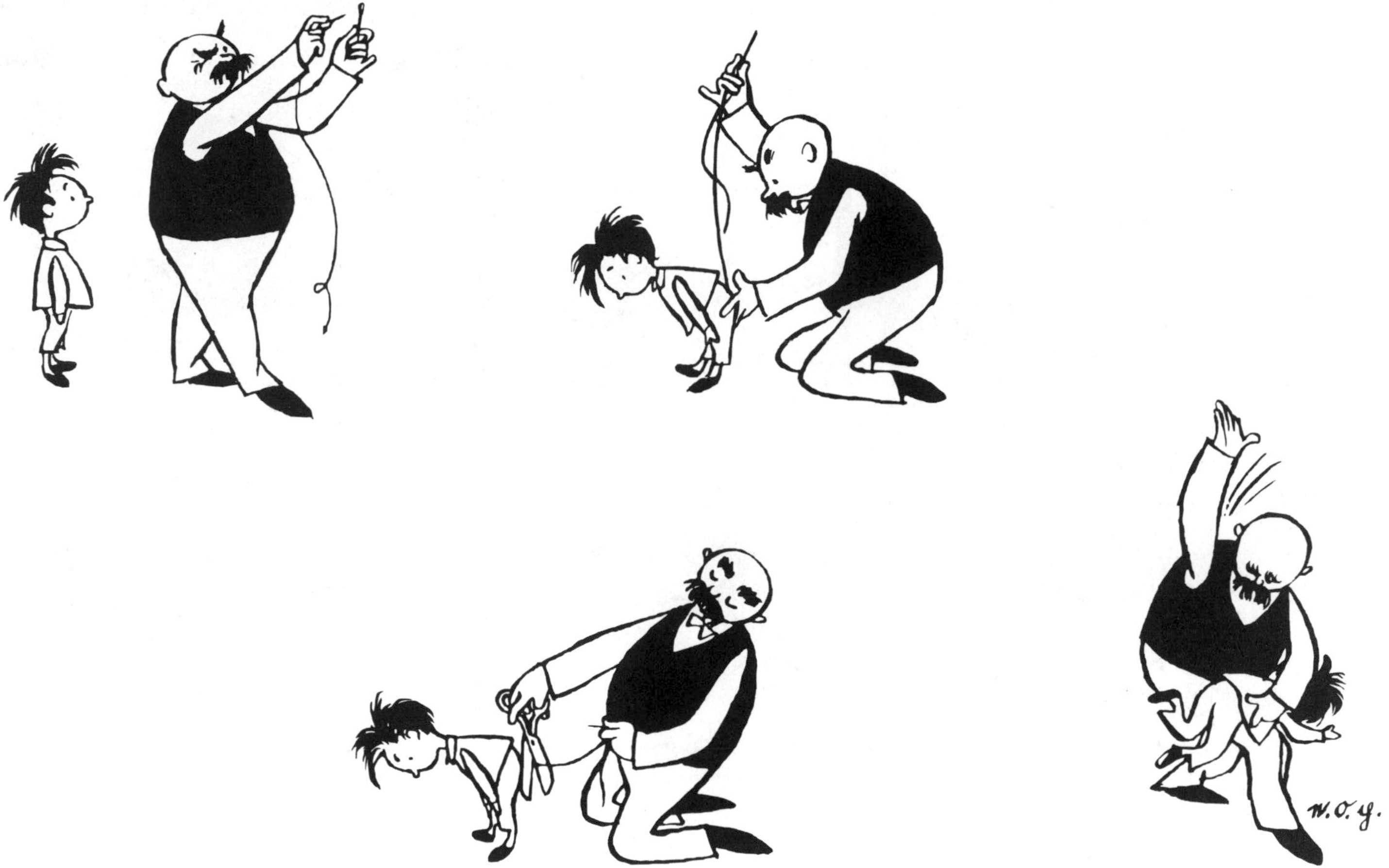

First things first

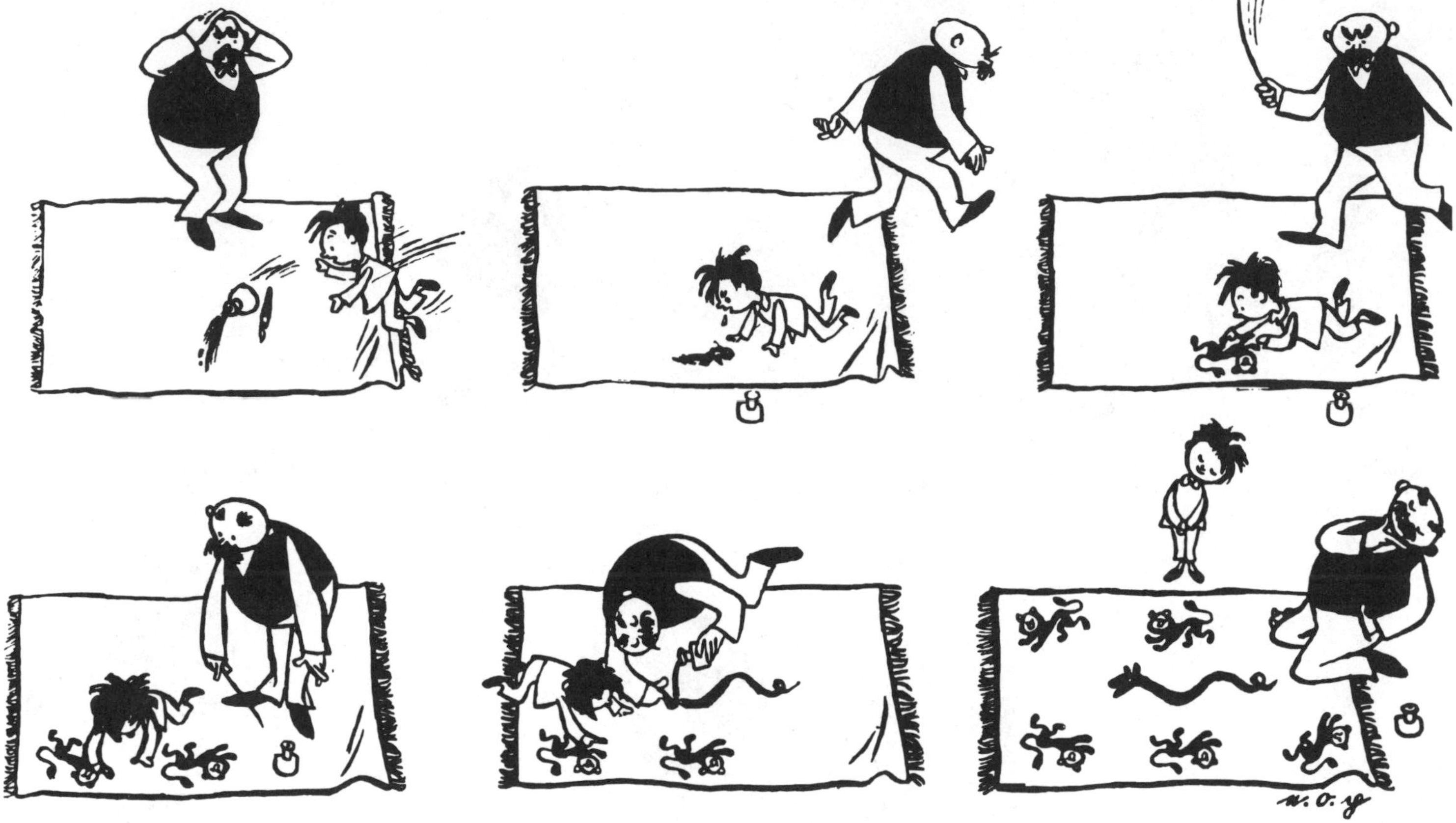

"Art wins favor"

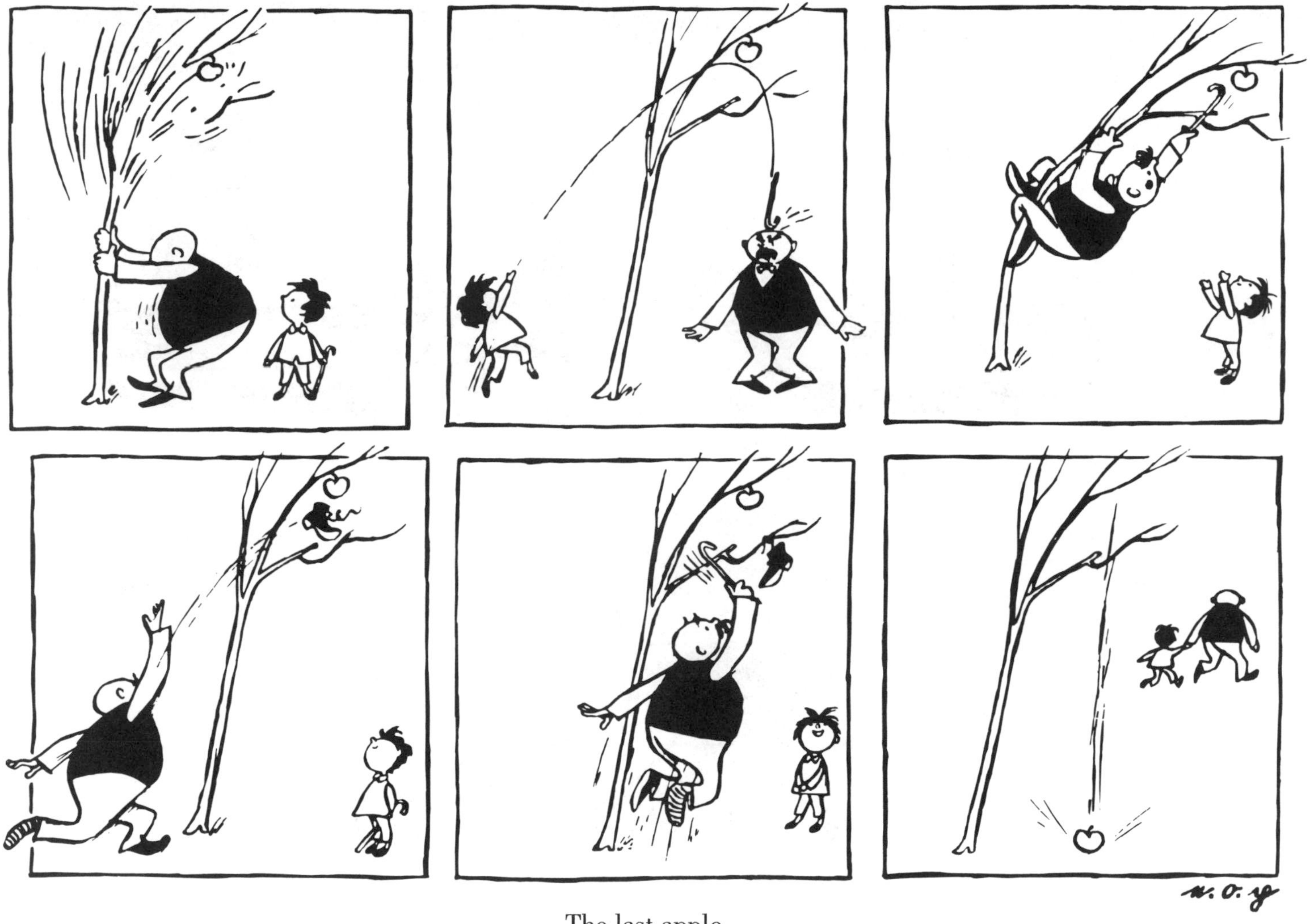
w. o. y

The last apple

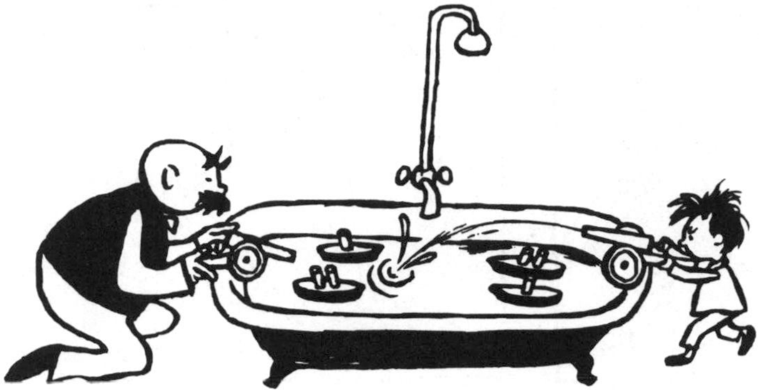

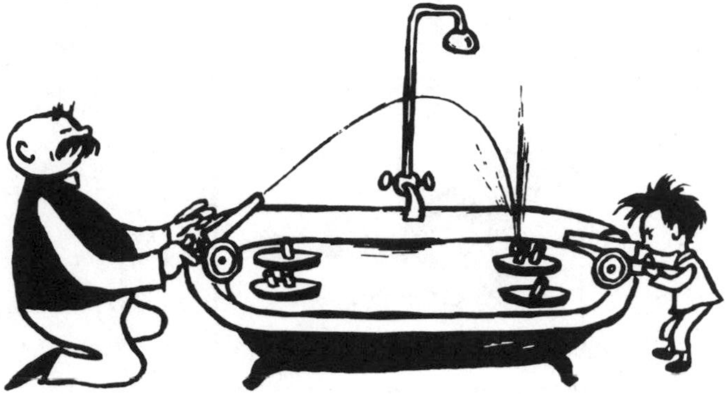

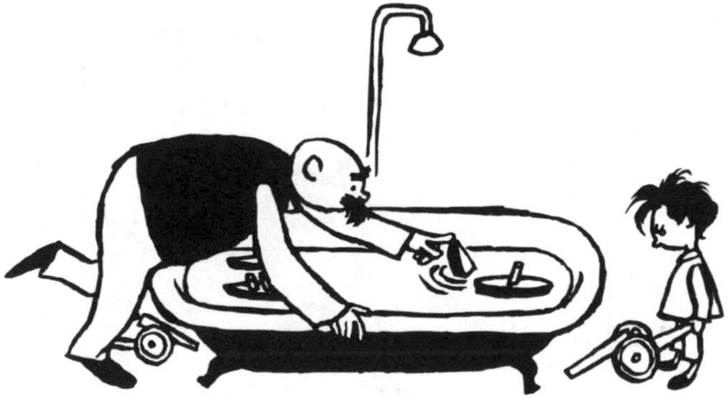

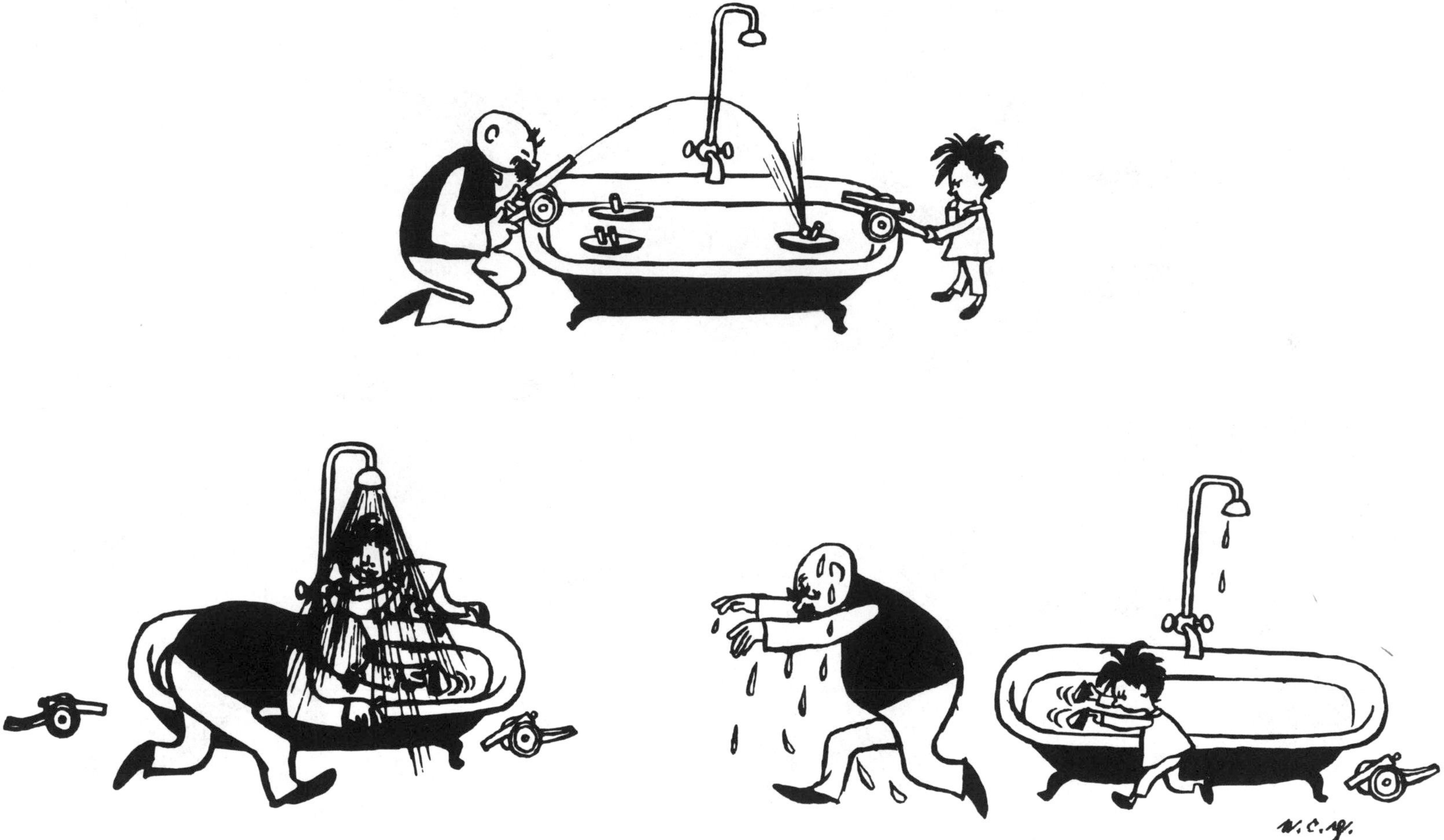

All's fair in war

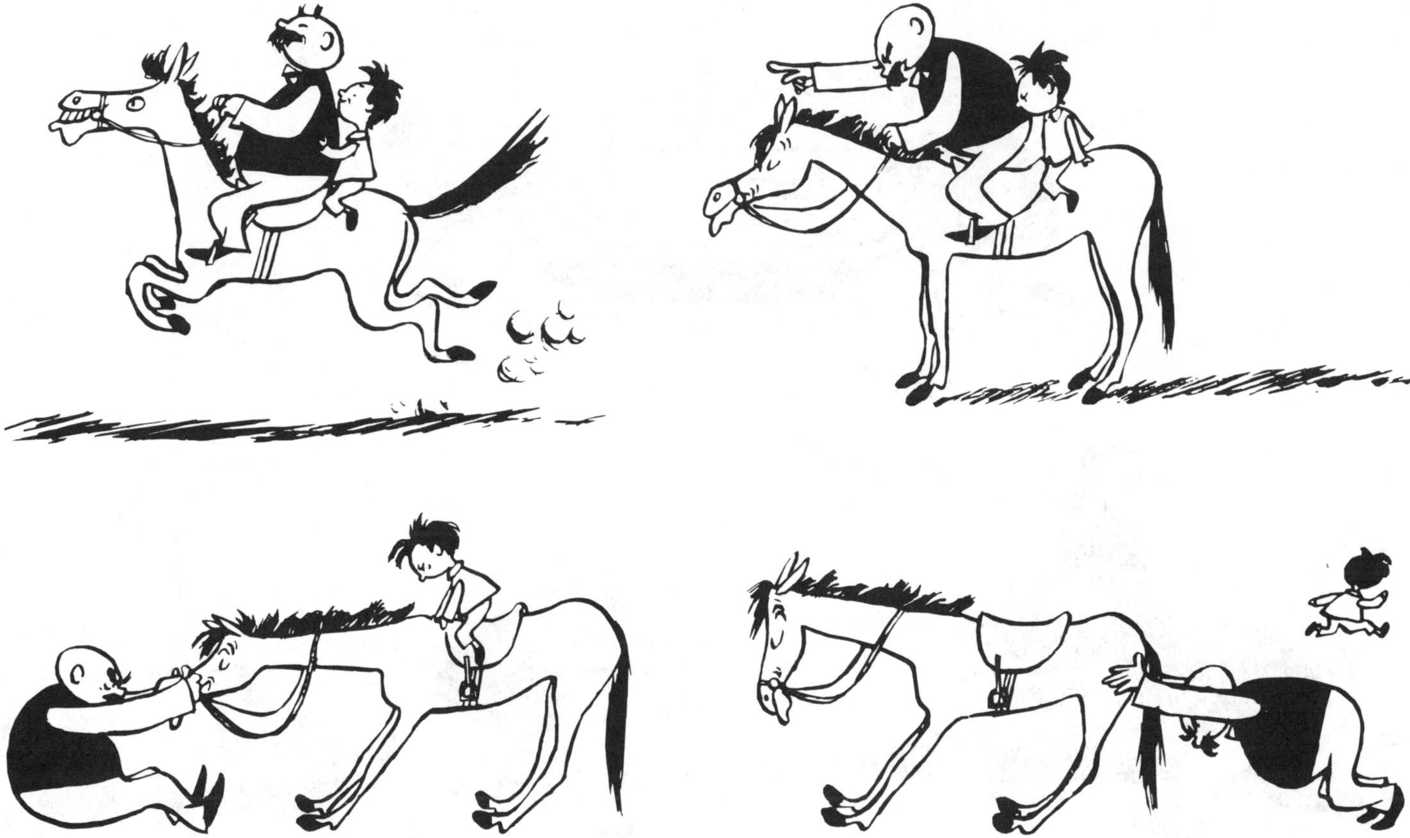

The taming of the shrew

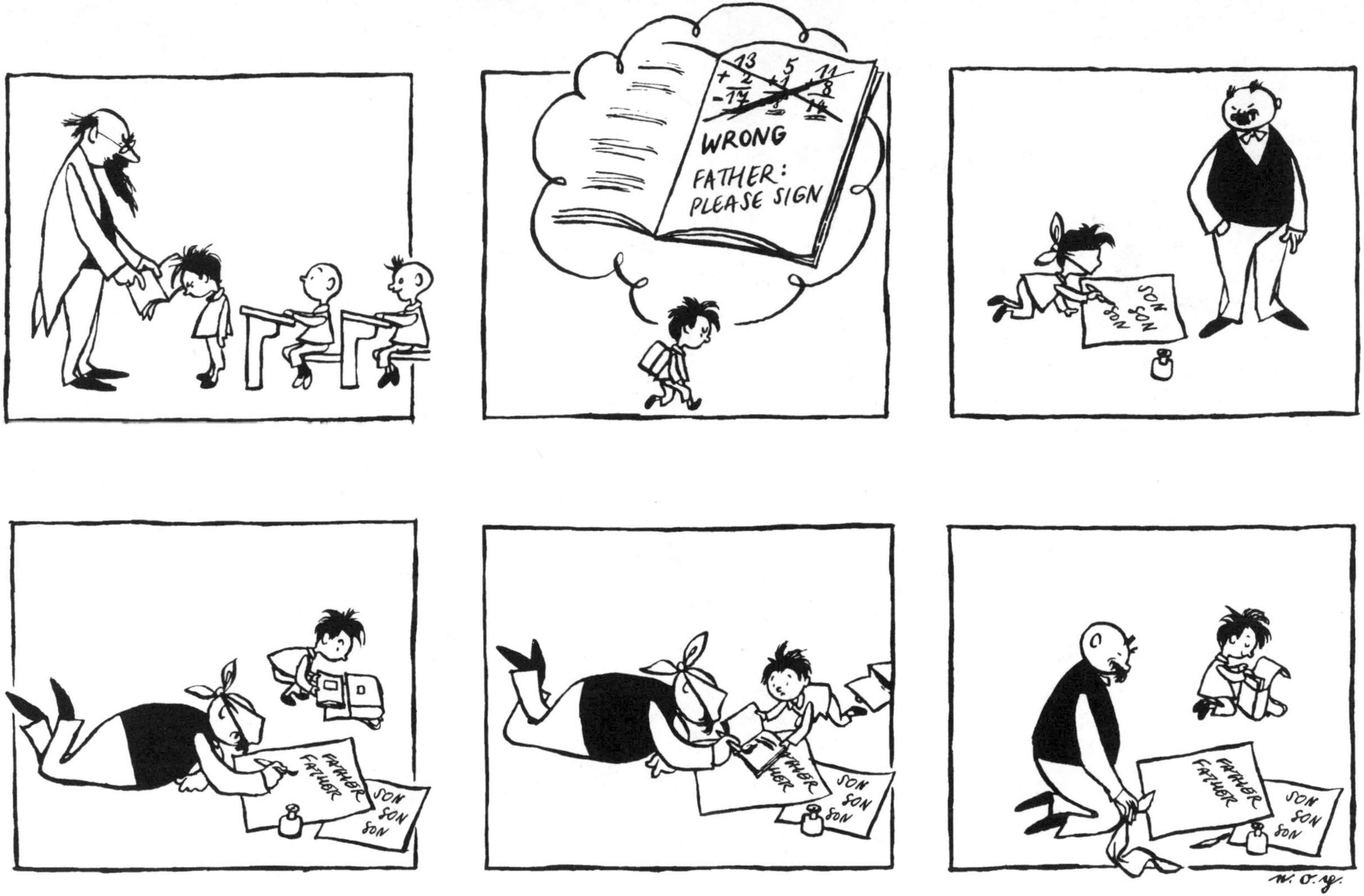
WRONG
FATHER: PLEASE SIGN
SON SON SON
FATHER FATHER
SON SON SON
FATHER FATHER
SON SON SON

Father's signature

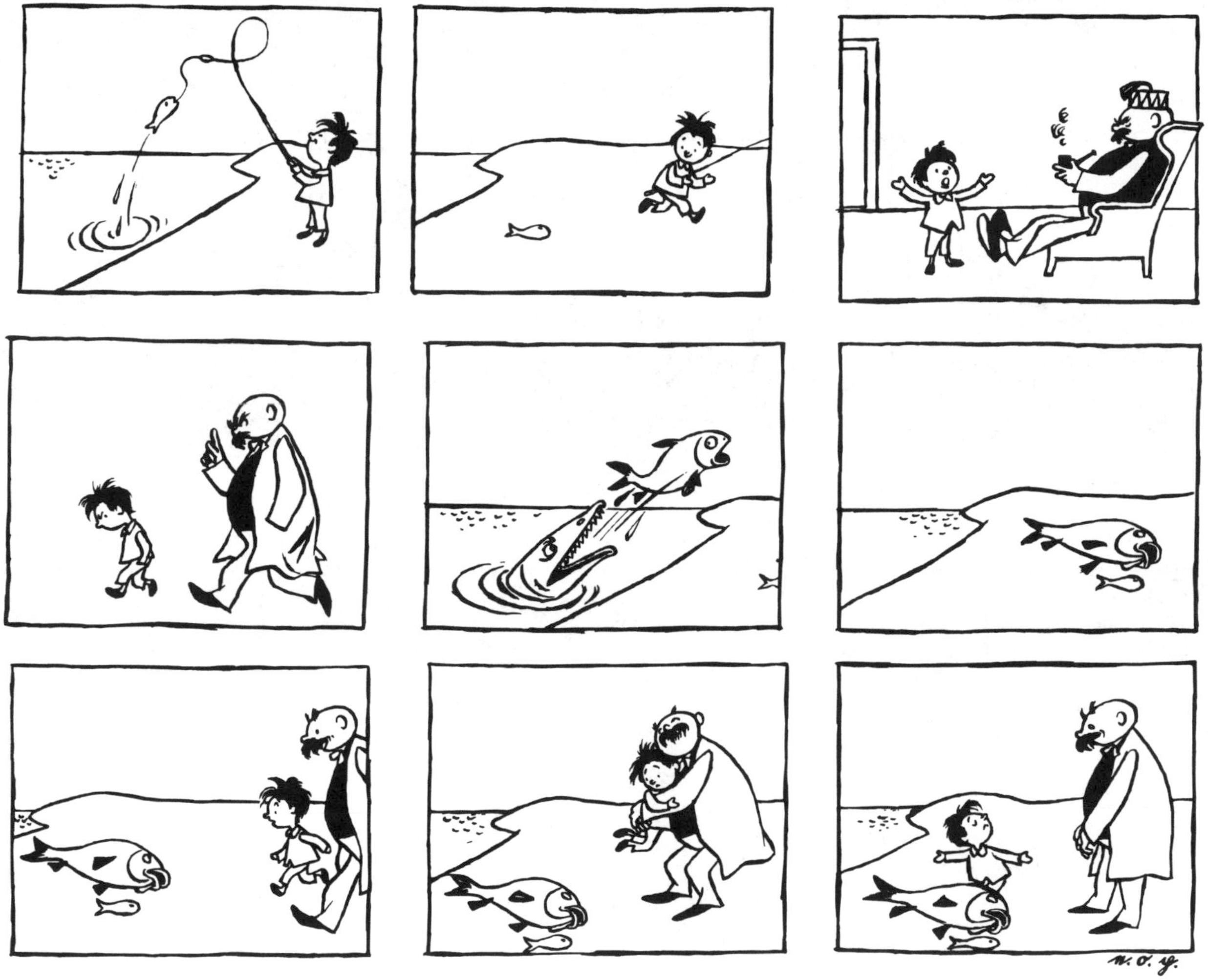

“Really it was THIS BIG!”

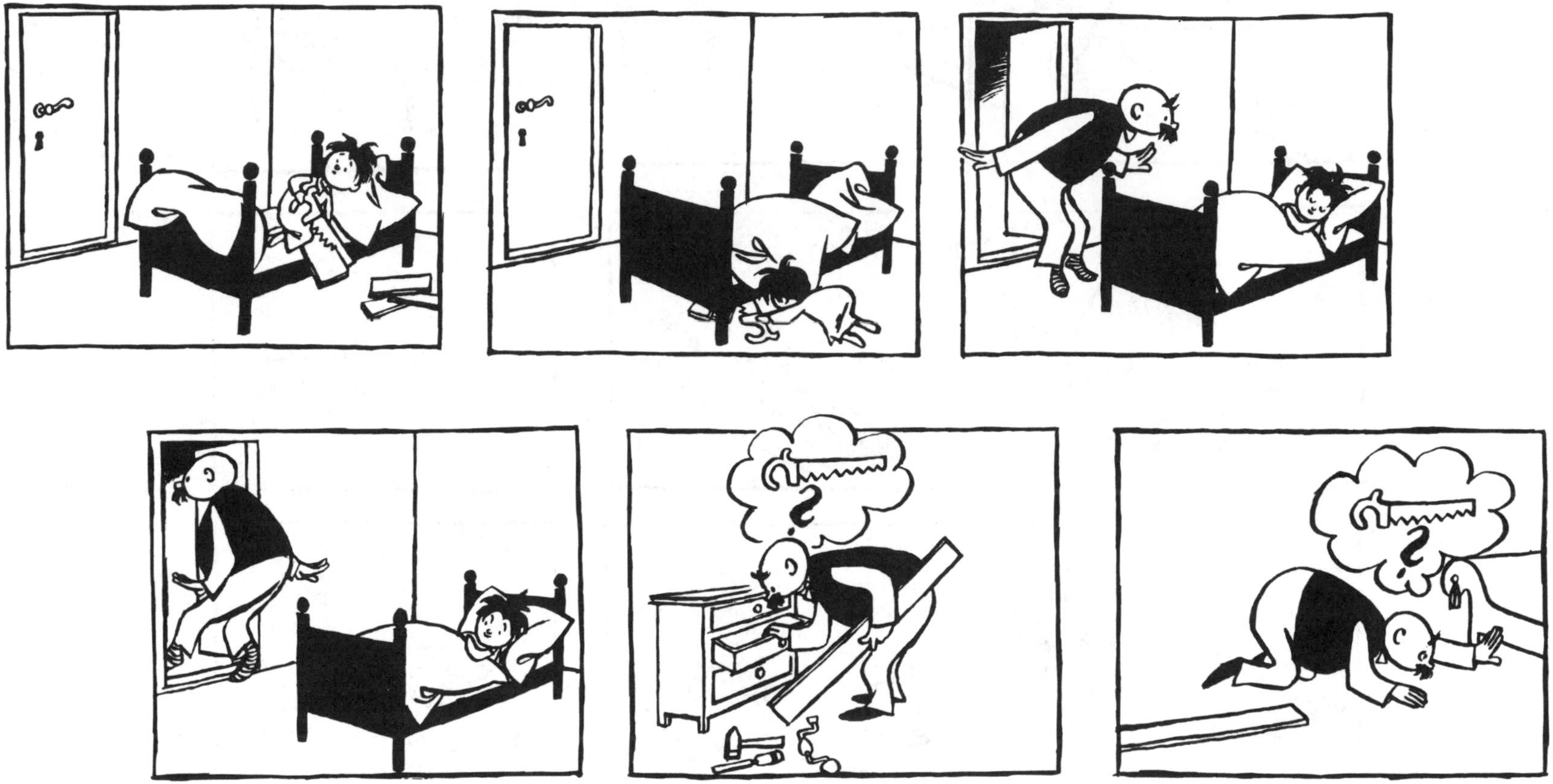

Secret Christmas project

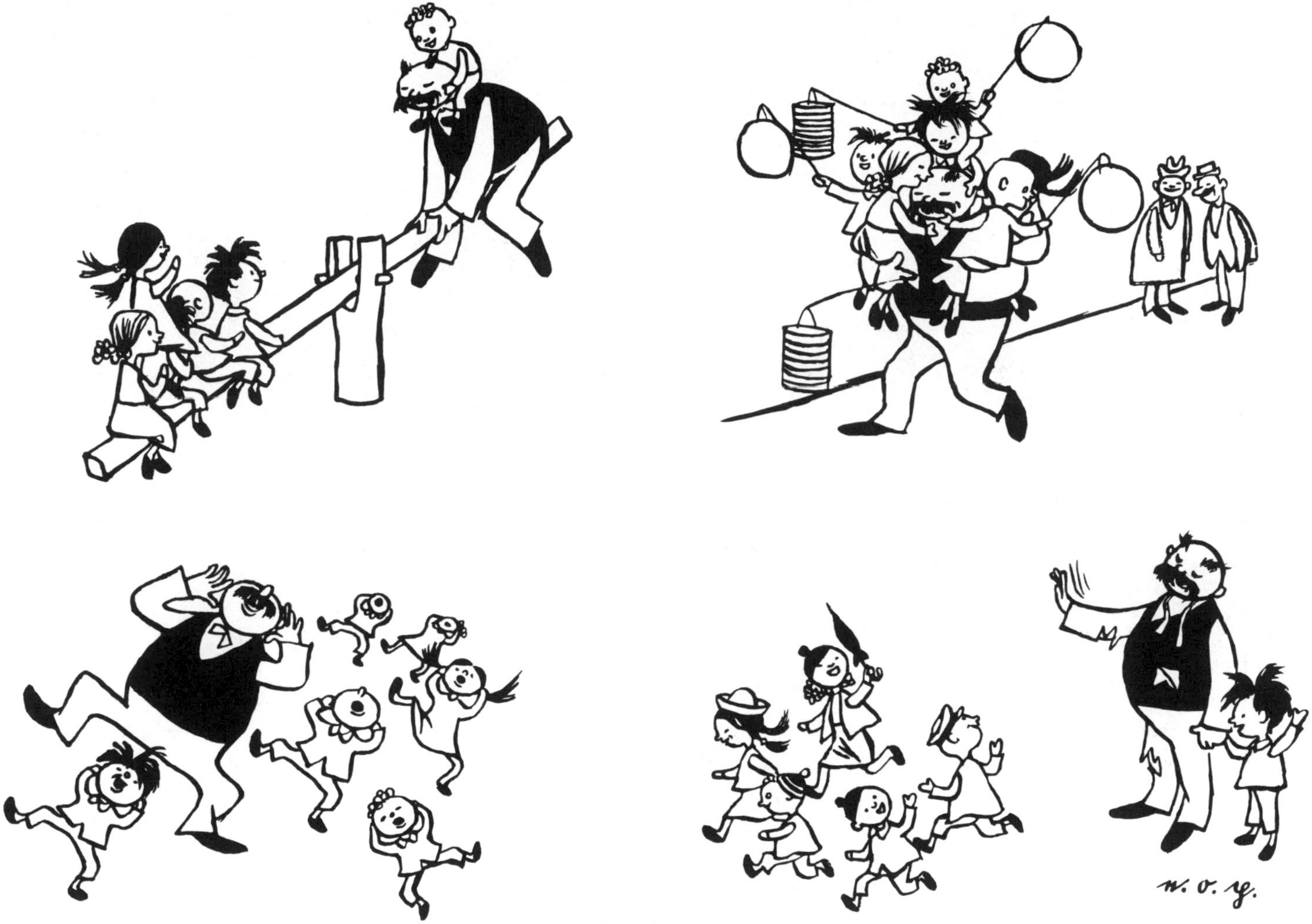
w. o. g.

Birthday party

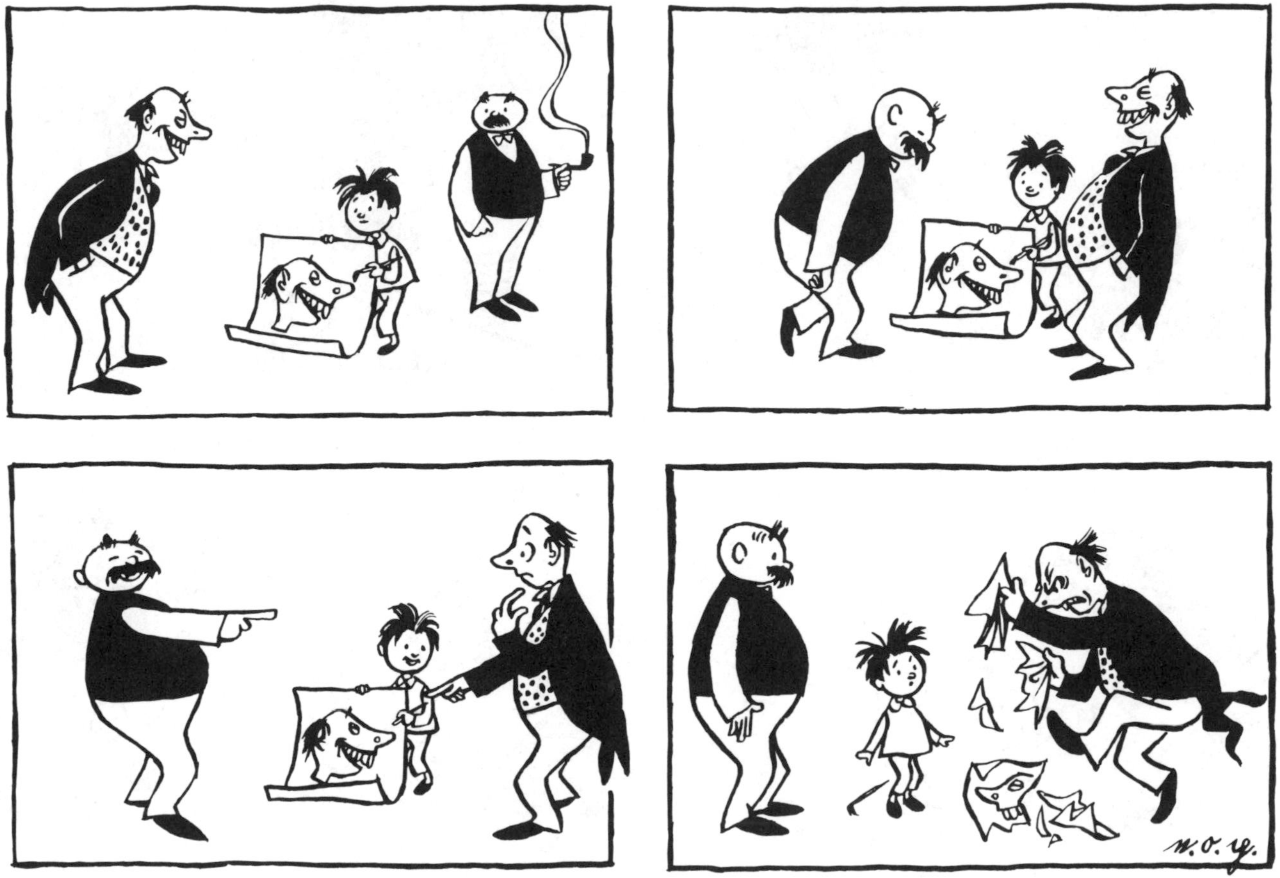

“What! That’s supposed to be me?”

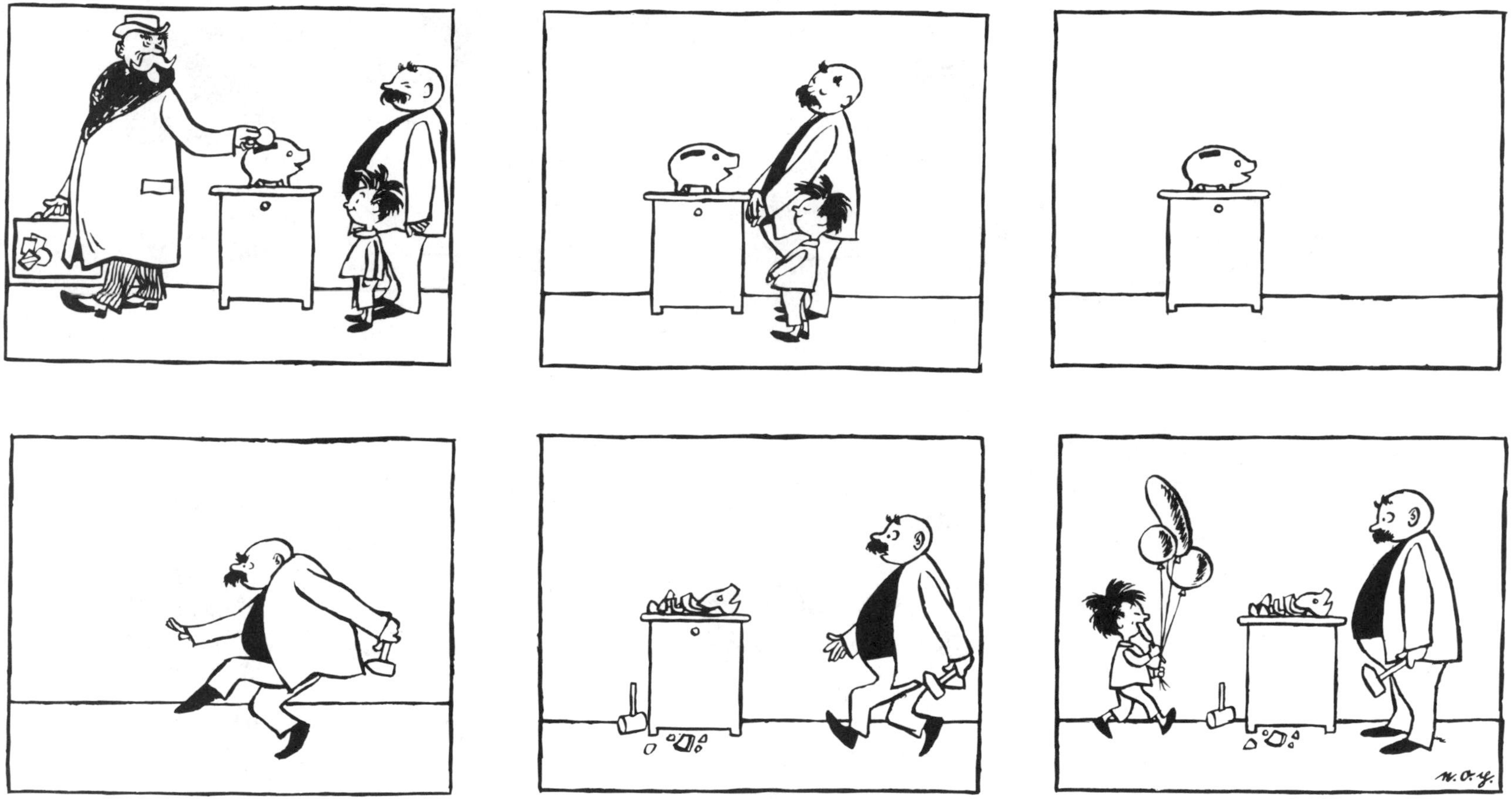

Got there first

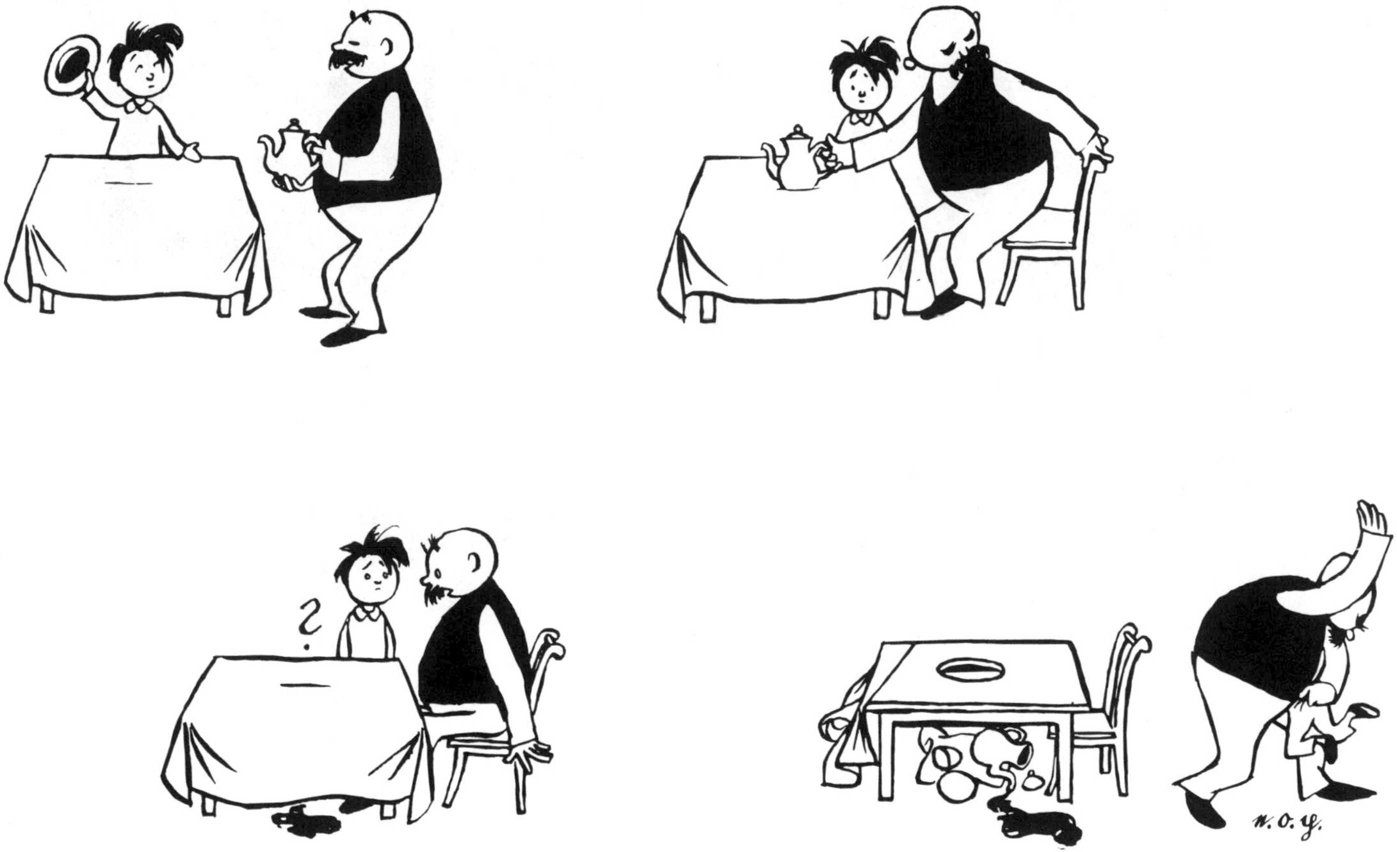

Abracadabra

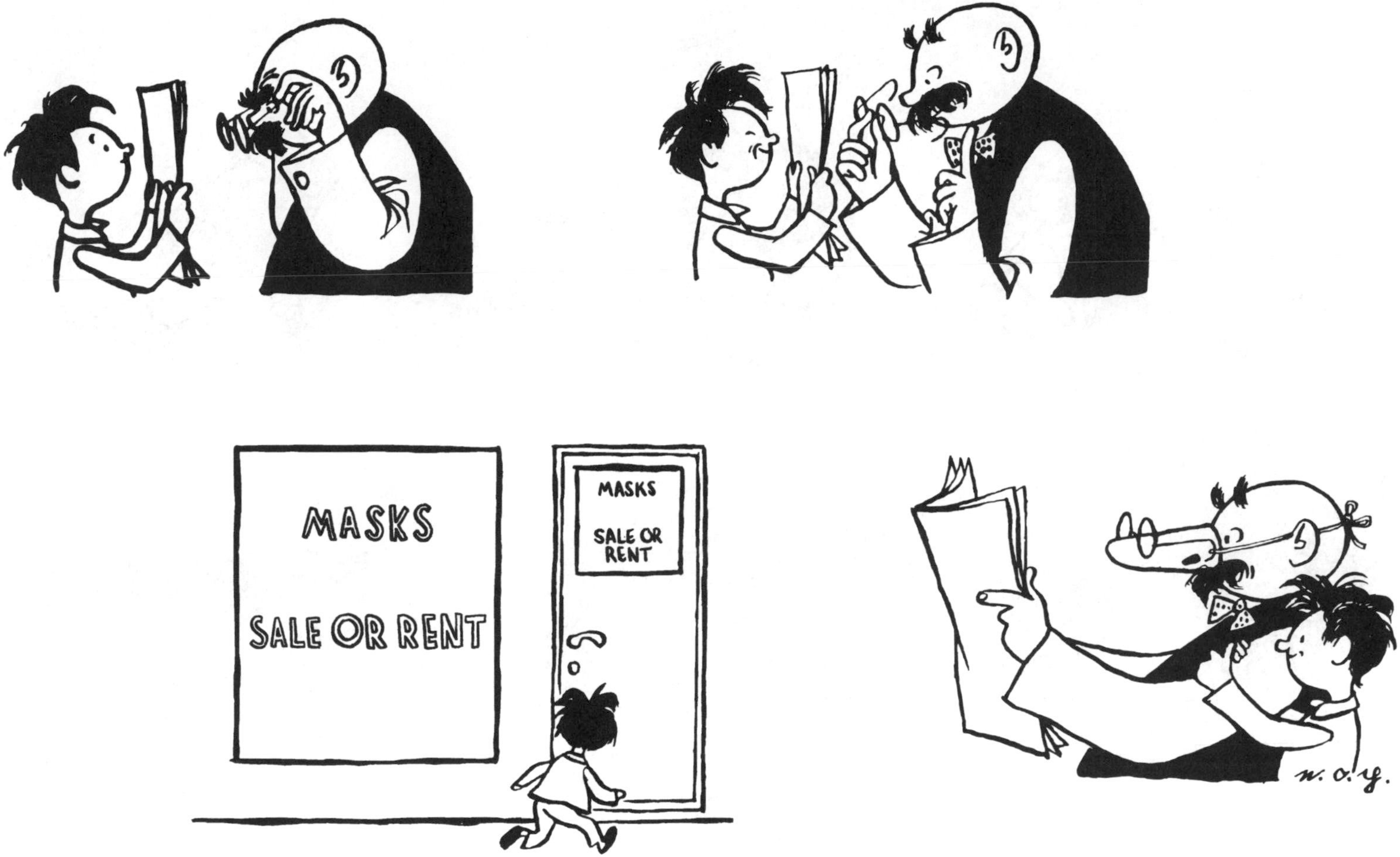
MASKS
SALE OR RENT
MASKS
SALE OR RENT
w. o. y.

The right distance

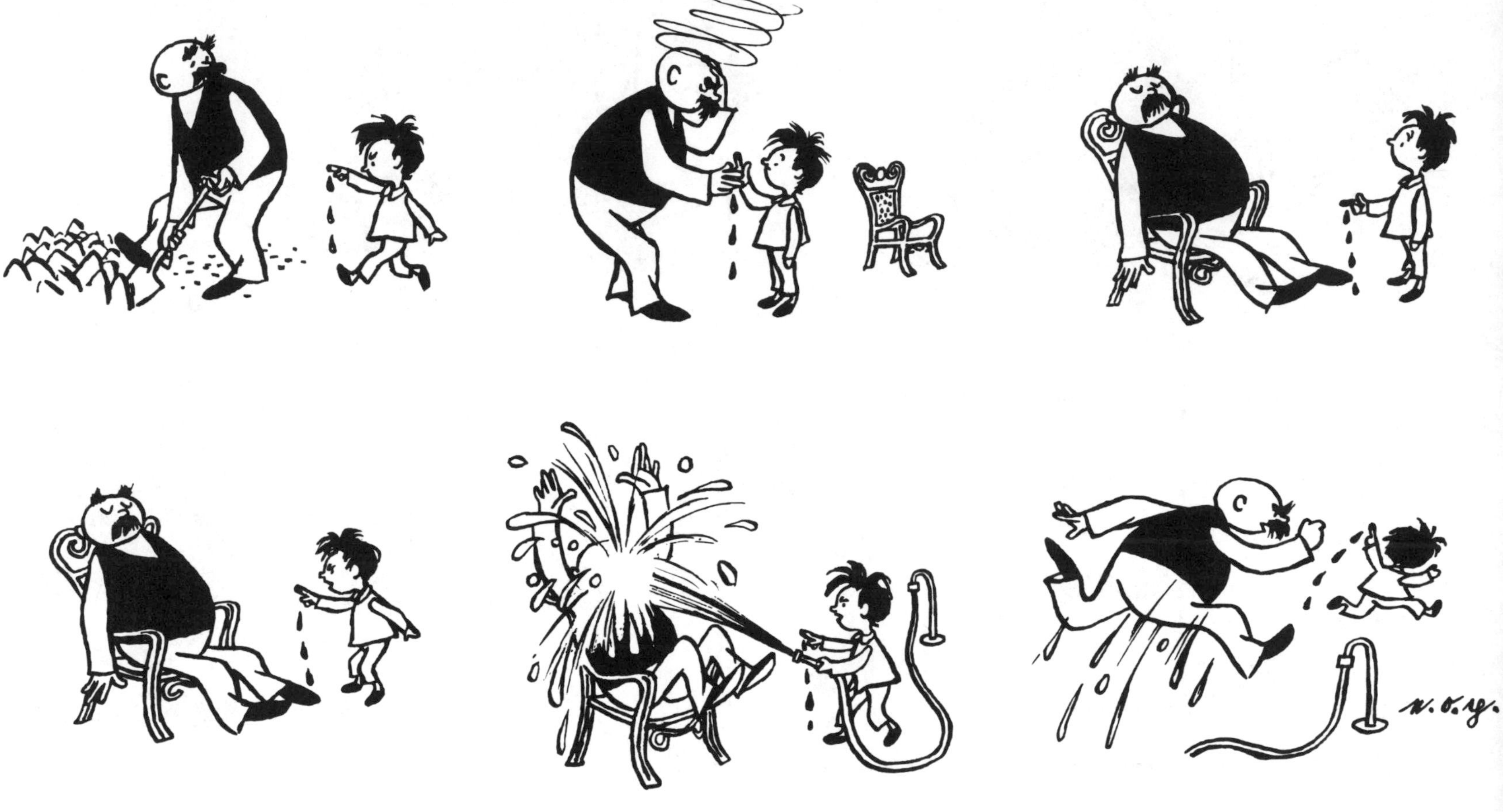

Father can't bear the sight of blood

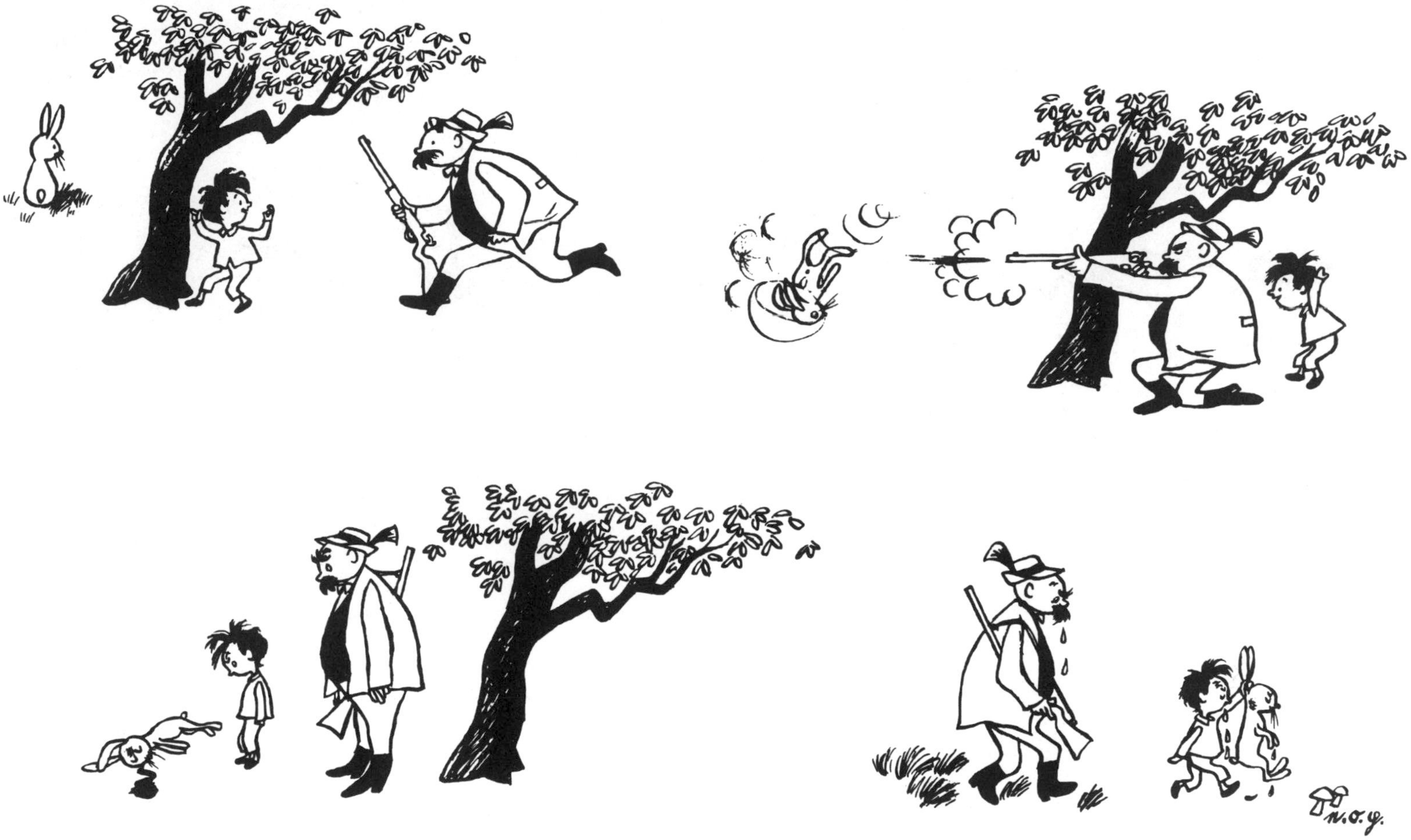

Hunter's remorse

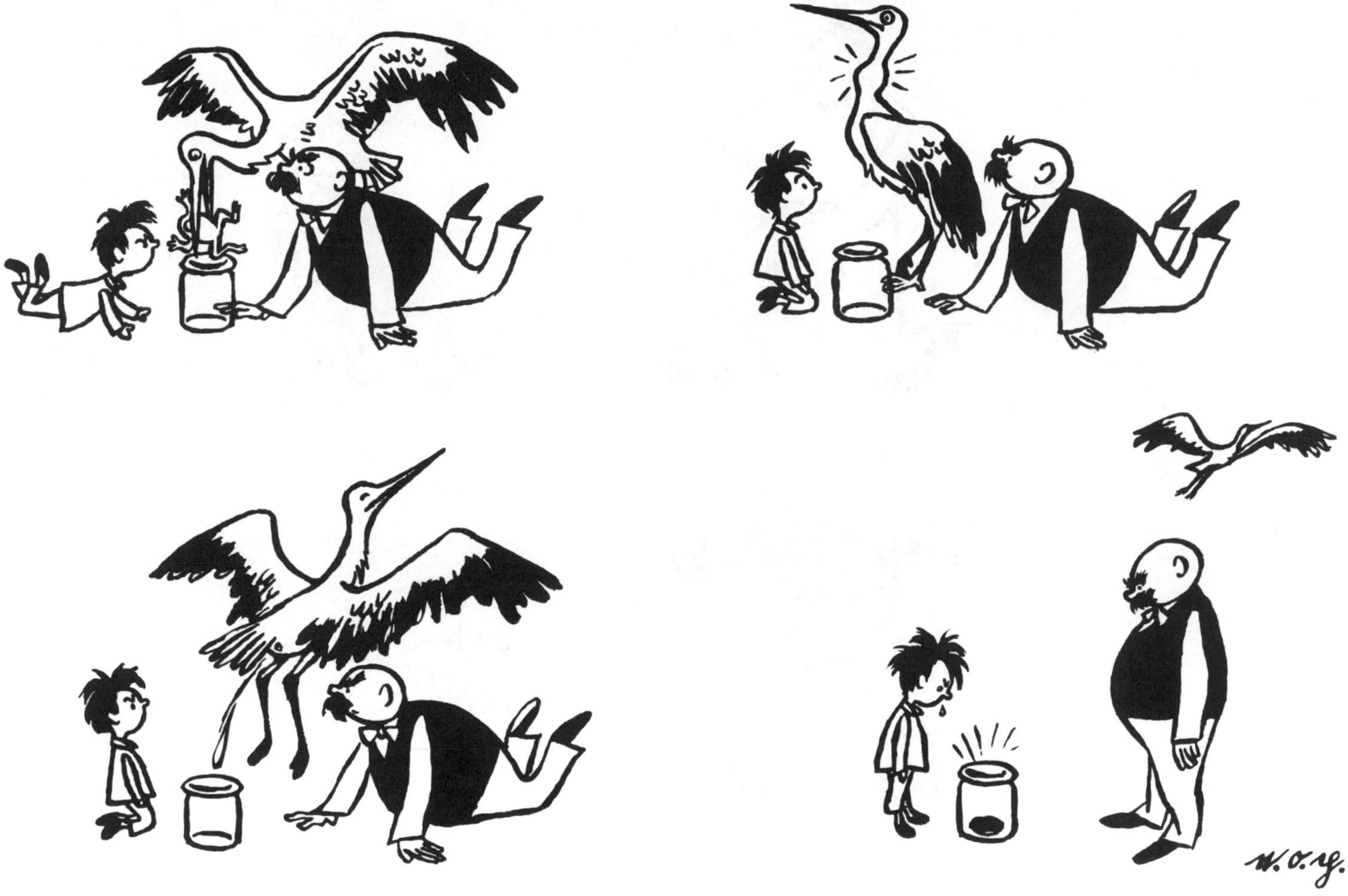

All things must pass

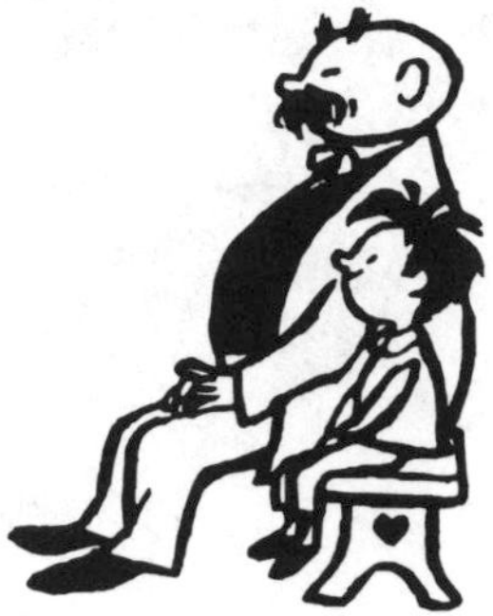
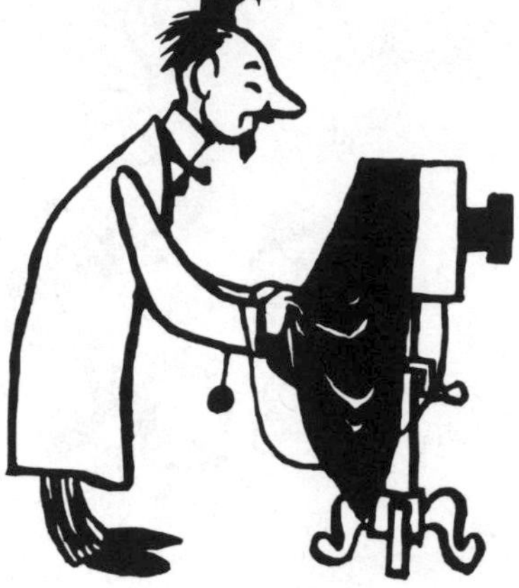
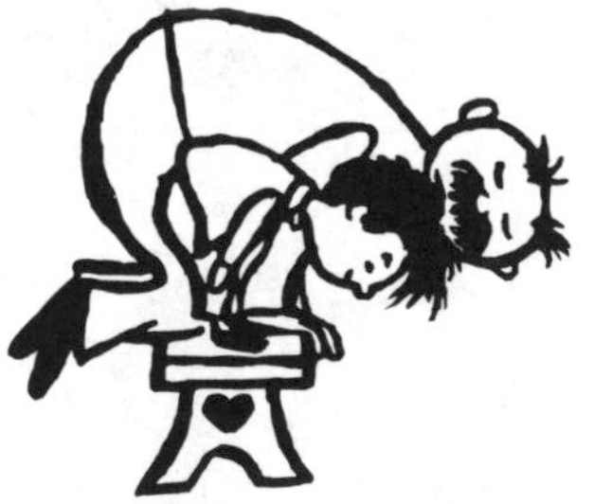
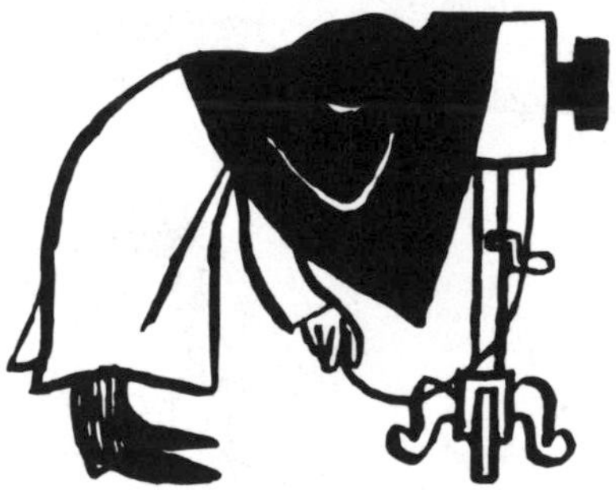

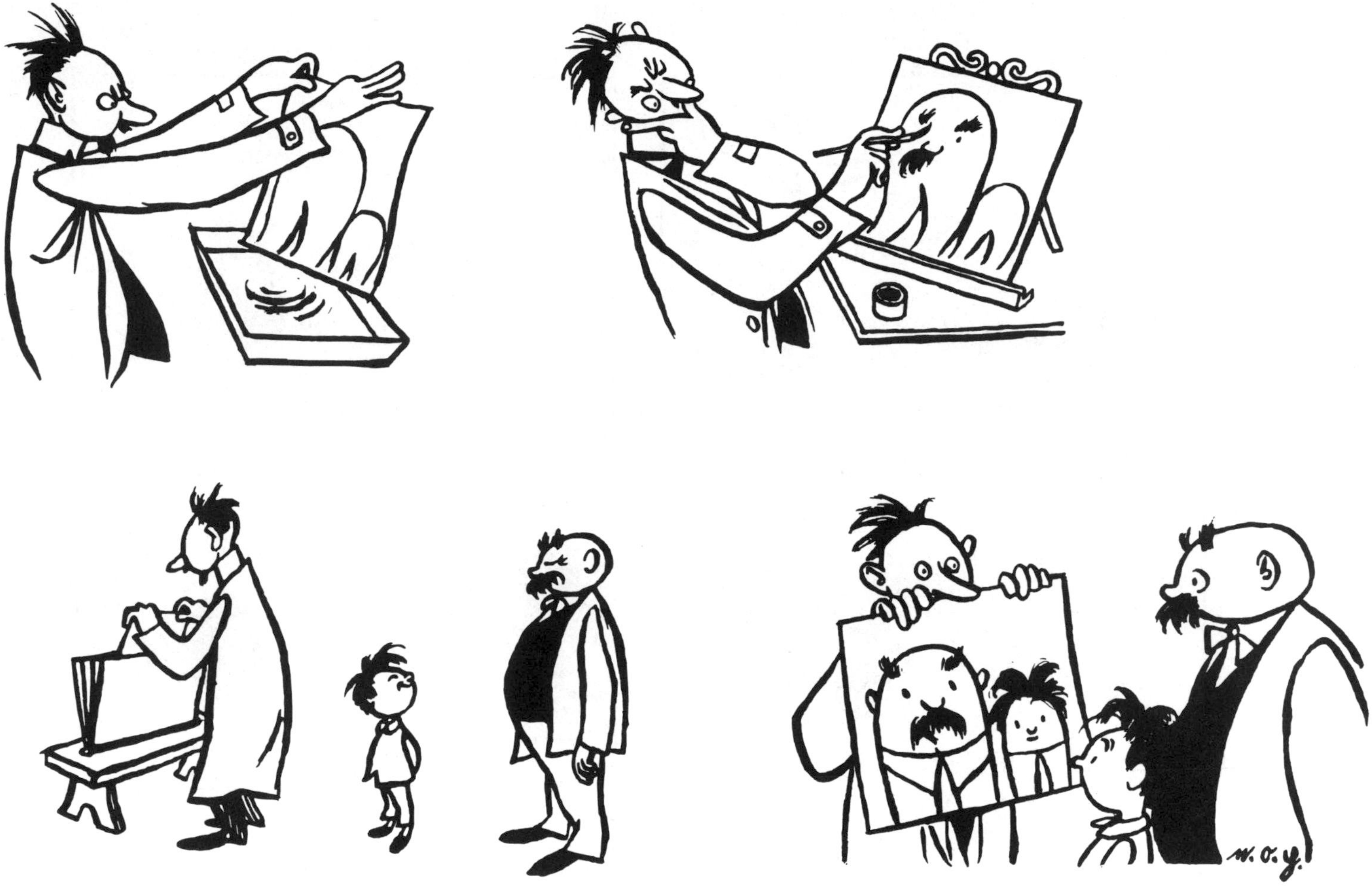
w. o. y.

Portrait photography

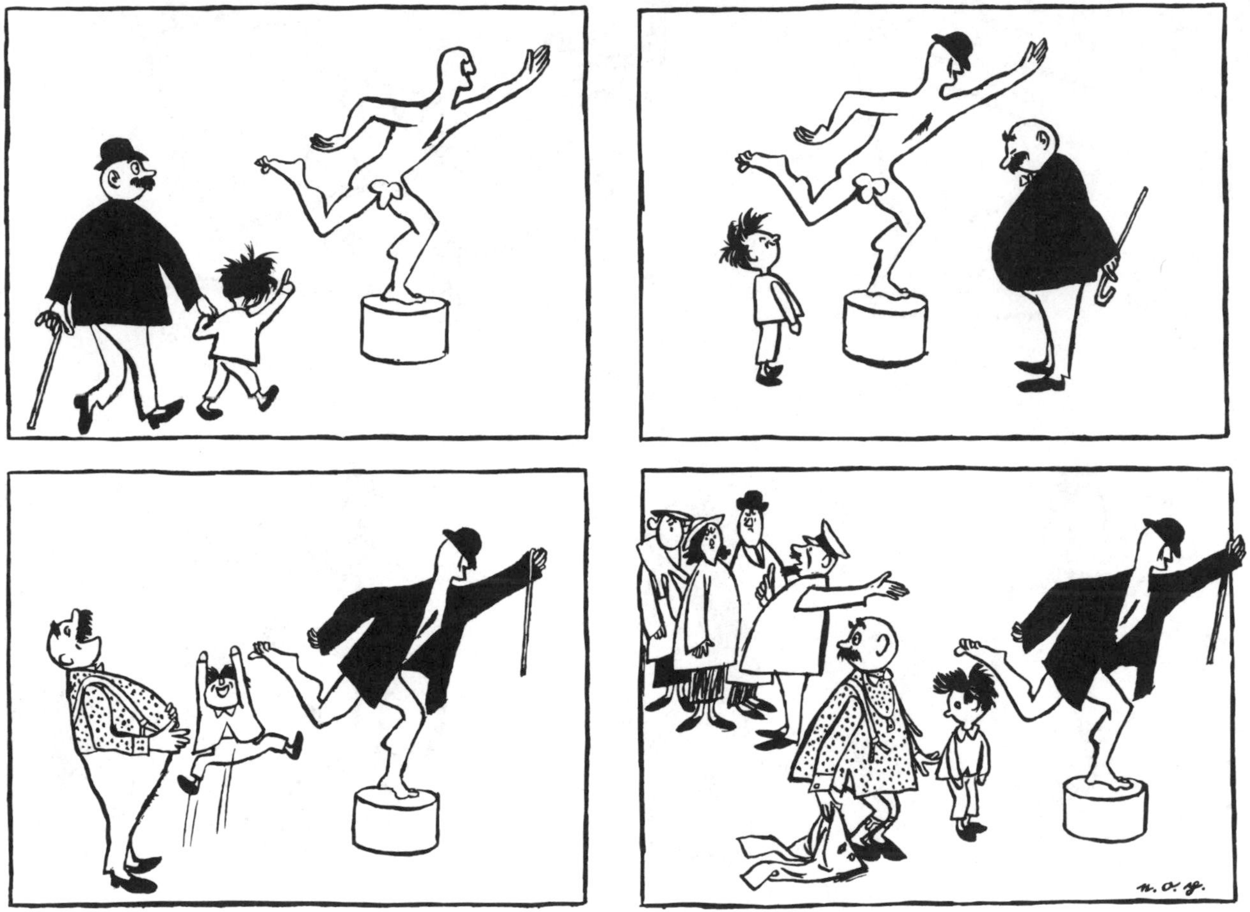

Fun at the museum

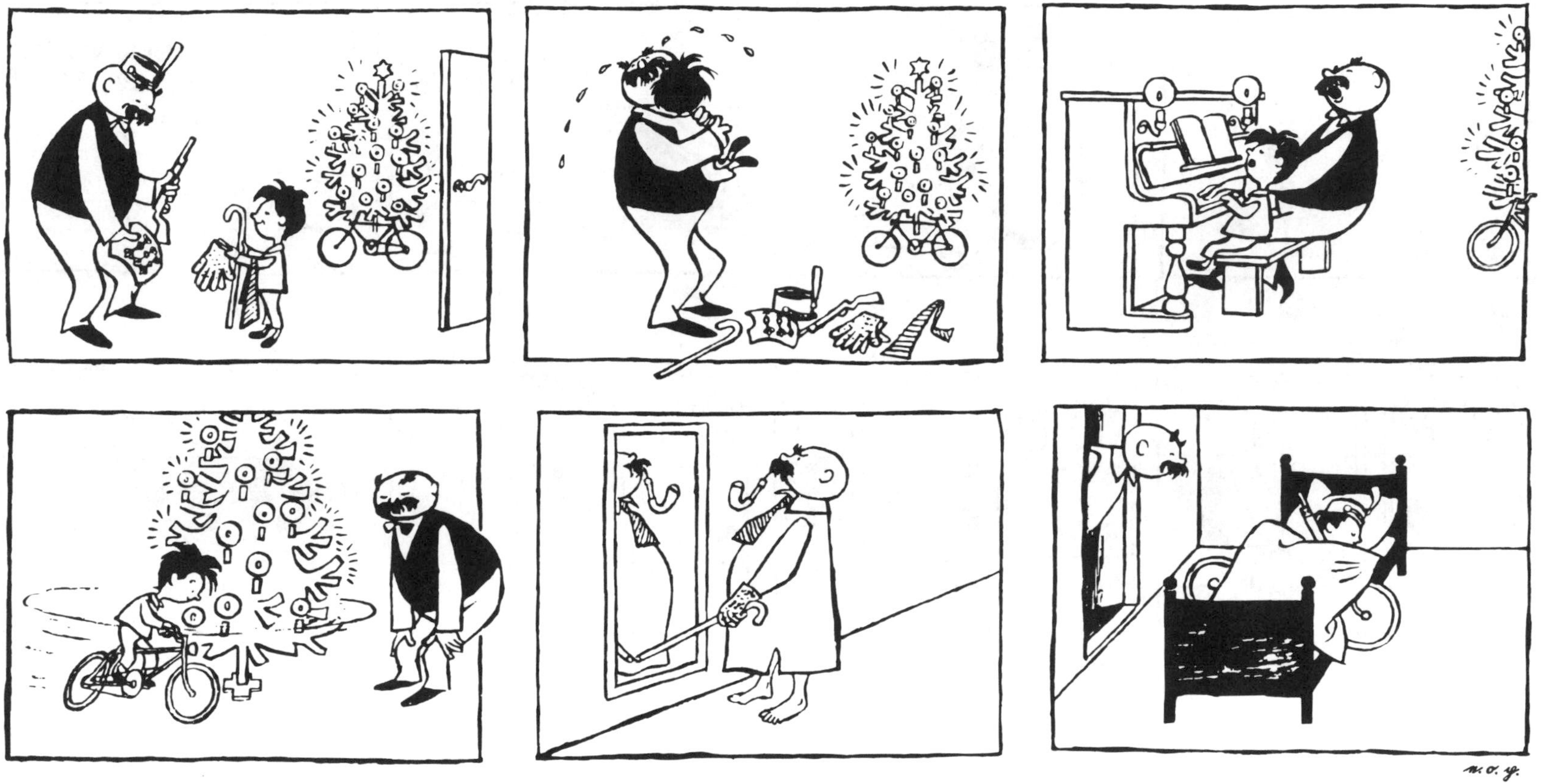

Christmas presents

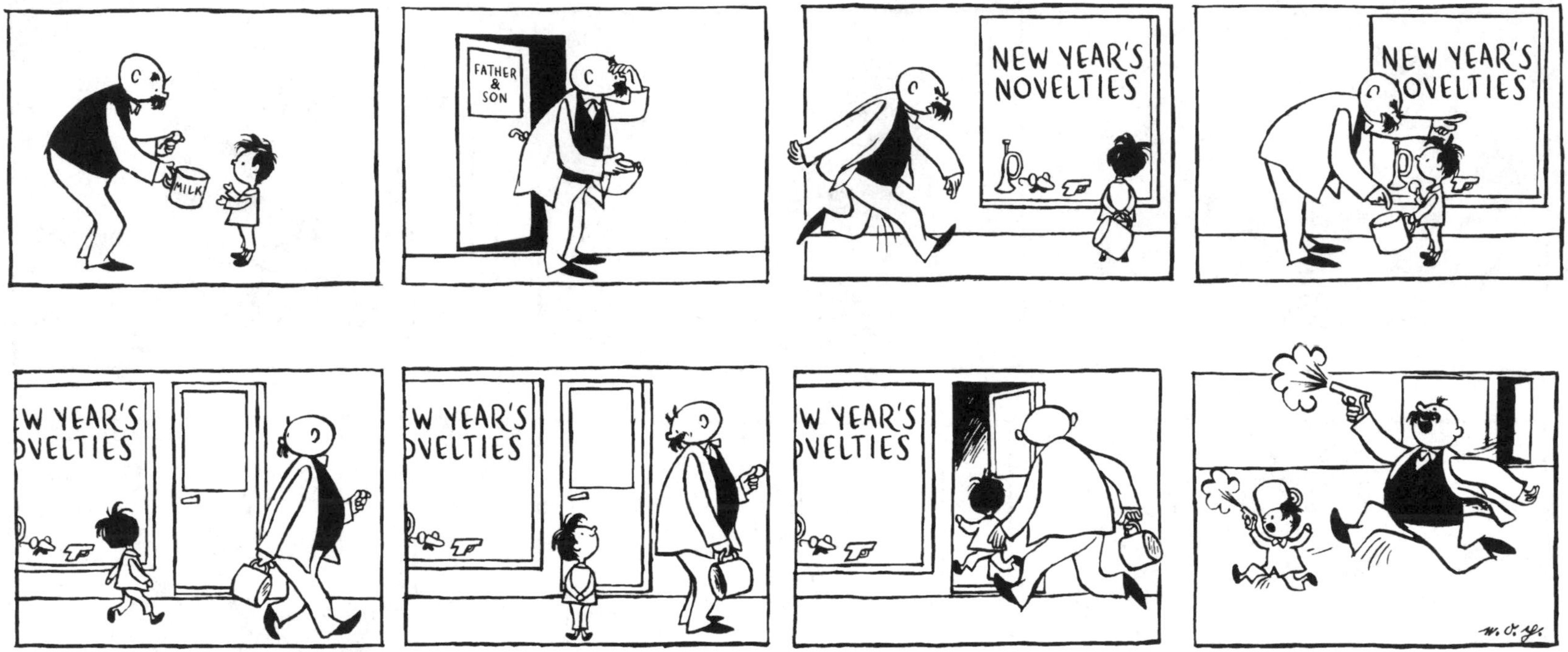
MILK
FATHER & SON
NEW YEAR'S NOVELTIES
NEW YEAR'S OVELTIES
EW YEAR'S VELTIES
W YEAR'S VELTIES
W YEAR'S VELTIES

Out with a bang

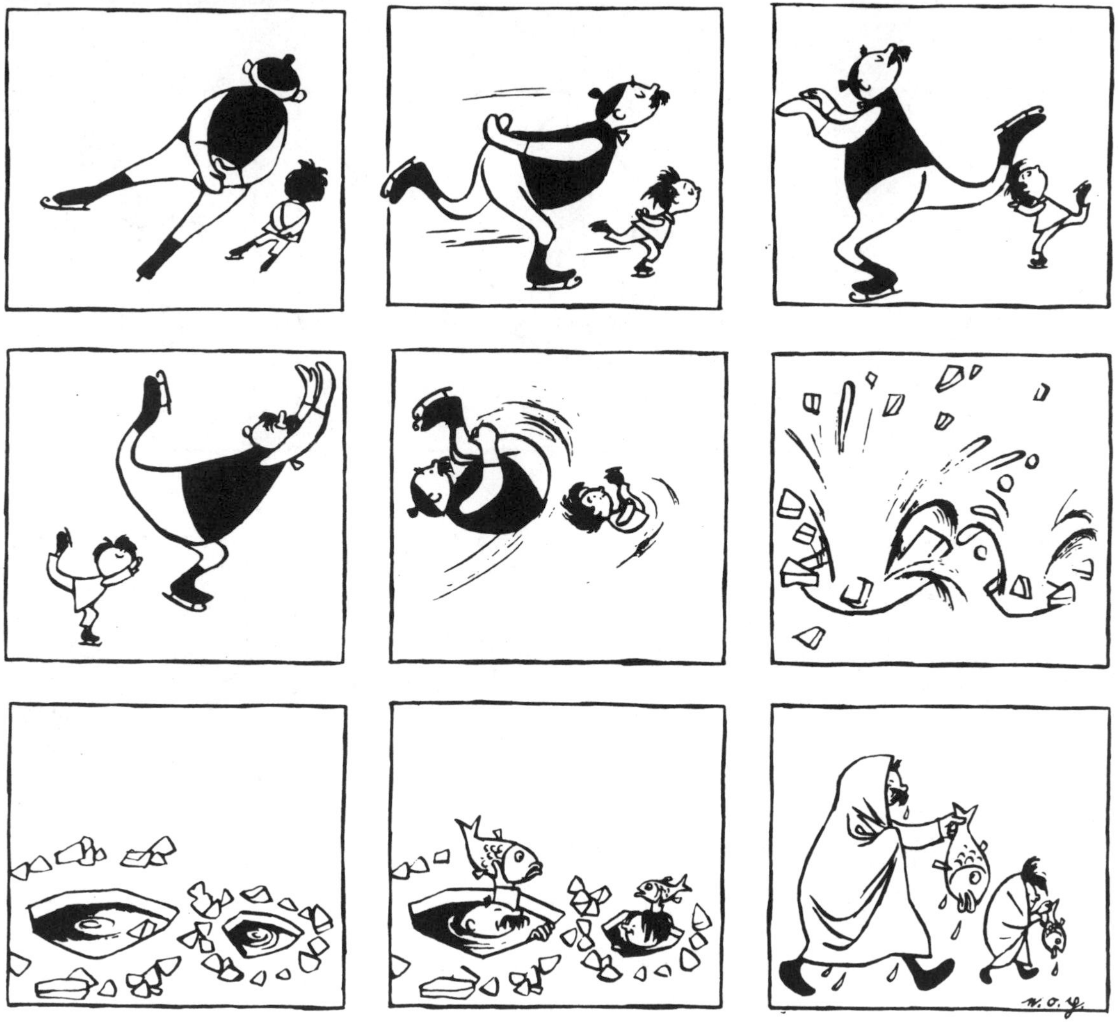

All's well that ends well

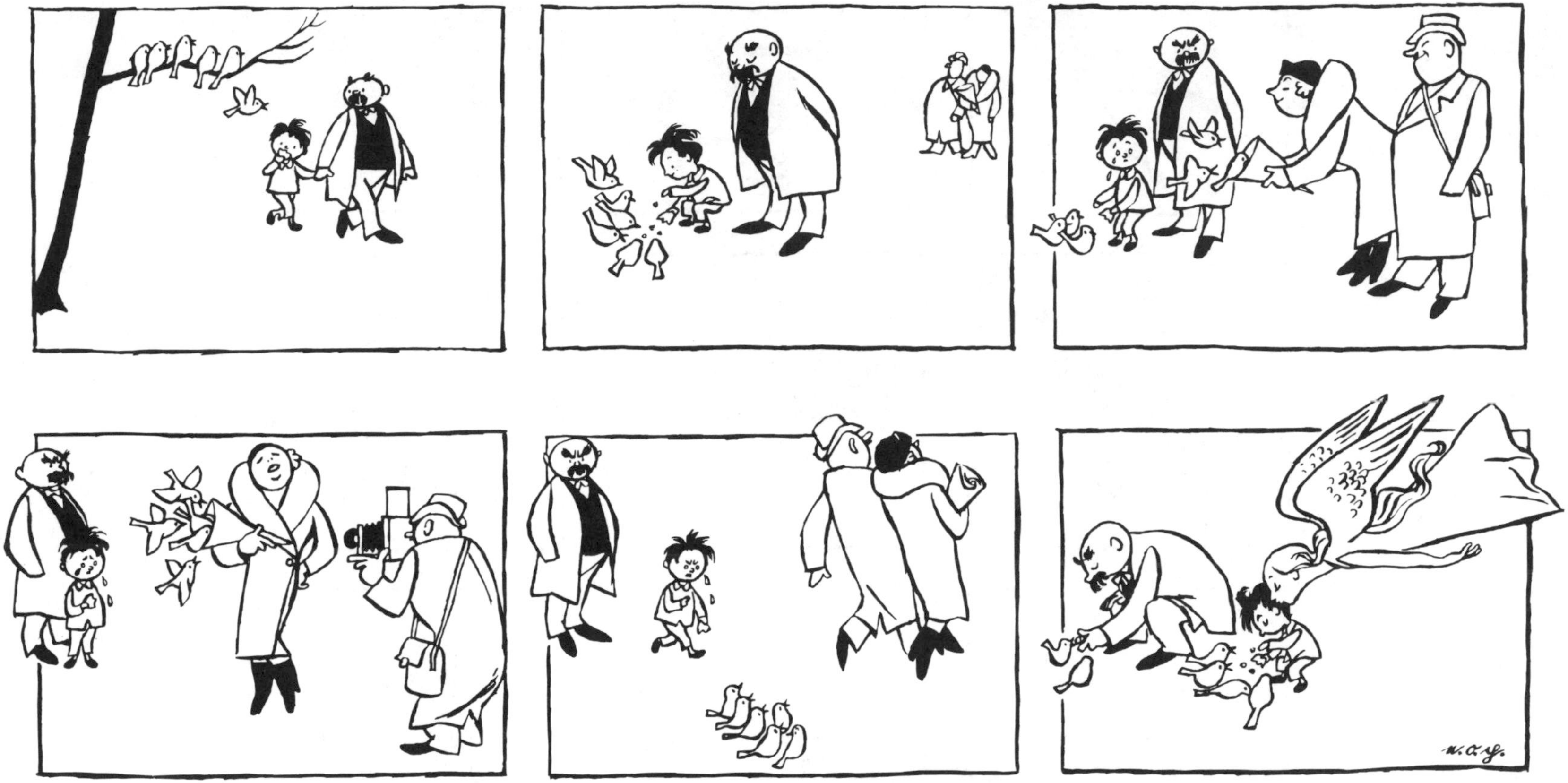

For show and for real

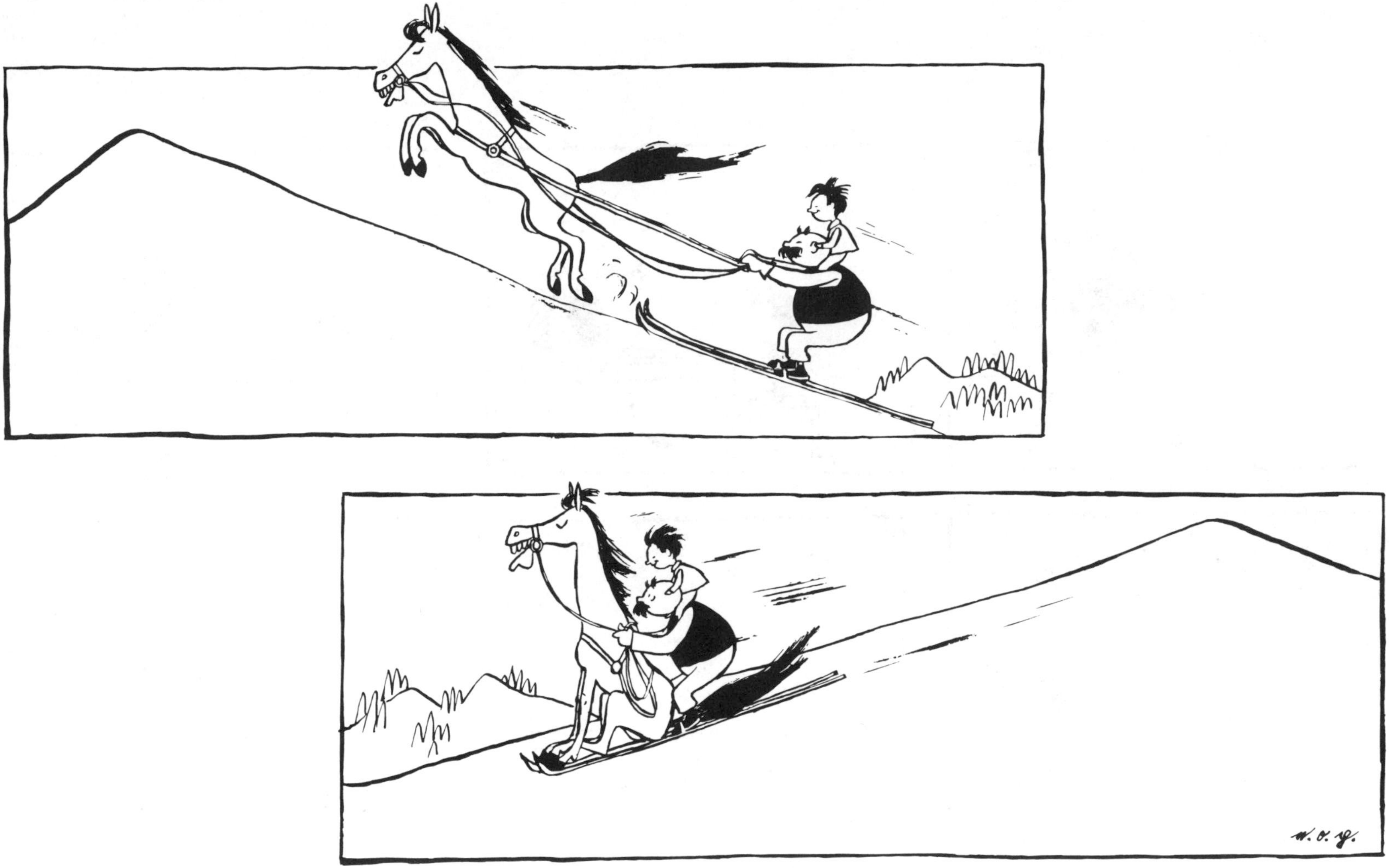

The clever horse

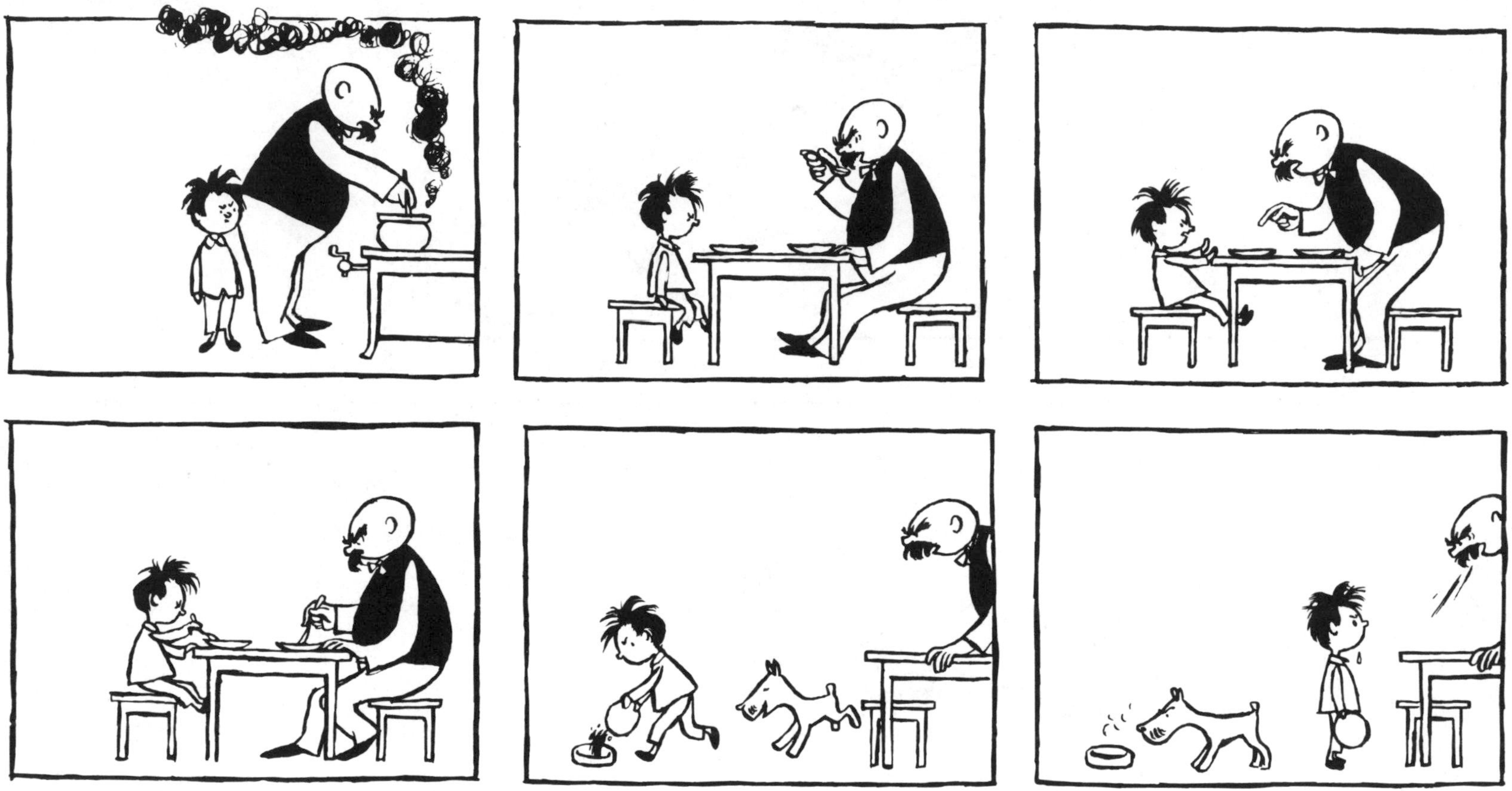

The lesson of the burned beans

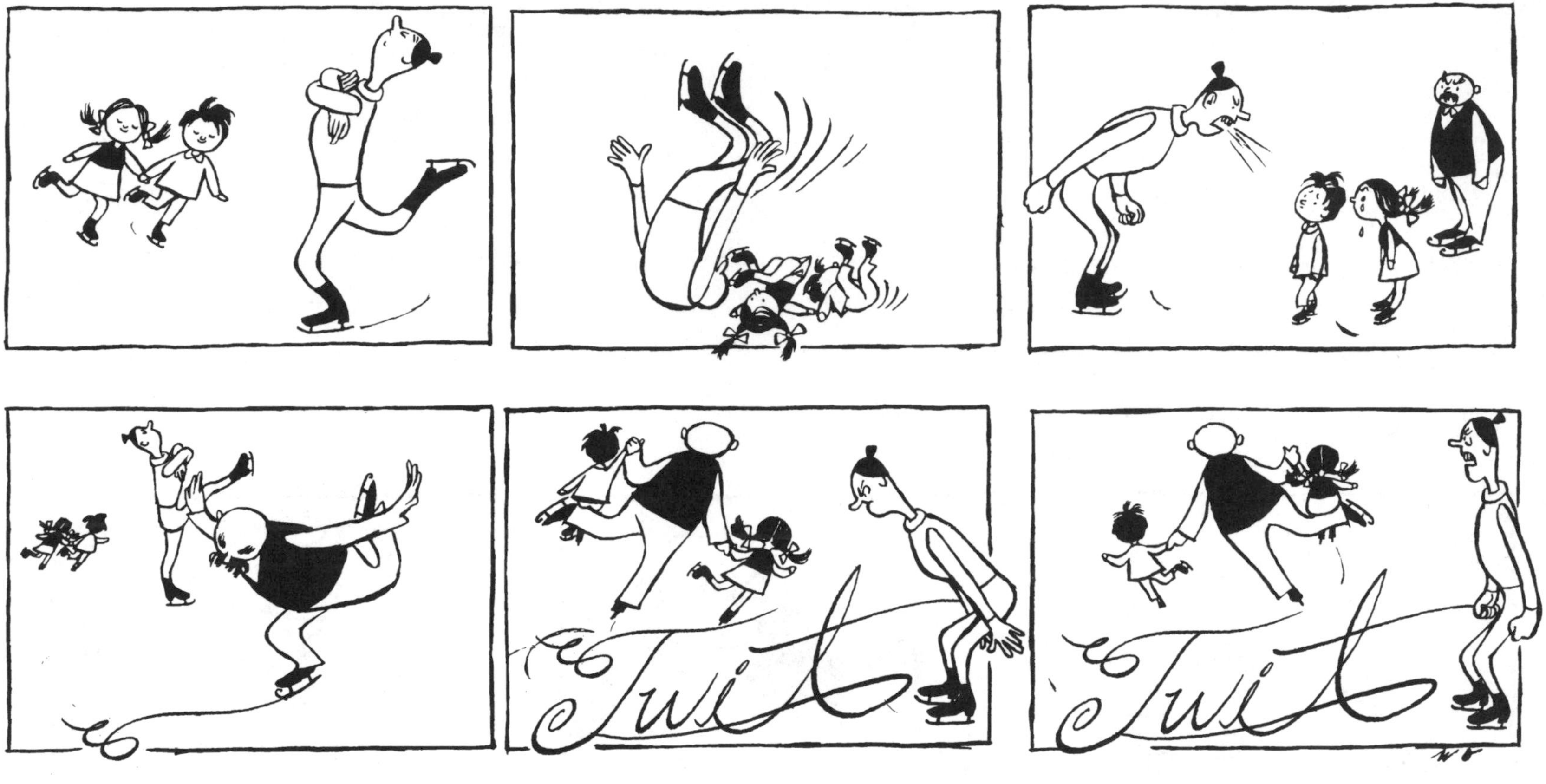
Twist
Twist

That's devotion

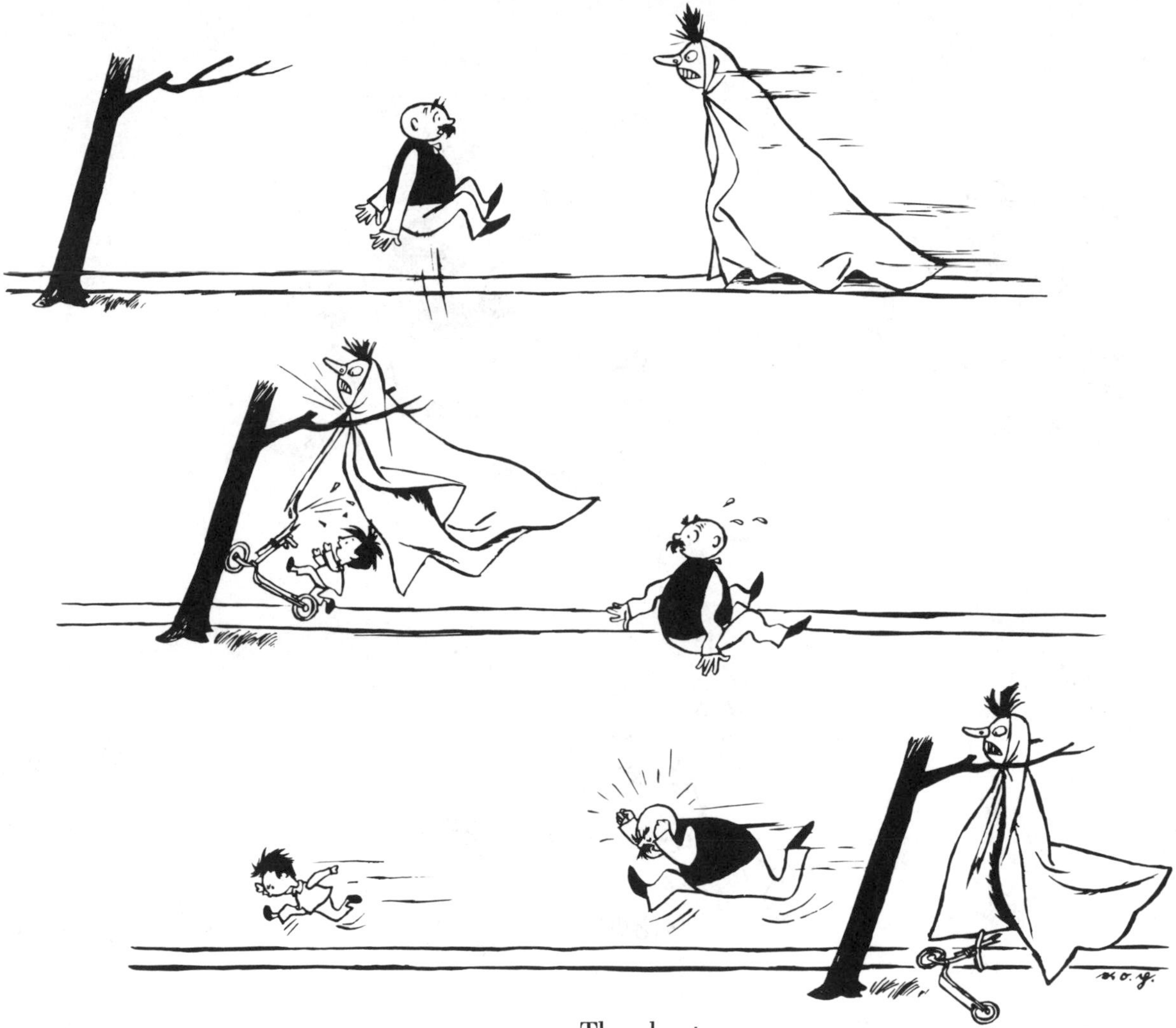

The ghost

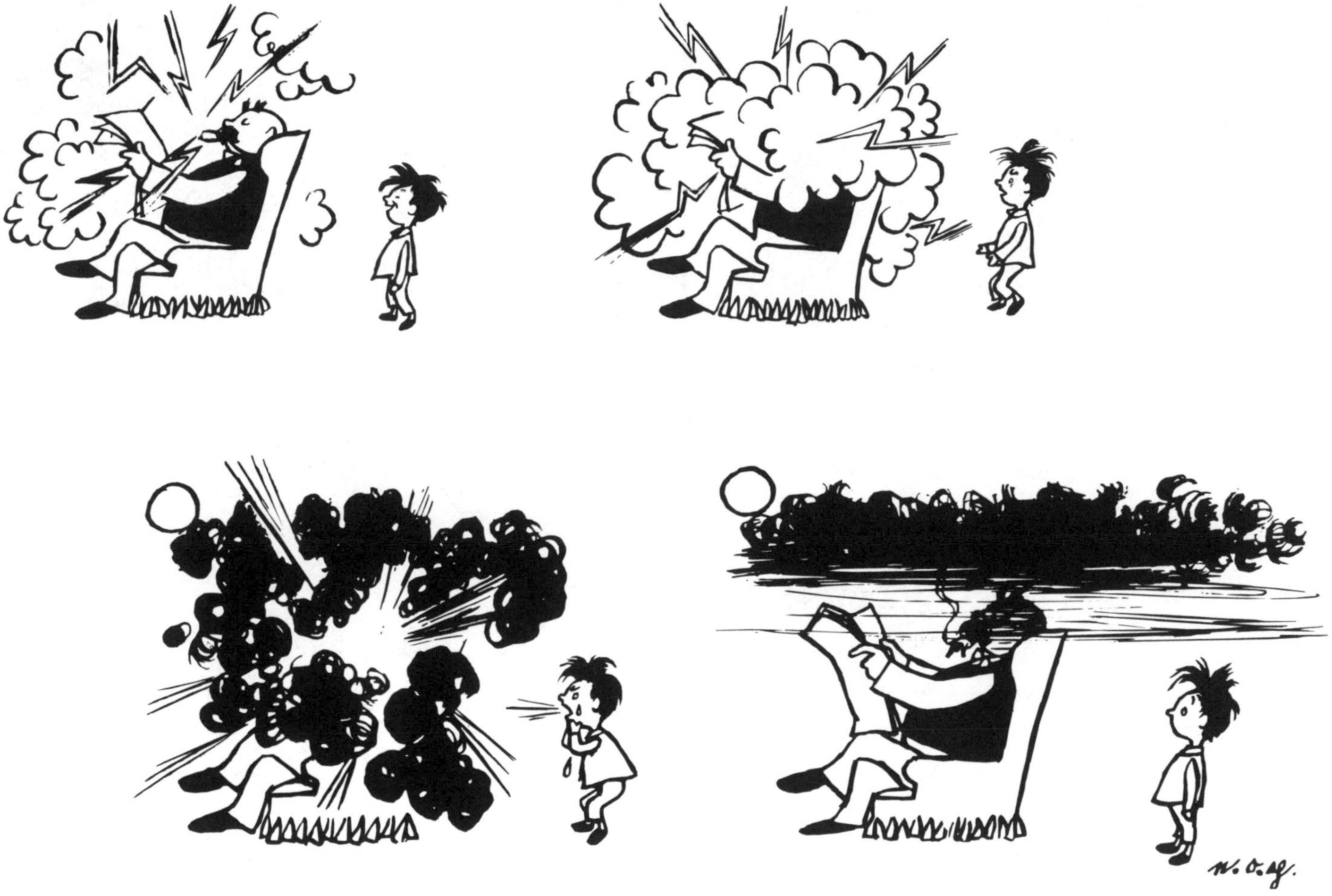

The exploding cigar

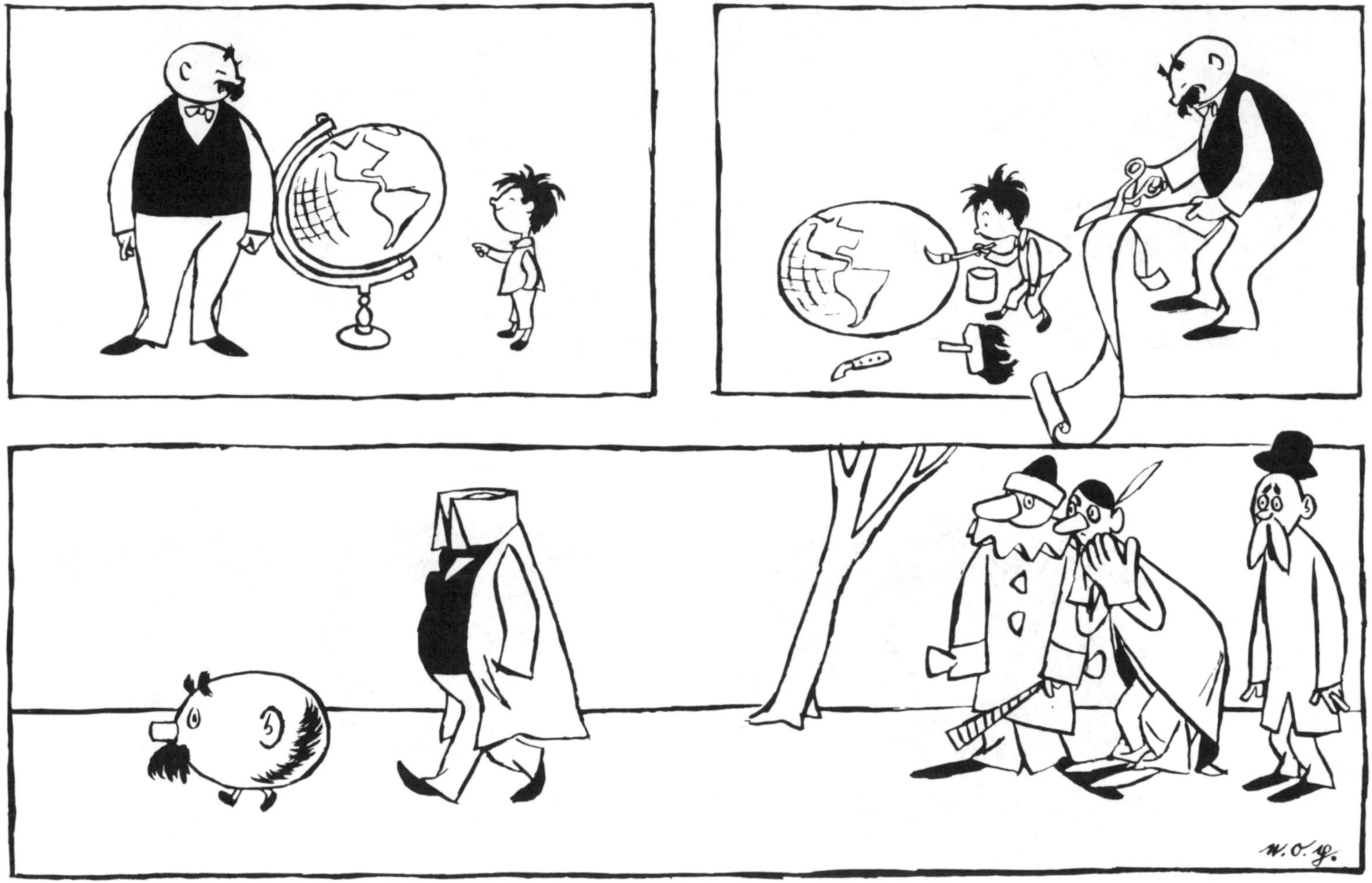
W.O.G.

Masquerade

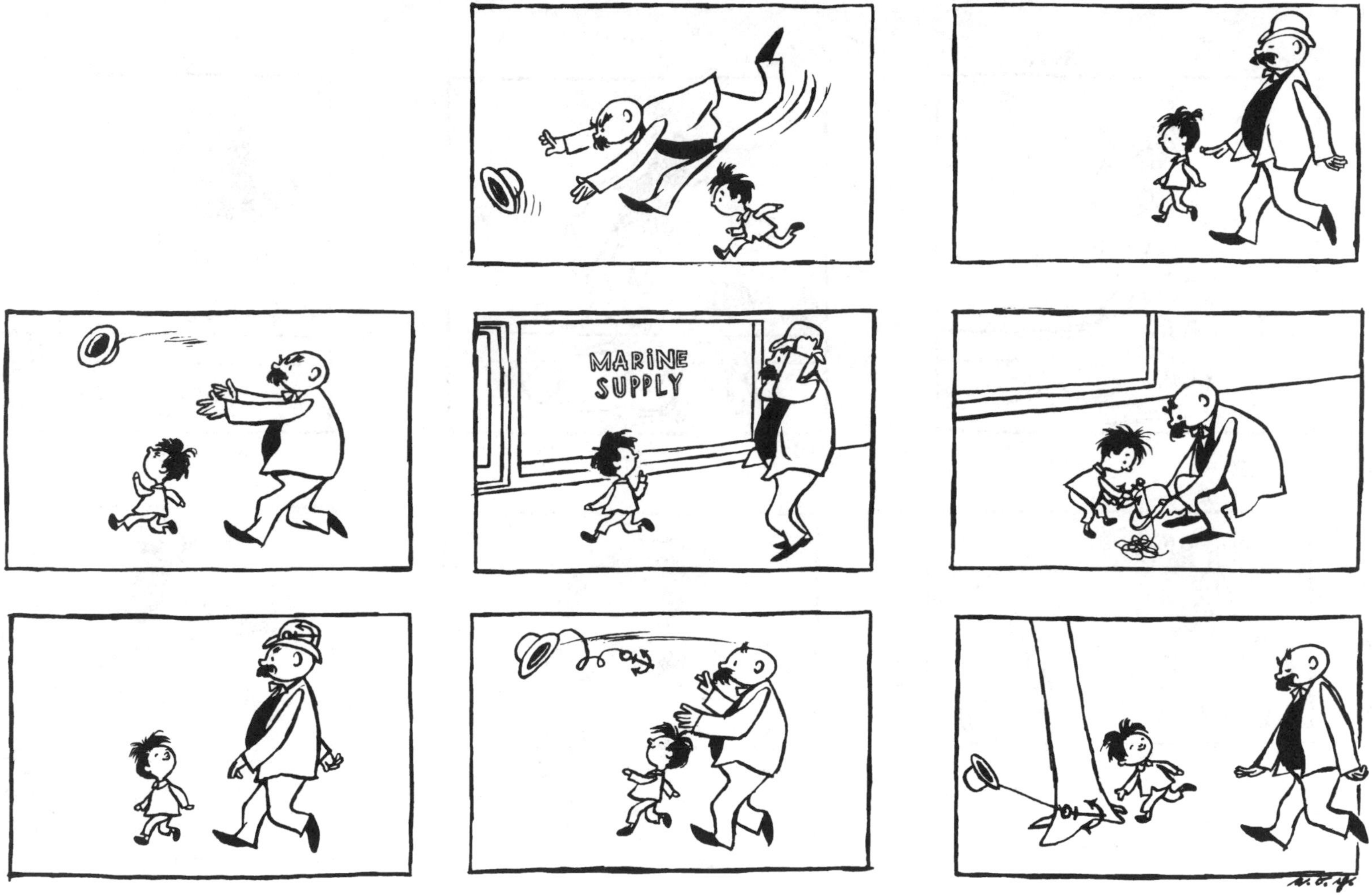
MARINE
SUPPLY

For windy days

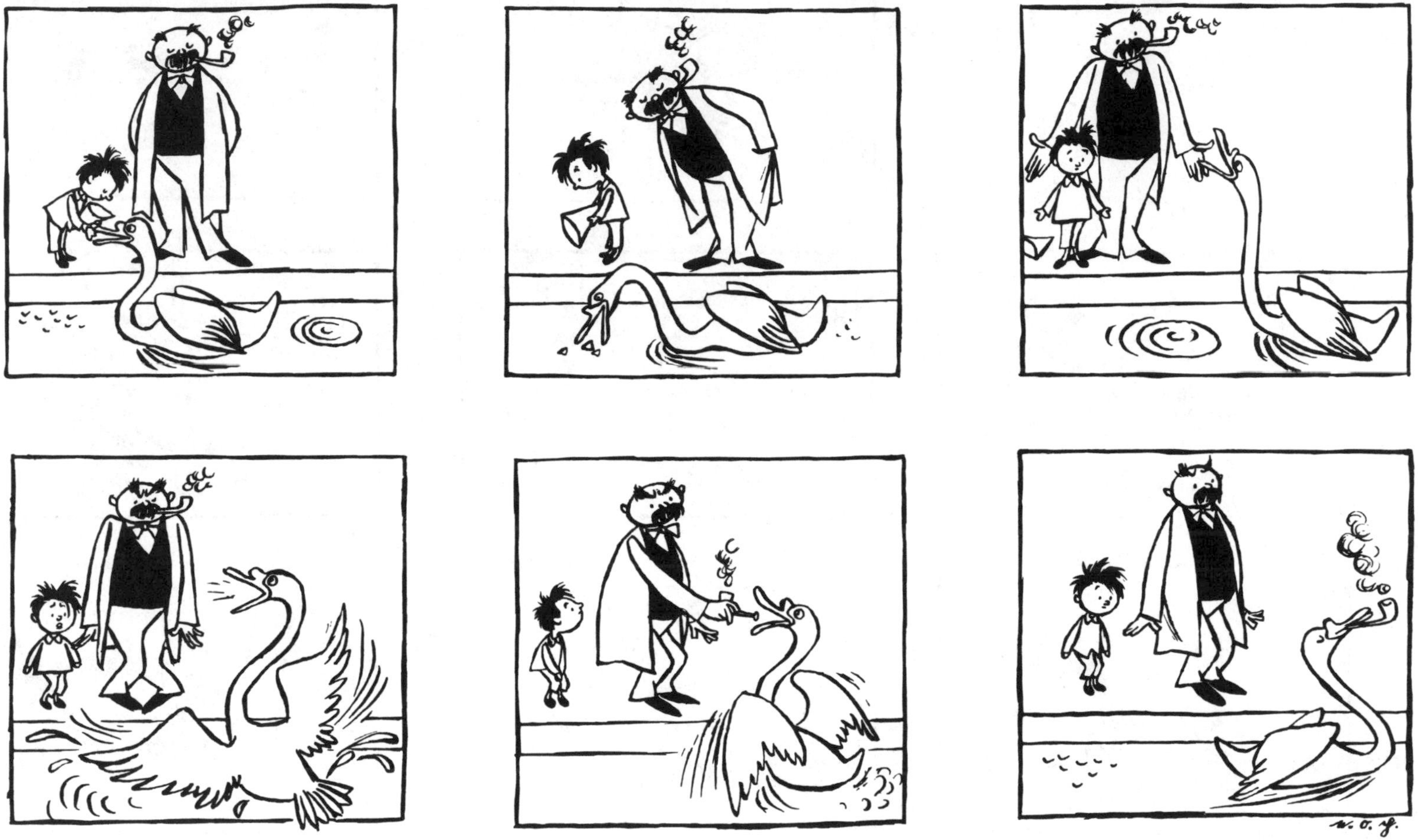

Watch out for swans!

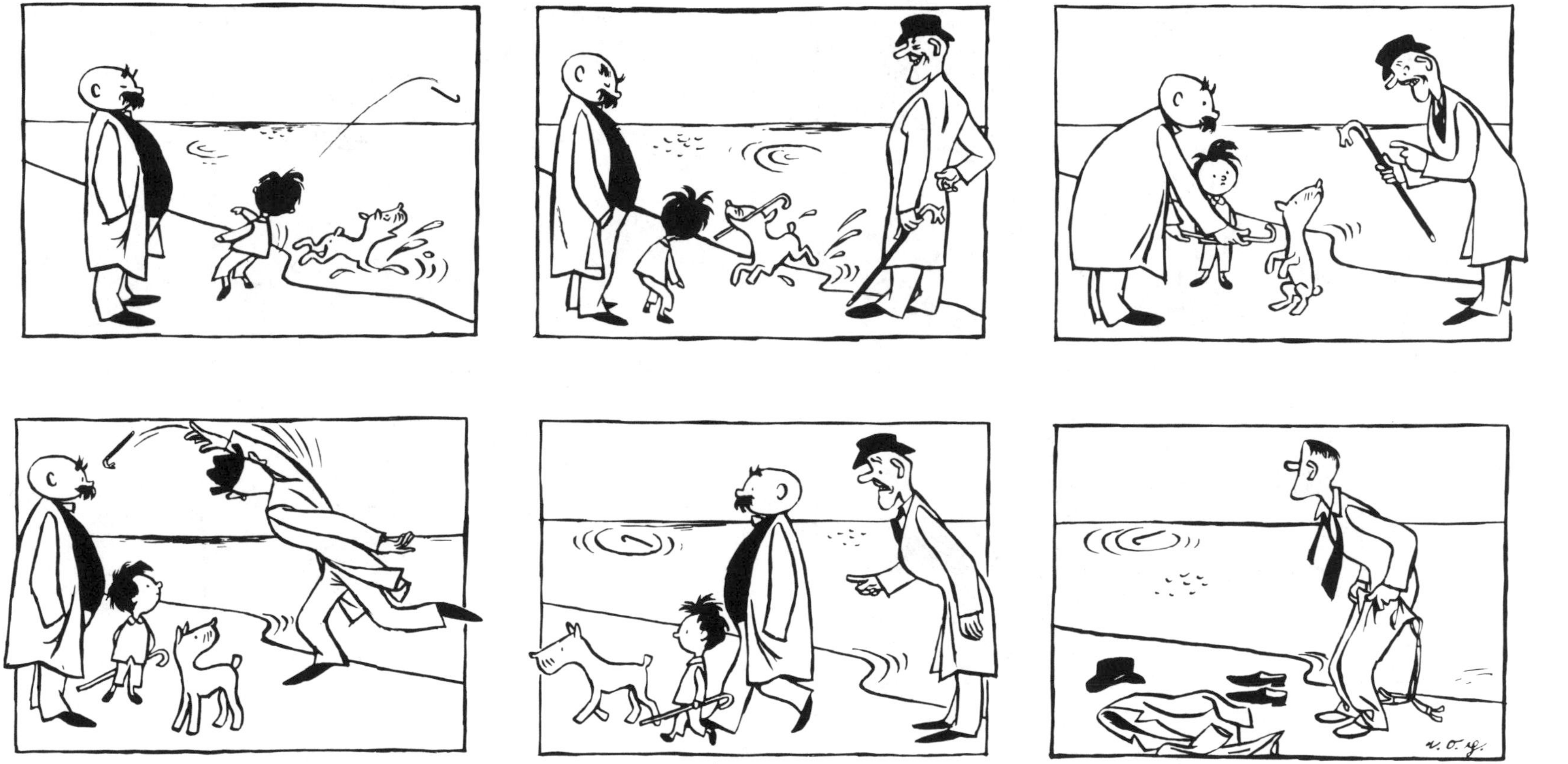

Unsuccessful overture

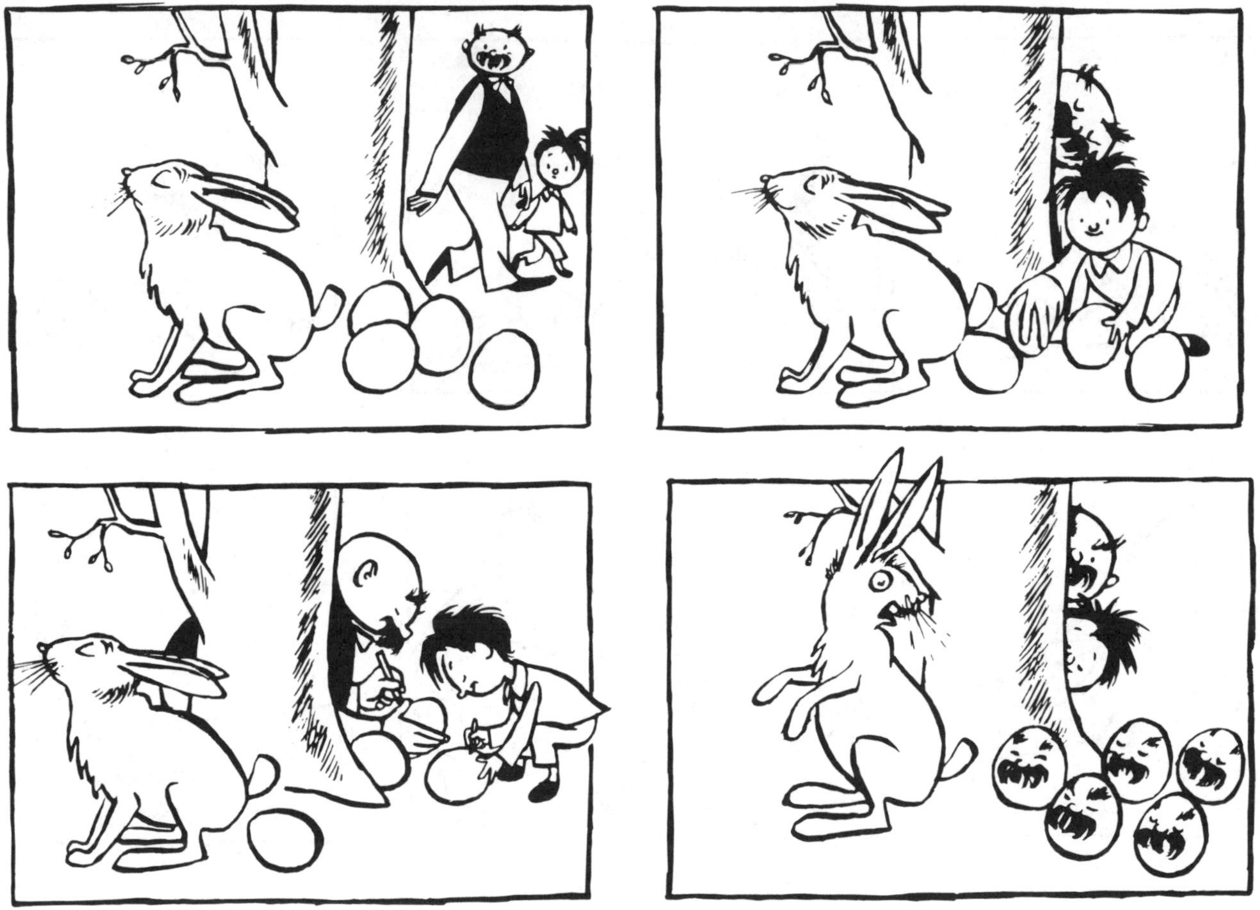

A surprise for the Easter bunny

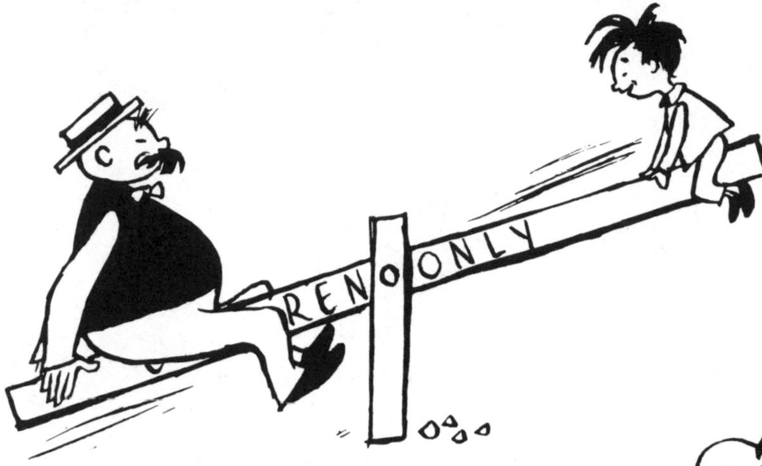
REN ONLY

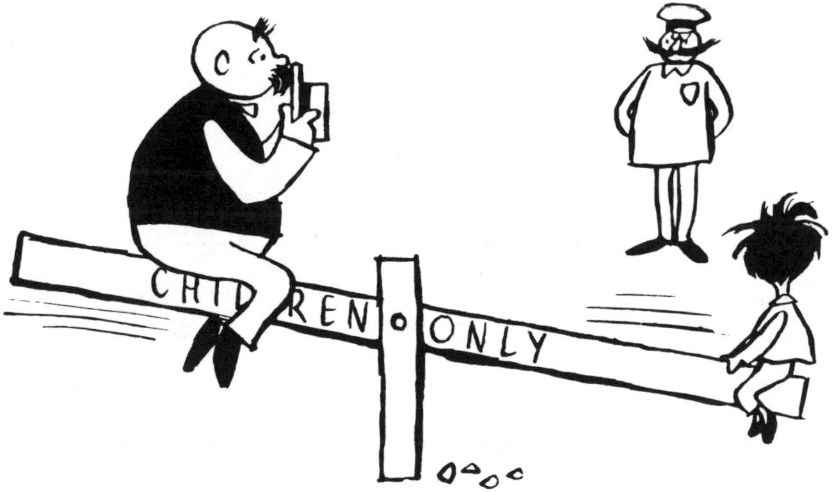
CHI REN ONLY

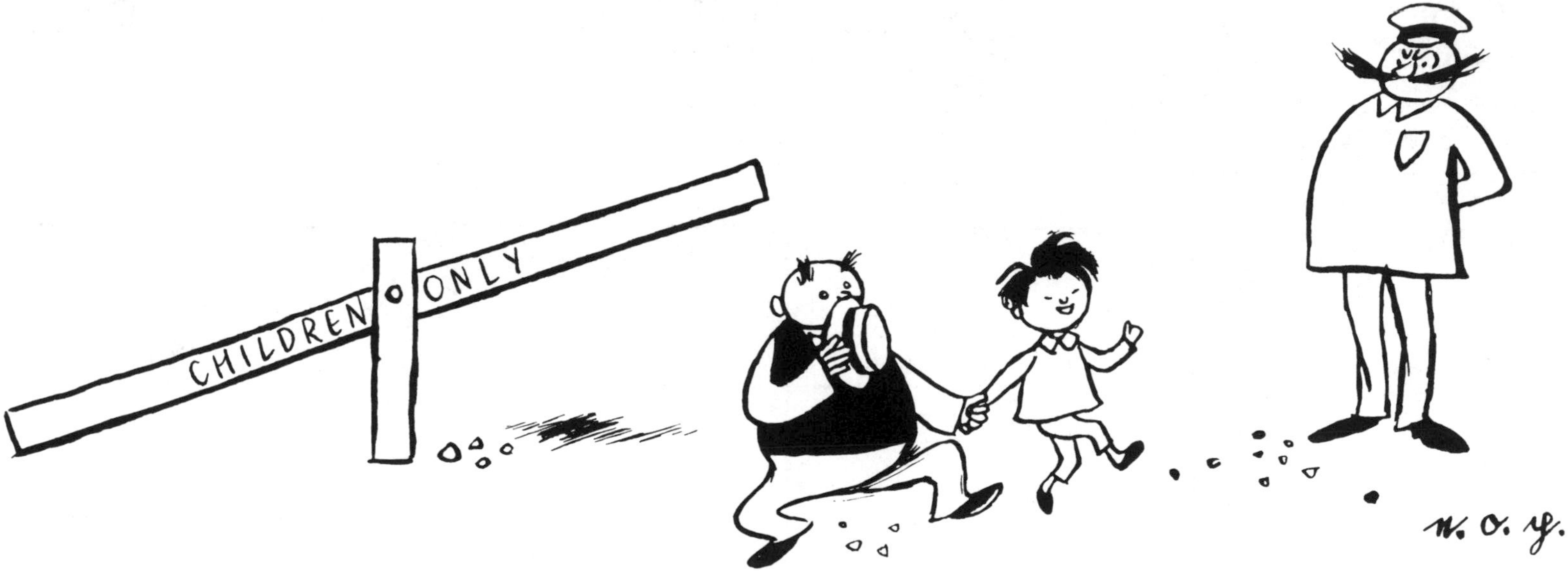
CHILDREN ONLY
W. O. G.

Impersonating a child

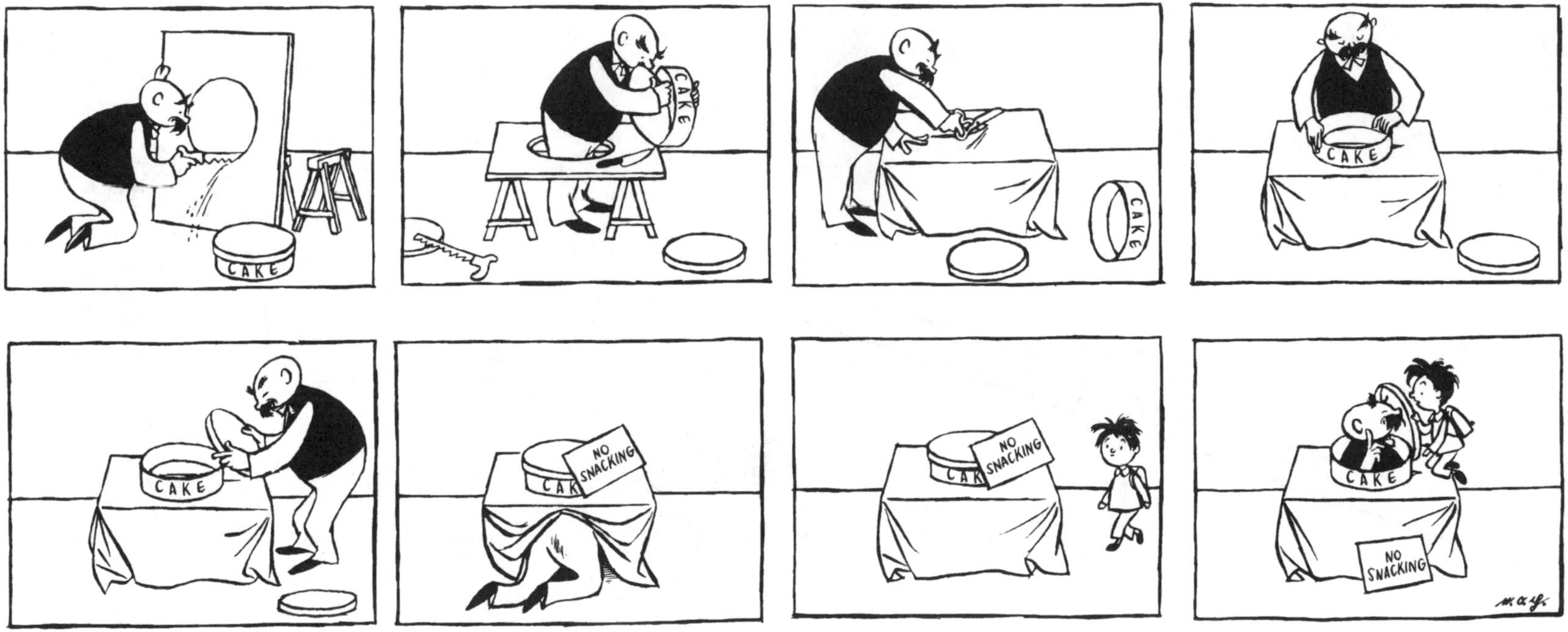
CAKE
CAKE
CAKE
CAKE
CAKE
NO SNACKING
NO SNACKING
CAKE
NO SNACKING

The cake

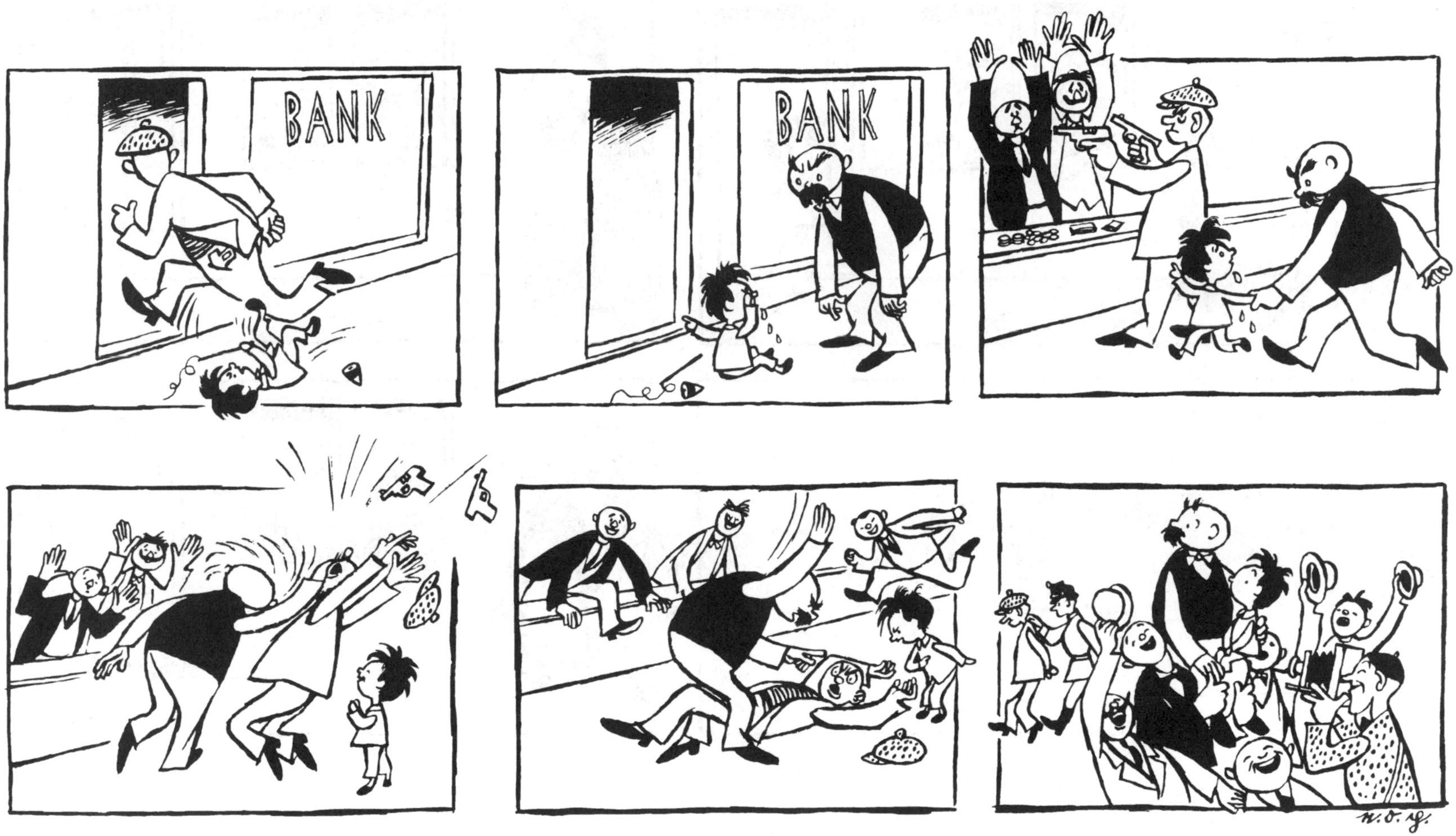
BANK
BANK

Accidental heroes

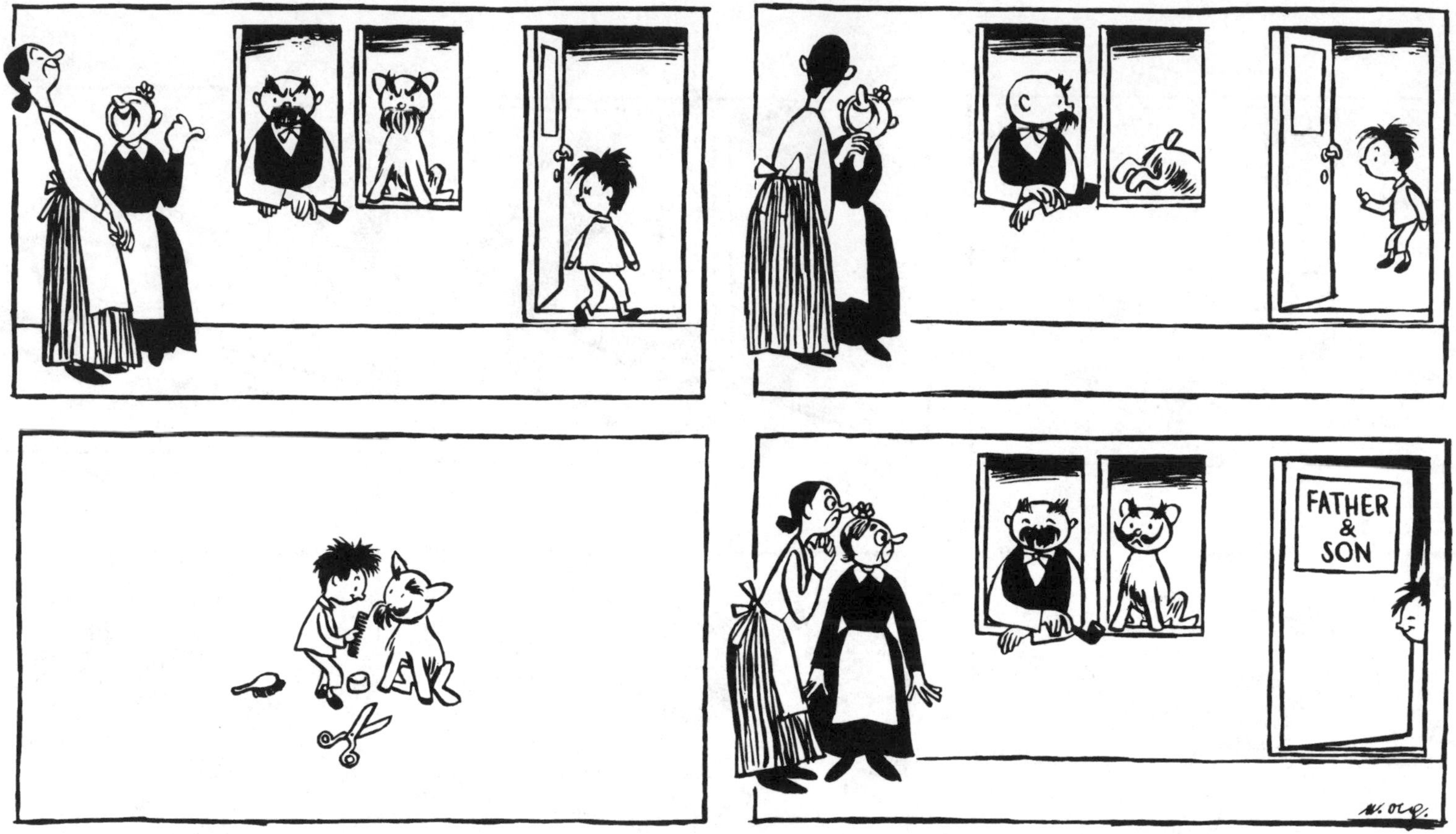
FATHER
&
SON

Resemblance corrected

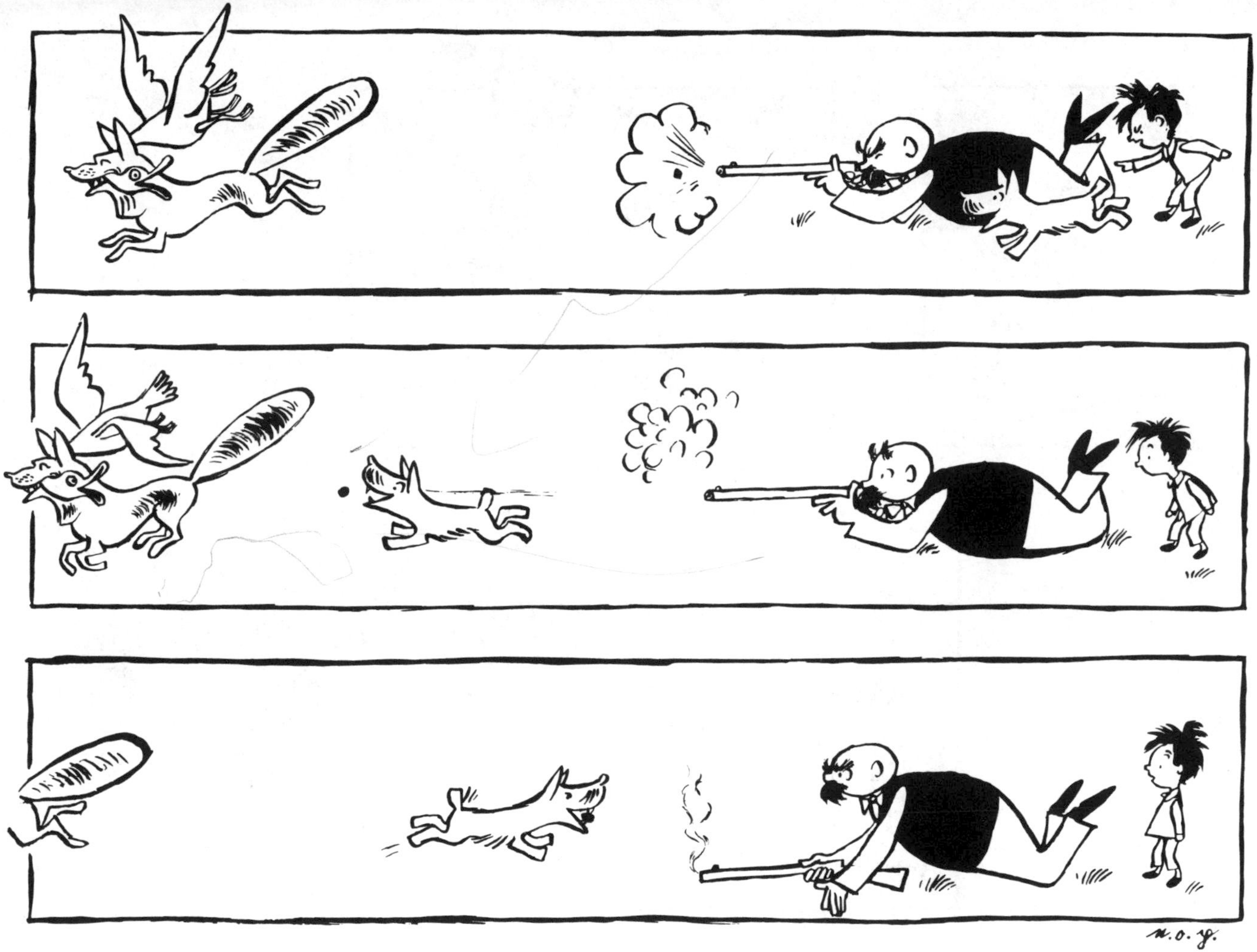
M.O.Y.

The bullet retriever

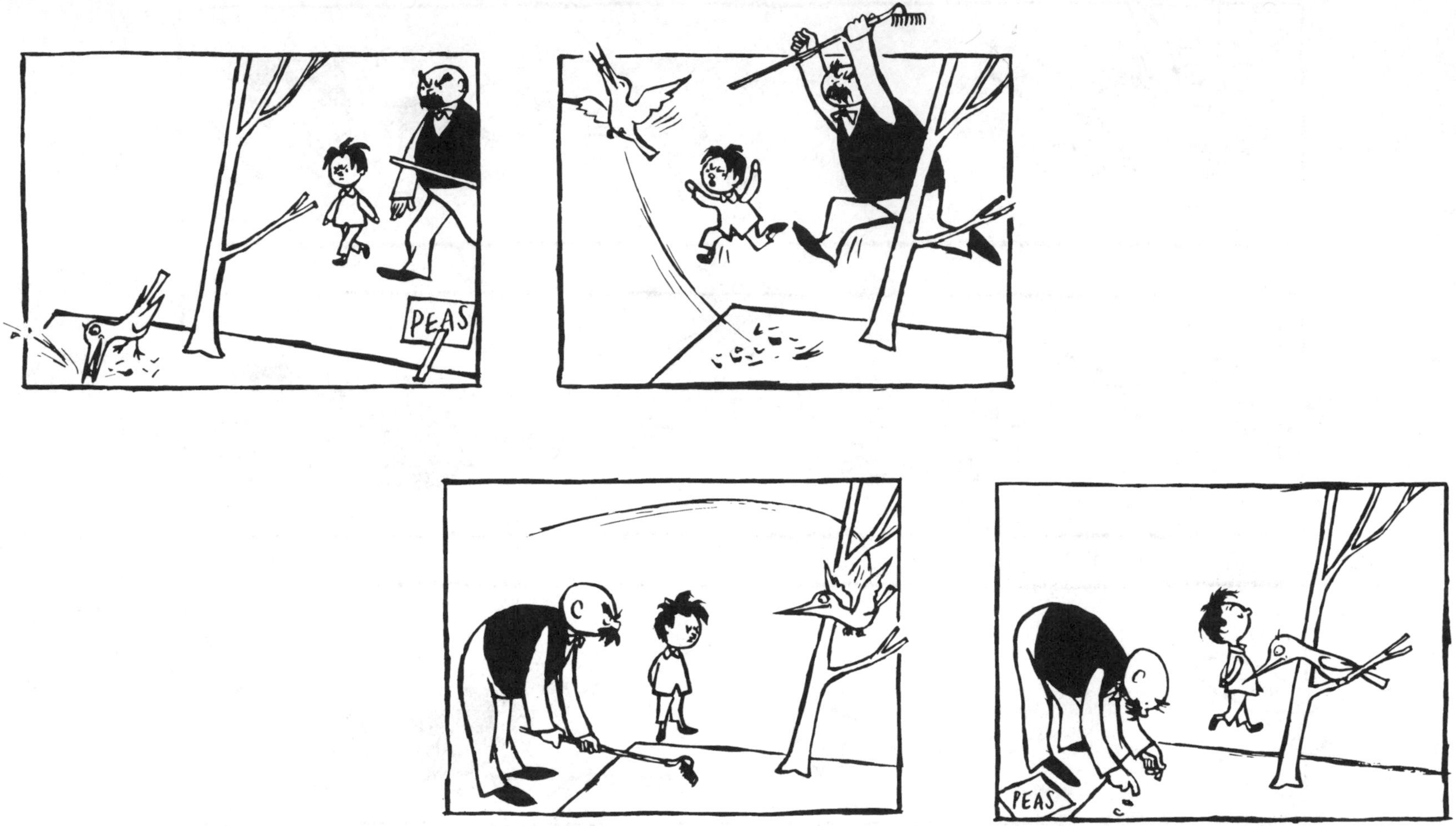
PEAS
PEAS

PEAS
W.O.J.

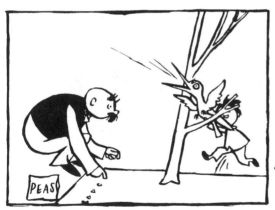

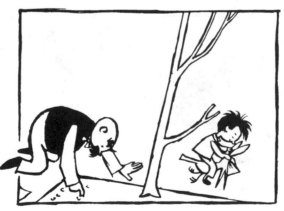

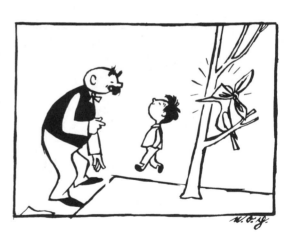

Disarmed

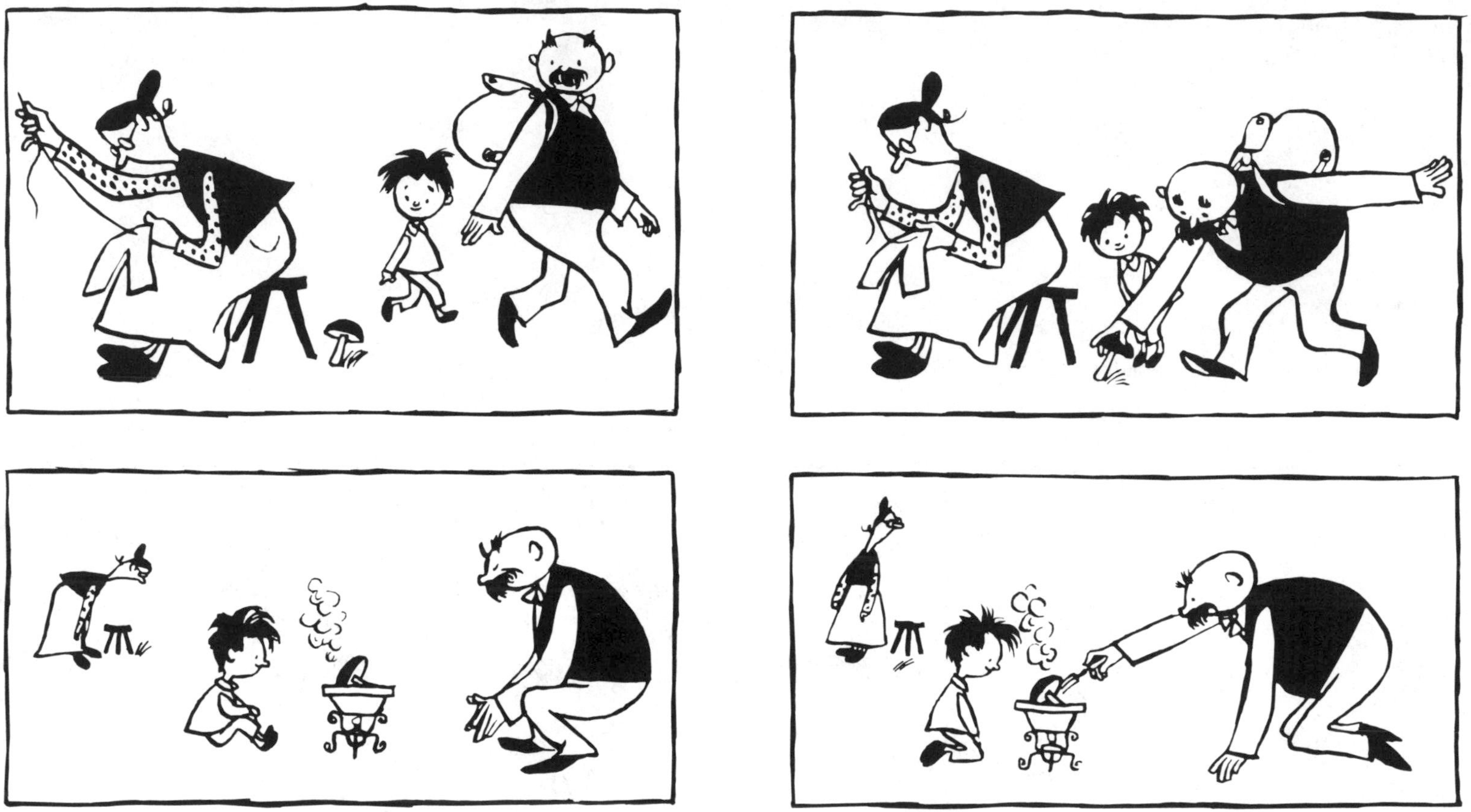

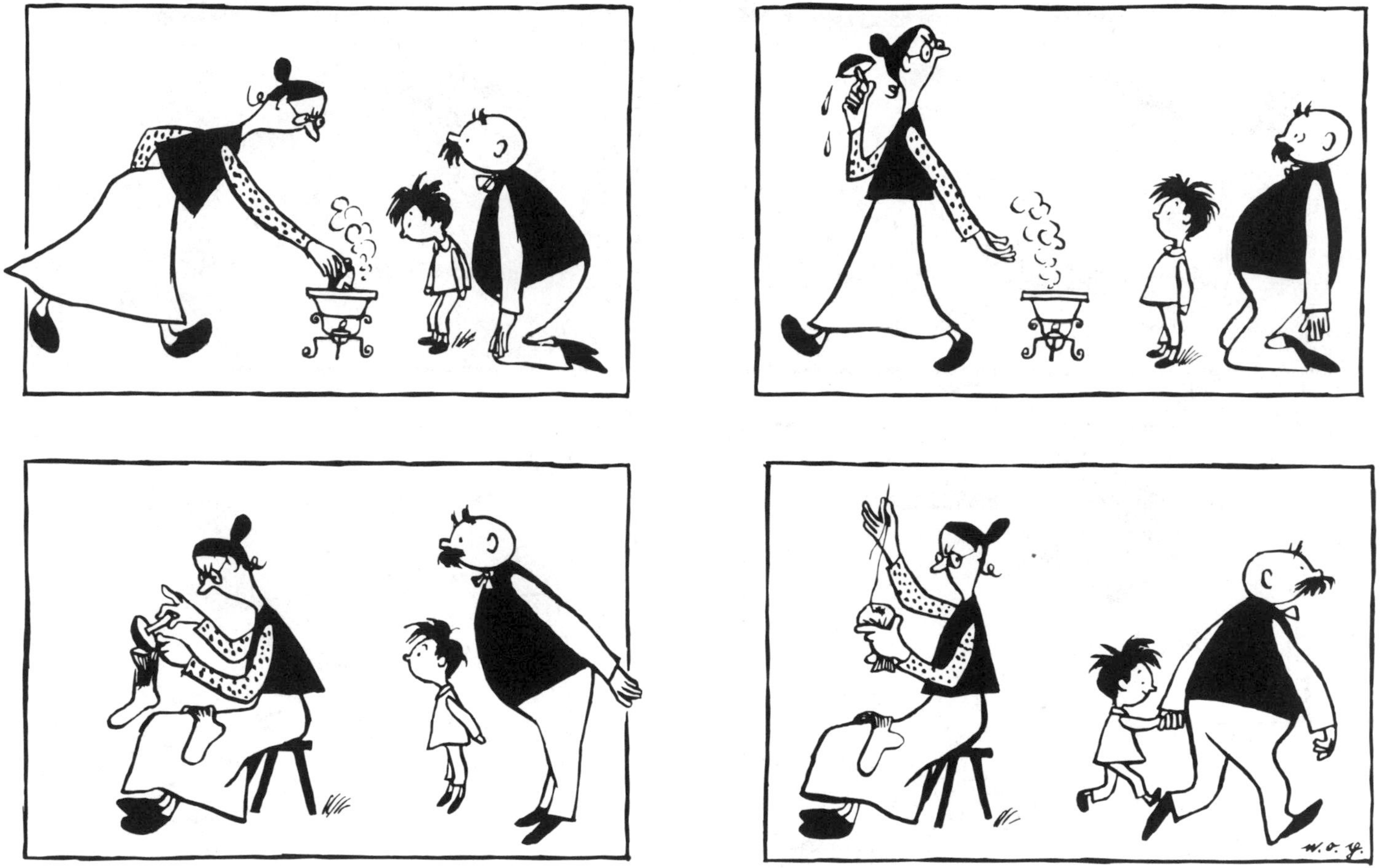

The mushroom

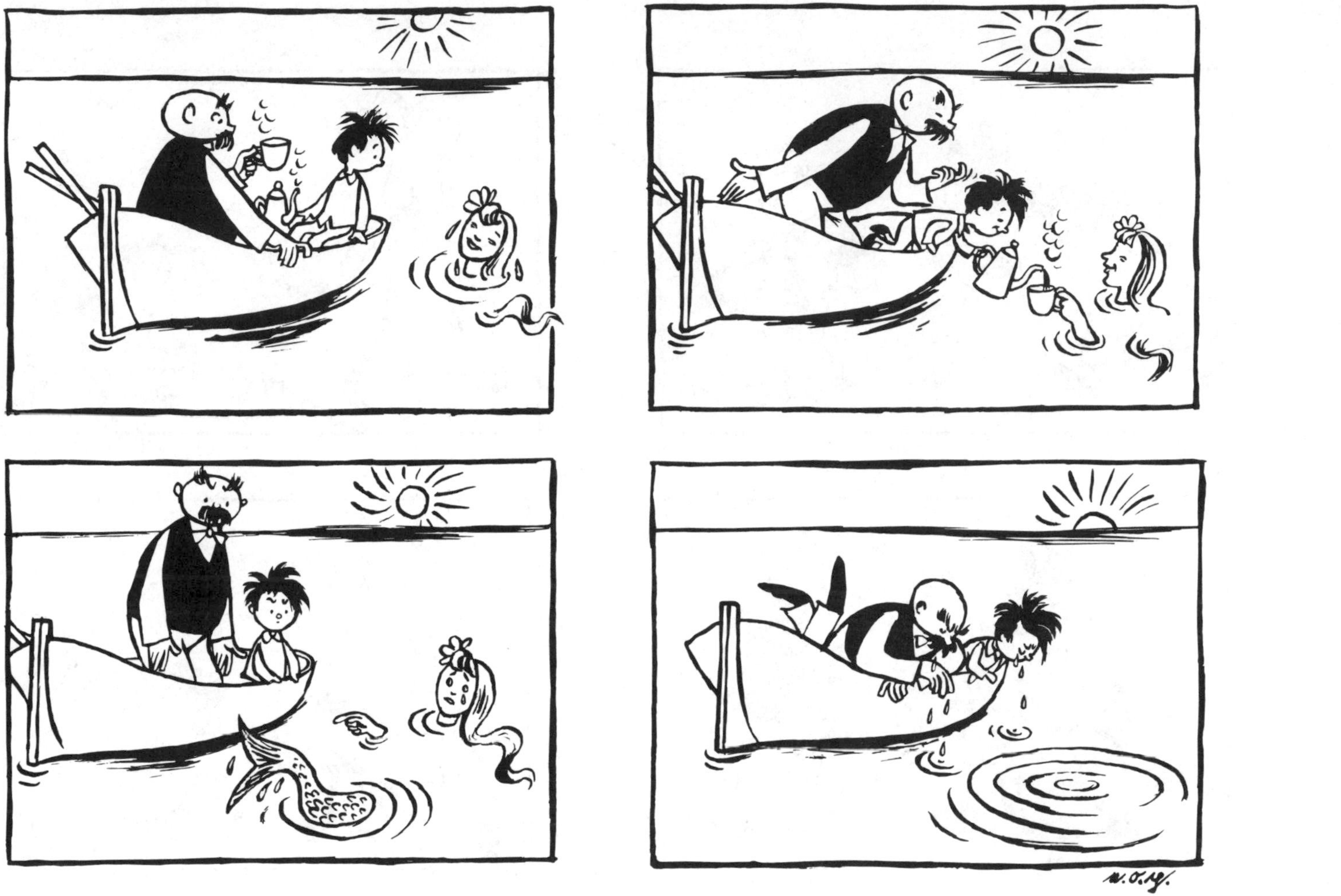

Too bad!

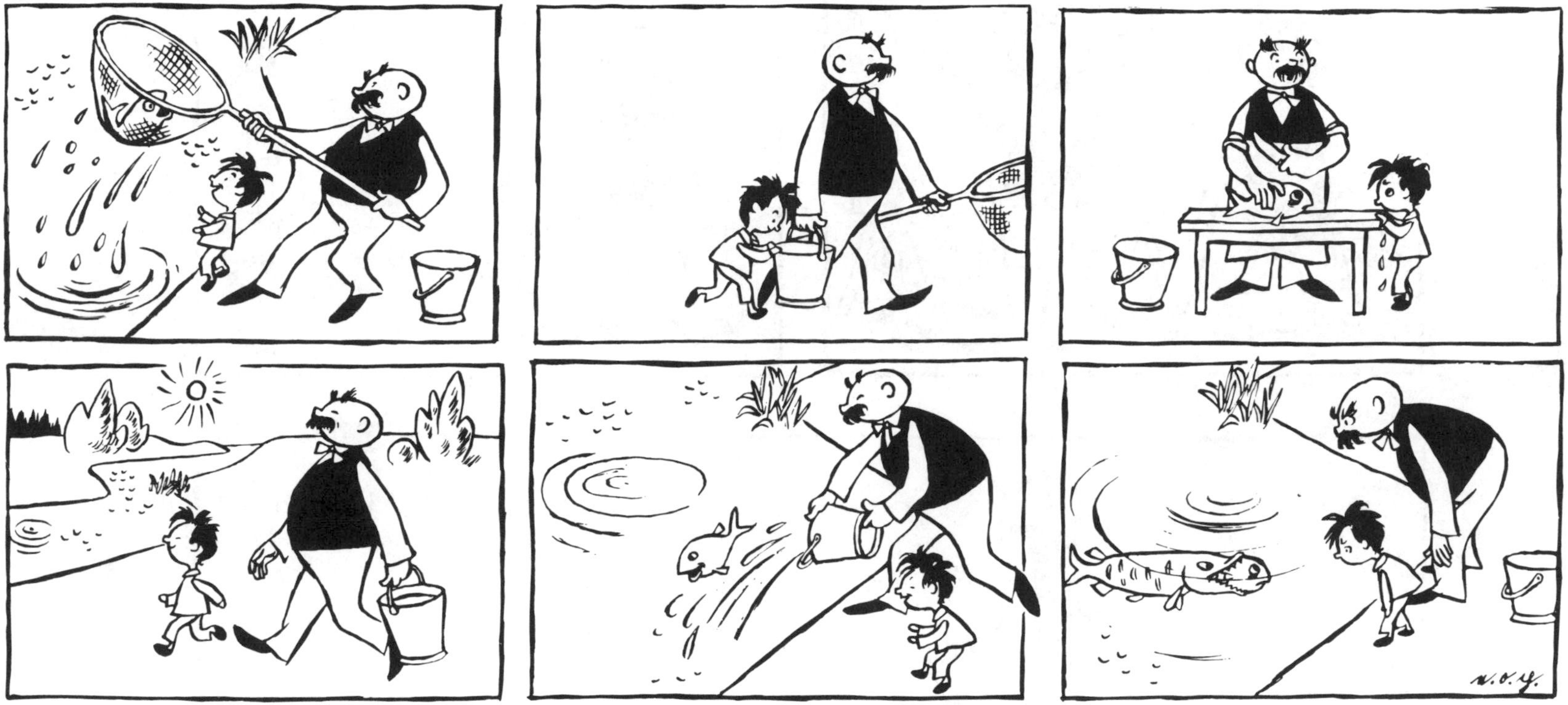

Back to nature

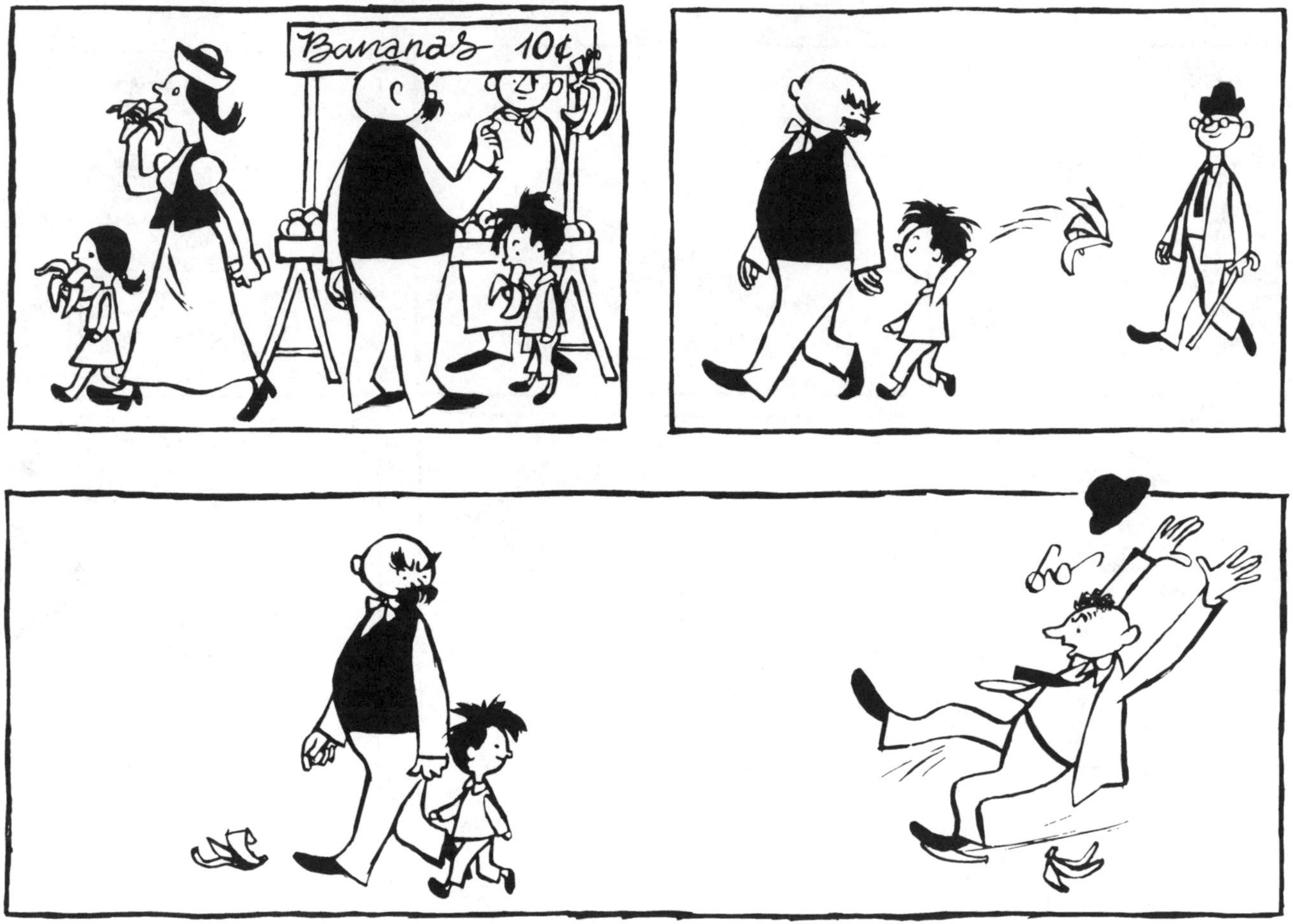
Bananas 10¢

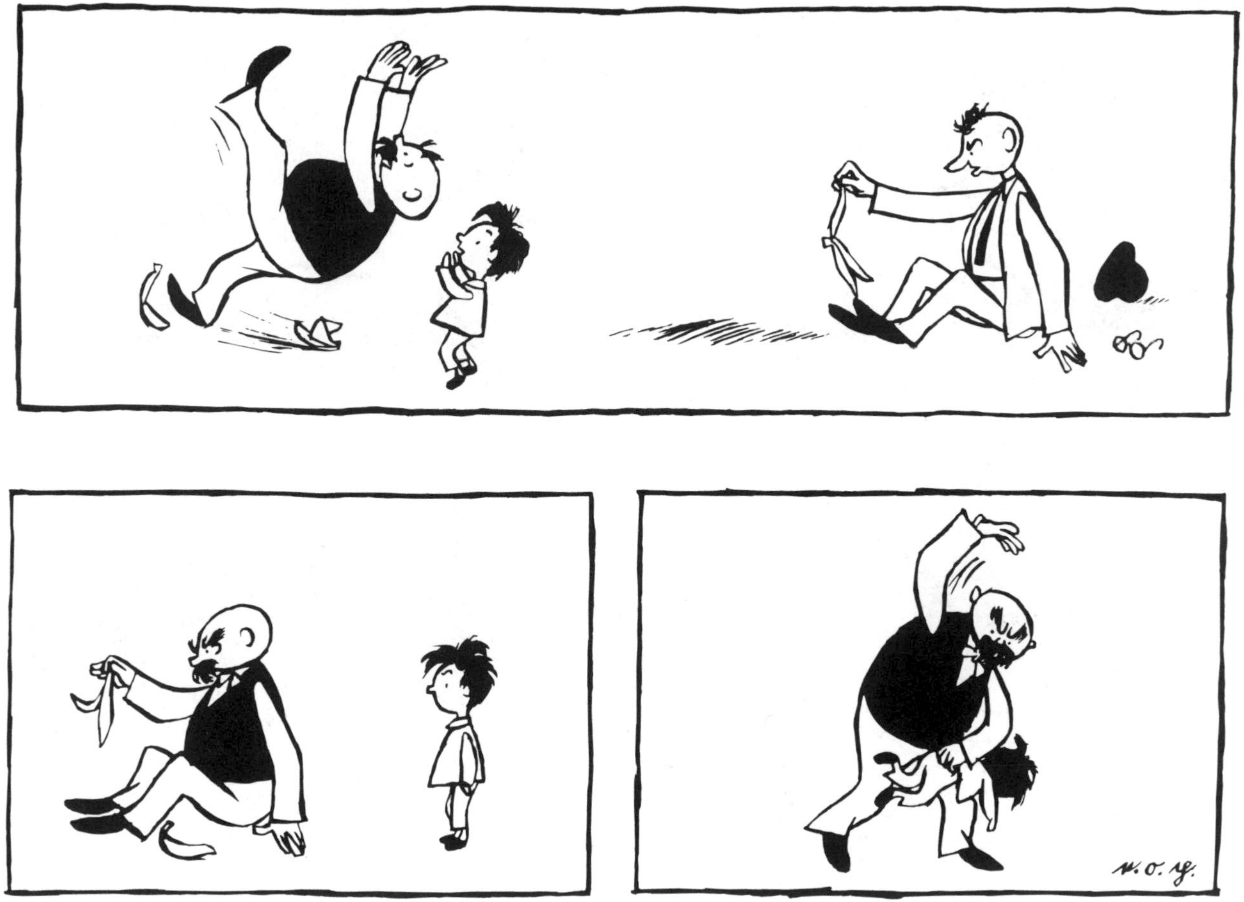

A disciplined upbringing . . . eventually

Countermeasure

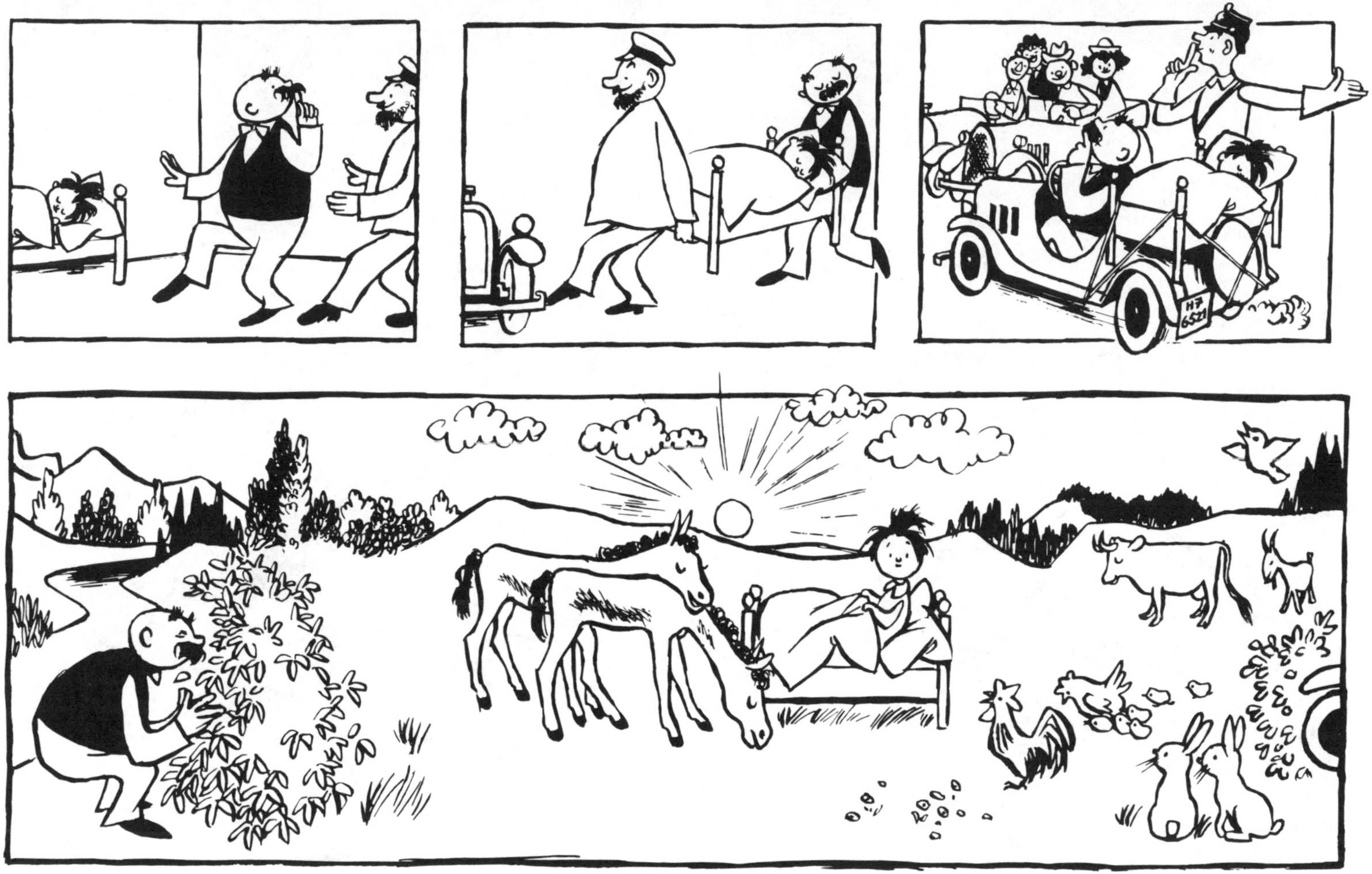
H7
6521

The first day of vacation

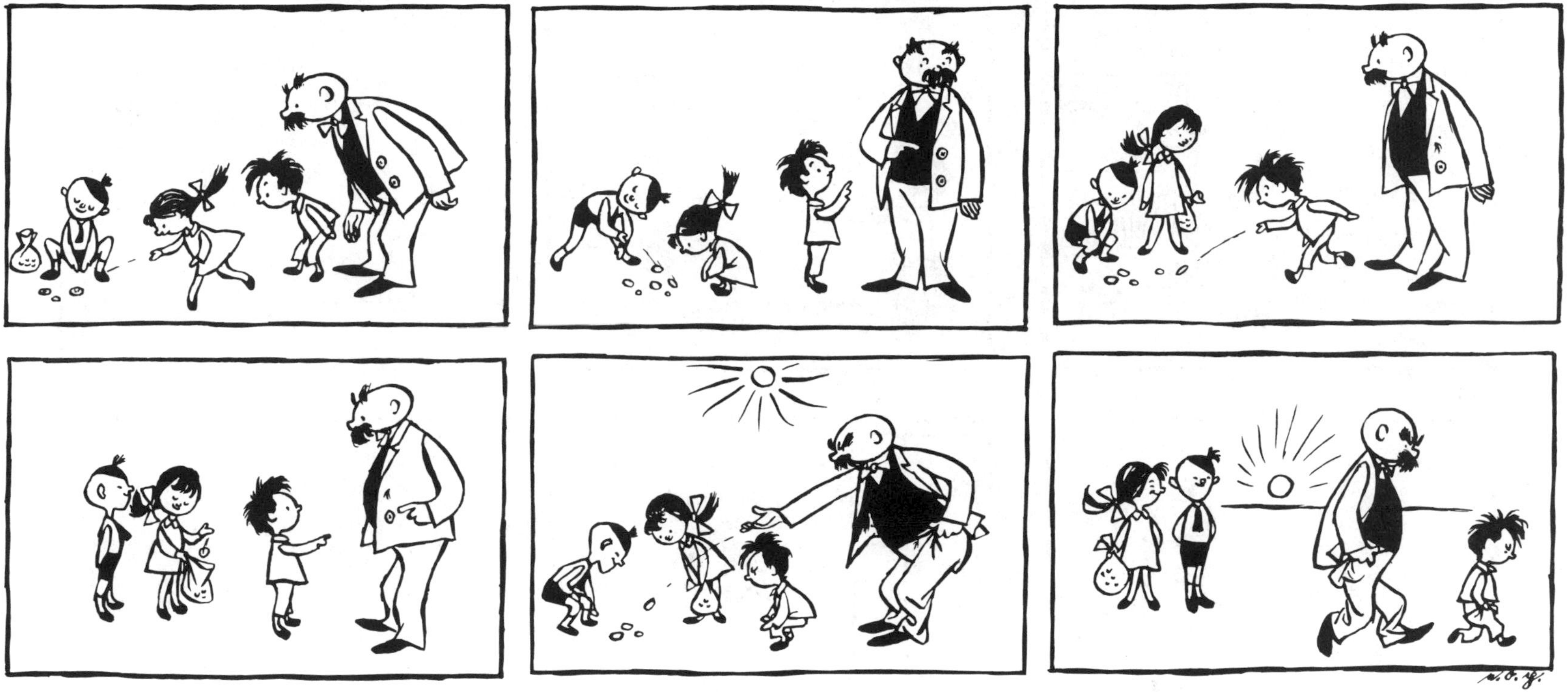

Betting his buttons

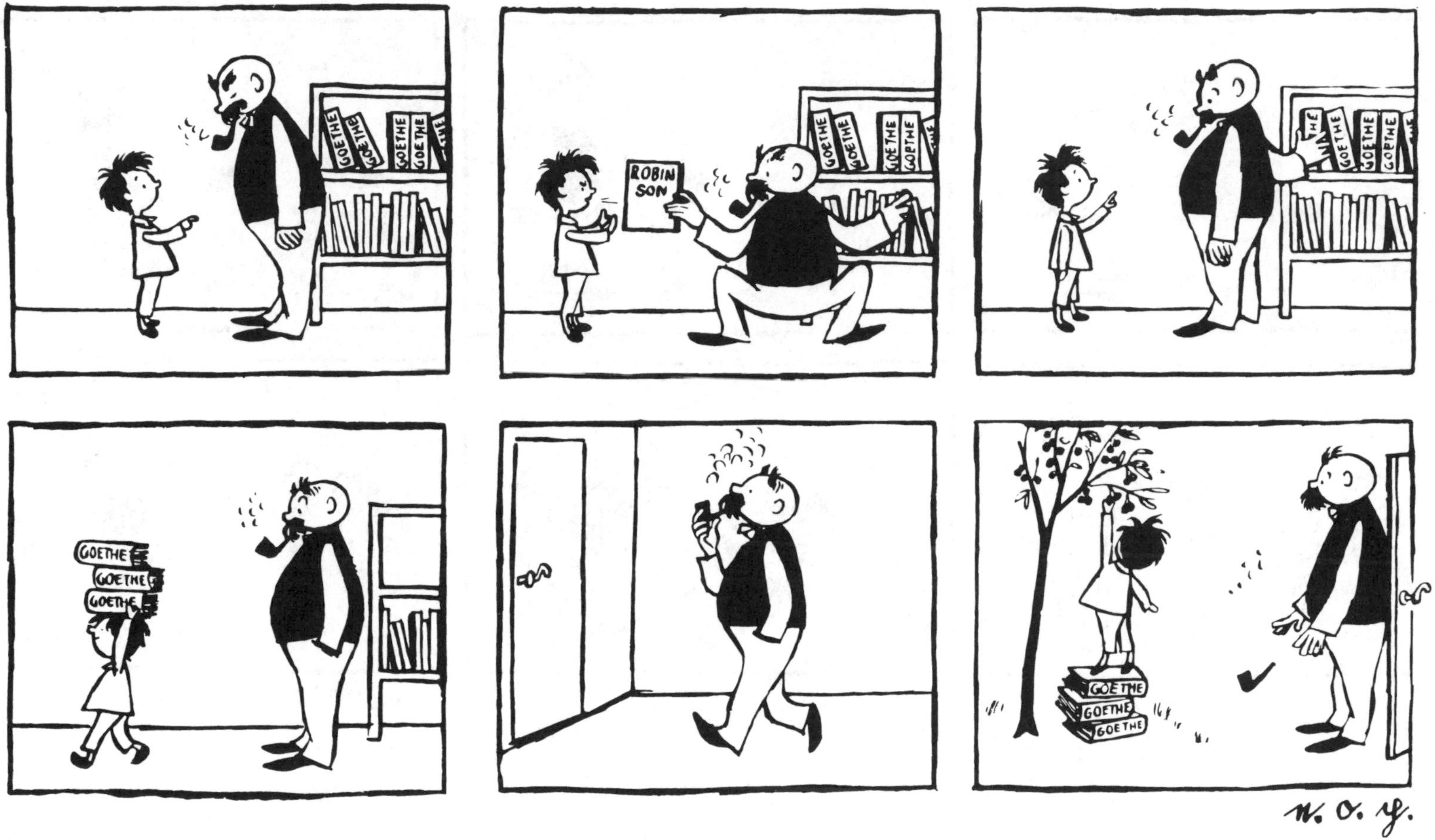
GOETHE
GOETHE
GOETHE
GOETHE
ROBIN SON
GOETHE
GOETHE
GOETHE
GOETHE
GOETHE
GOETHE
GOETHE
GOETHE
GOETHE
GOETHE

Hats off to Goethe!

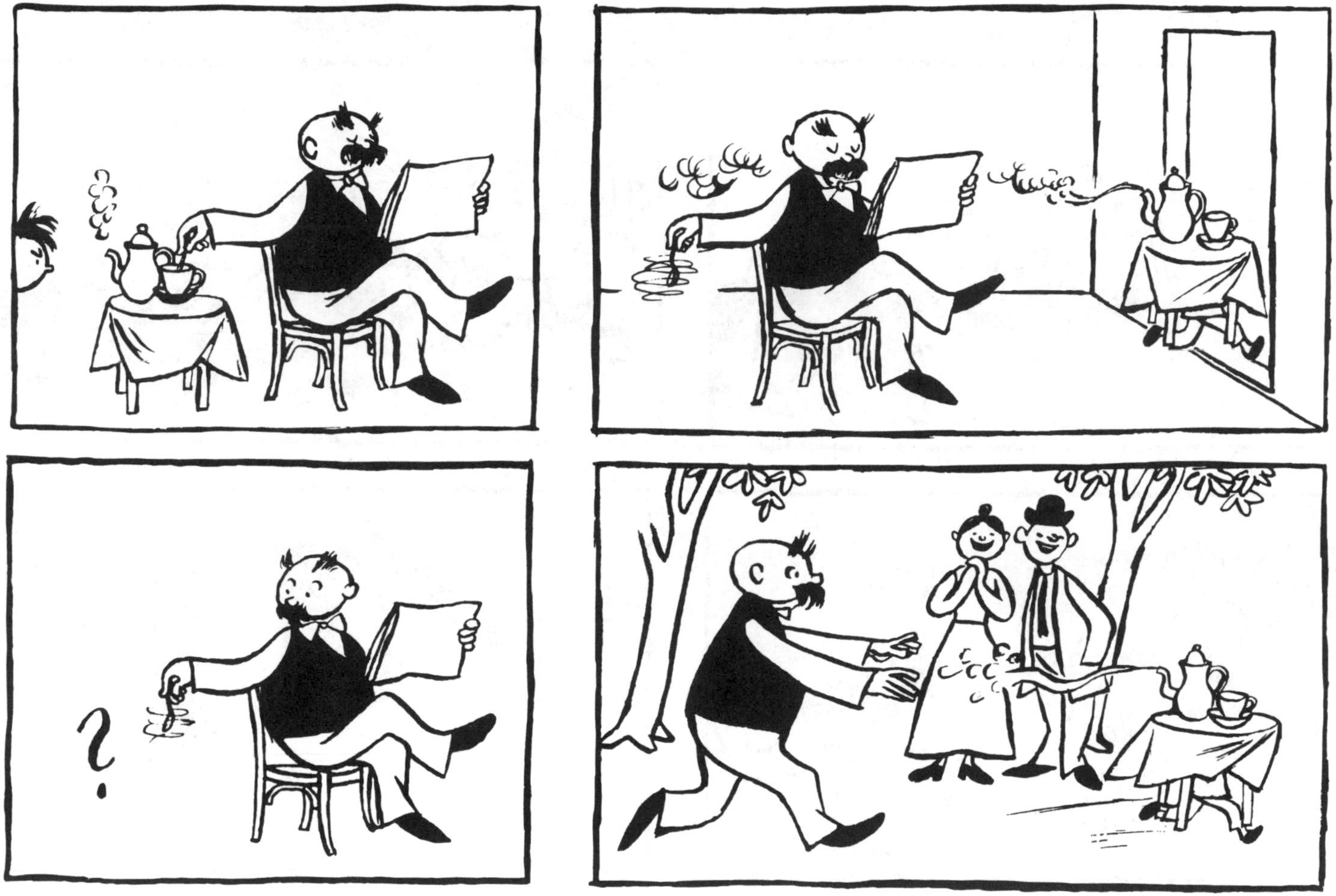

Doctor's orders: no strong coffee

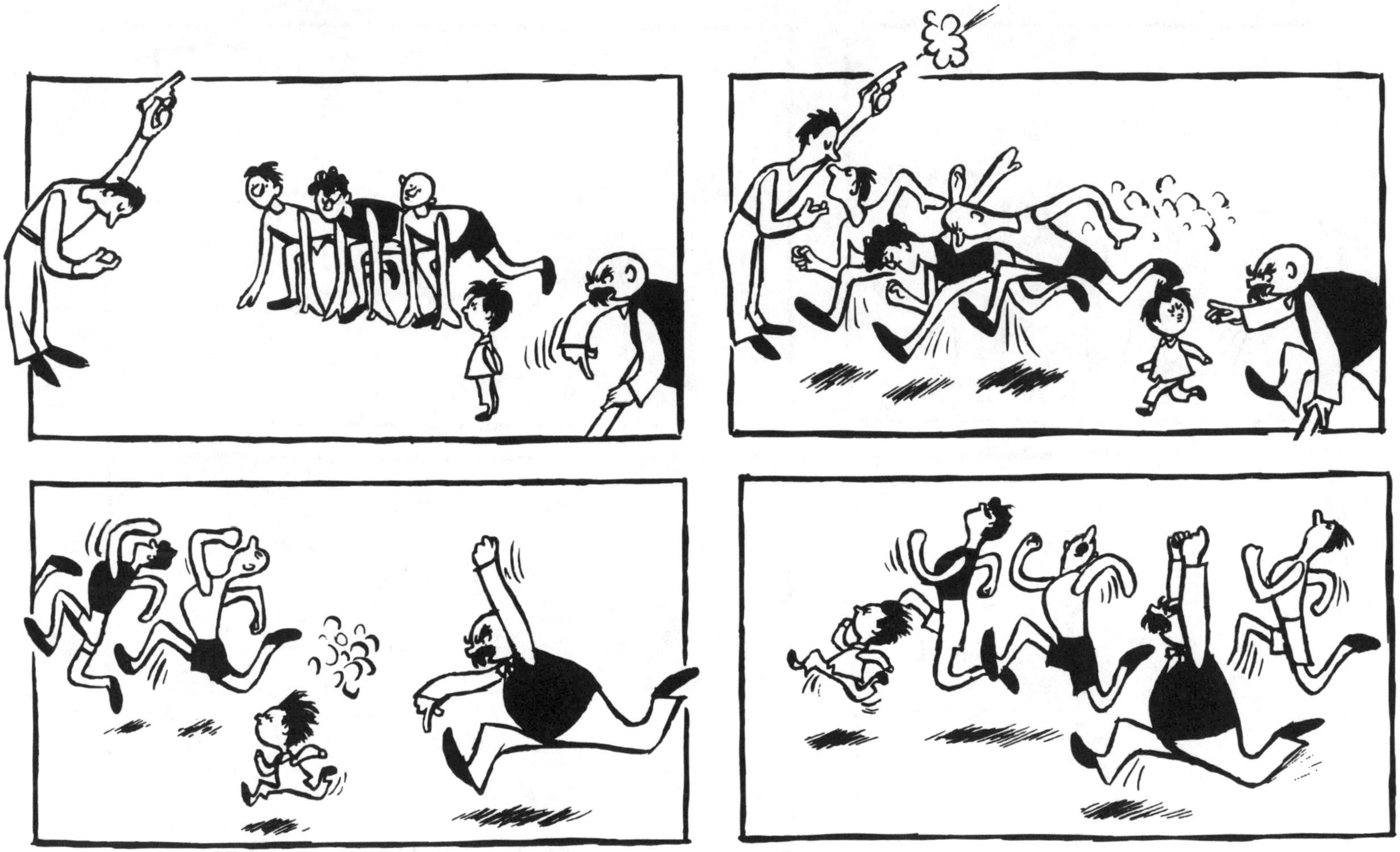

FINISH

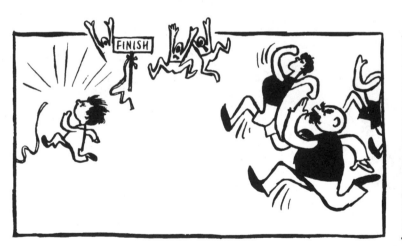

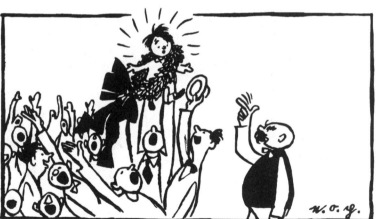

Fear makes you faster

WELCOM

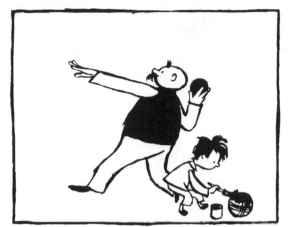

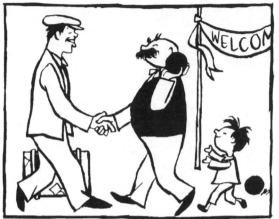

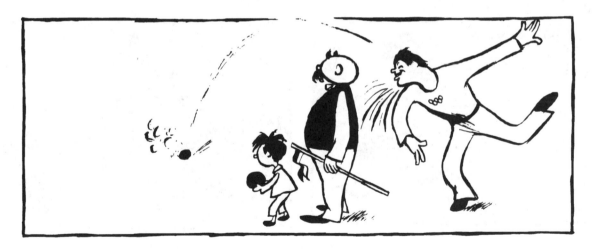

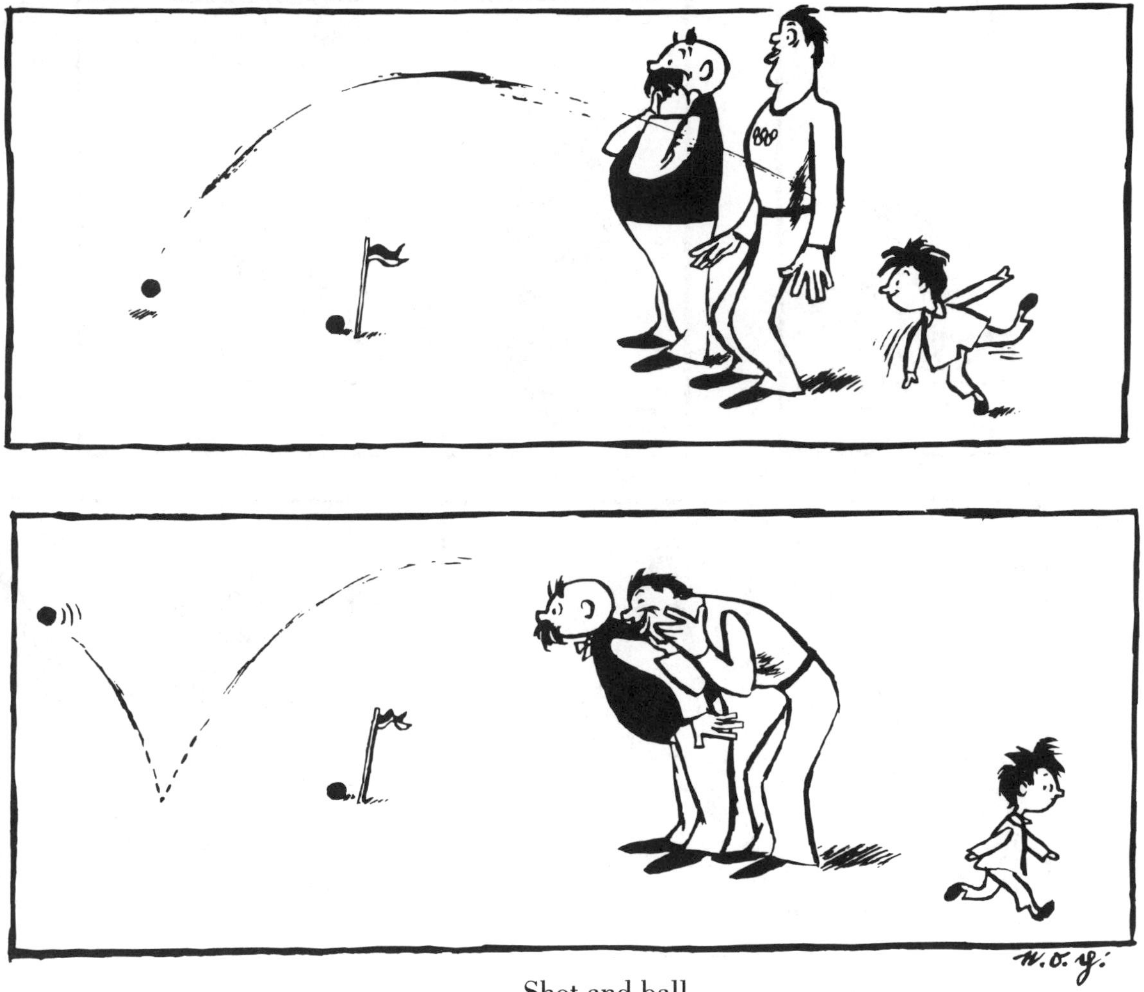

Shot and ball

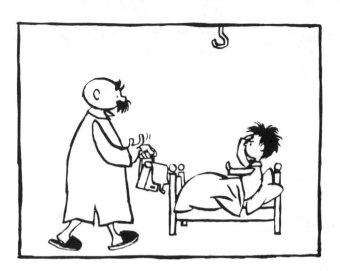

TEE

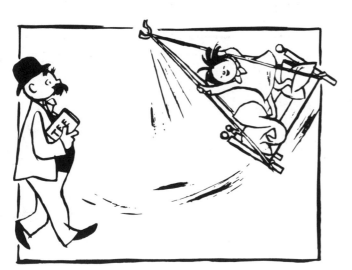

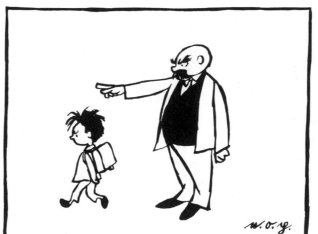

The malingerer

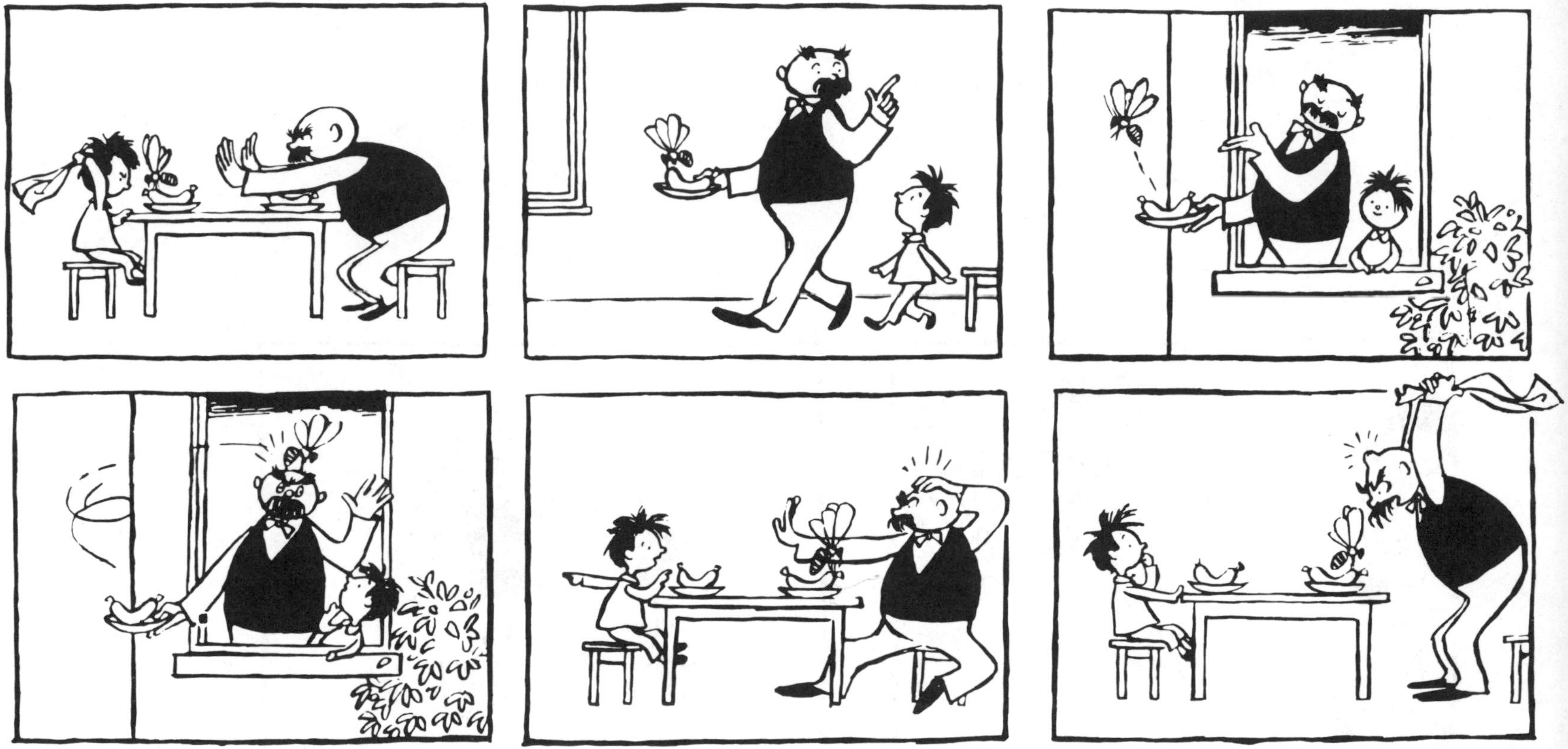

Be kind to wasps

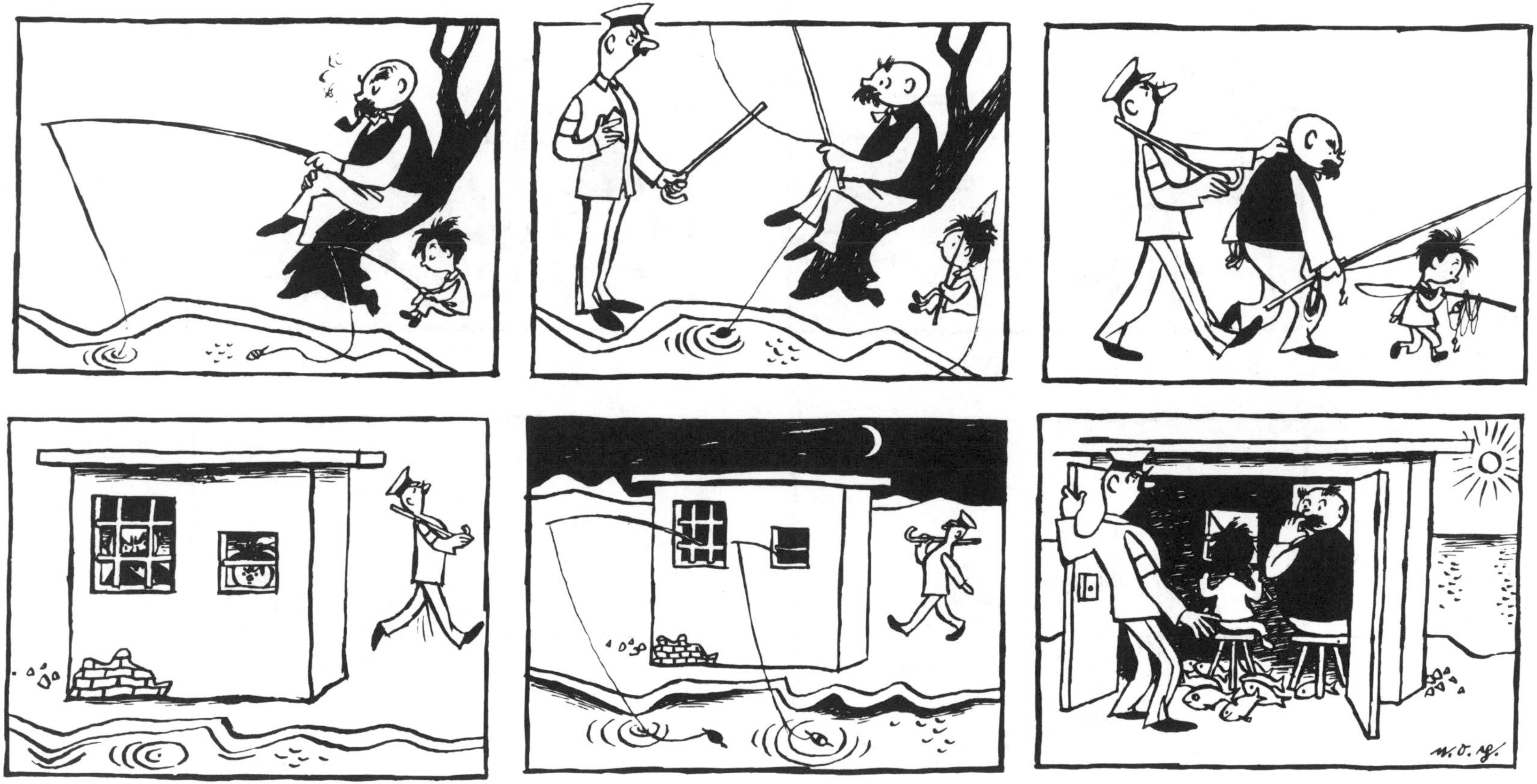

Incorrigible enthusiasts

The gift

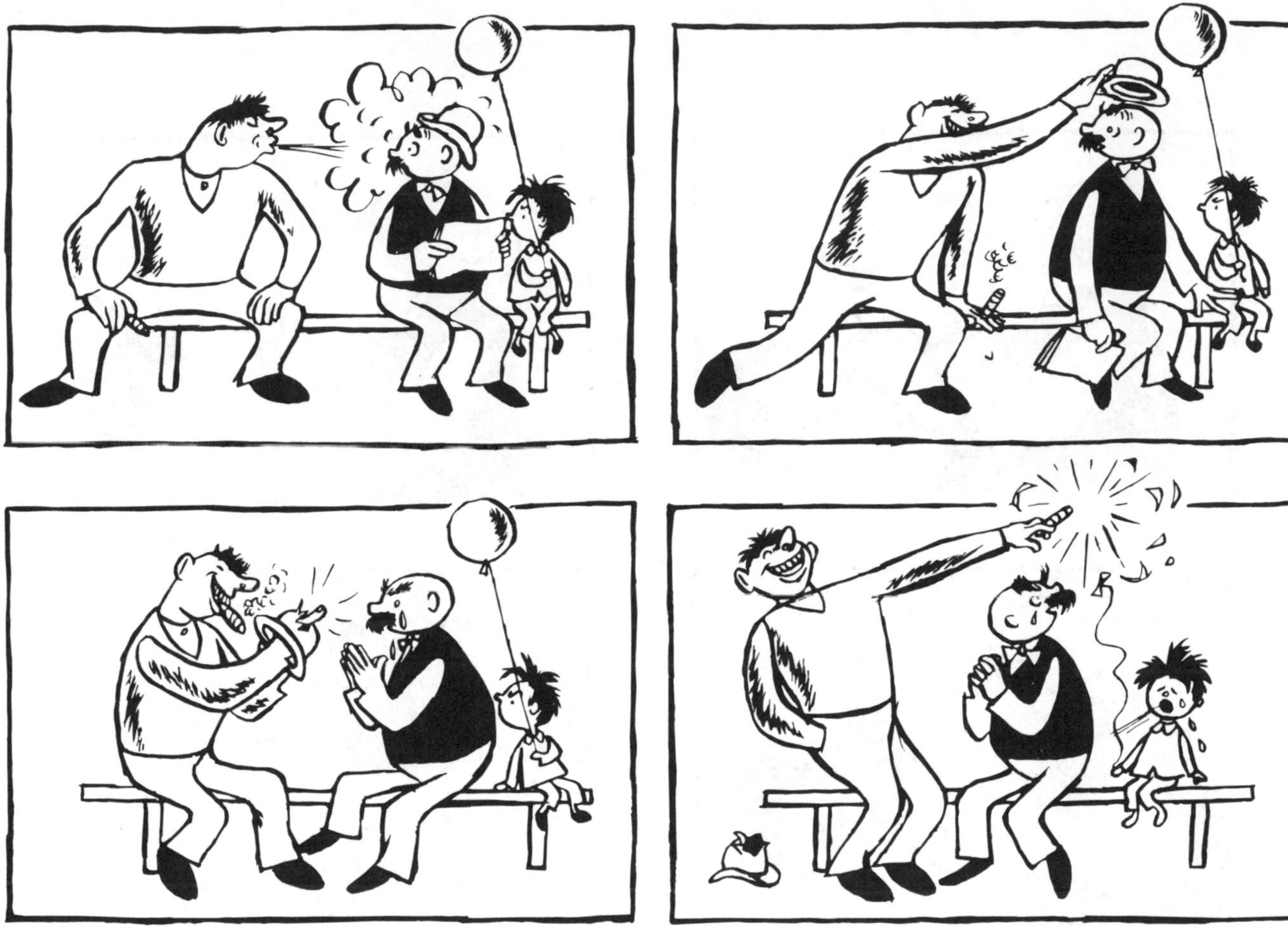

The last straw

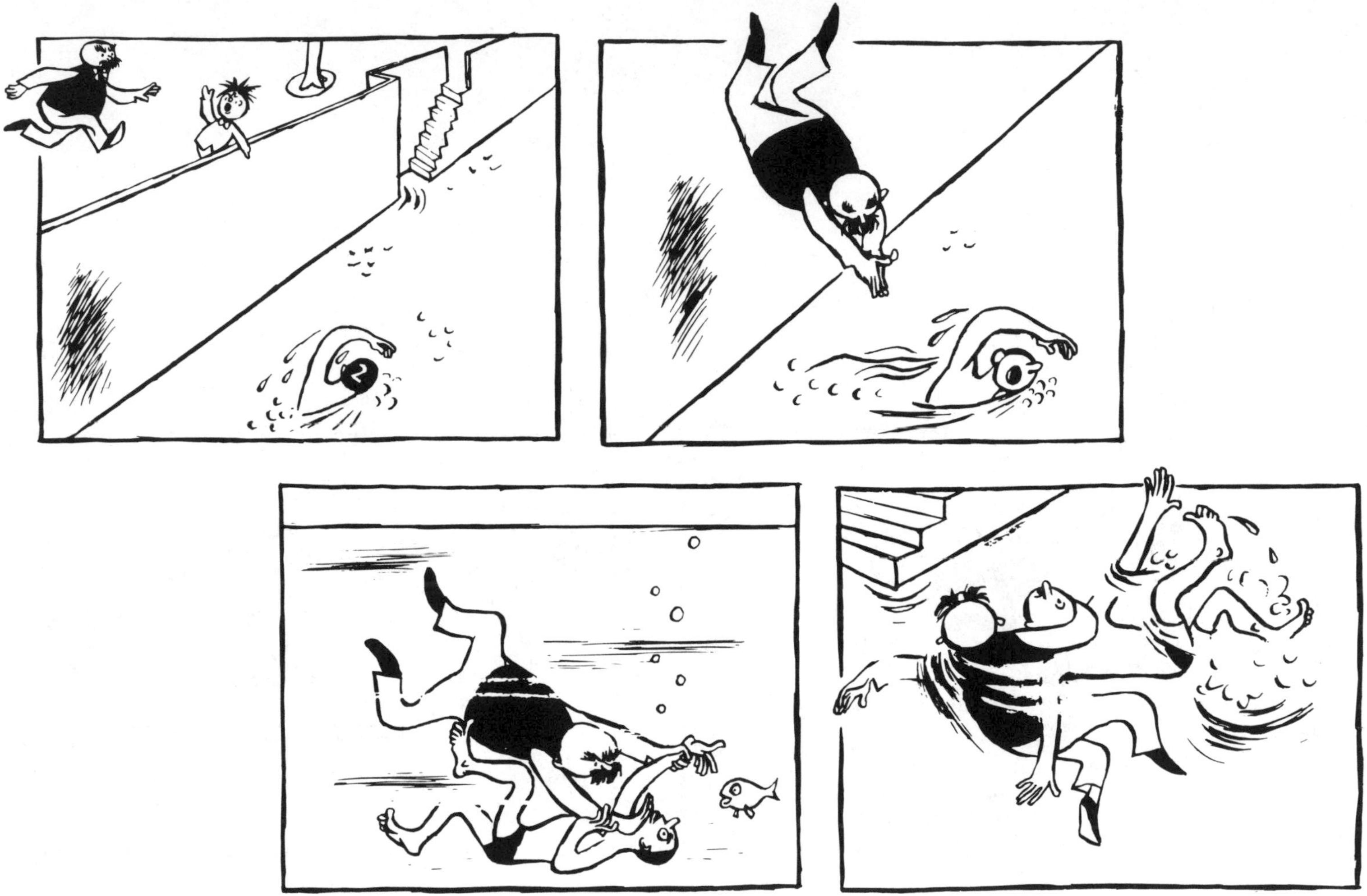

FINISH

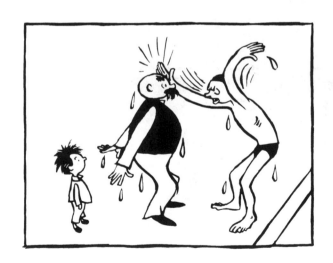

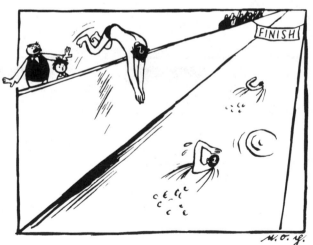

Ingrate

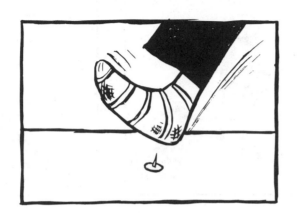

The thumbtack

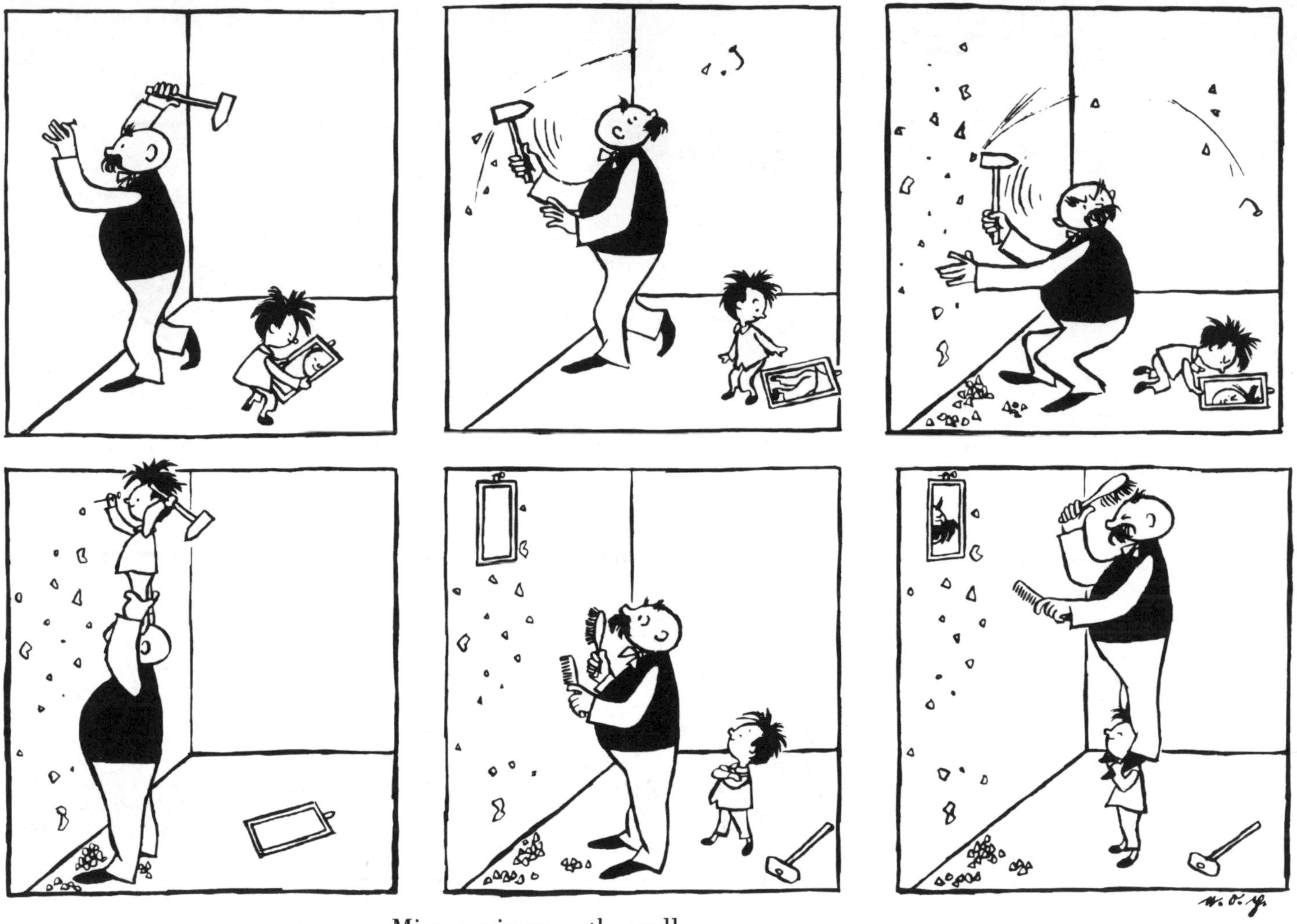

Mirror, mirror on the wall

Life is short

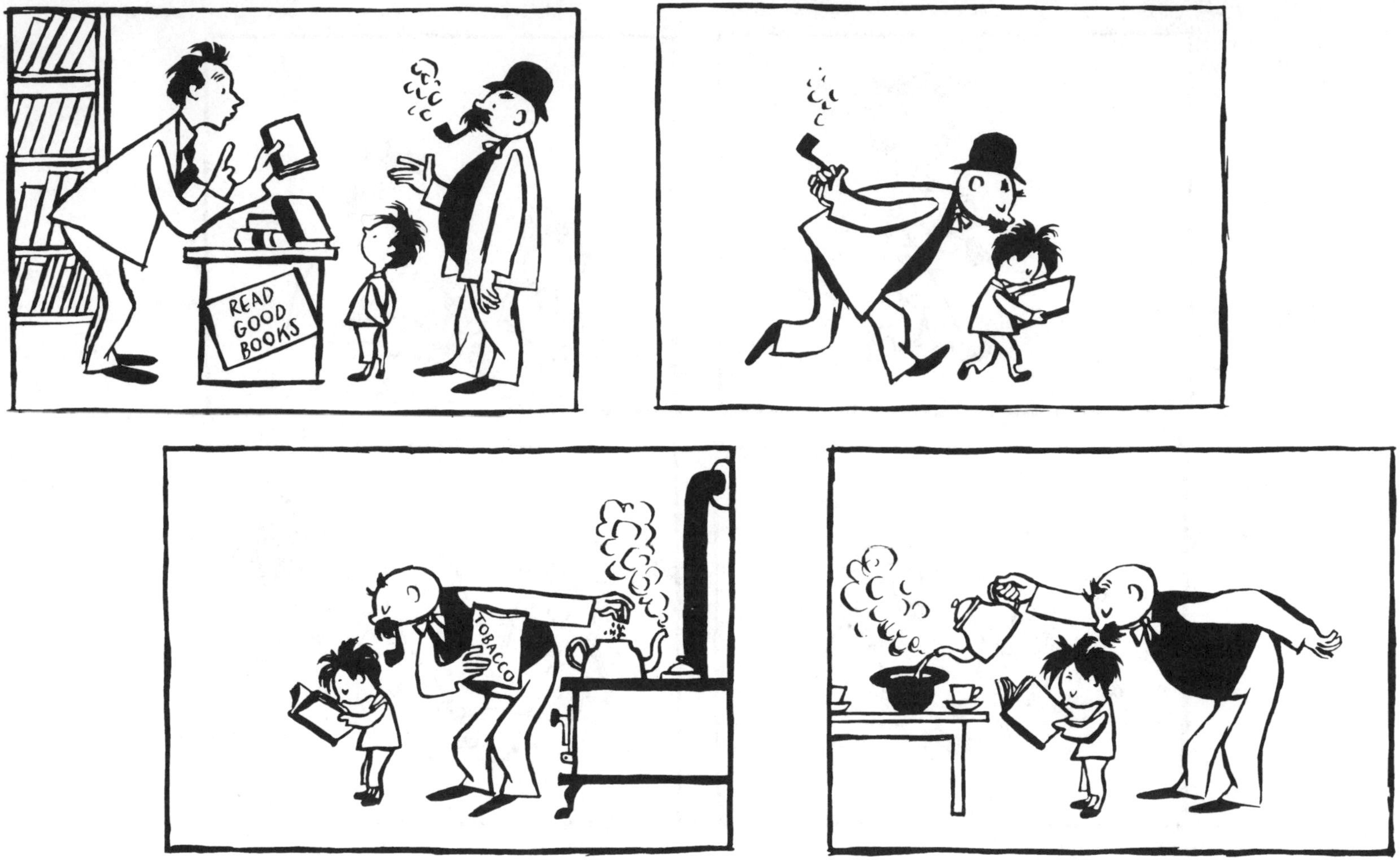
READ
GOOD
BOOKS
TOBACCO

Glued to the page

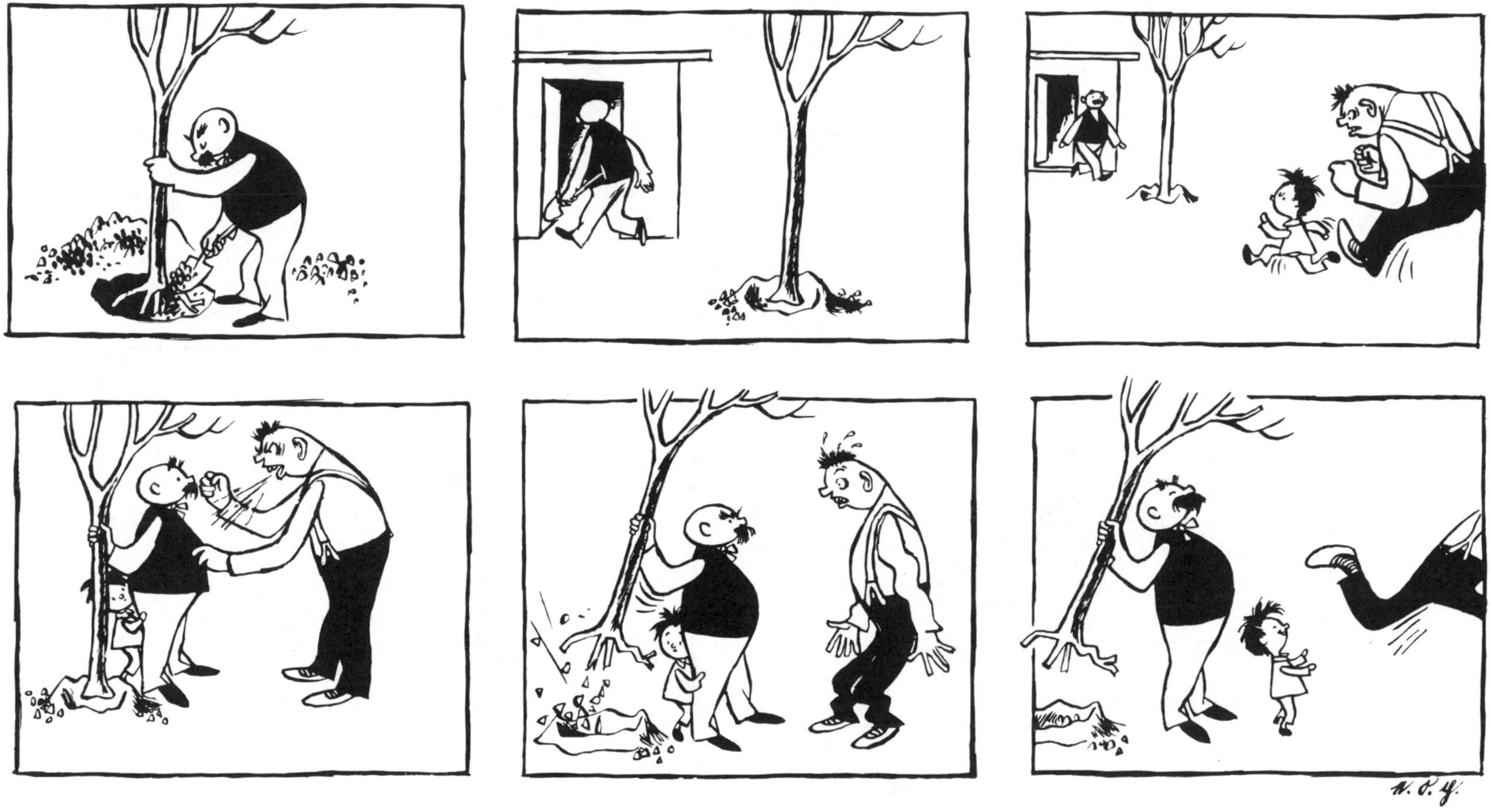
e. o. p.

Feigned strength

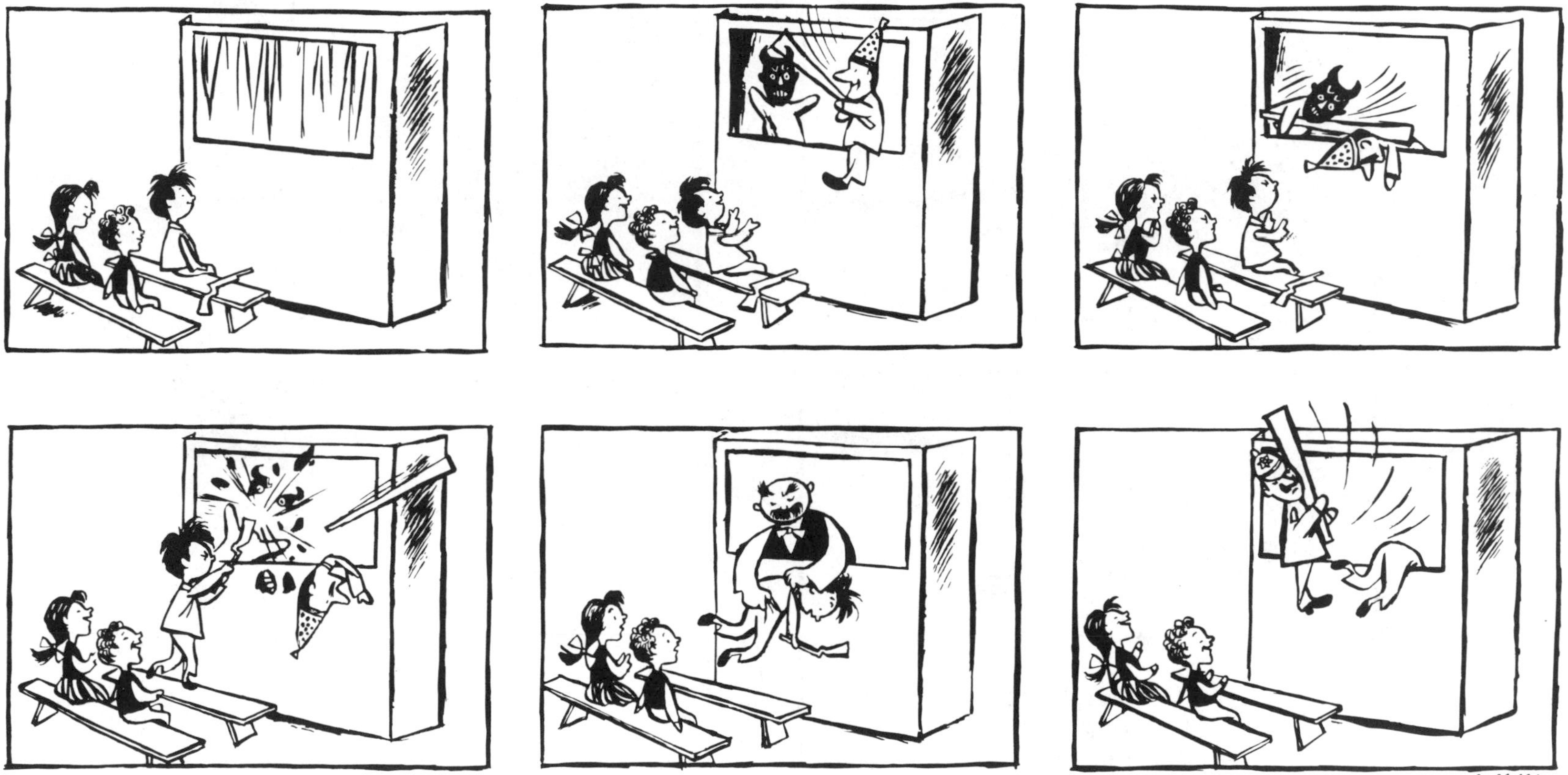

Punch and Judy show

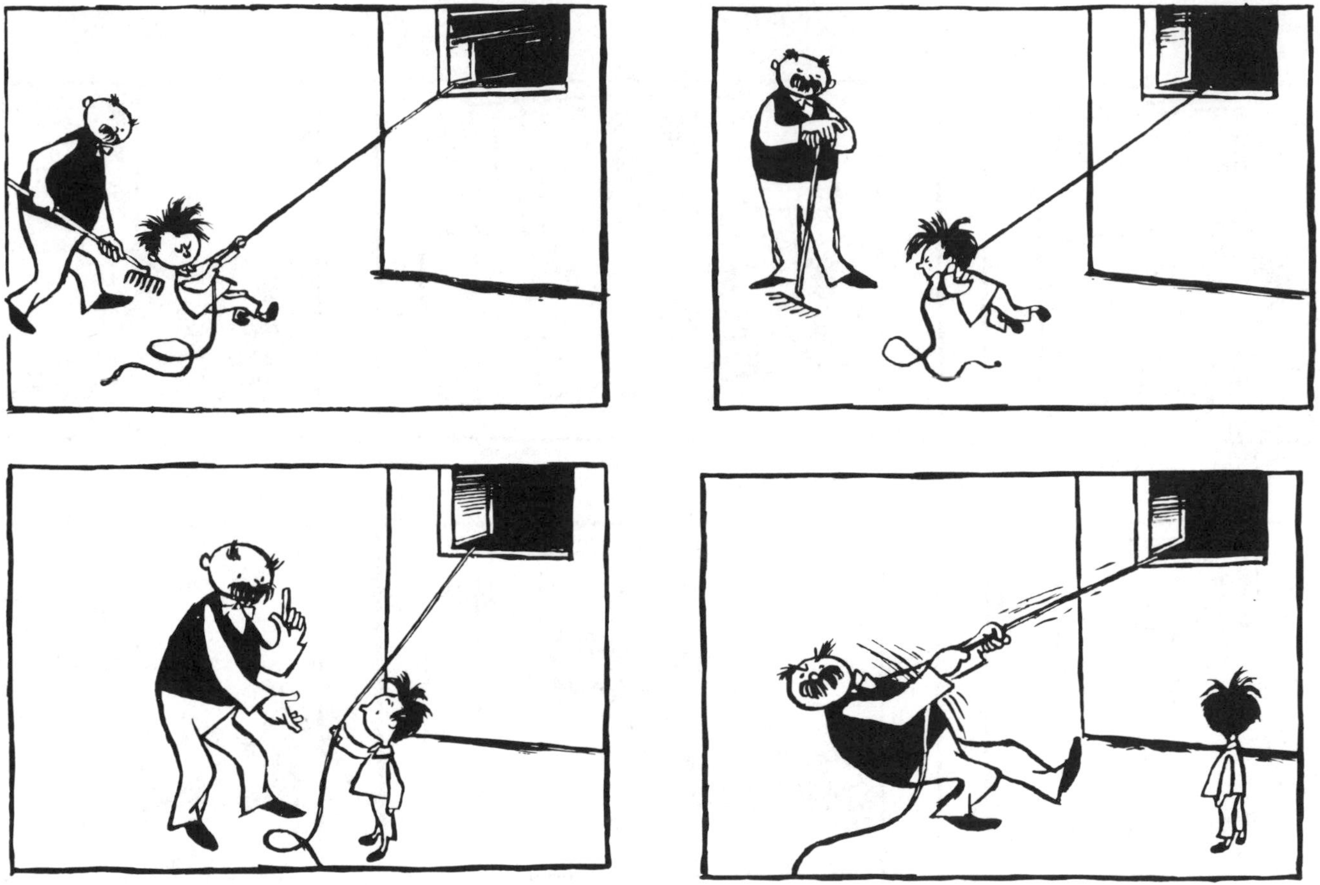

Help unwisely given

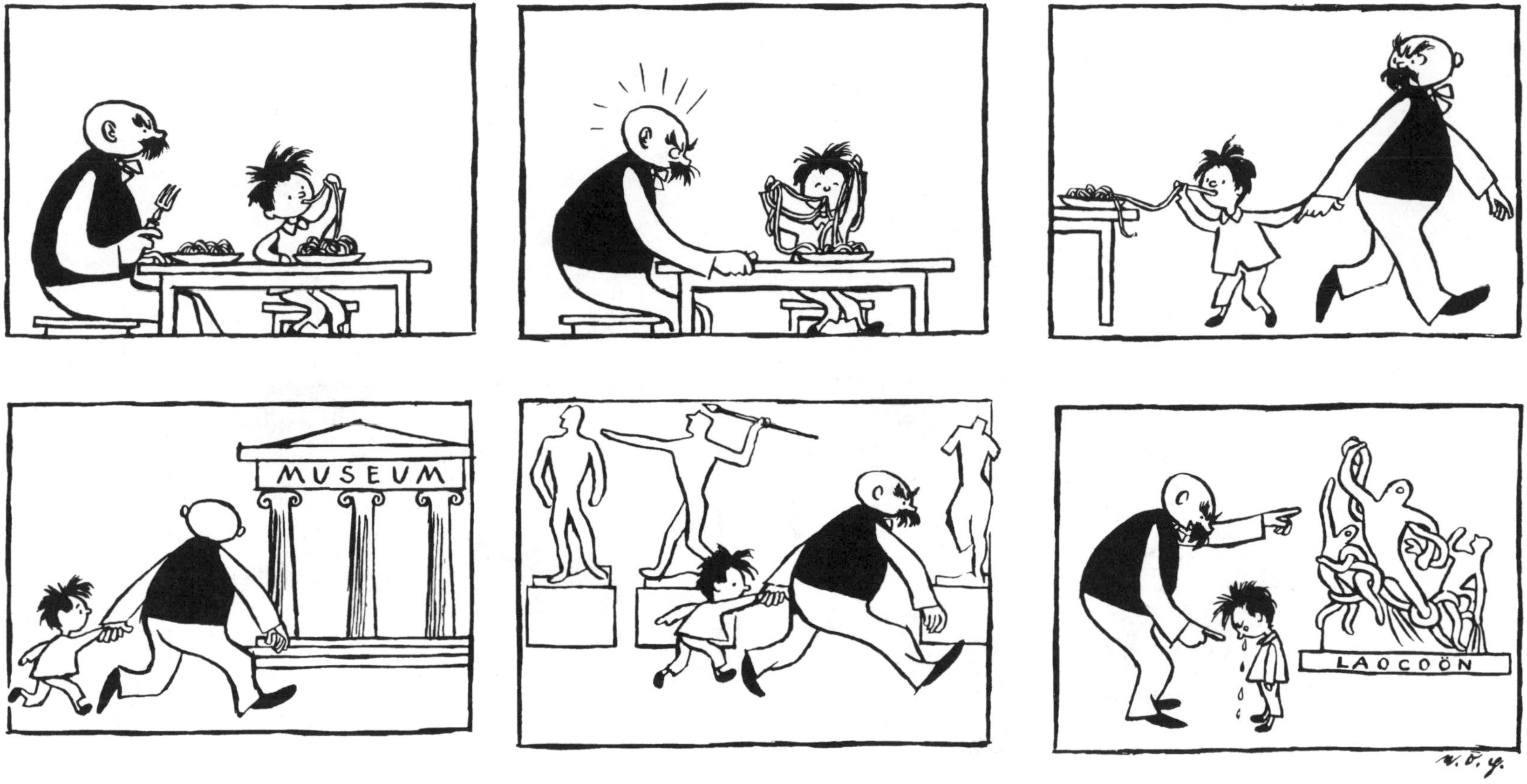
MUSEUM
LAOCOÖN

Cautionary example

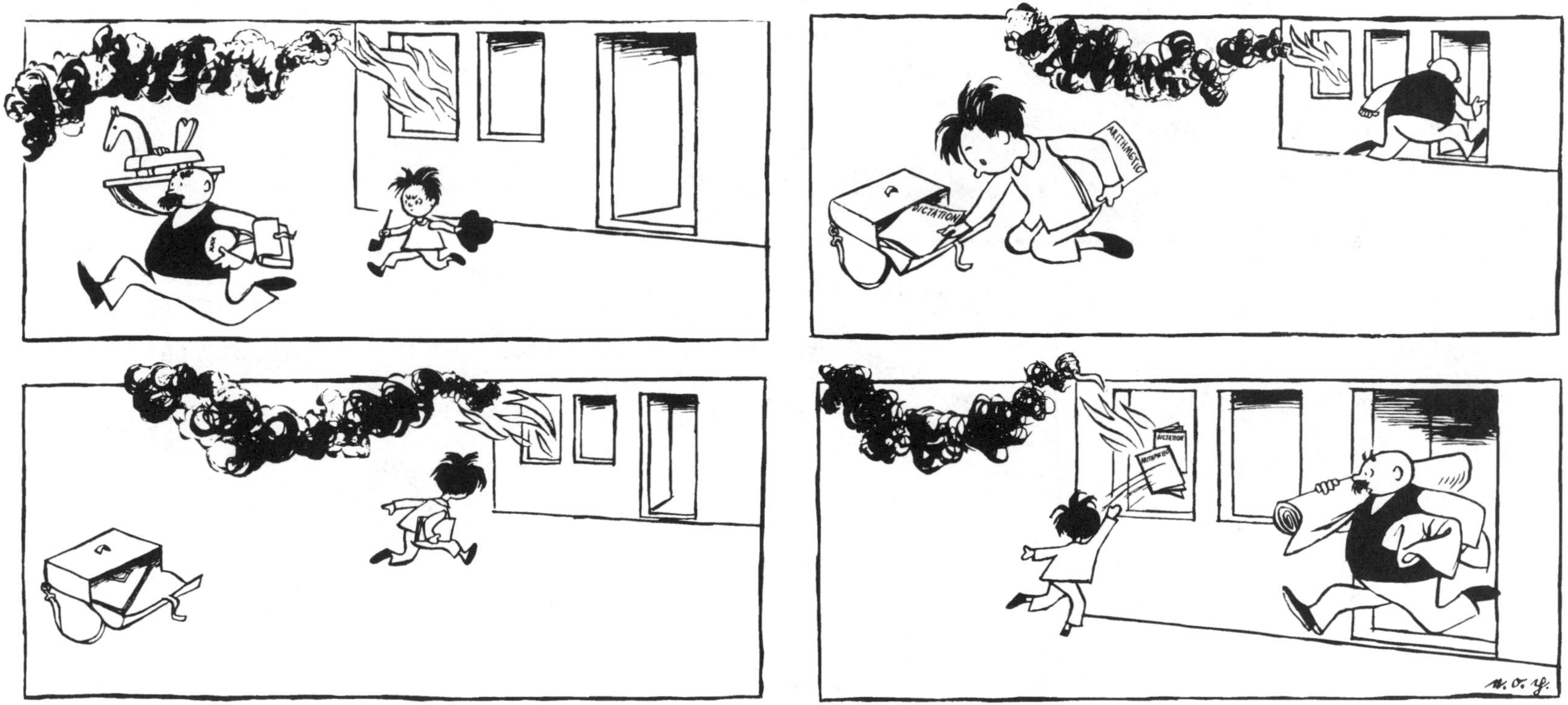
ARITHMETIC
DICTATION

Good opportunity

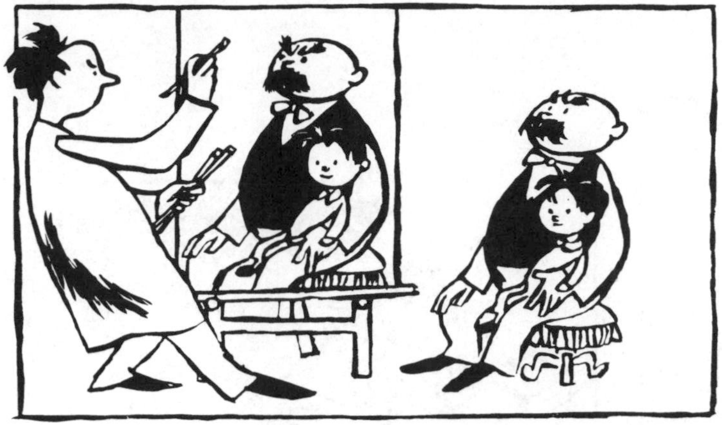

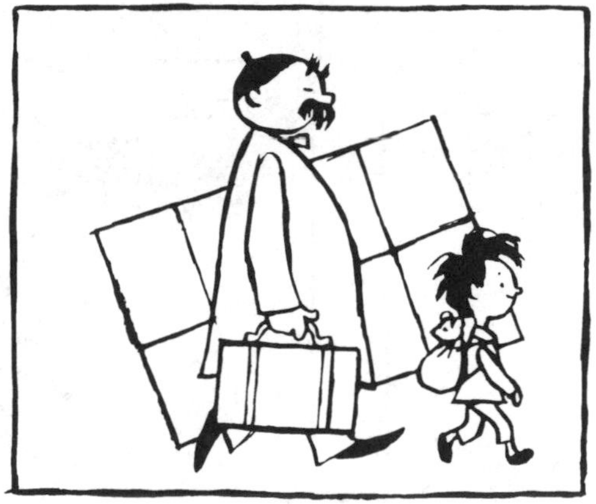

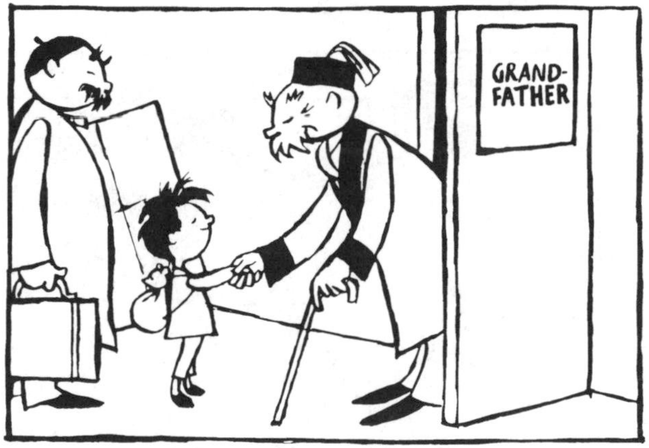

GRAND-
FATHER

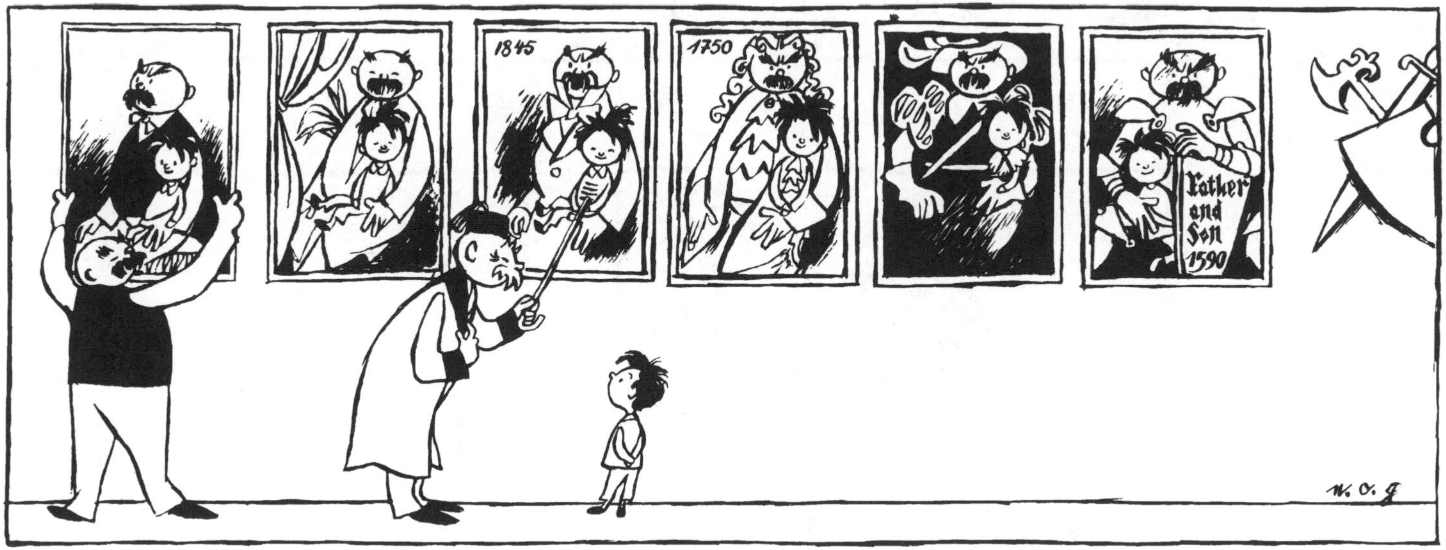
1845
1750
Father
and
Son
1590
W. O. G

The family portrait gallery

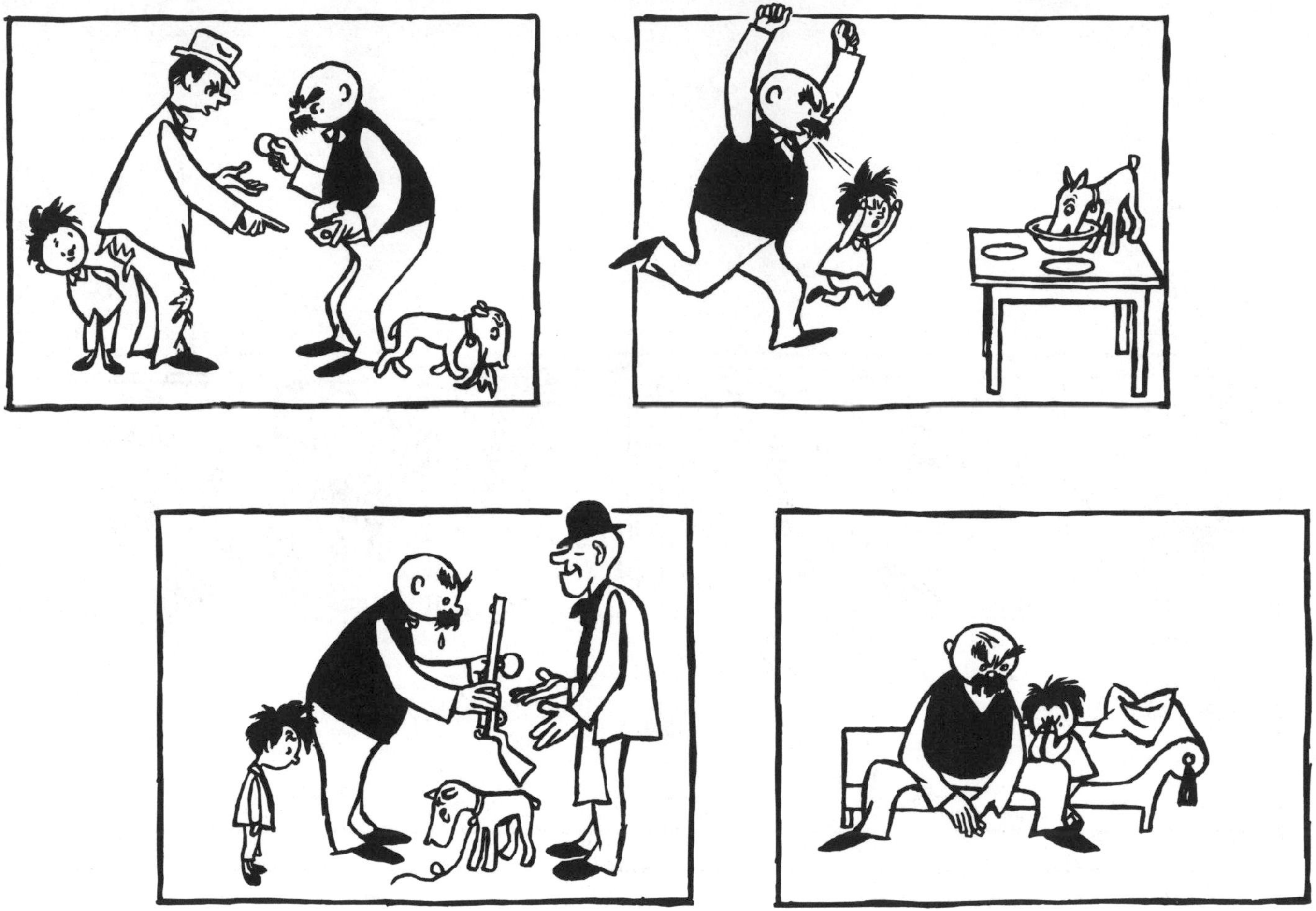

The expensive dog

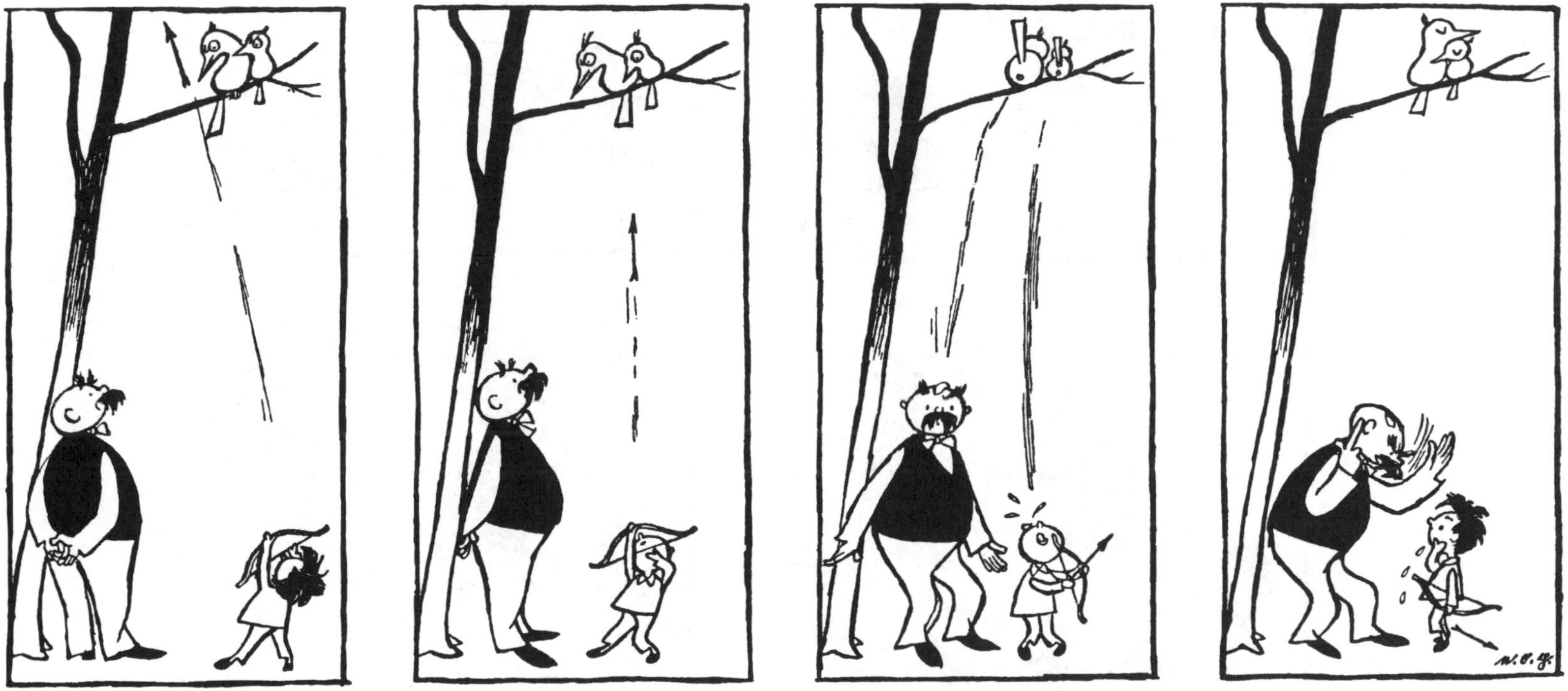

Response from on high

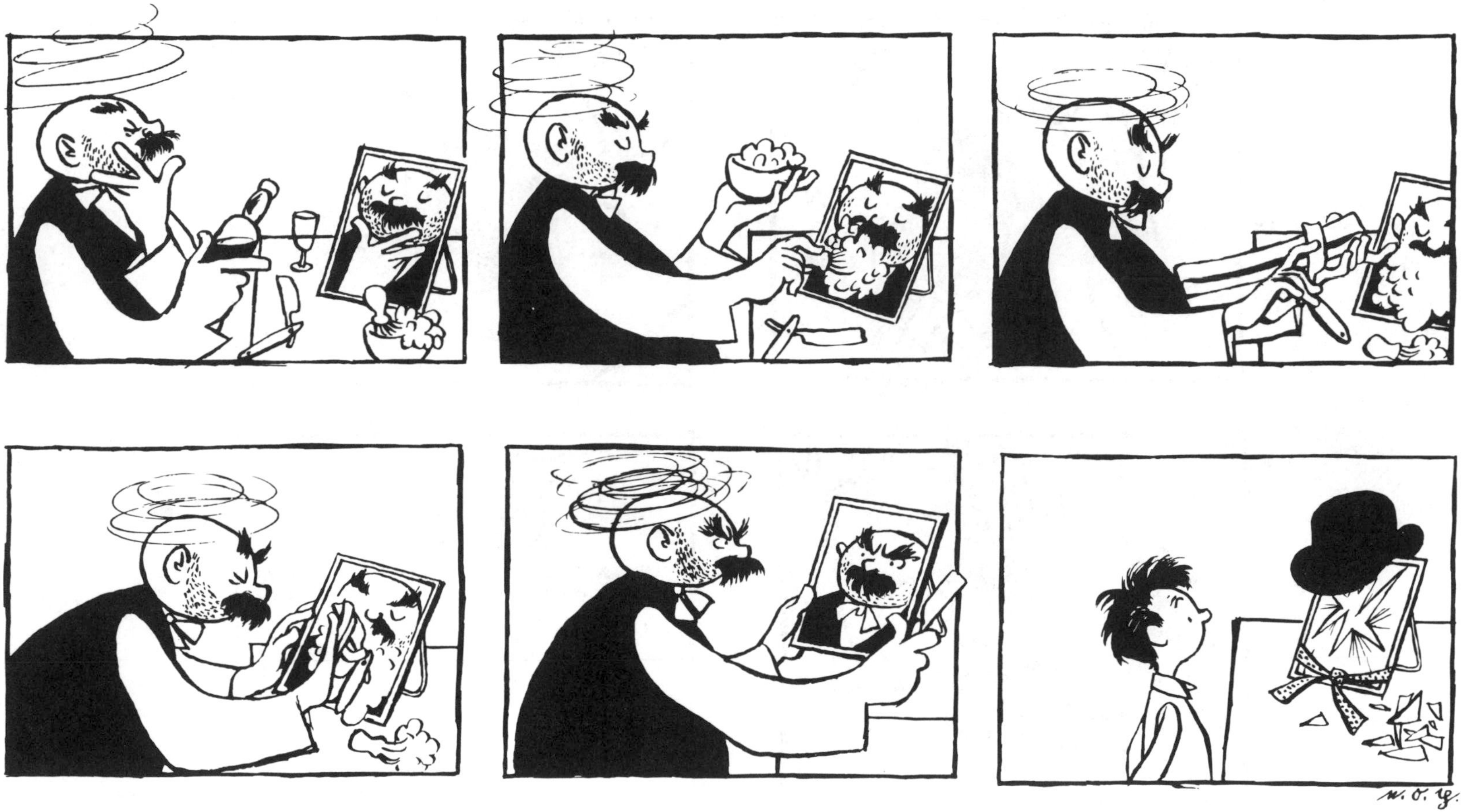

Shaving under the influence

Blessedness is the reward of effort

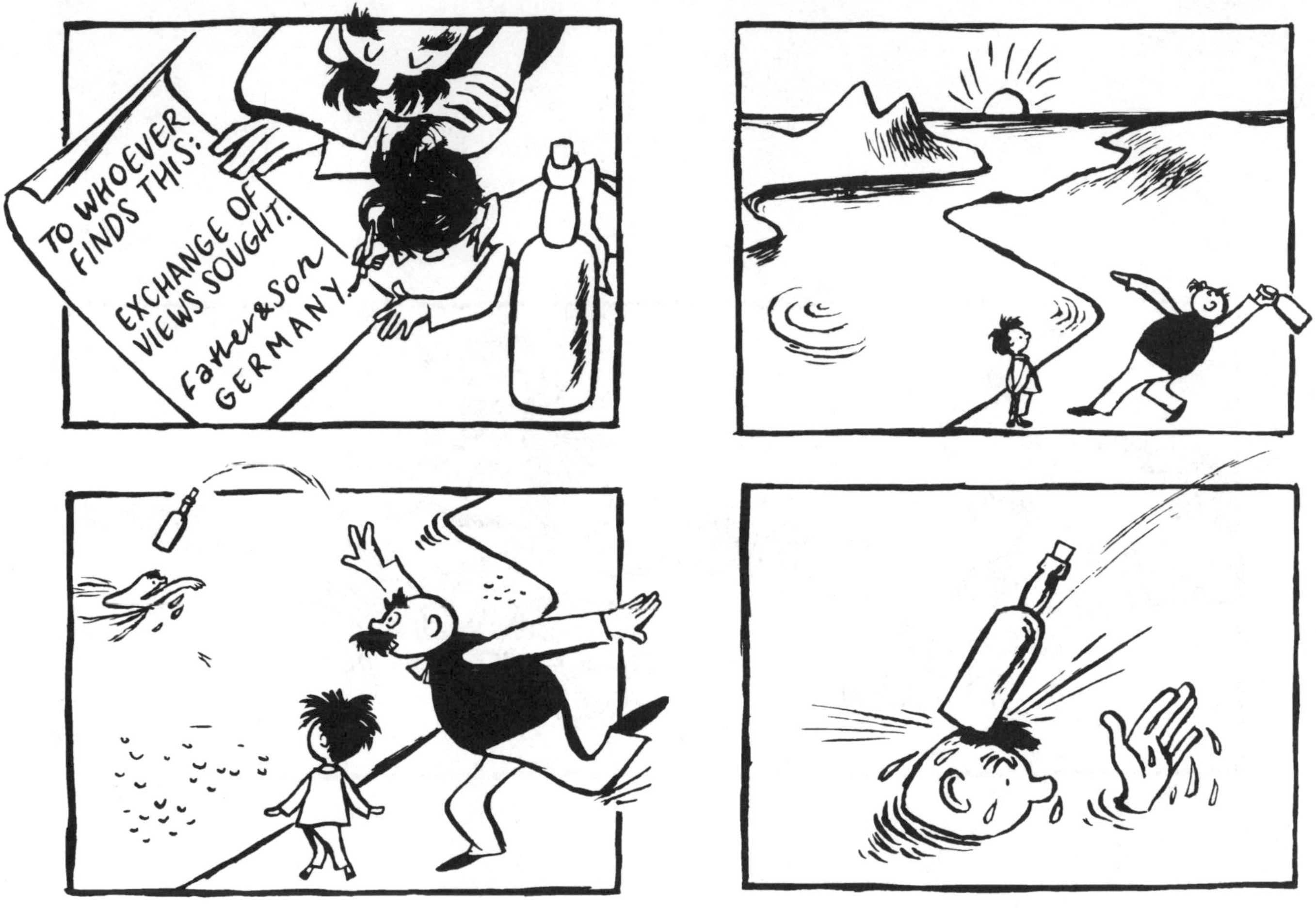
TO WHOEVER FINDS THIS:
EXCHANGE OF VIEWS SOUGHT.
Father & Son
GERMANY.

Wish quickly granted

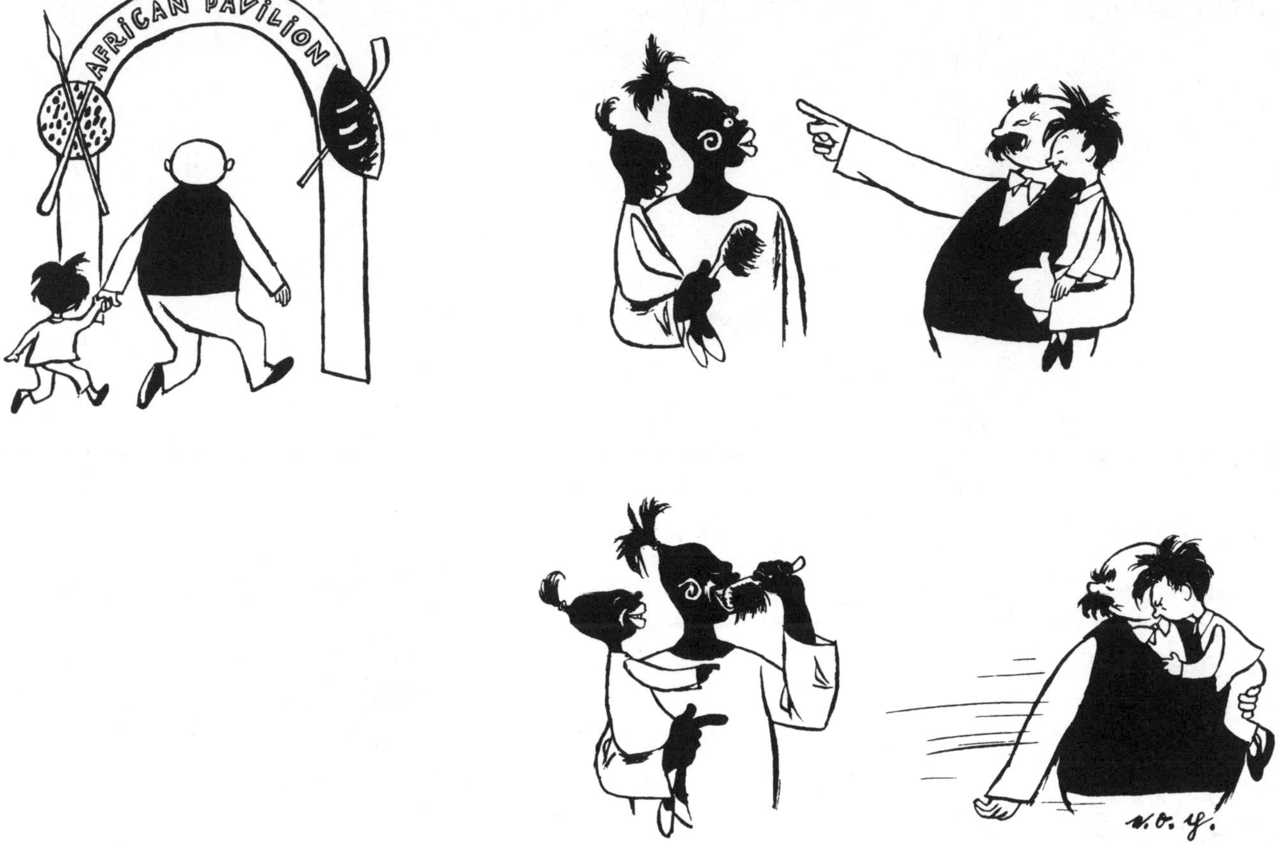
AFRICAN PAVILION

Paintbrush and scrub brush

Editor's note: Ethnographic attractions sometimes known as “human zoos” were common in Europe and the United States in the late nineteenth century and early twentieth century. Native peoples of non-European countries were put on display, often in settings that were presented as authentic recreations of life in their native countries.

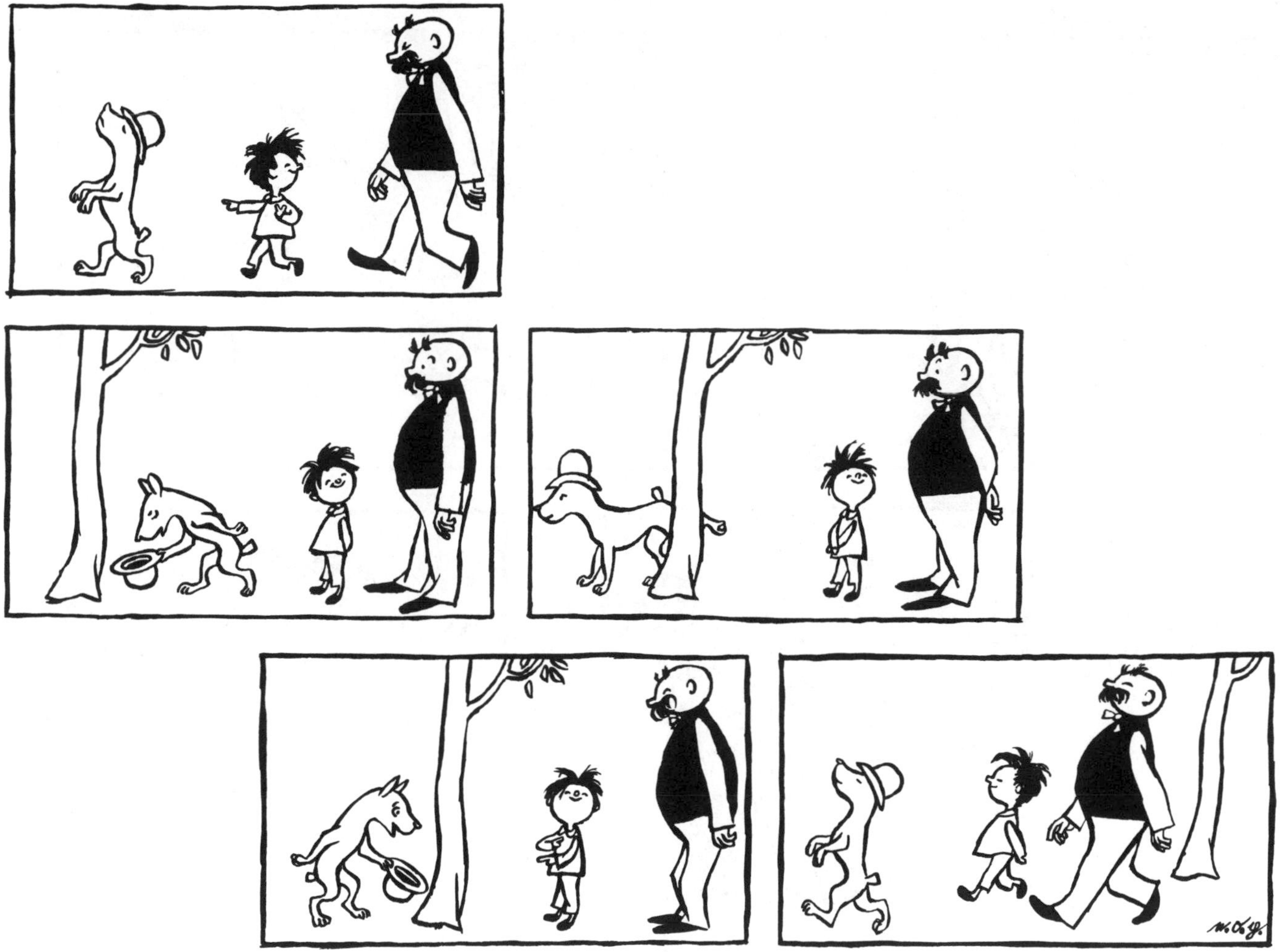

Training in good manners

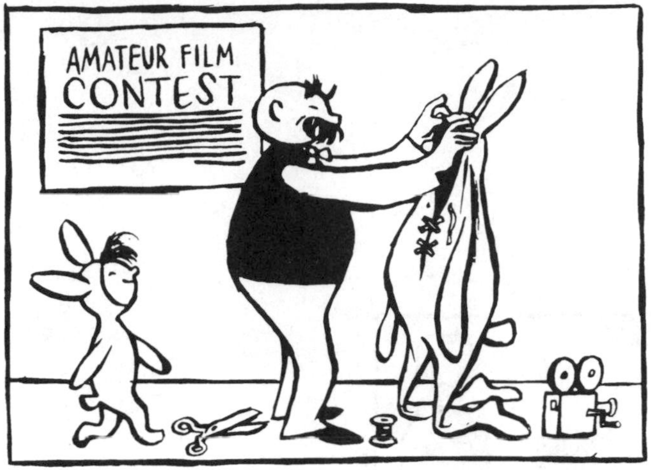
AMATEUR FILM
CONTEST
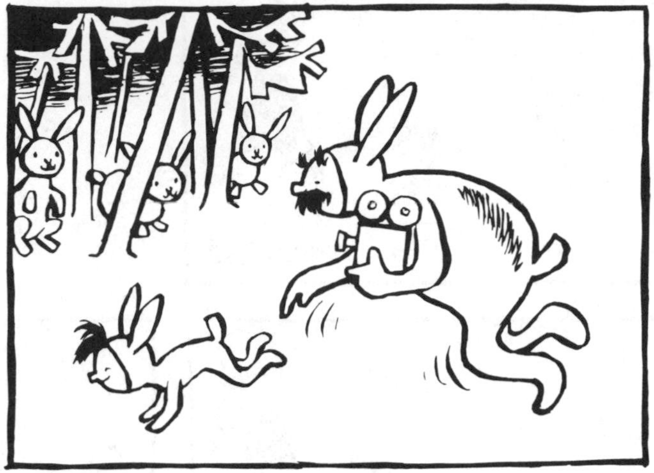
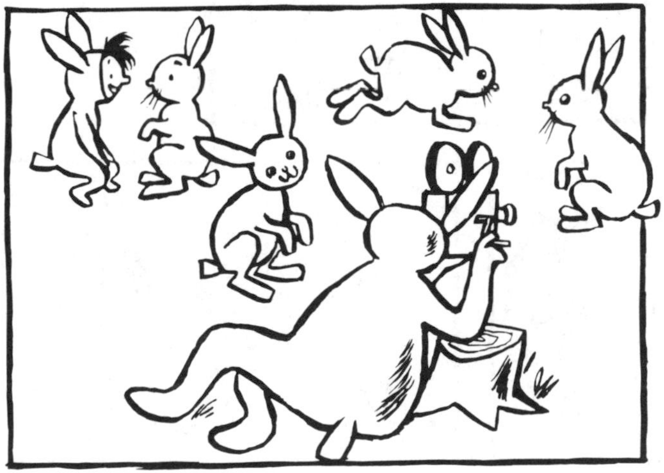
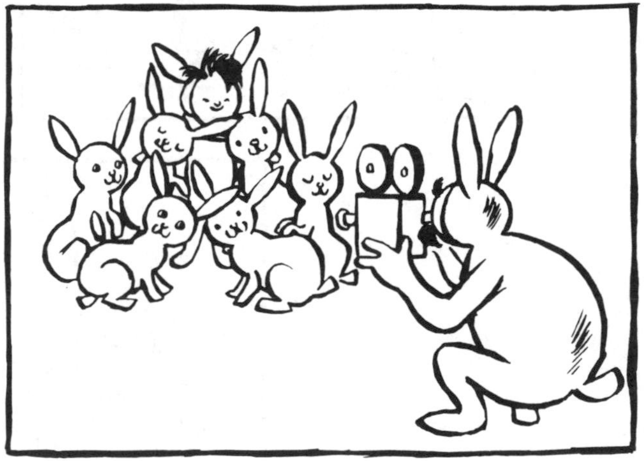

Undercover documentary

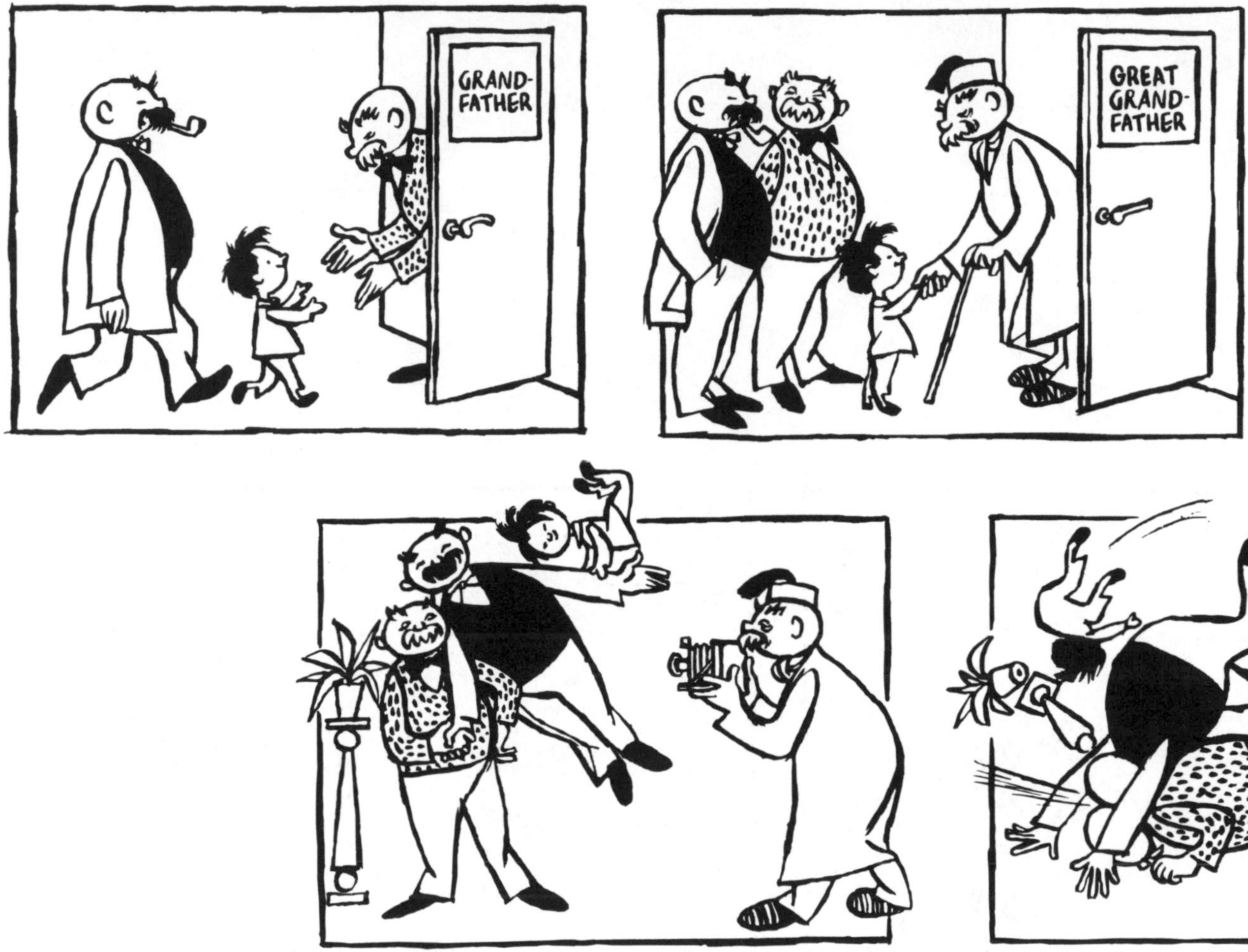
GRAND-FATHER
GREAT GRAND-FATHER

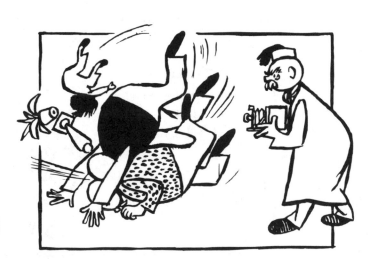

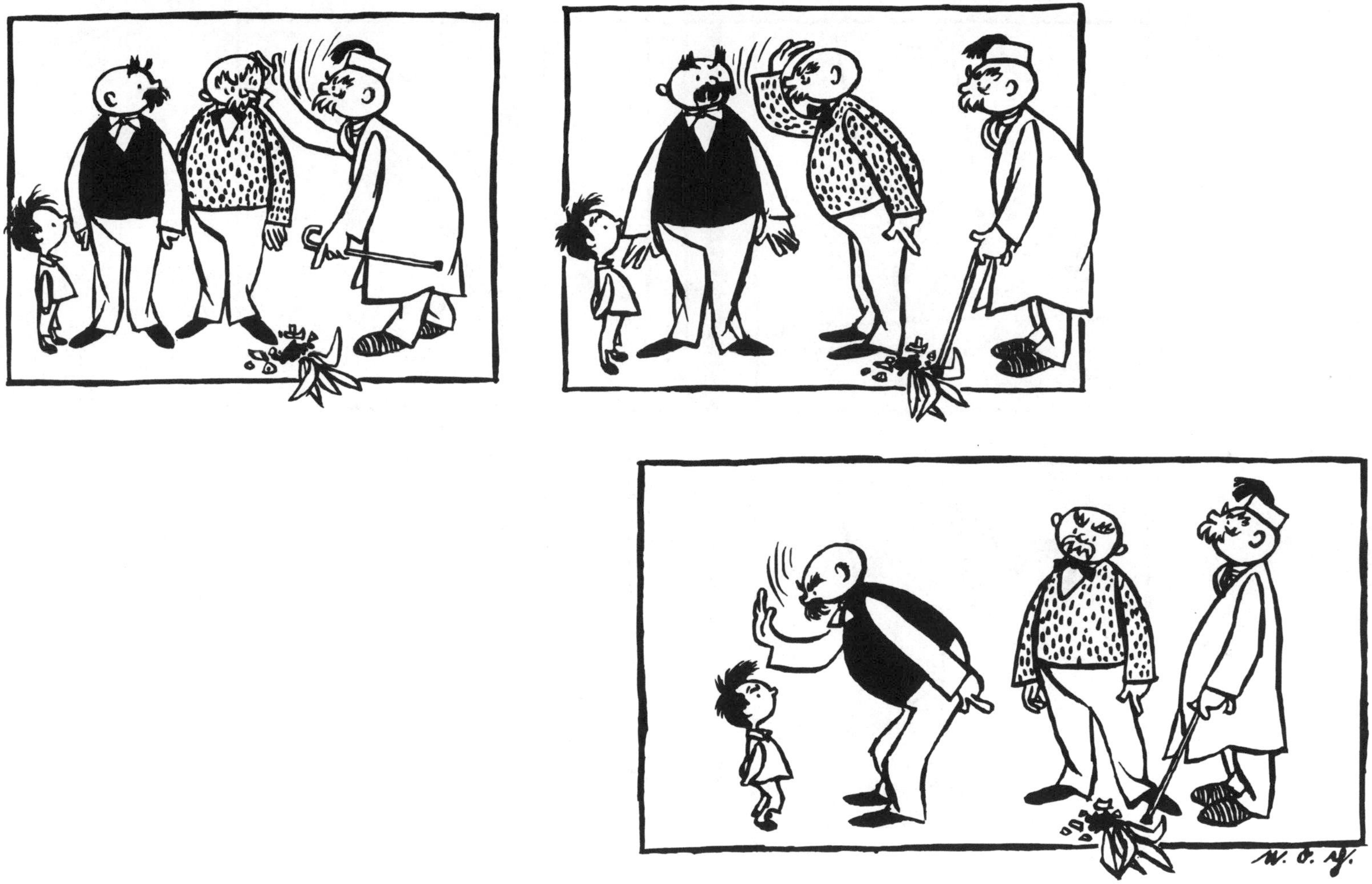

The ancestral slap

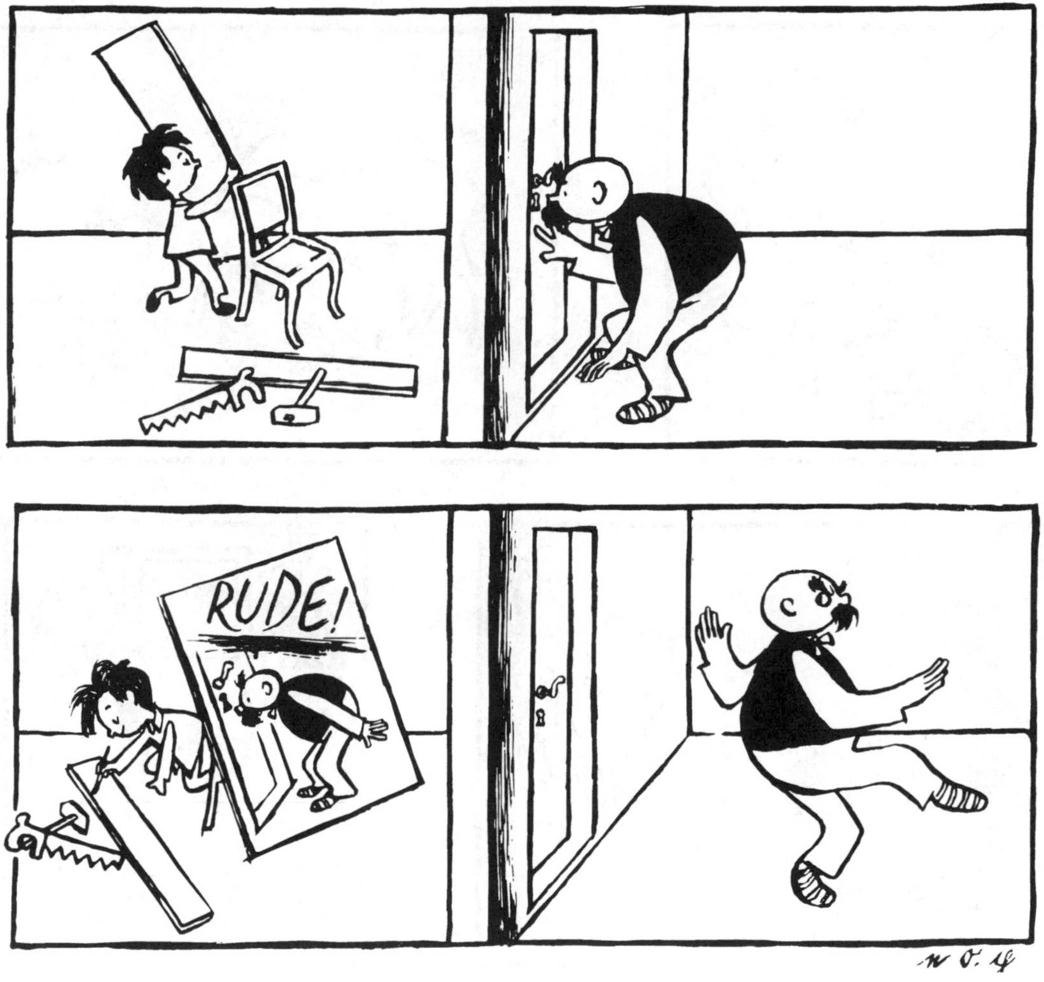
RUDE!

Mysterious doings before the party

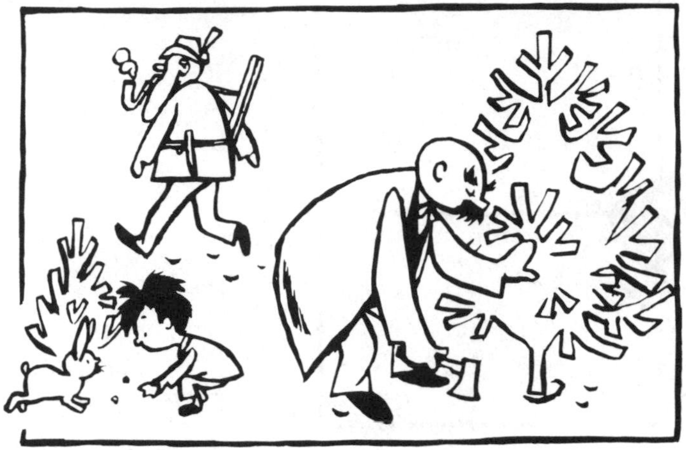

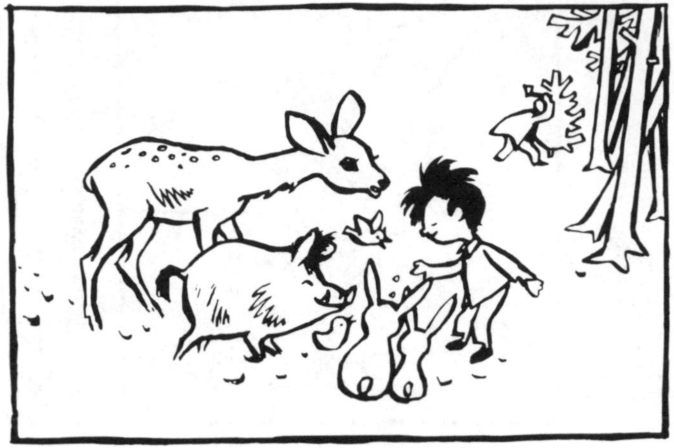

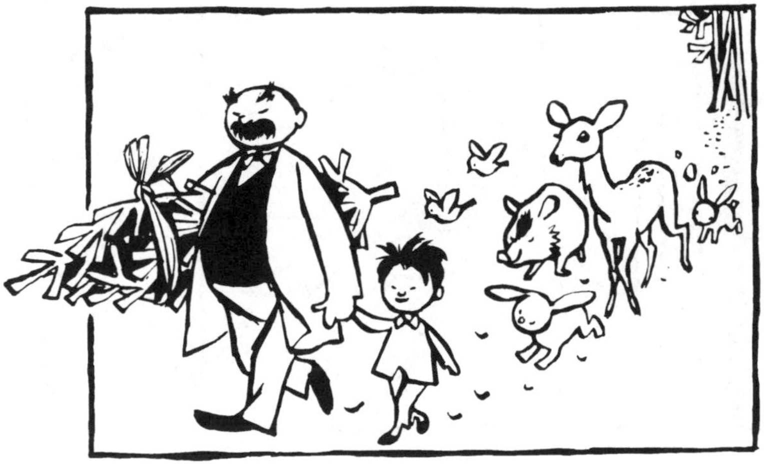

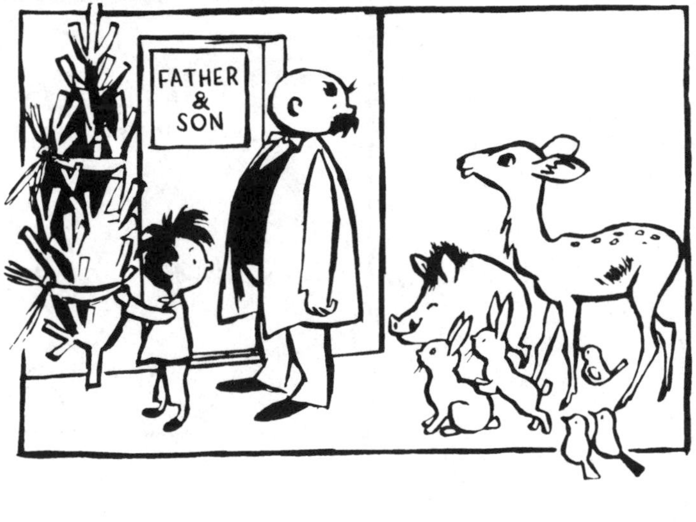
FATHER & SON

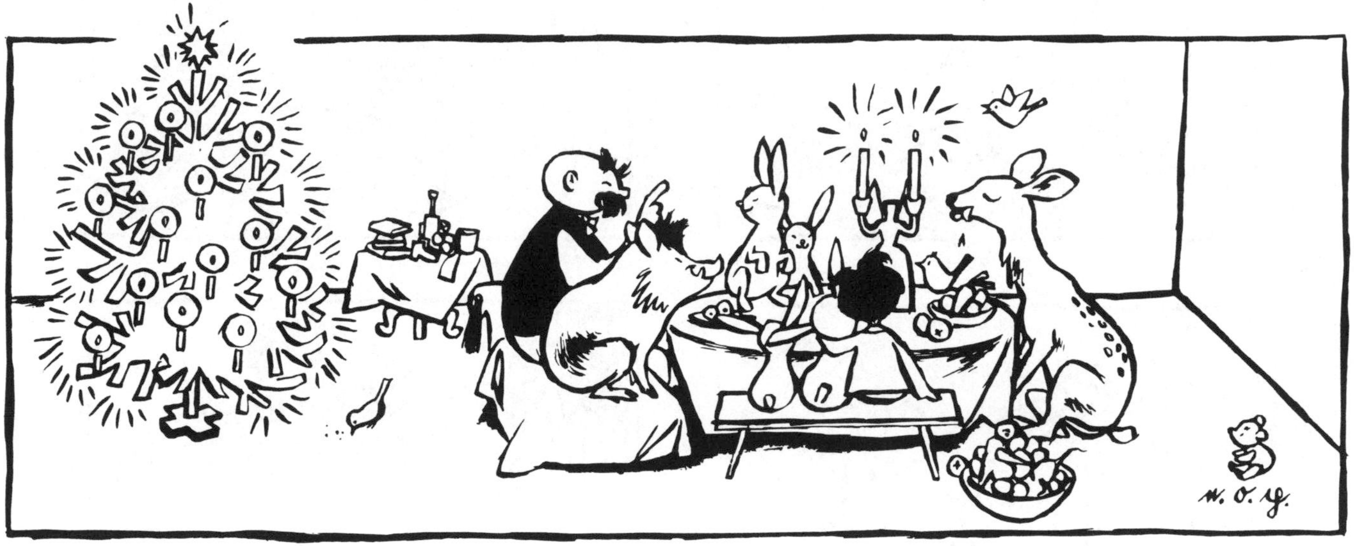
w. o. g.

Christmas with friends

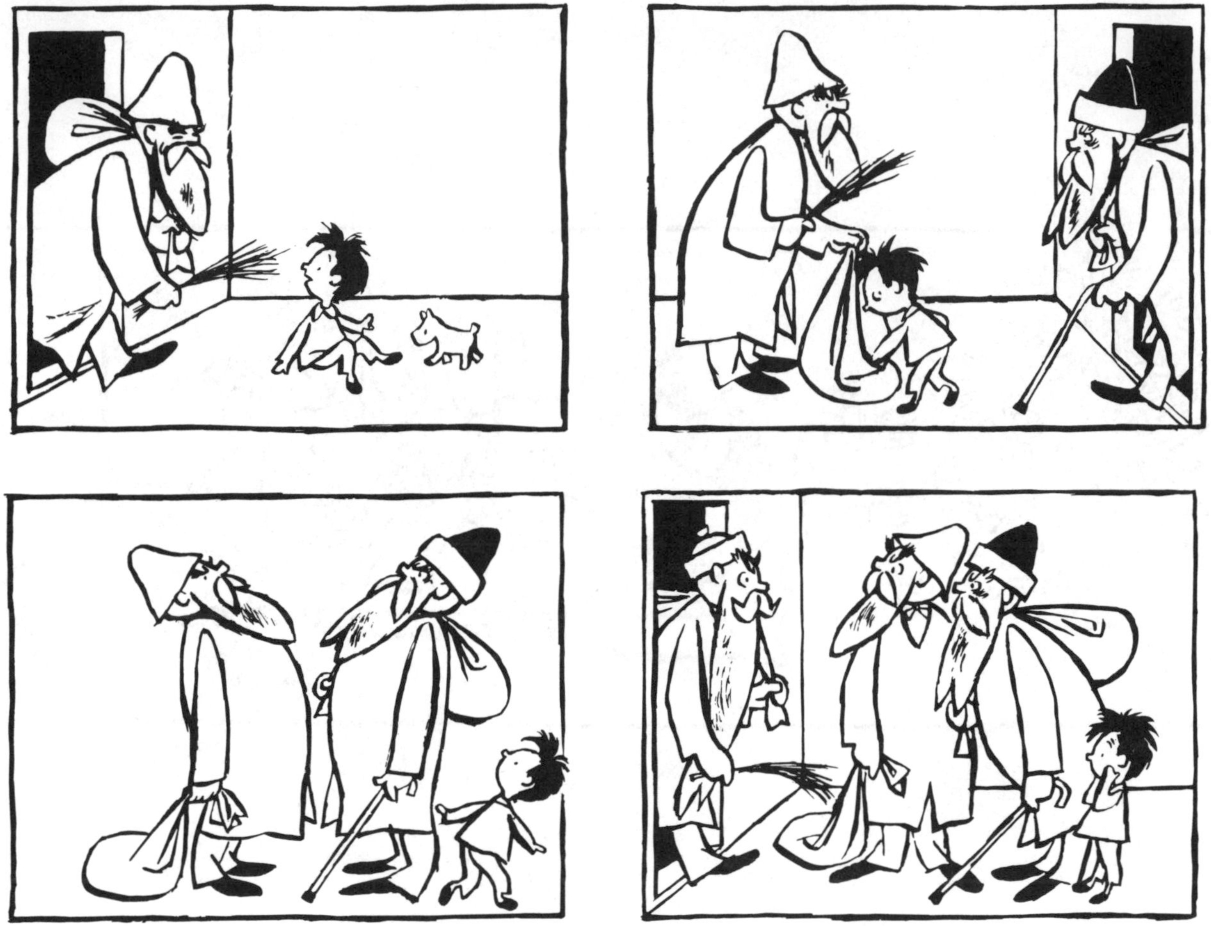

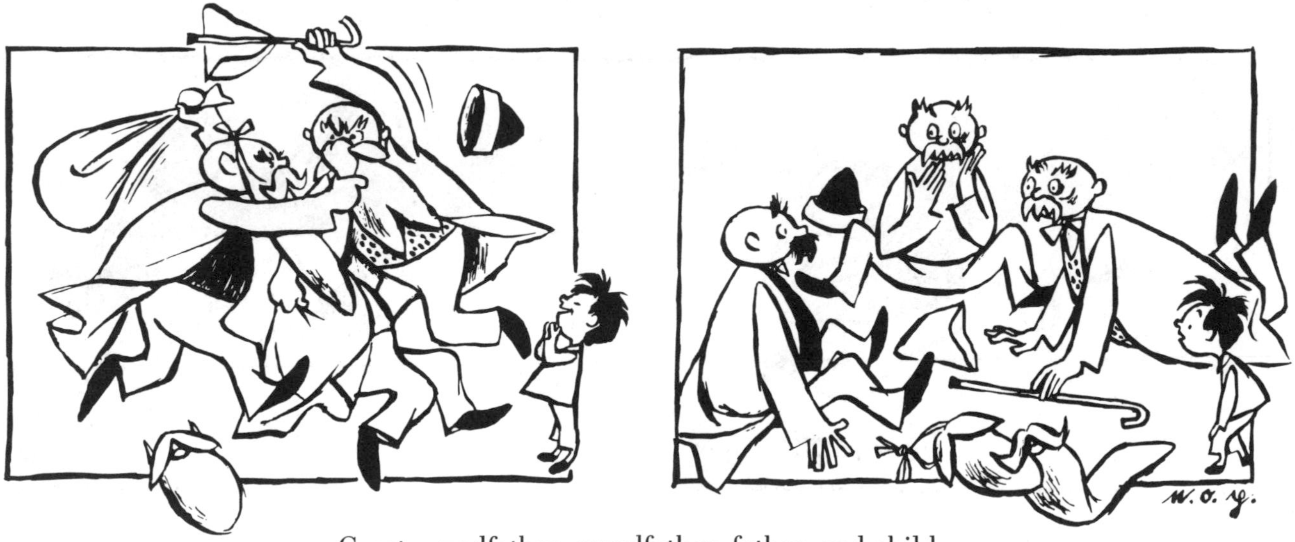
w.o.g.

Great-grandfather, grandfather, father, and child

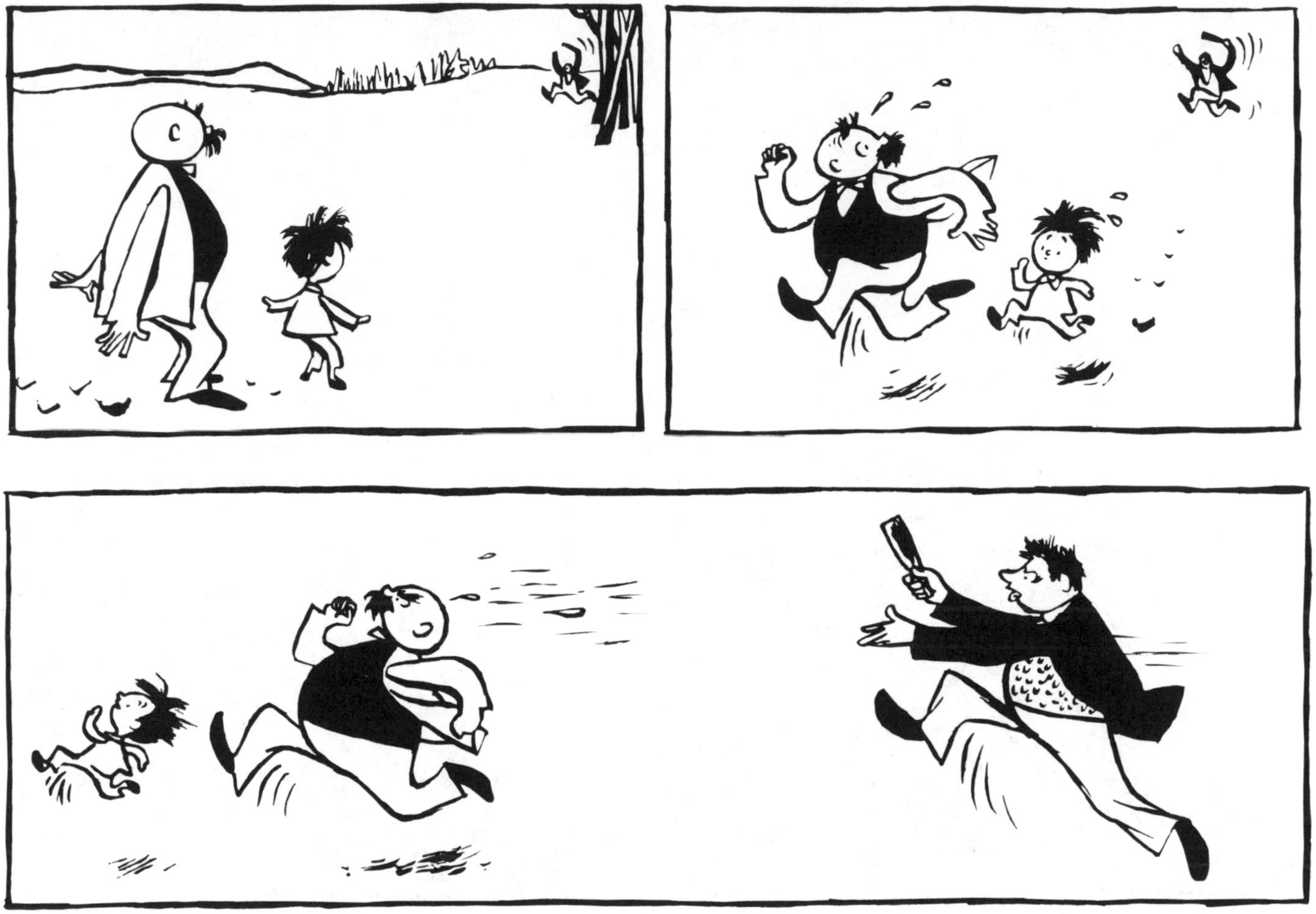

Happy New Year
W.O.G.

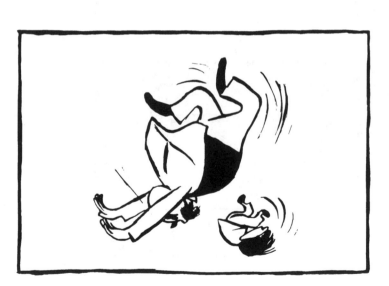

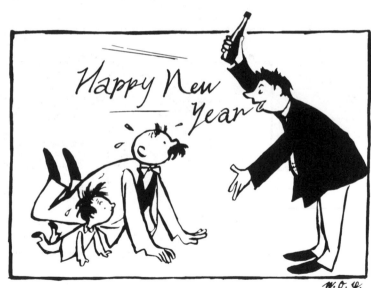

New Year's adventure

The clock struck two, away she flew

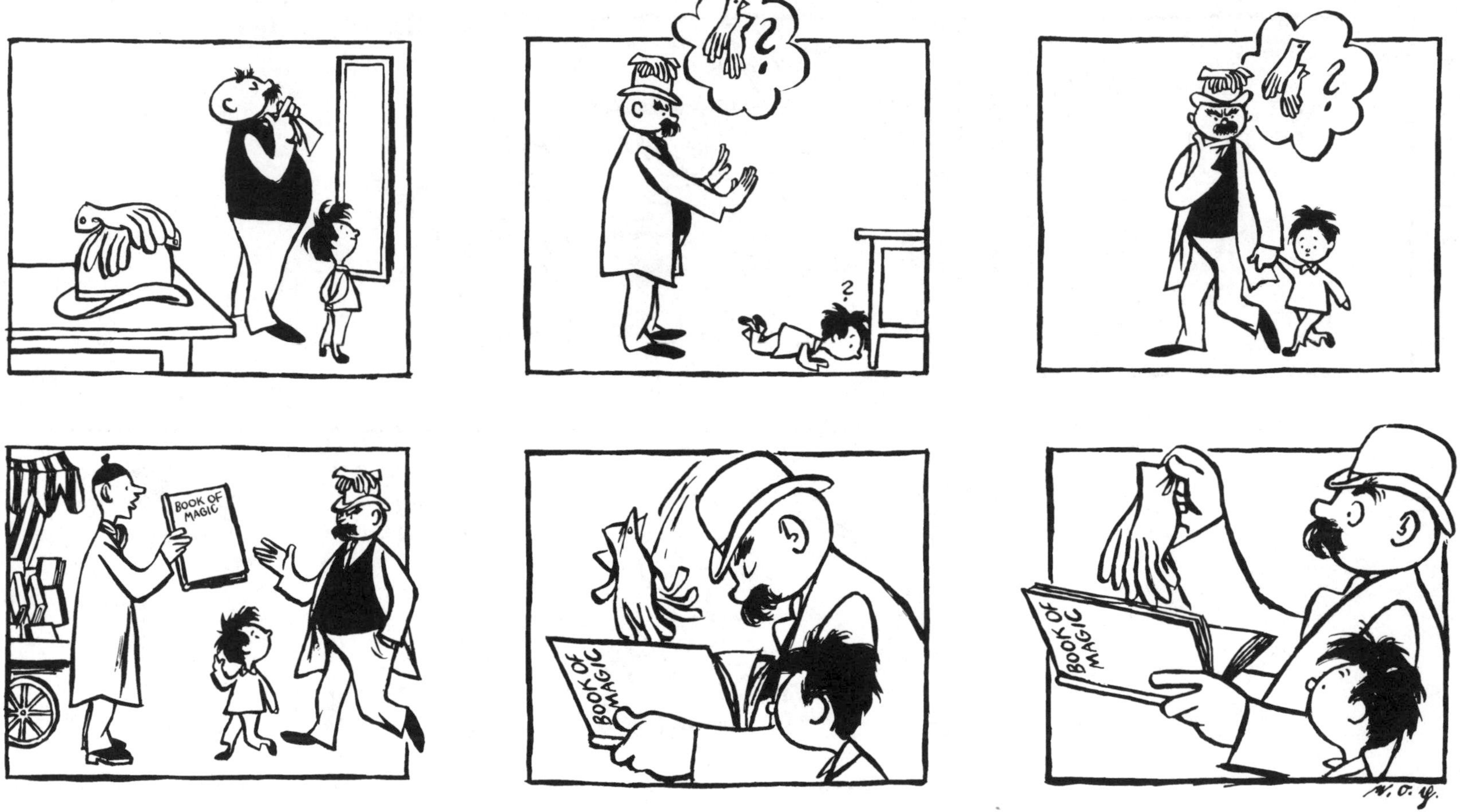
?
?
?
BOOK OF MAGIC
BOOK OF MAGIC
BOOK OF MAGIC
W. O. G.

Now he believes

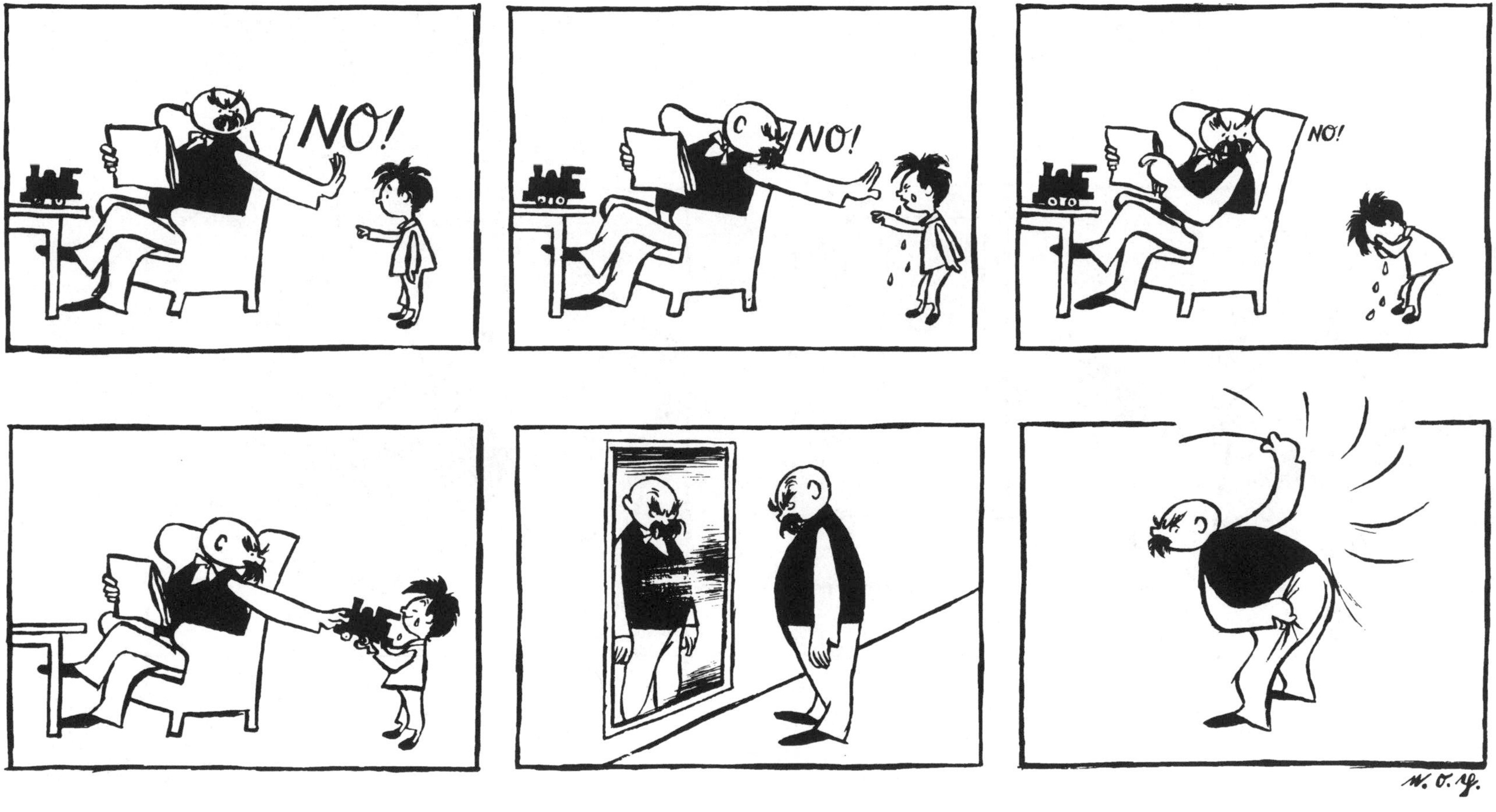
NO!
NO!
NO!

Scathing self-criticism

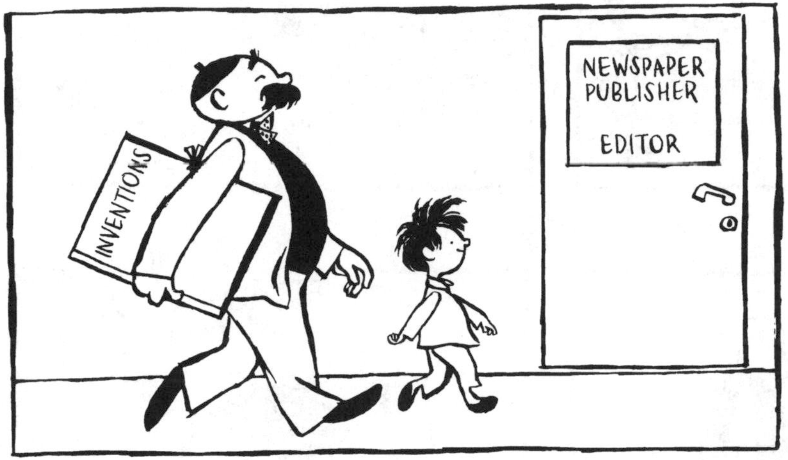
INVENTIONS
NEWSPAPER
PUBLISHER
EDITOR

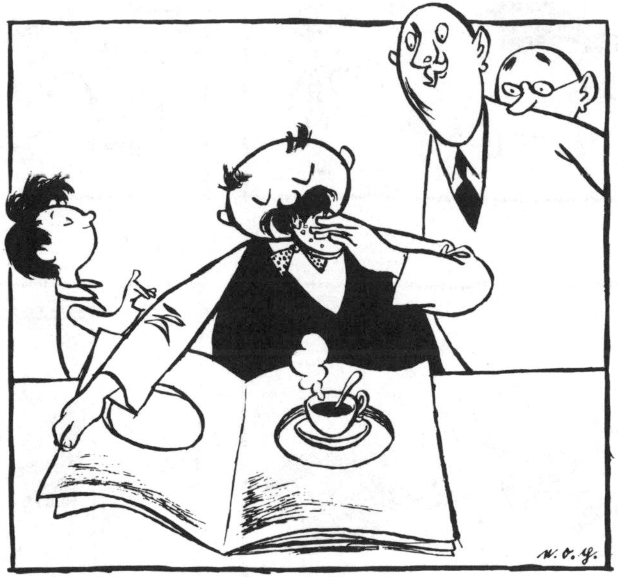

The morning paper we've been looking for . . .

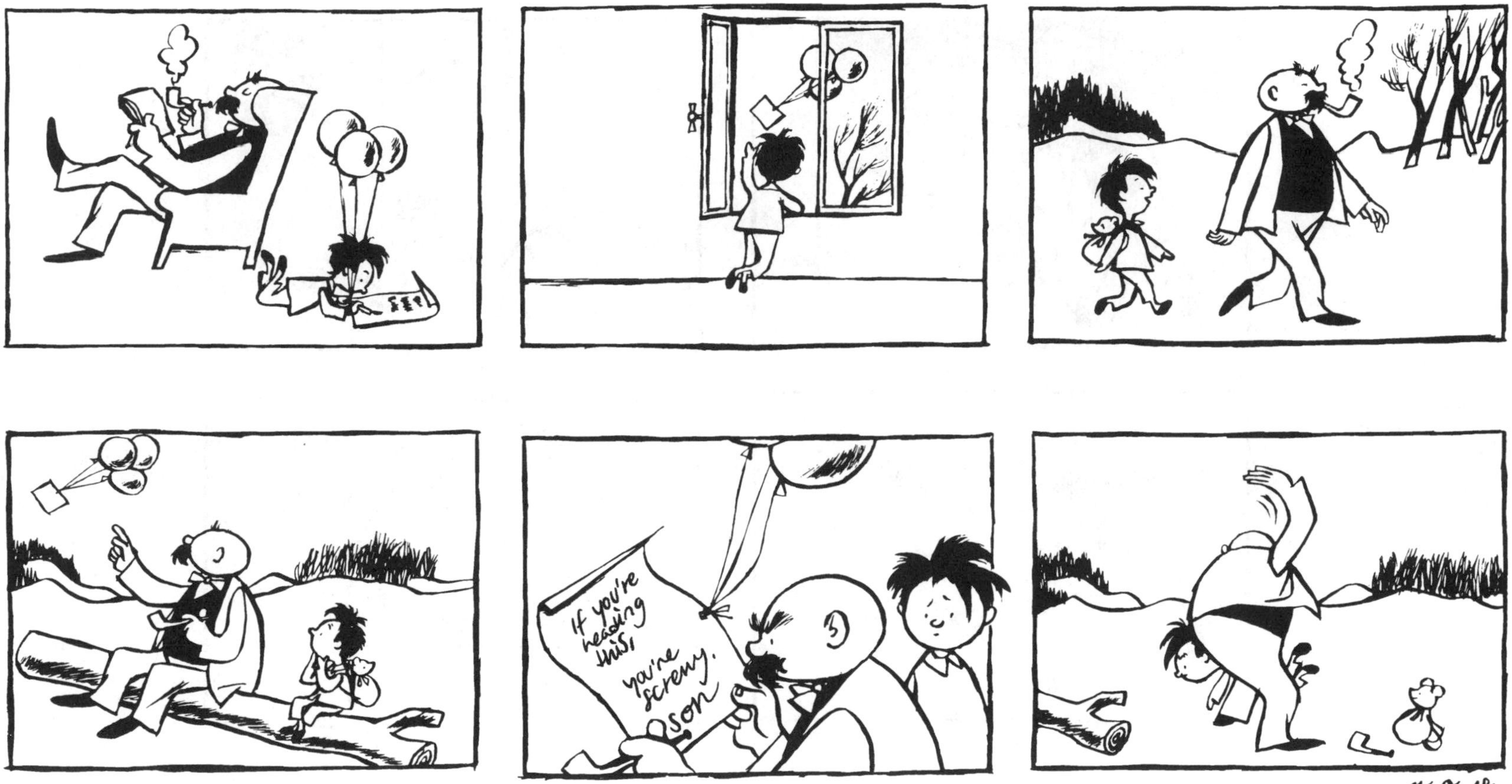
If you're reading this, you're screwy. son

Return to sender

The fighting snowman

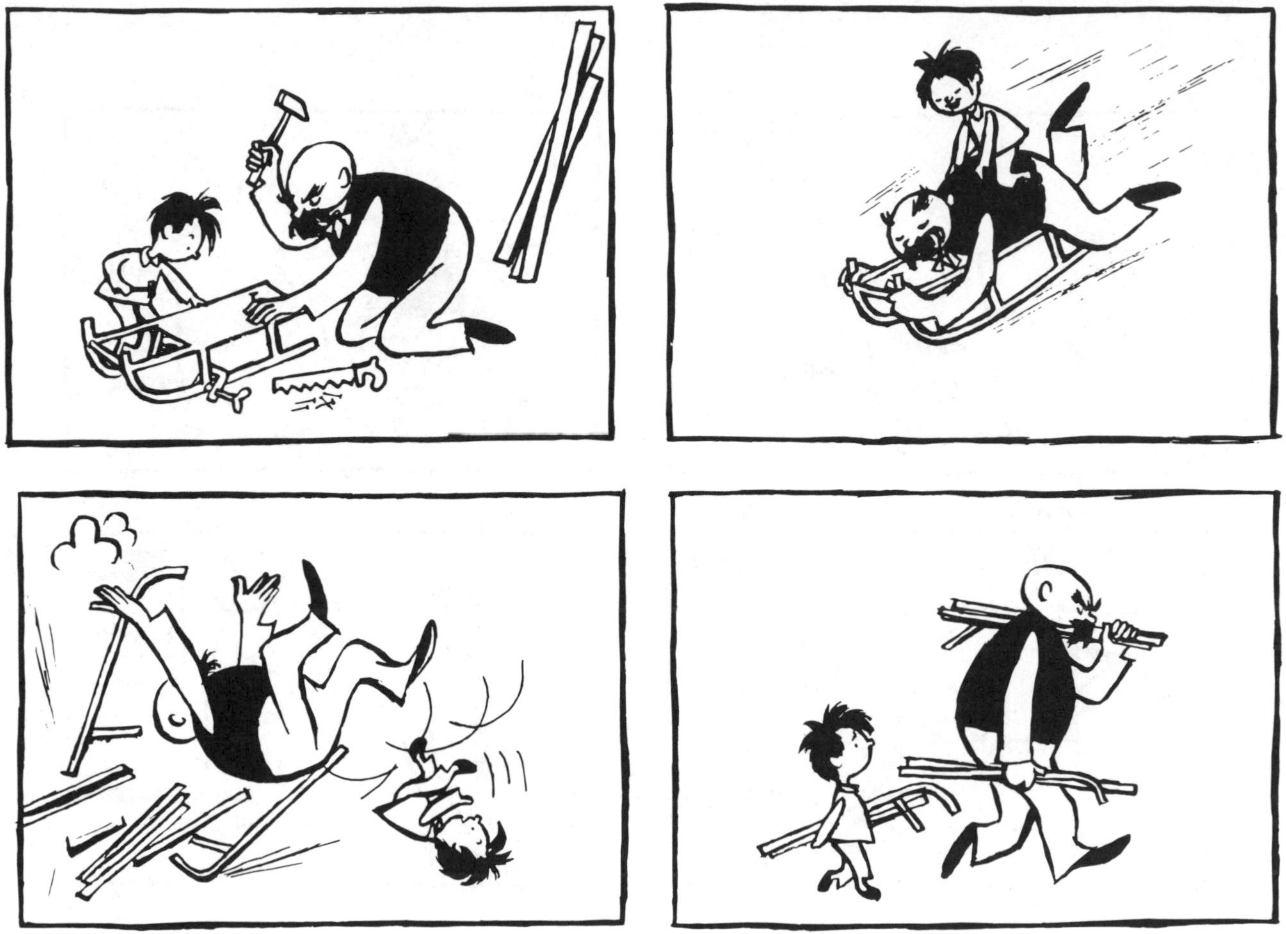

The homemade sled

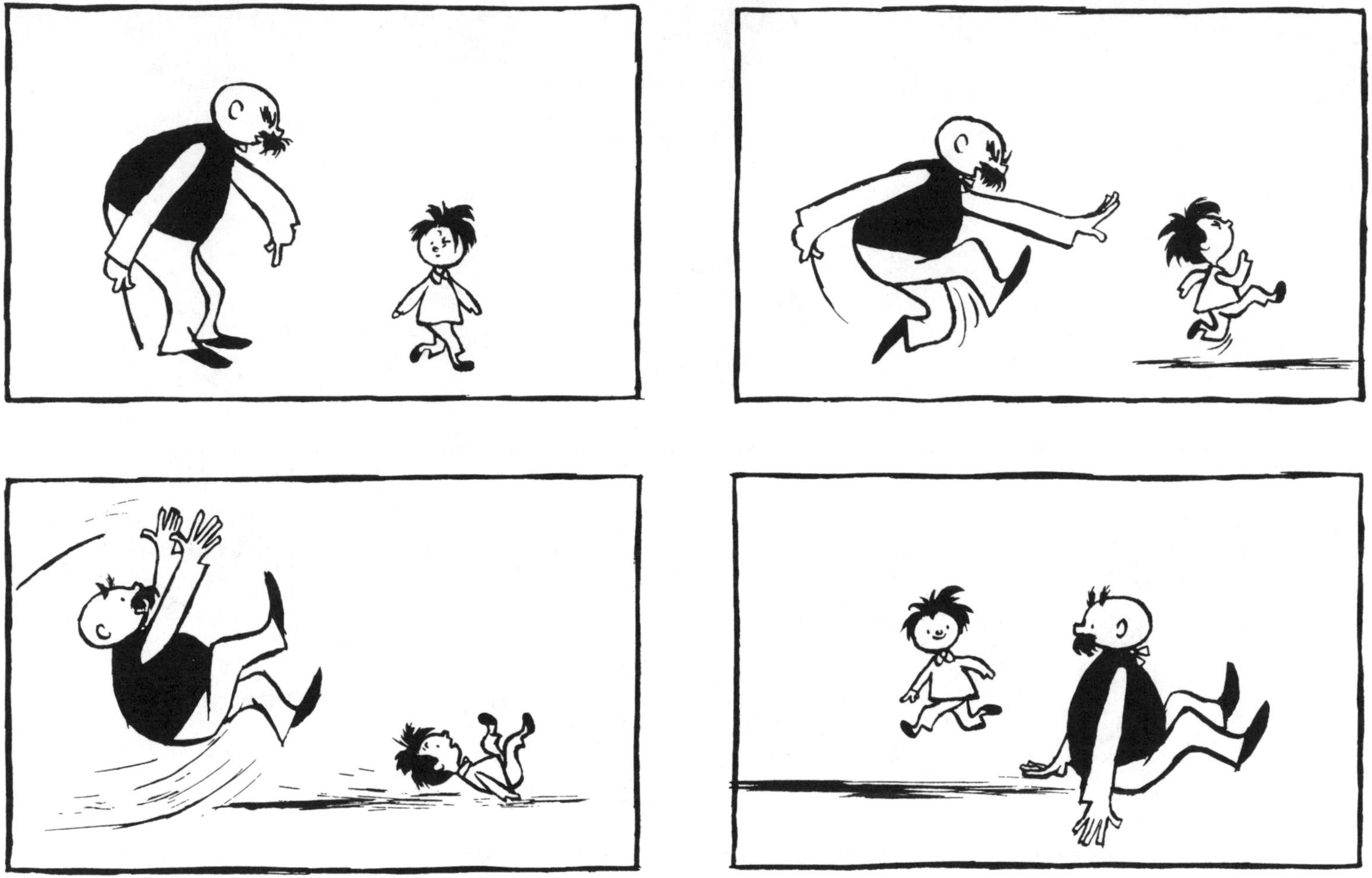

w. o. g.

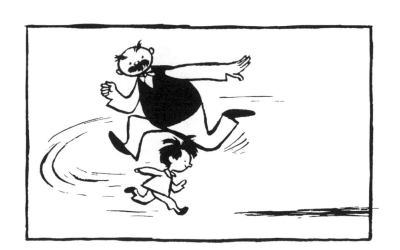

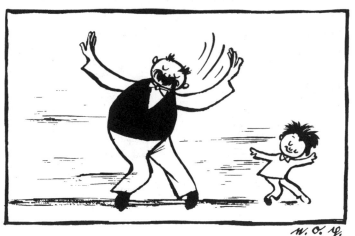

A good place to skate

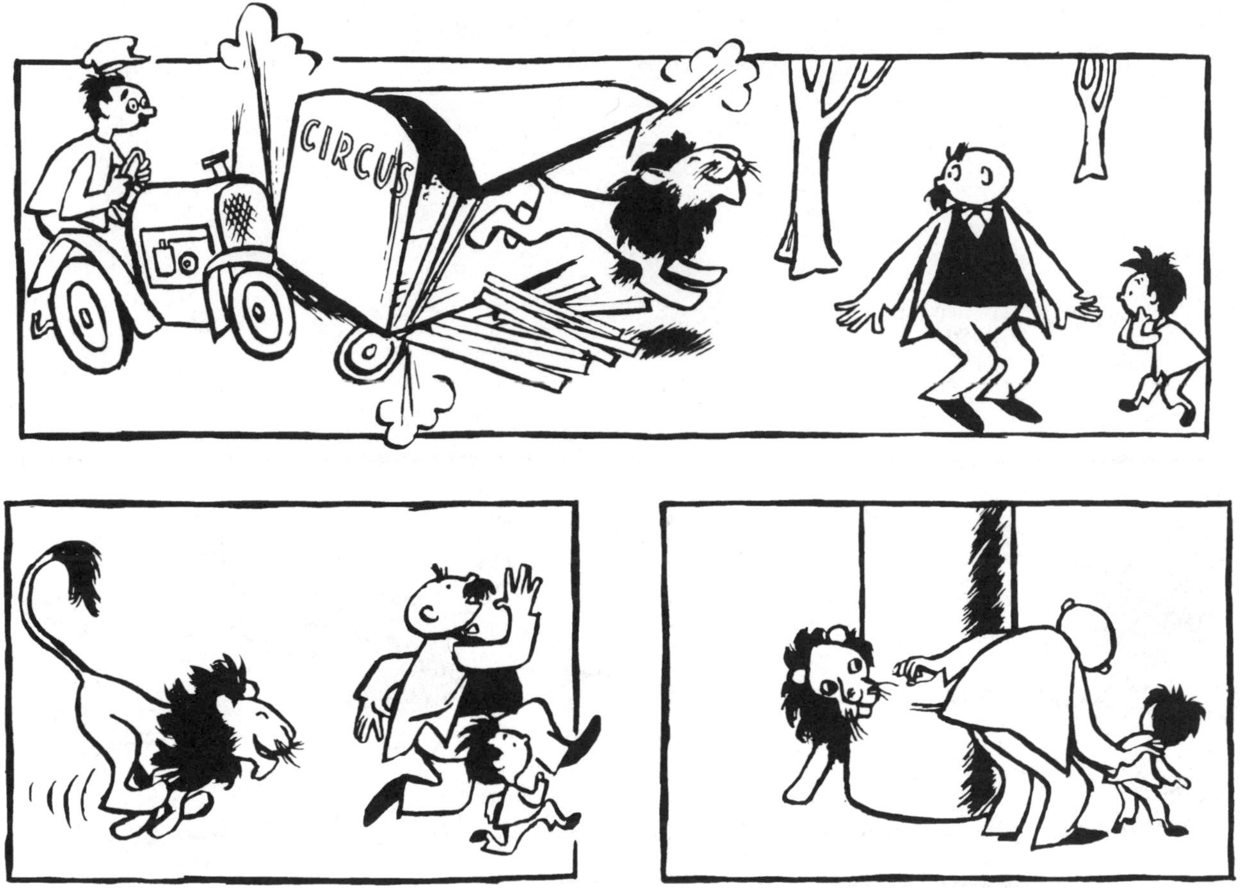
CIRCUS

FATHER & SON
FATHER & SON
OUT
M.O.Y.

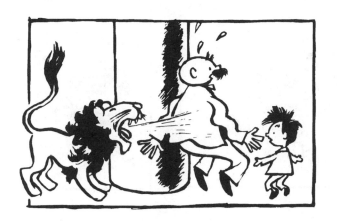

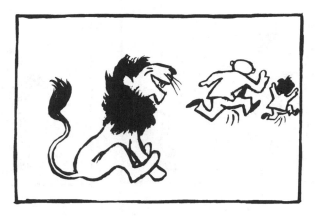

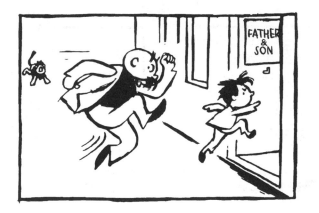

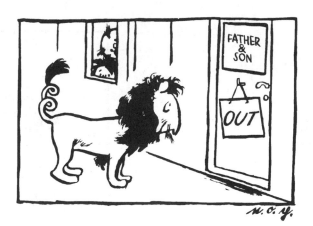

Escaped lion!

The goldfish that wasn't

The writing on the scroll reads:

Father
and Son
are hereby
named
sole heirs
of these
two million
marks and
the castle

FATHER
&
SON

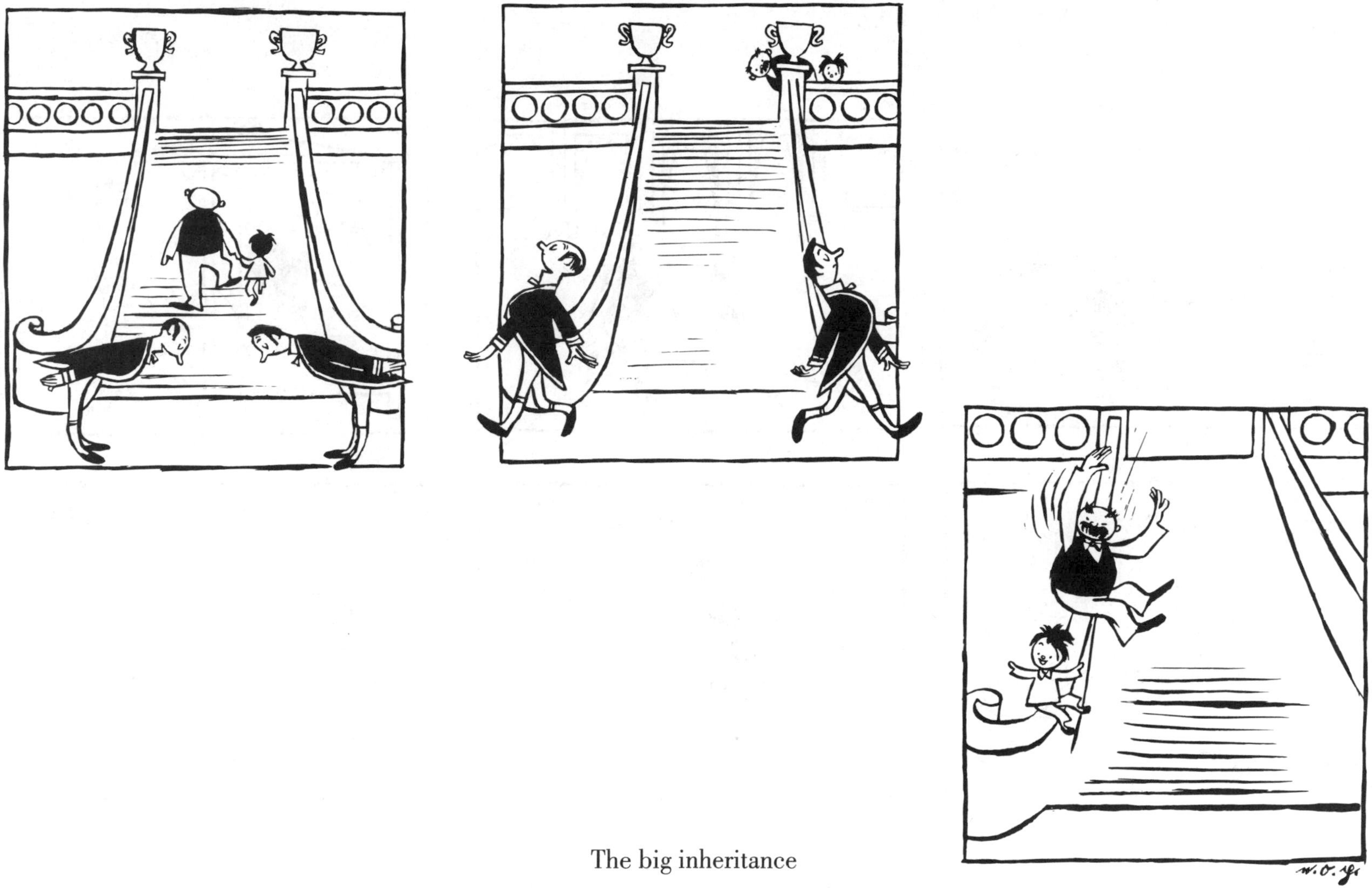

The big inheritance

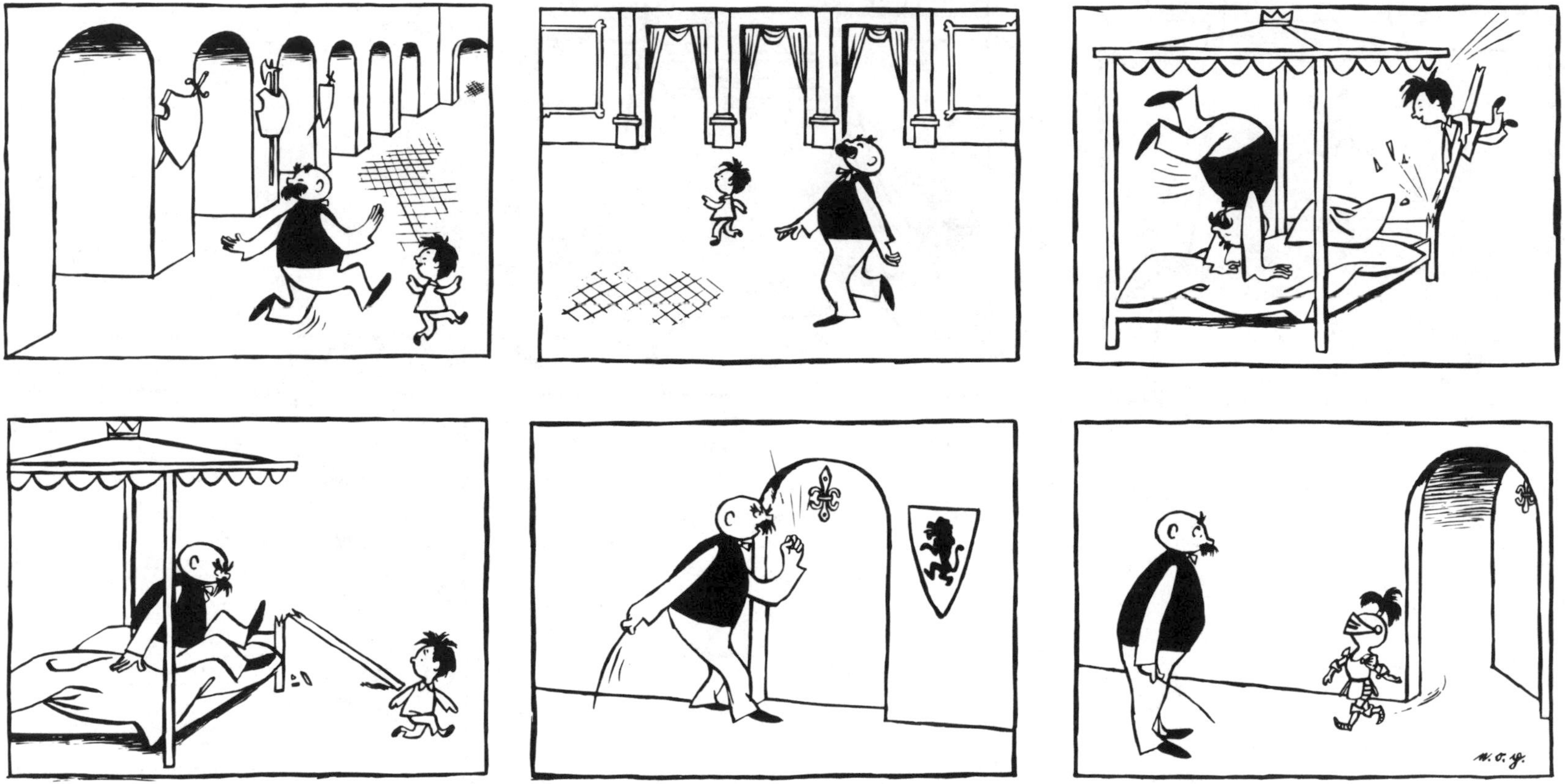

Fun in the castle

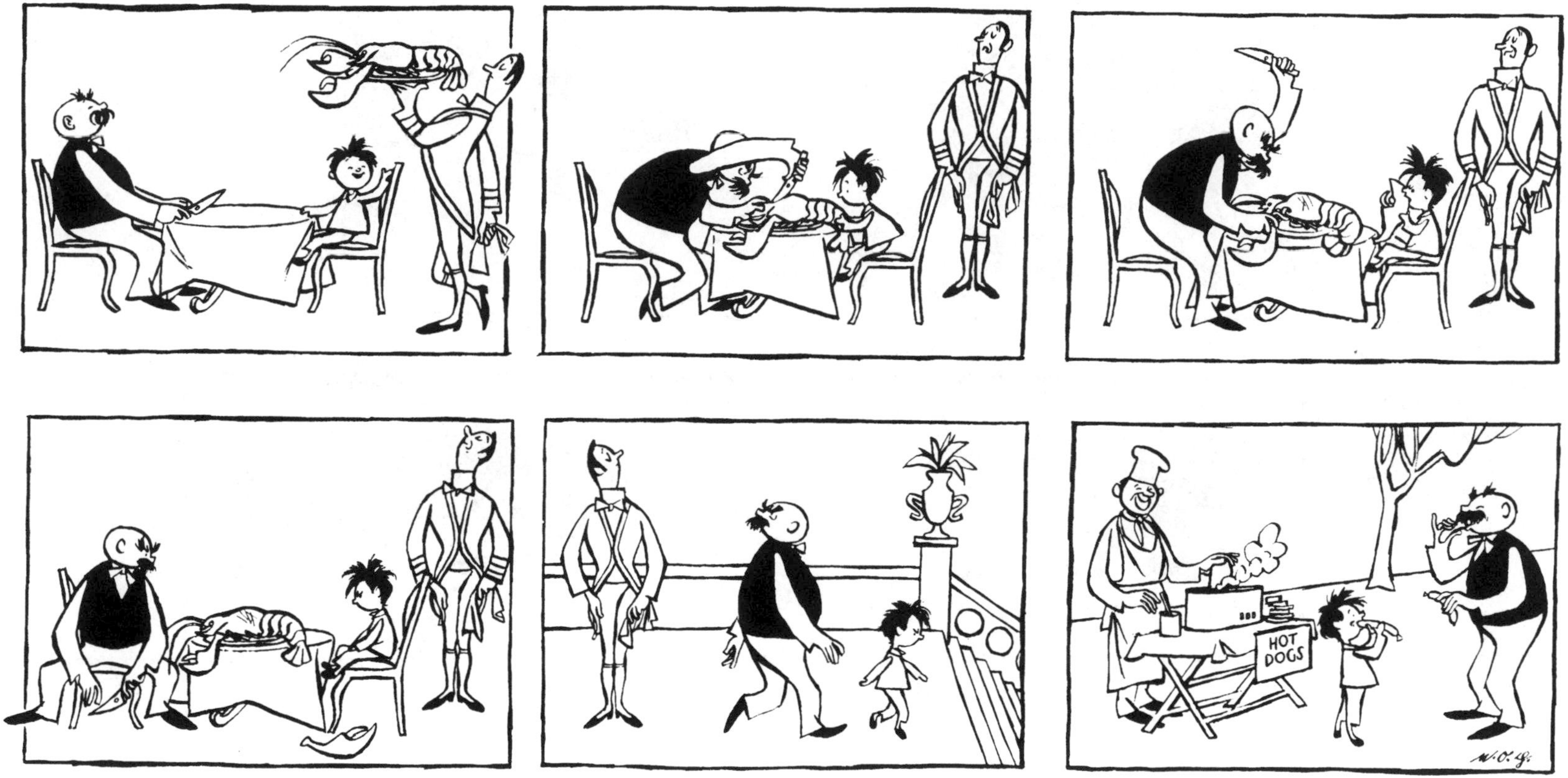
HOT DOGS

Shell shock

Easter present

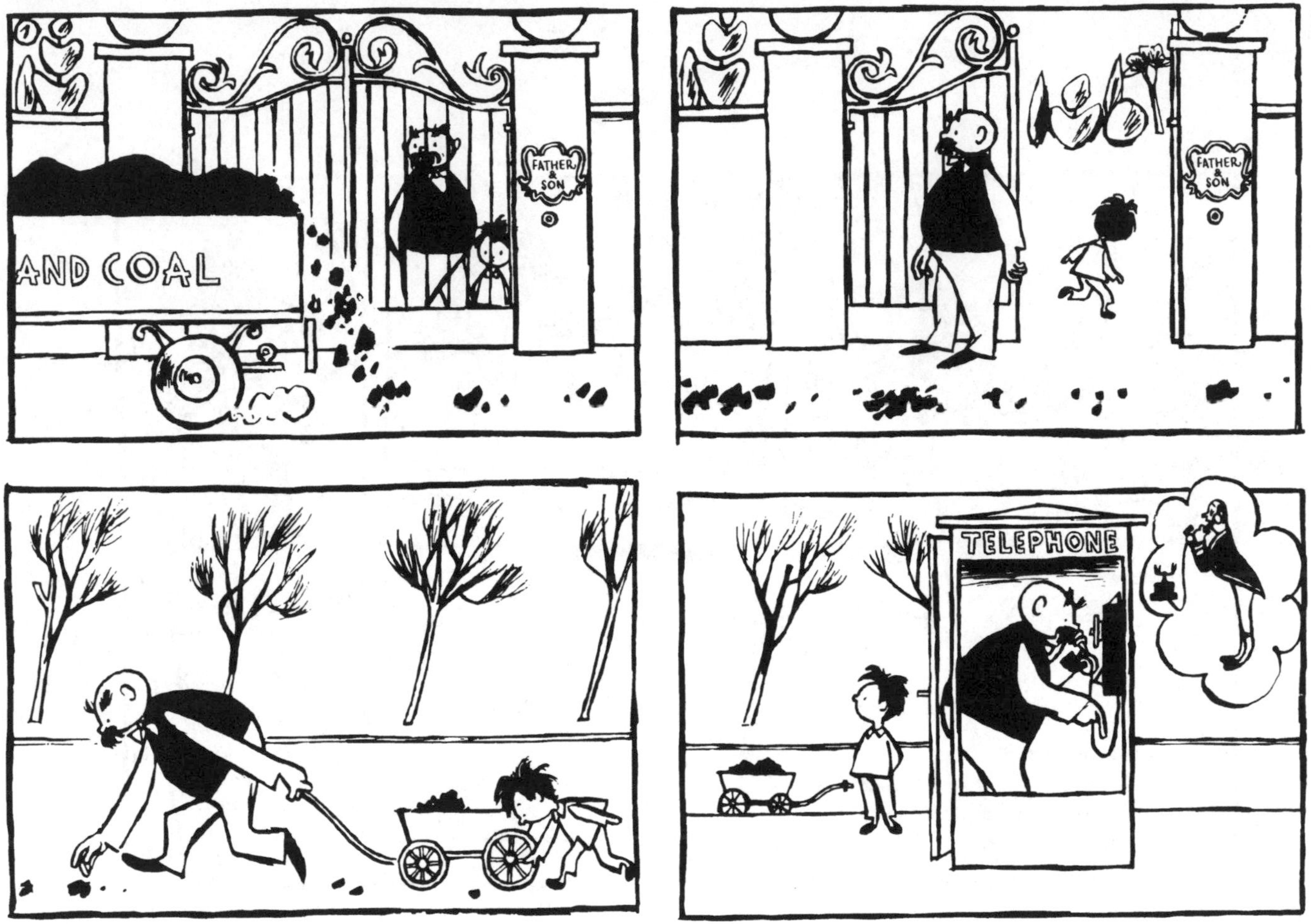
AND COAL
FATHER & SON
FATHER & SON
TELEPHONE

Force of habit

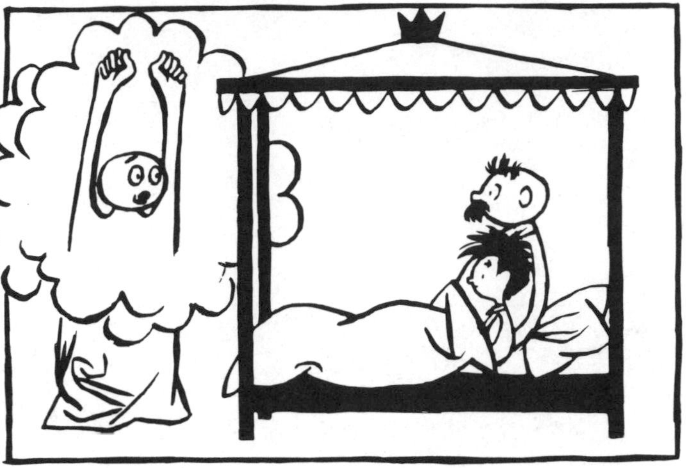
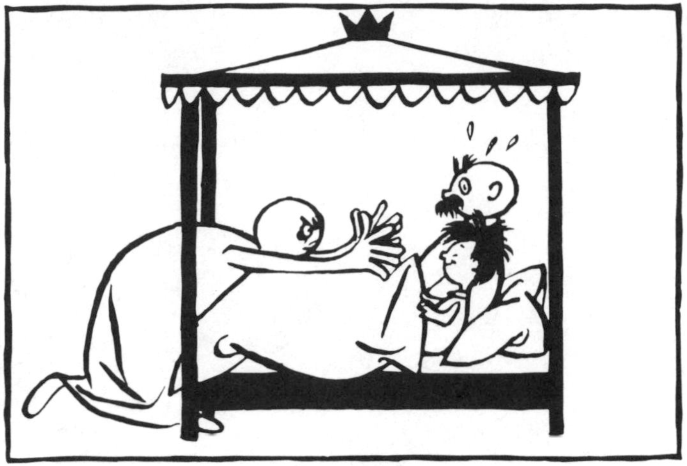
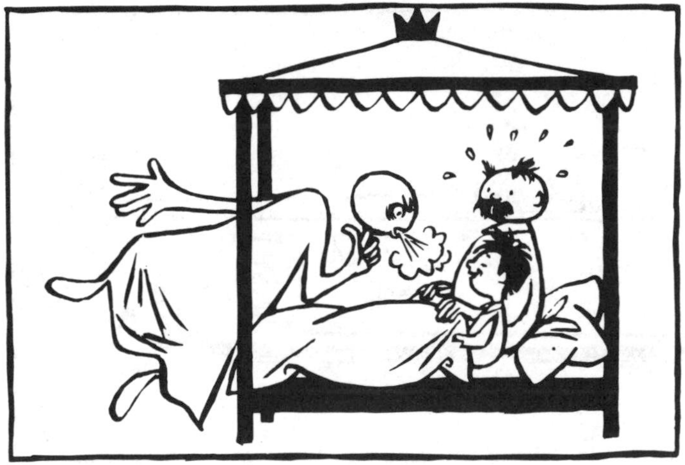
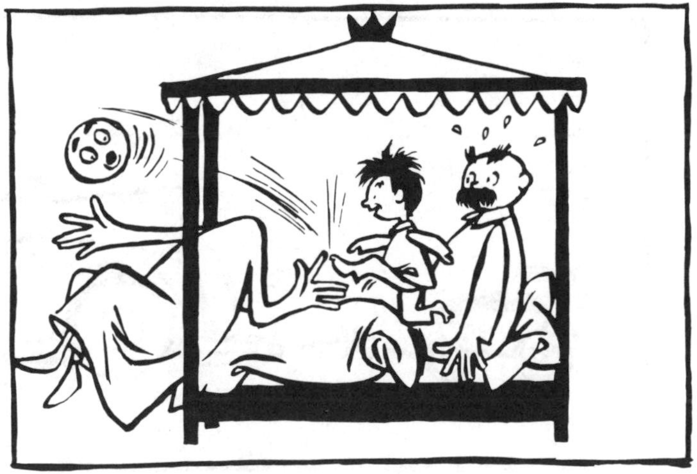

No respect for ghosts

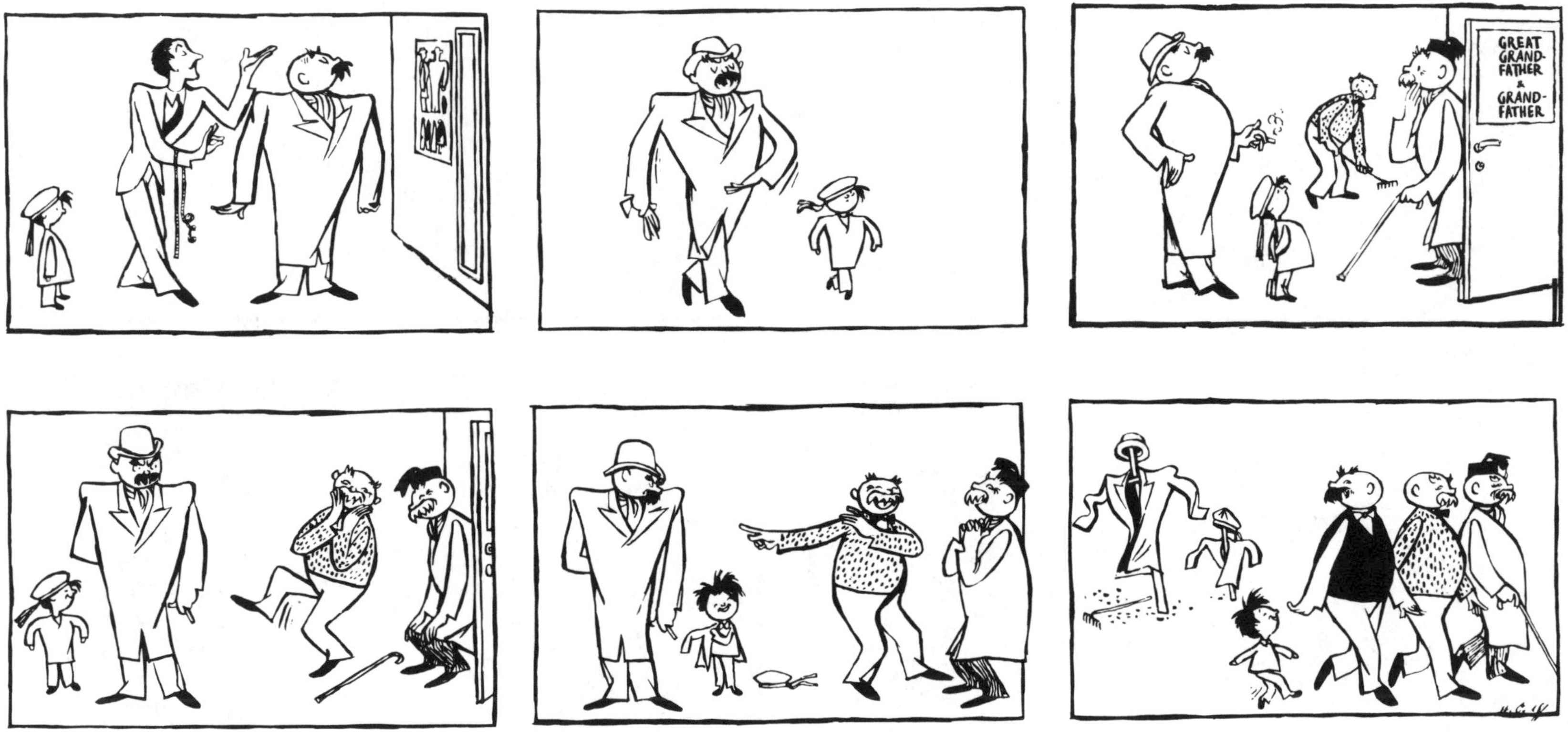
GREAT GRAND-FATHER & GRAND-FATHER

Vanity cured

HELP!
HELP!
HELP!

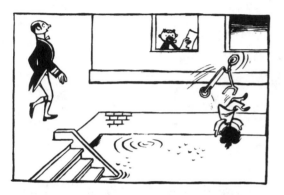

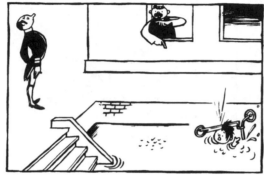

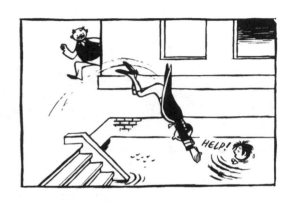

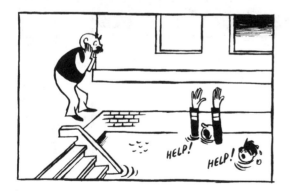

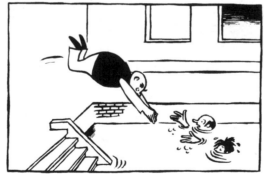

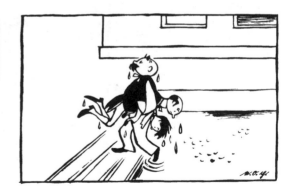

Just following orders

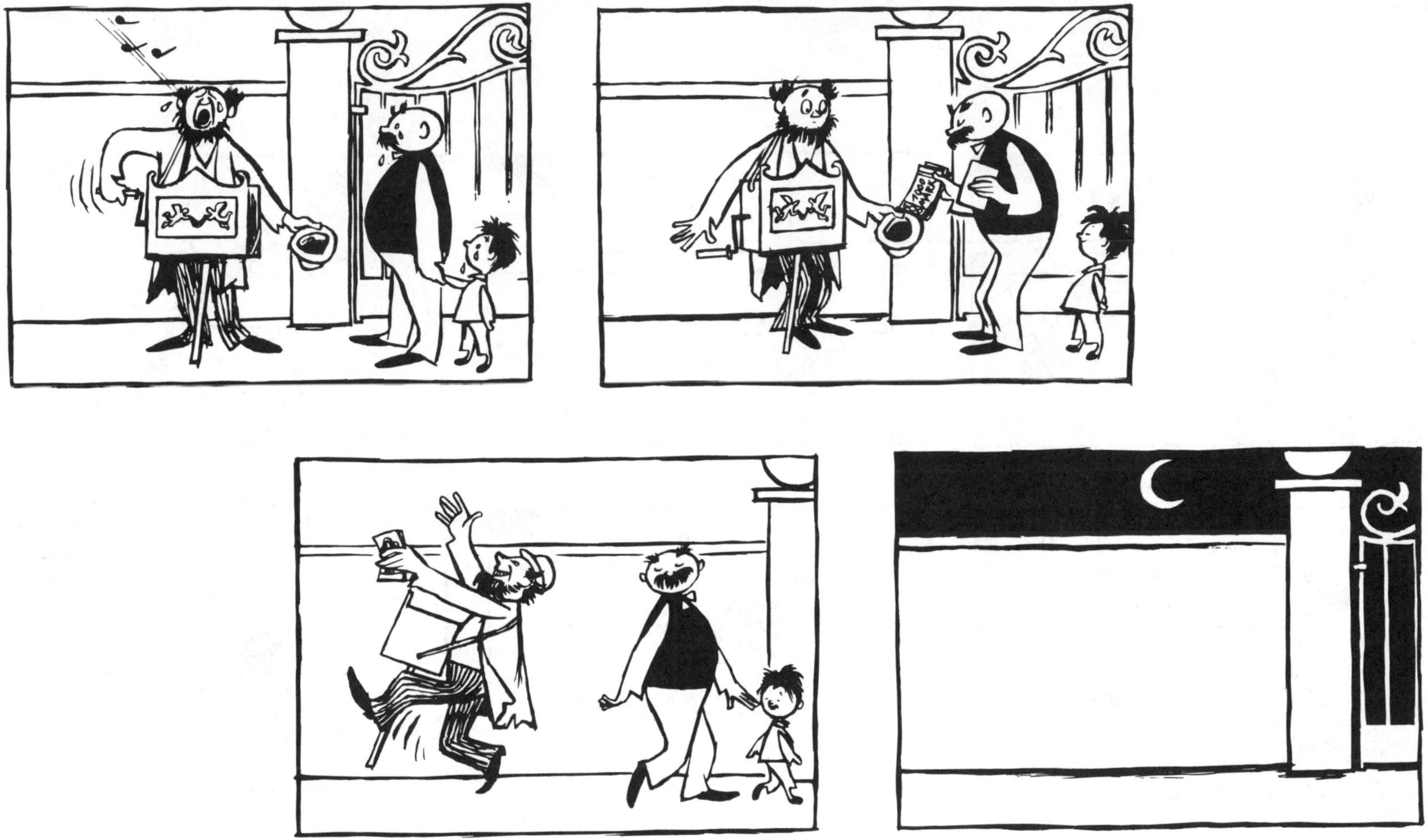
1000 MARK

A good deed and what comes of it

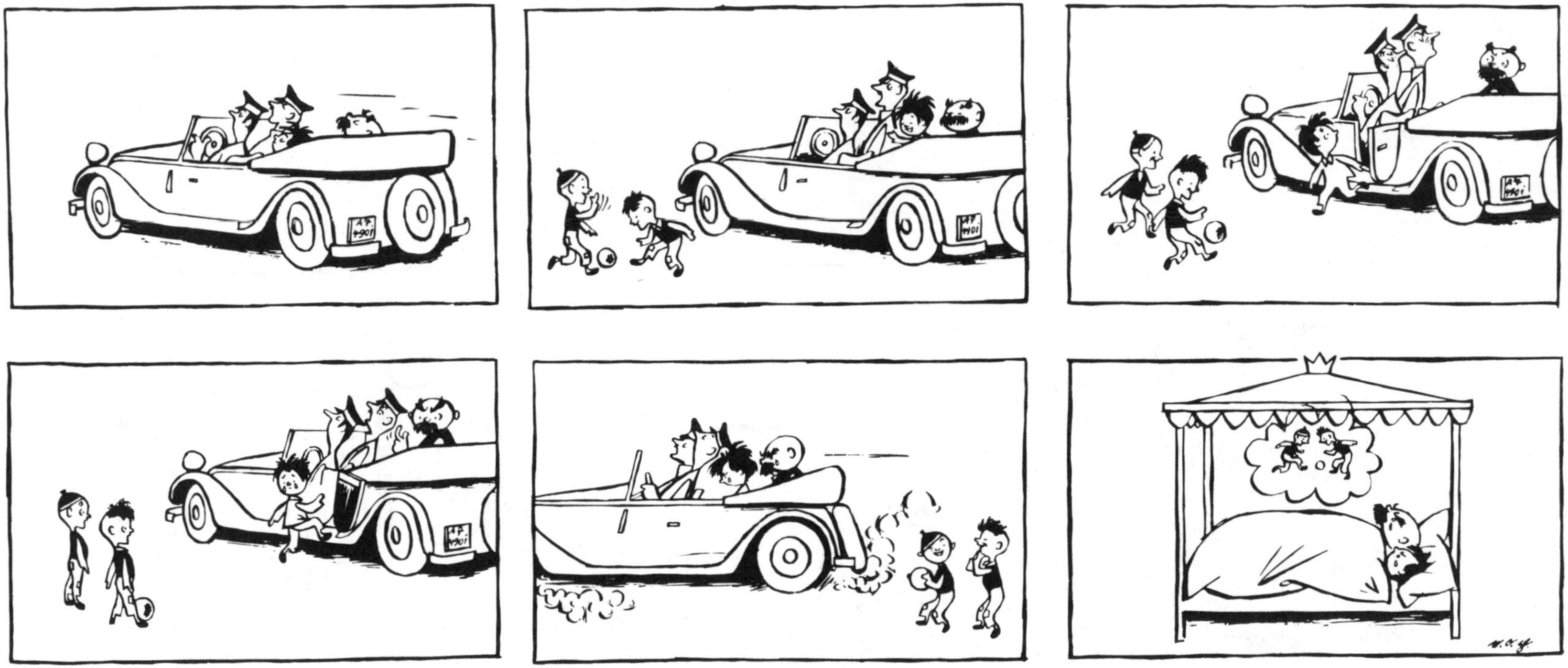

It’s not easy being a gentleman

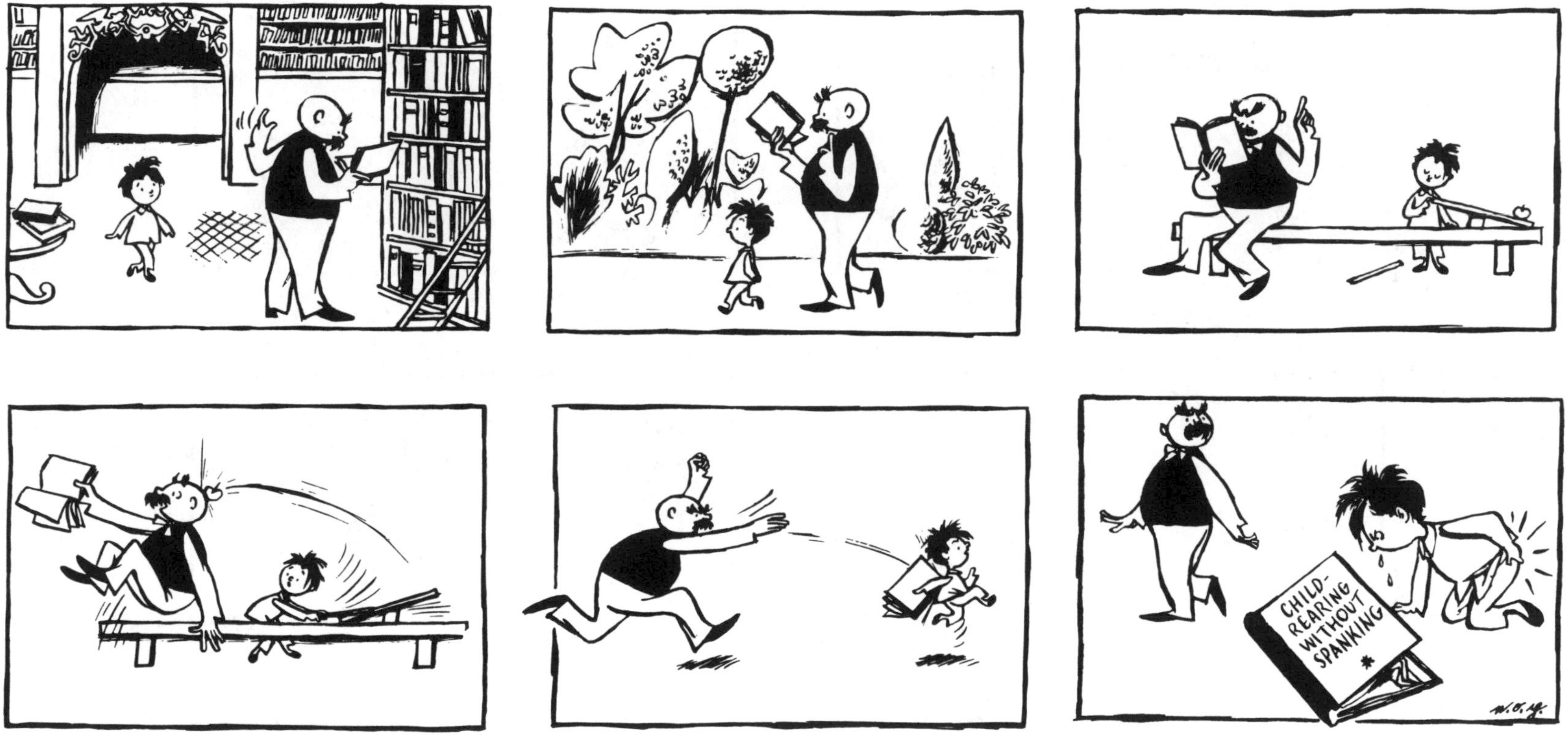
CHILD-
REARING
WITHOUT
SPANKING

"All theory is gray"

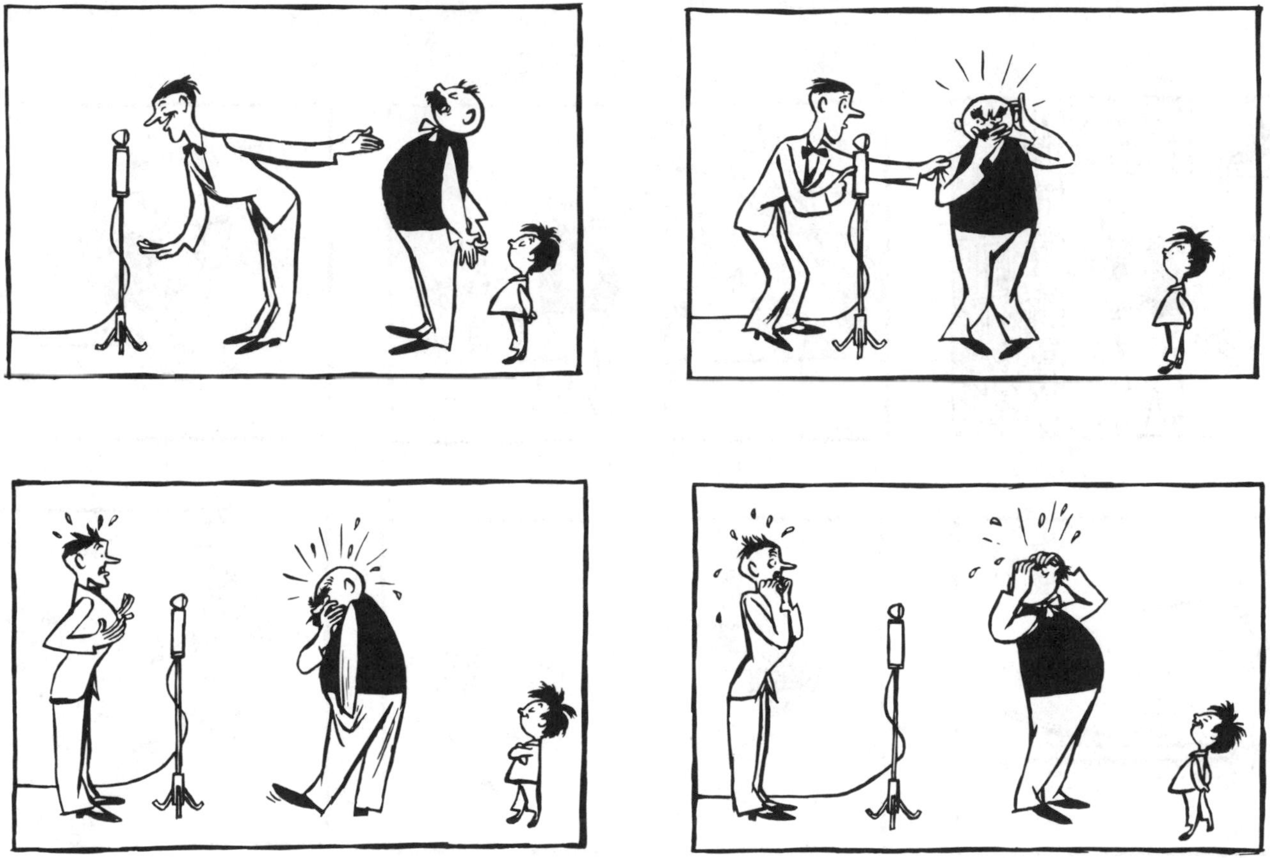

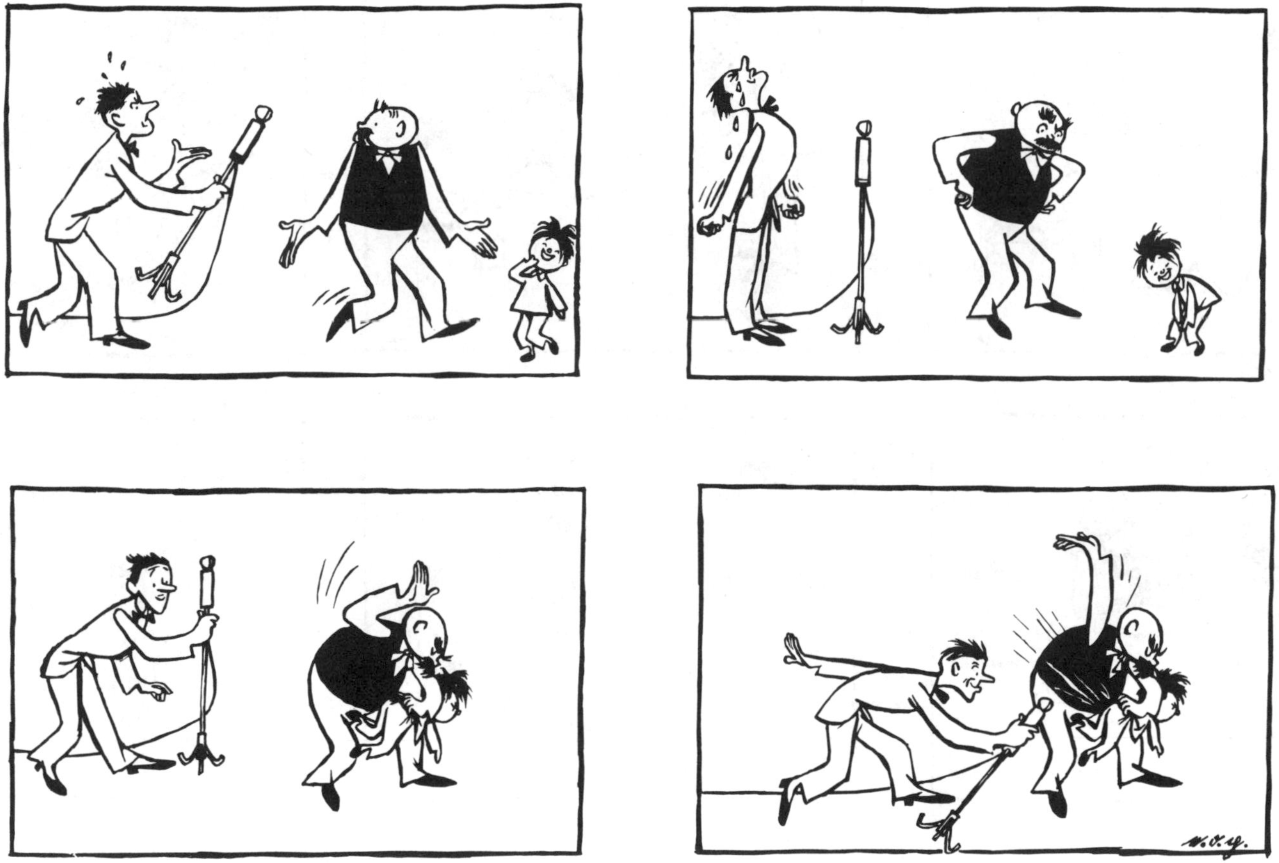

A bit more for the audience at home

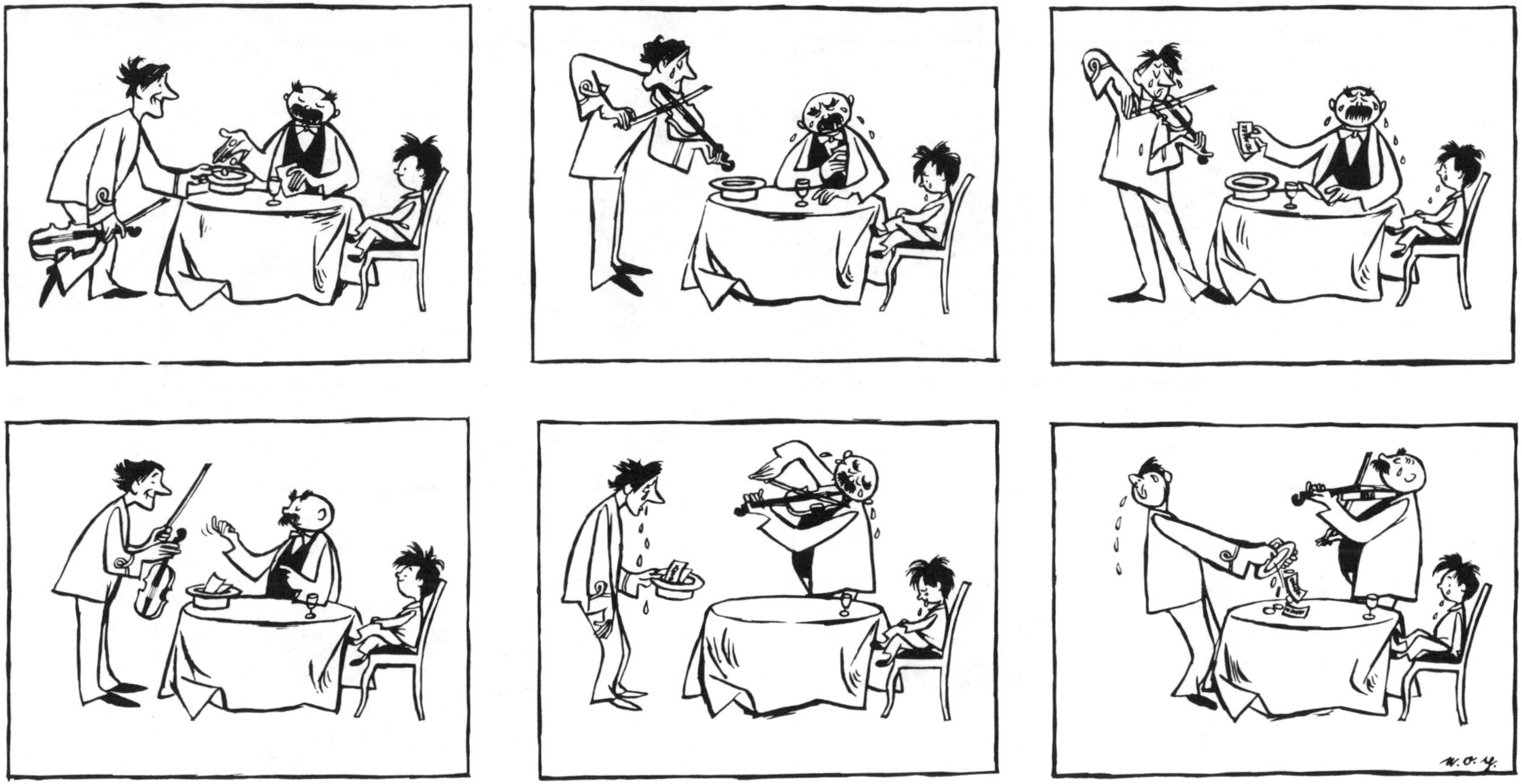

Trading sobs

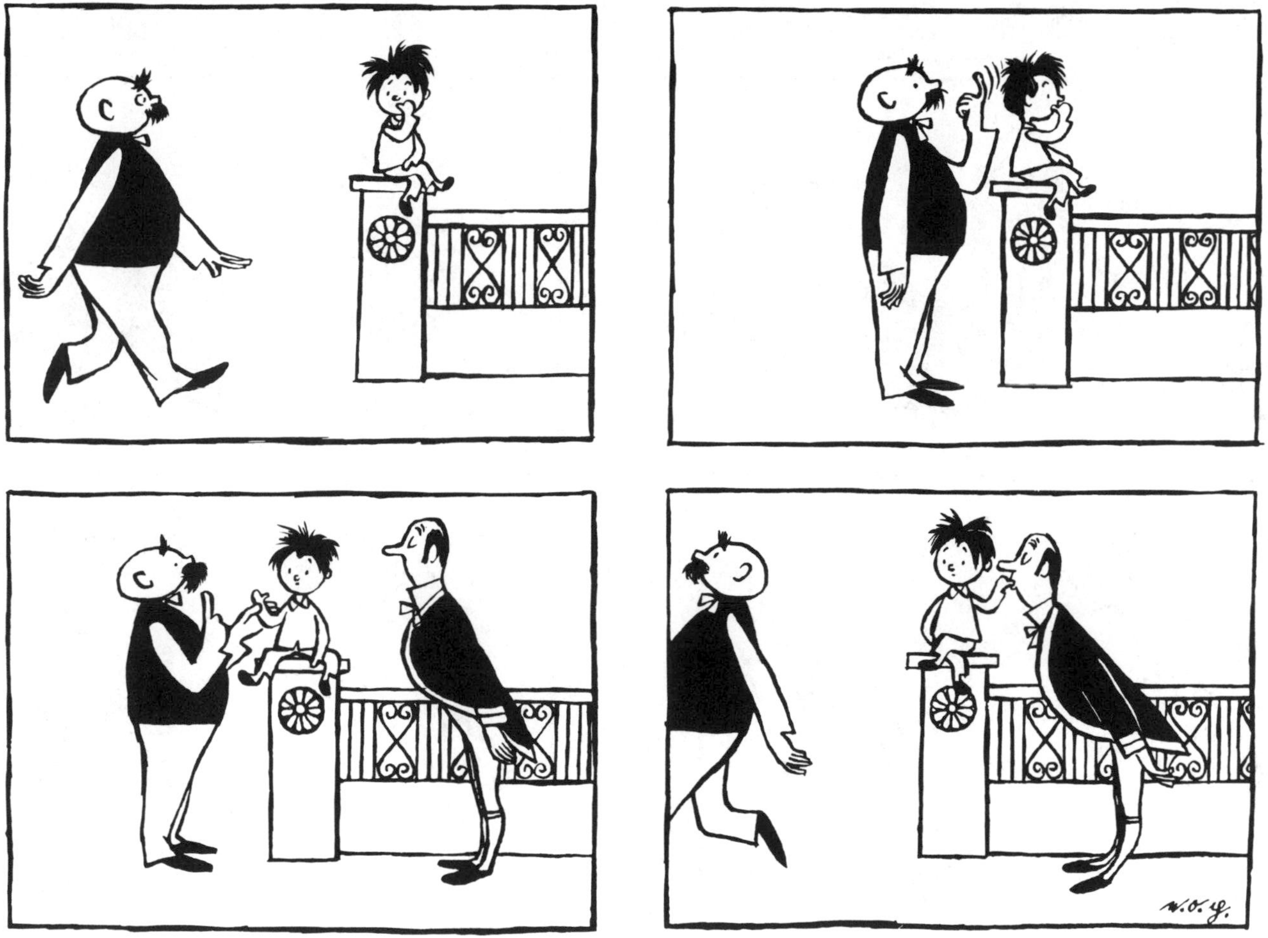

What else are servants for?

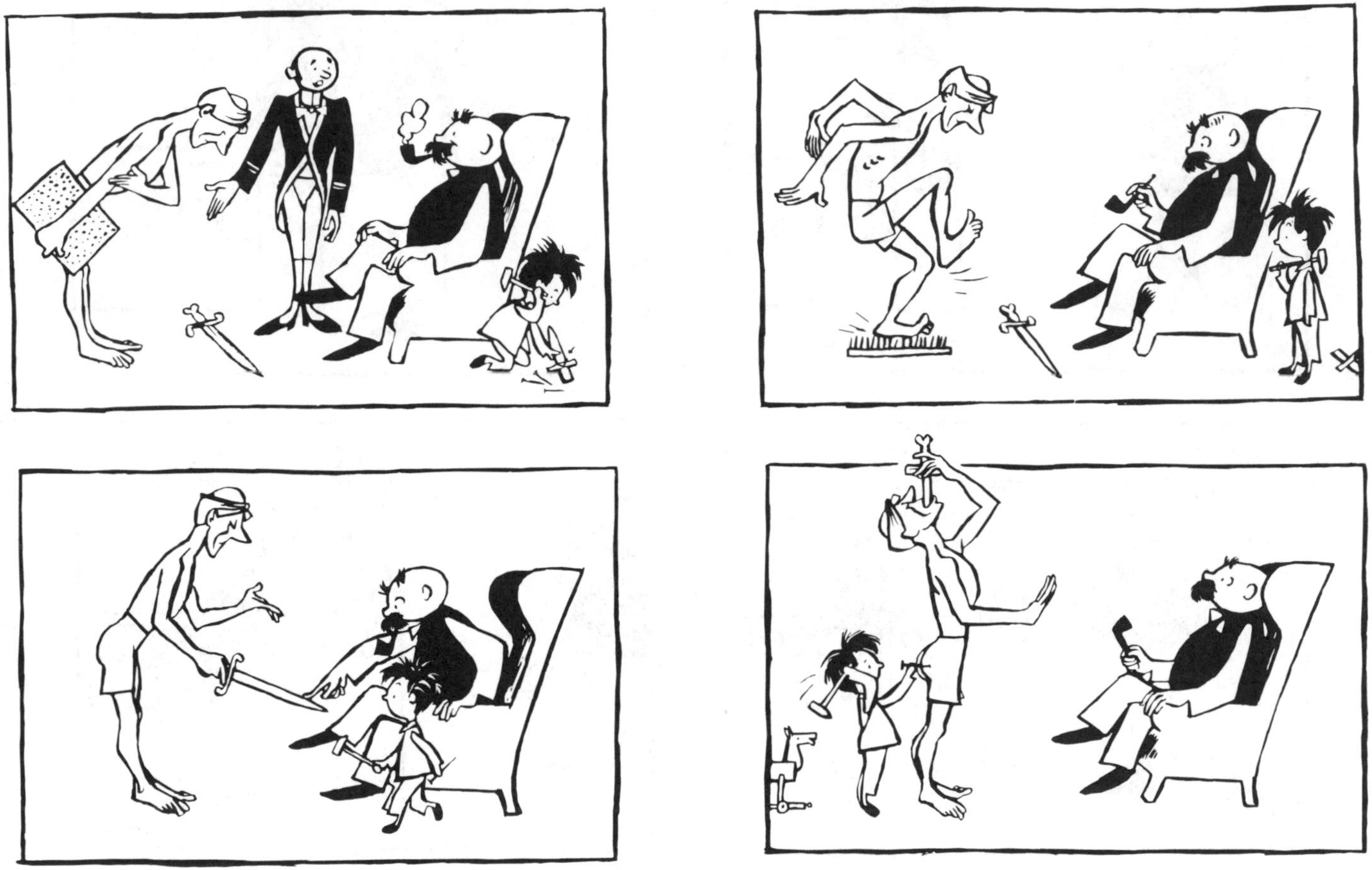

Point well taken

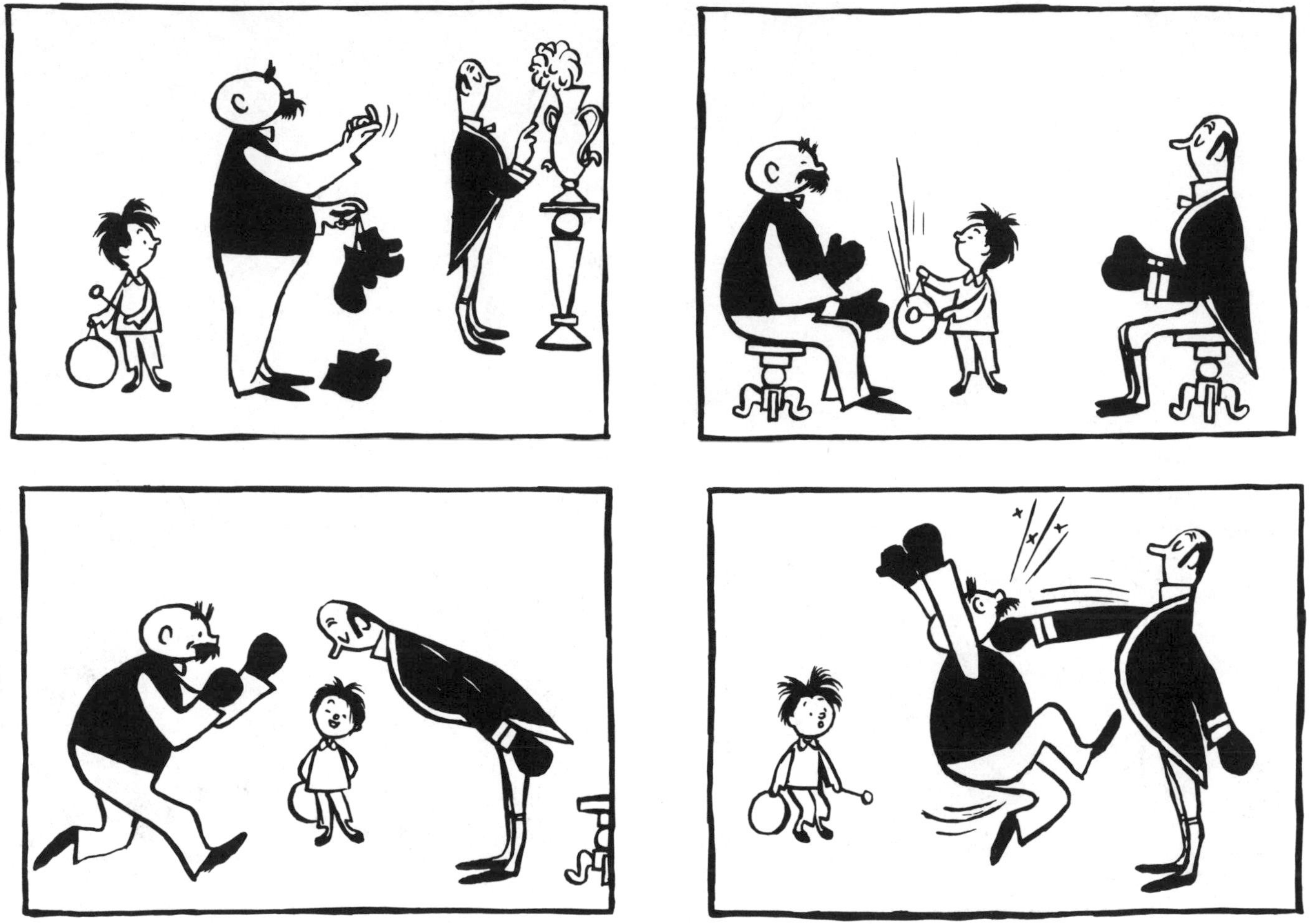

Most obedient servant

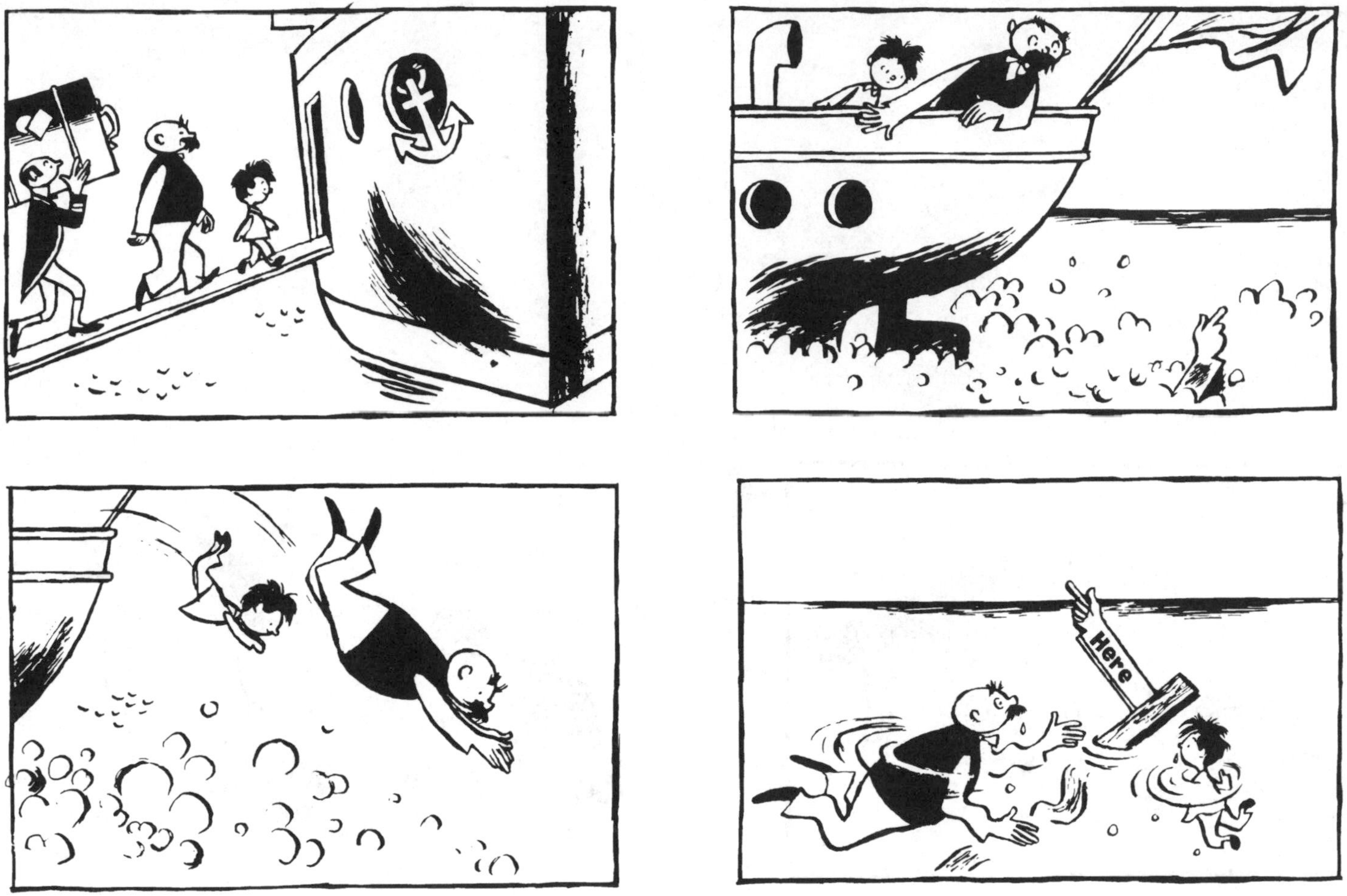
Here

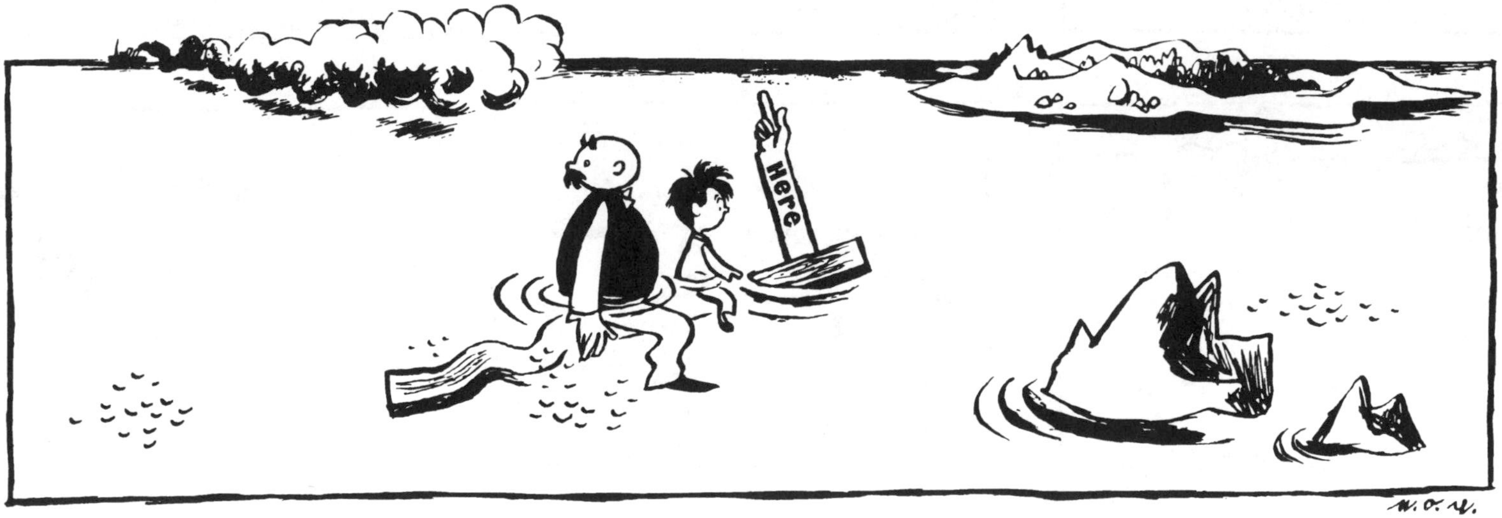
Here

Incident on a summer cruise

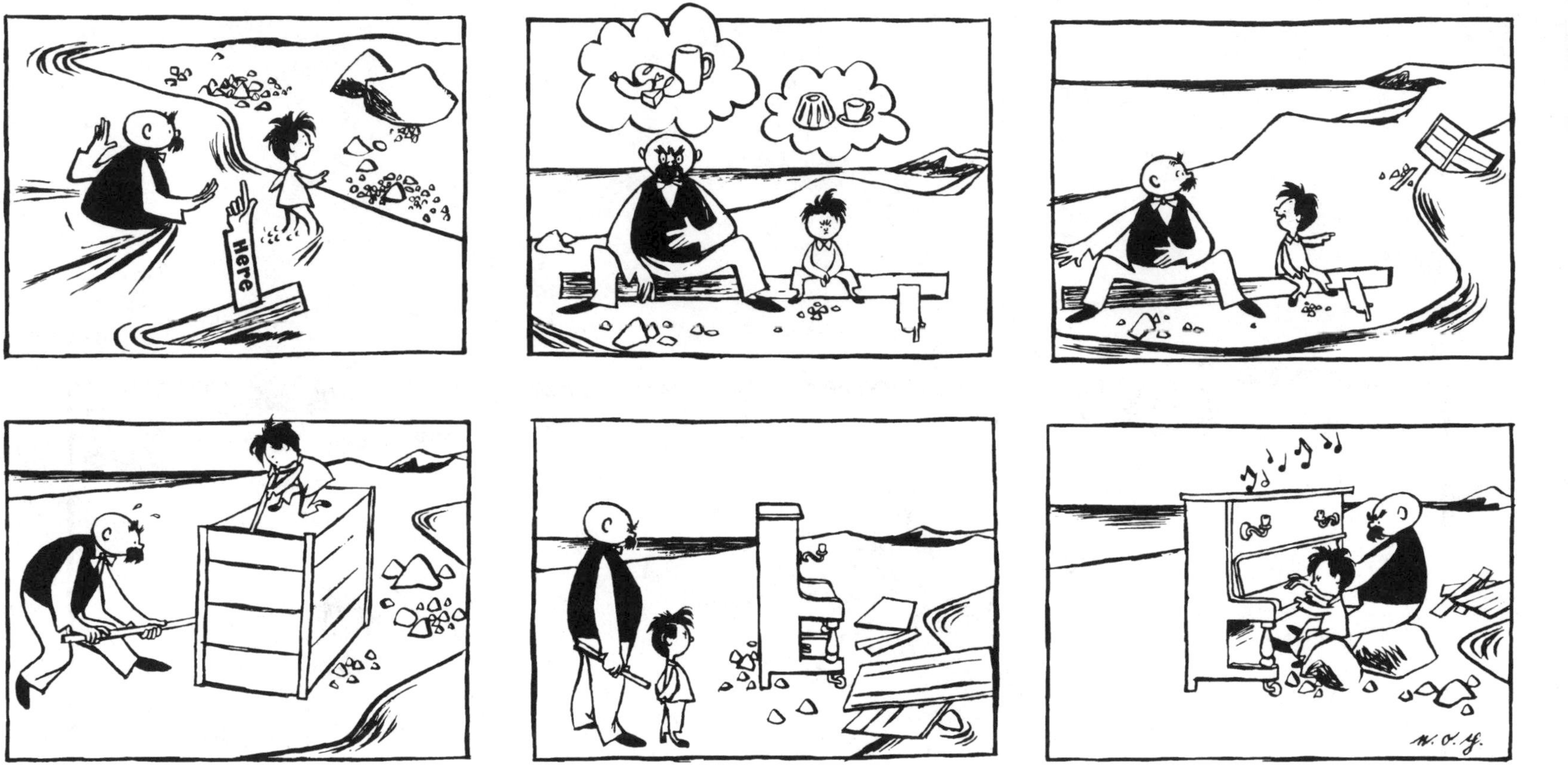
Here

Cast away on a desert island: The Hunger Sonata

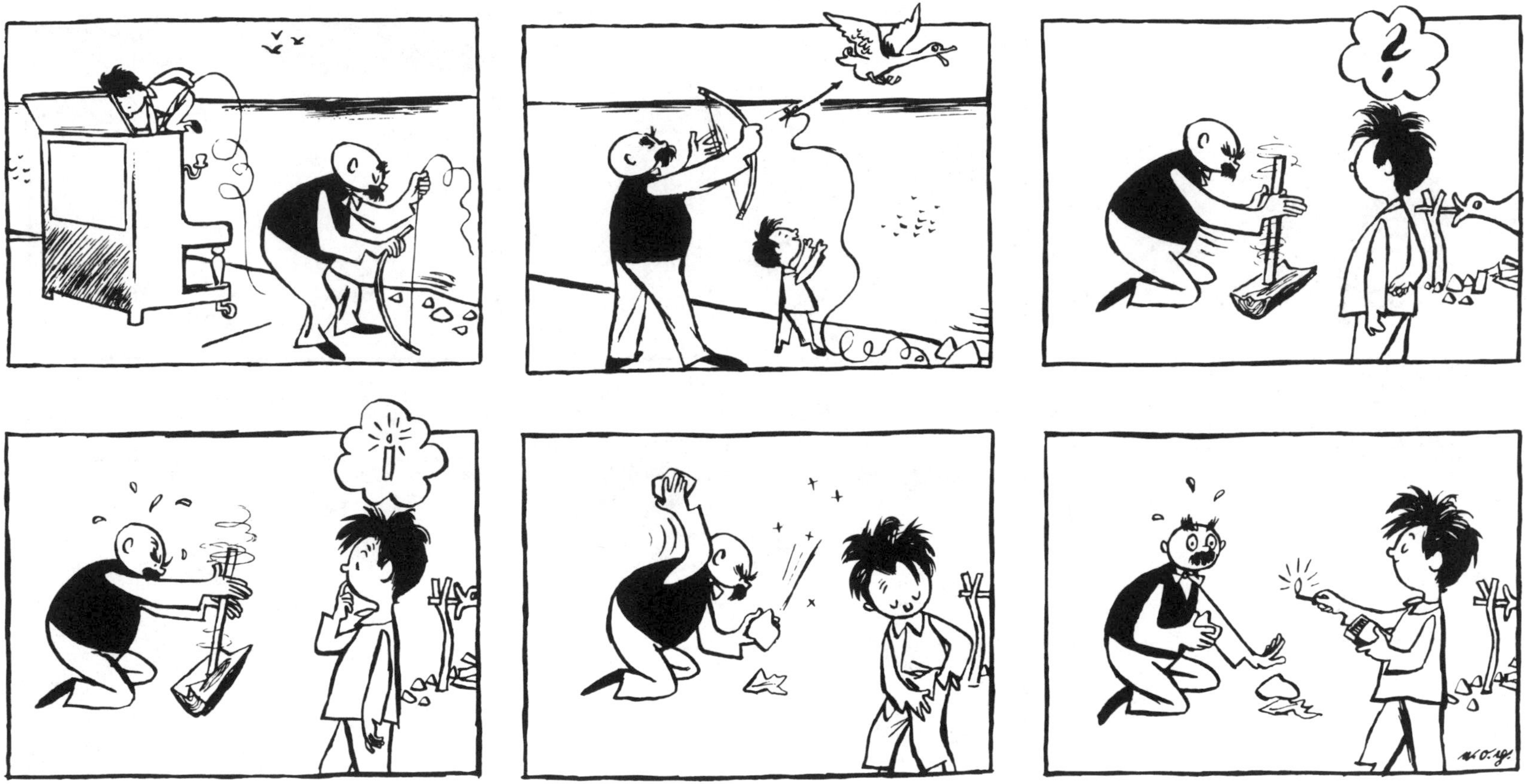

“Oh, we’re making a fire?”

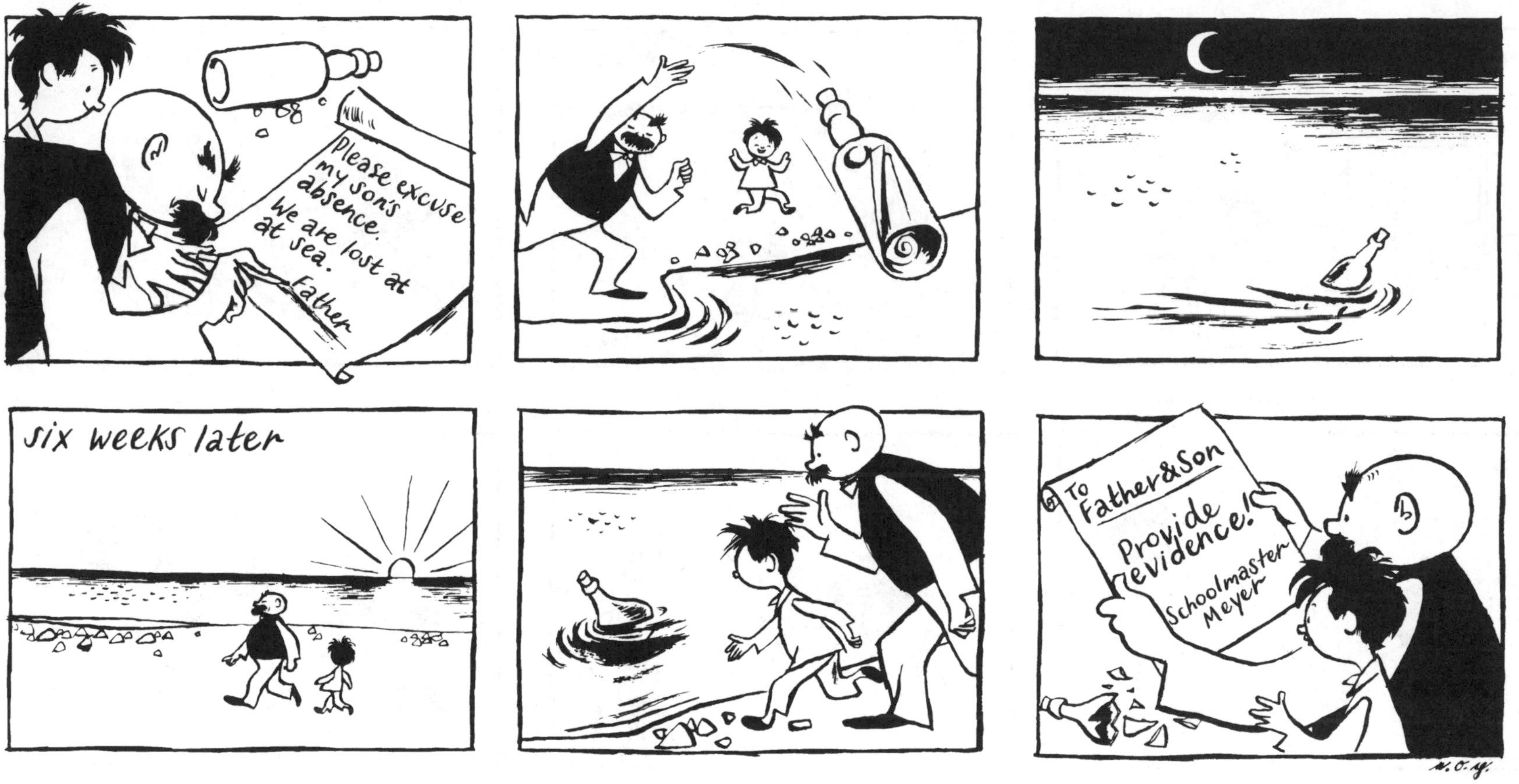
Please excuse my son's absence. We are lost at at sea. Father
six weeks later
To Father & Son
Provide evidence!
Schoolmaster Meyer
e.o.p.

First order of business

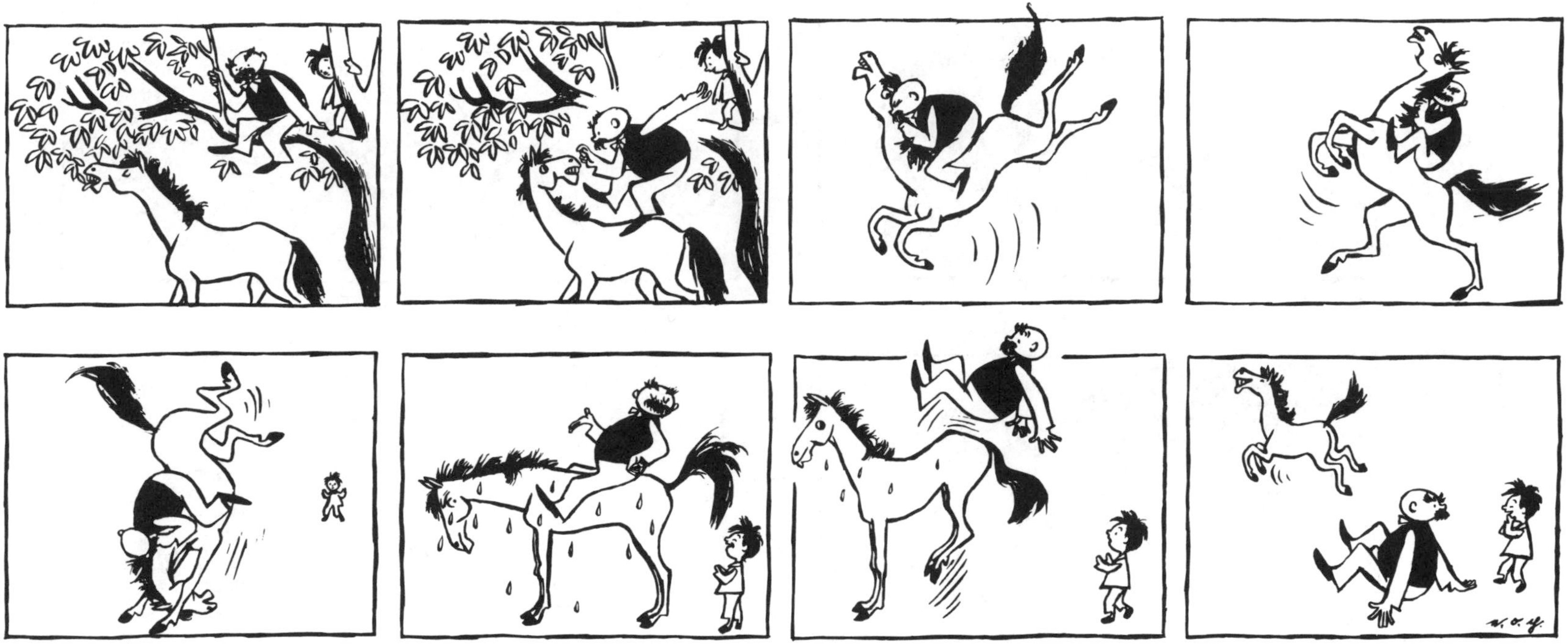

The wild horse

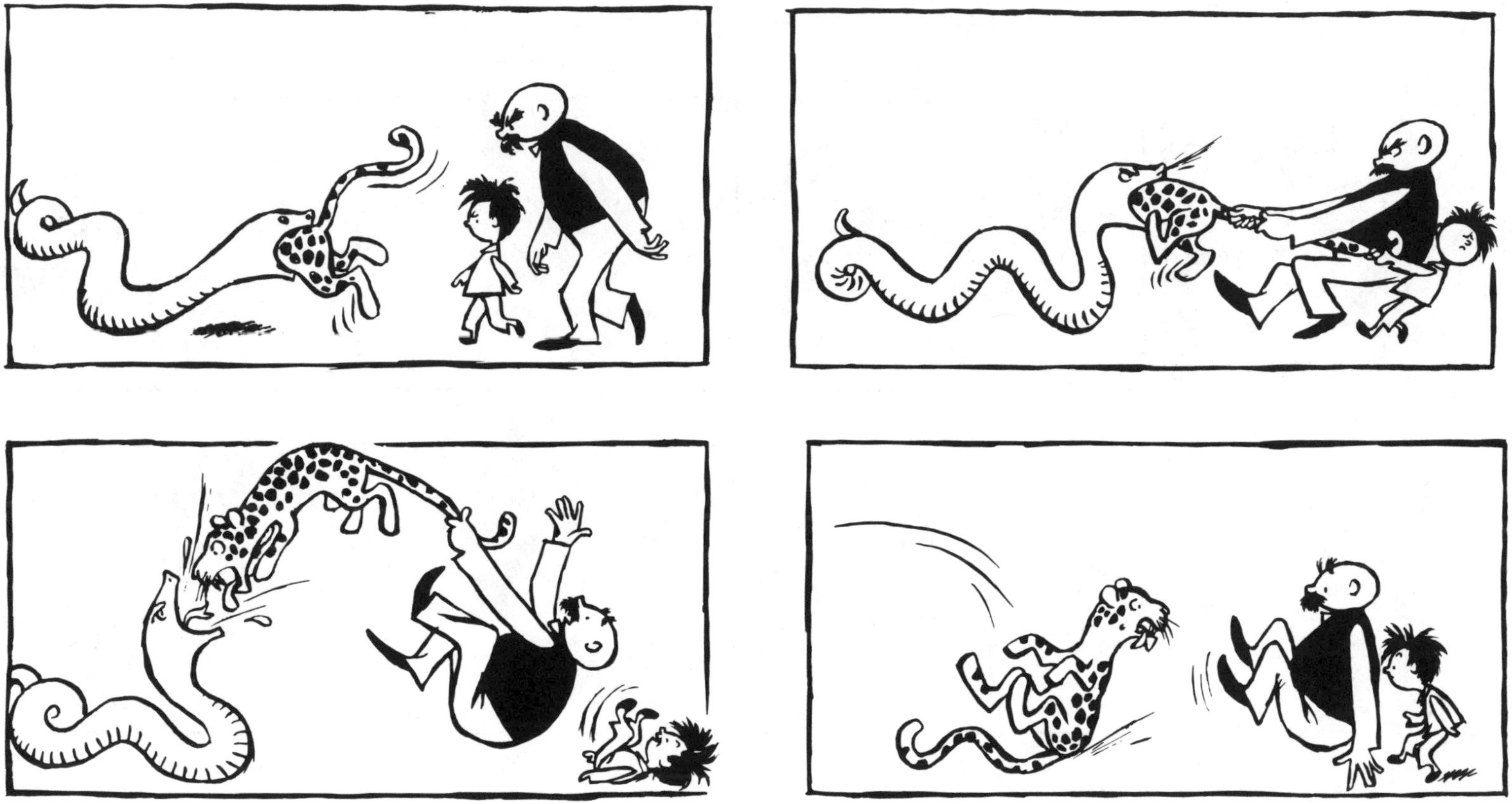

Gratitude

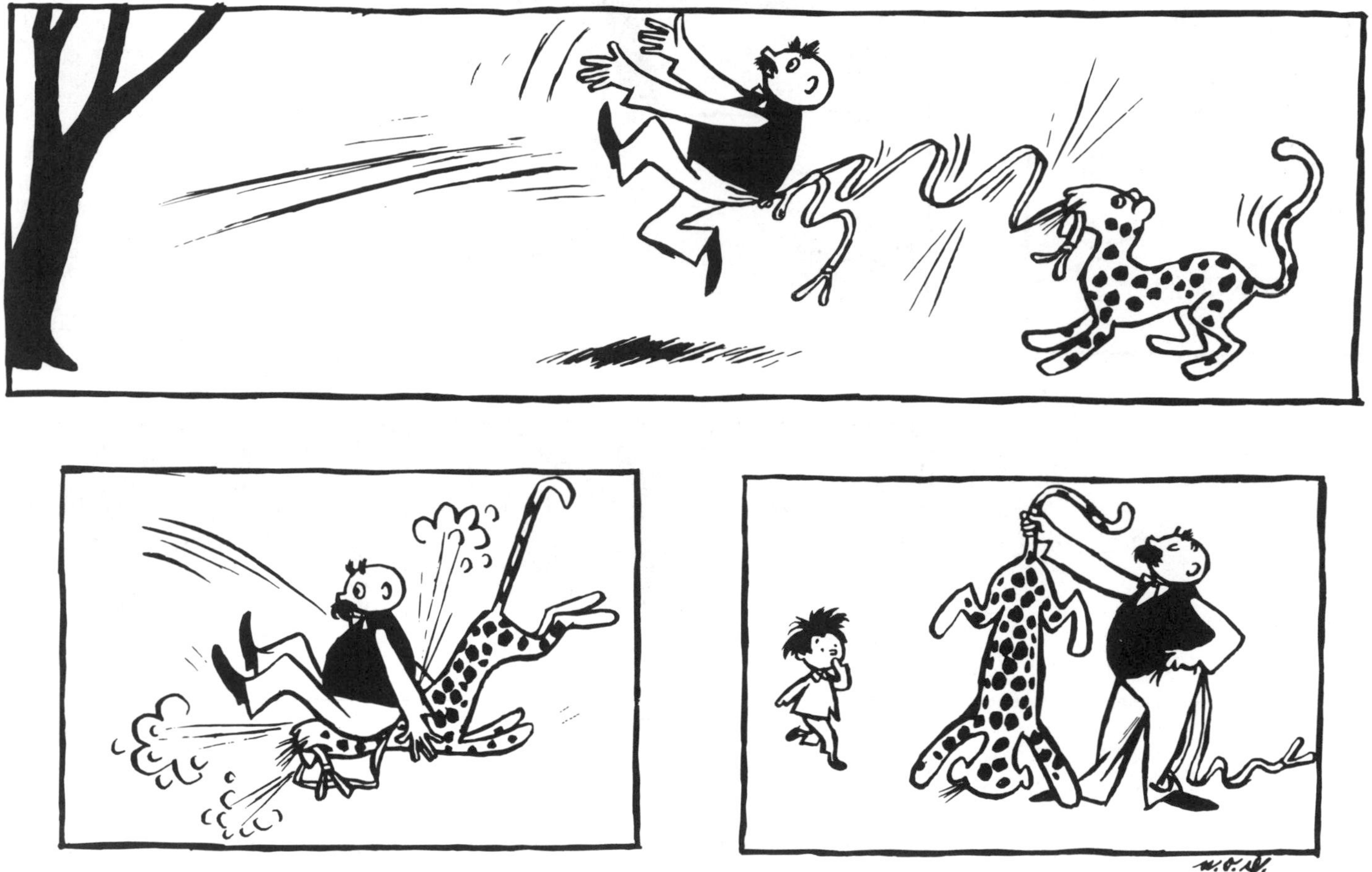

A hunter in spite of himself

Really incredible what father can do

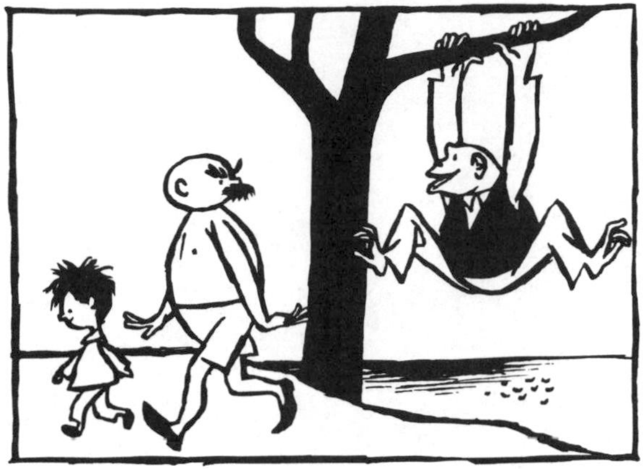
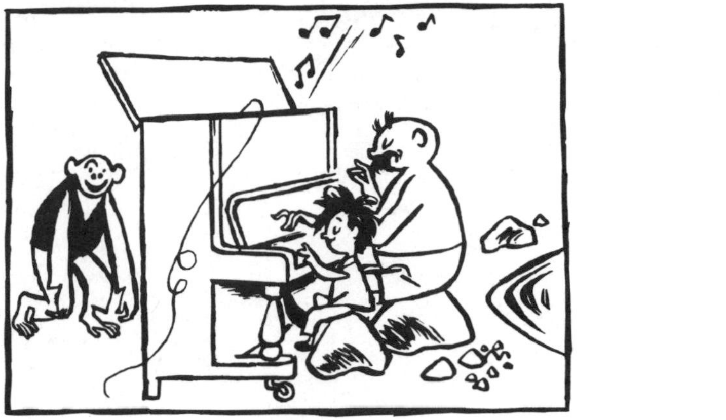
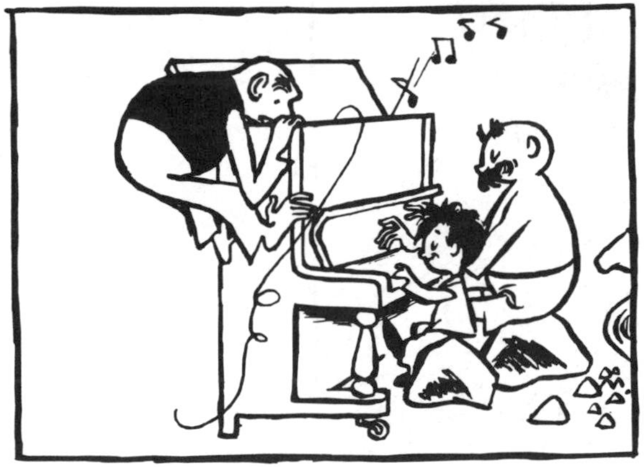
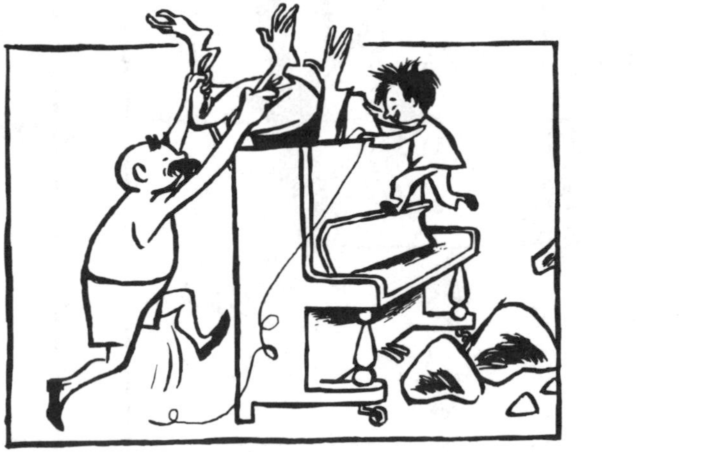

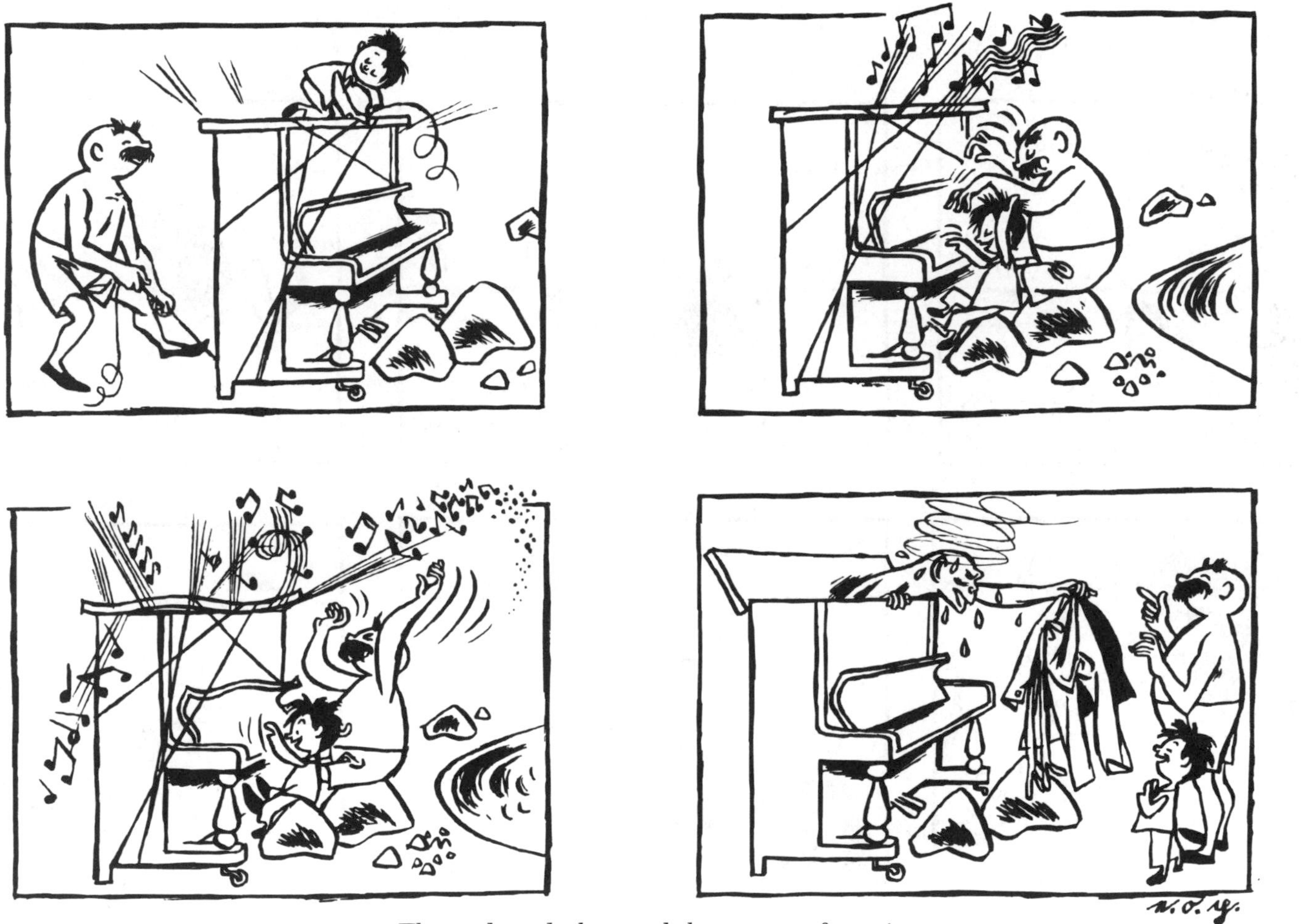

The stolen clothes and the power of music

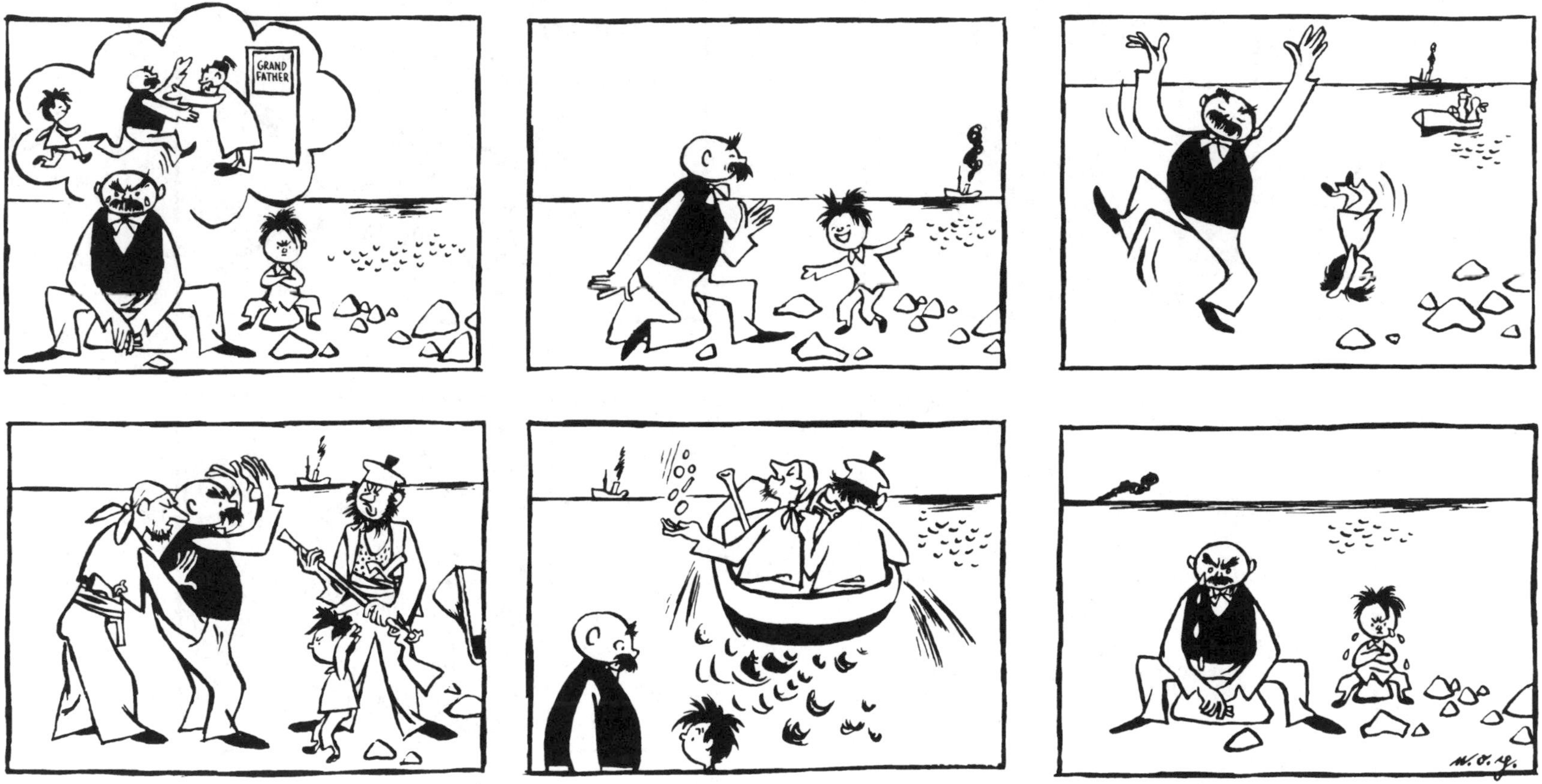
GRAND
FATHER

Picked up? Held up

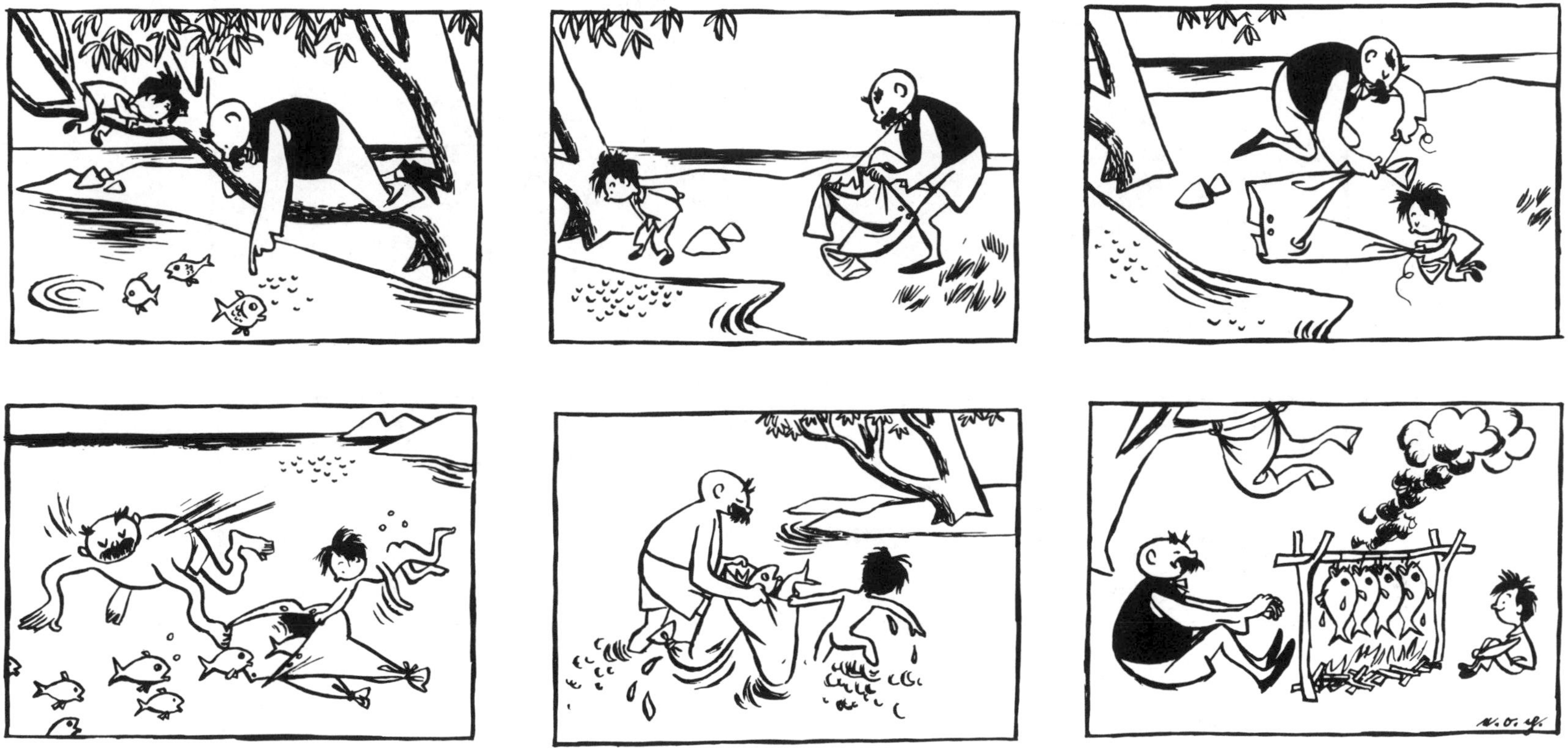

A big haul

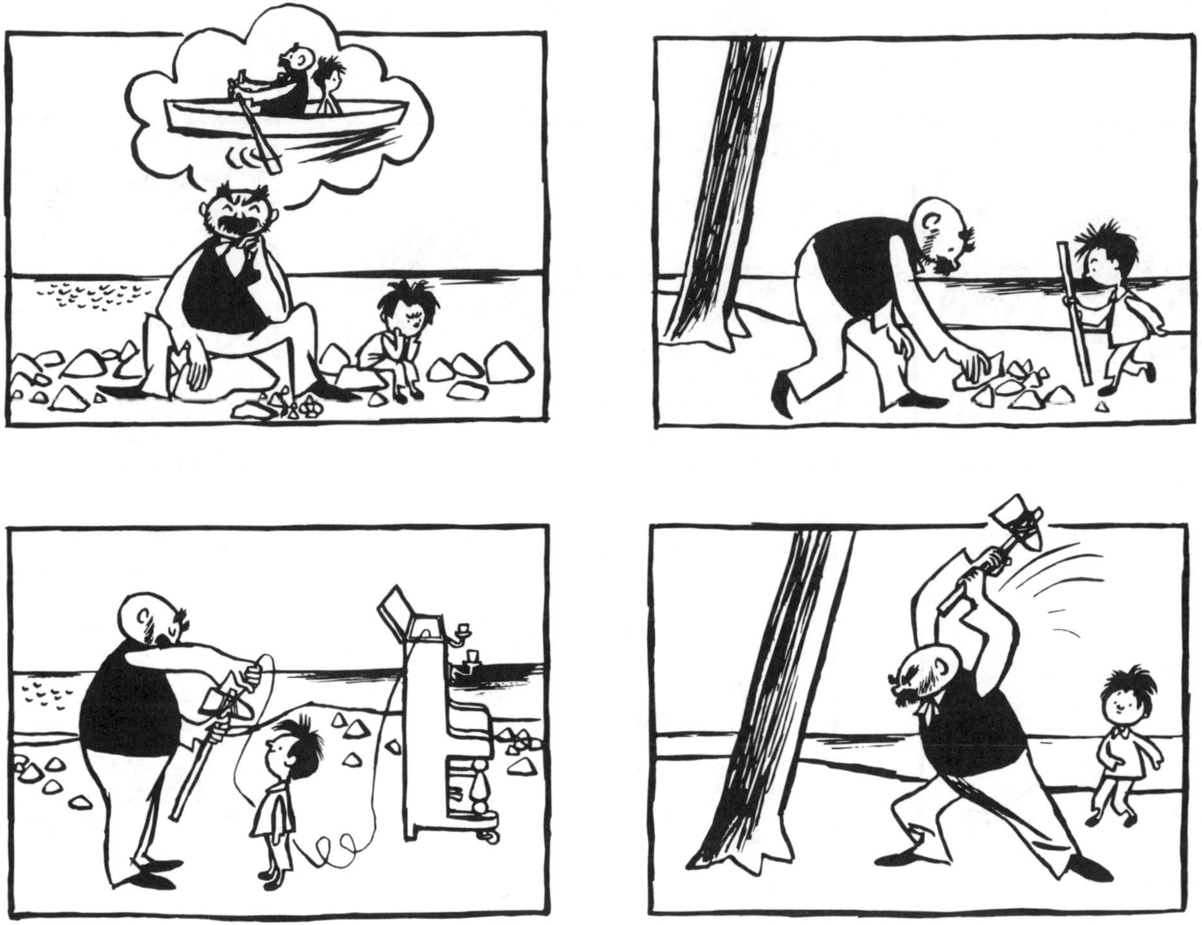

Boat, no — shave, yes

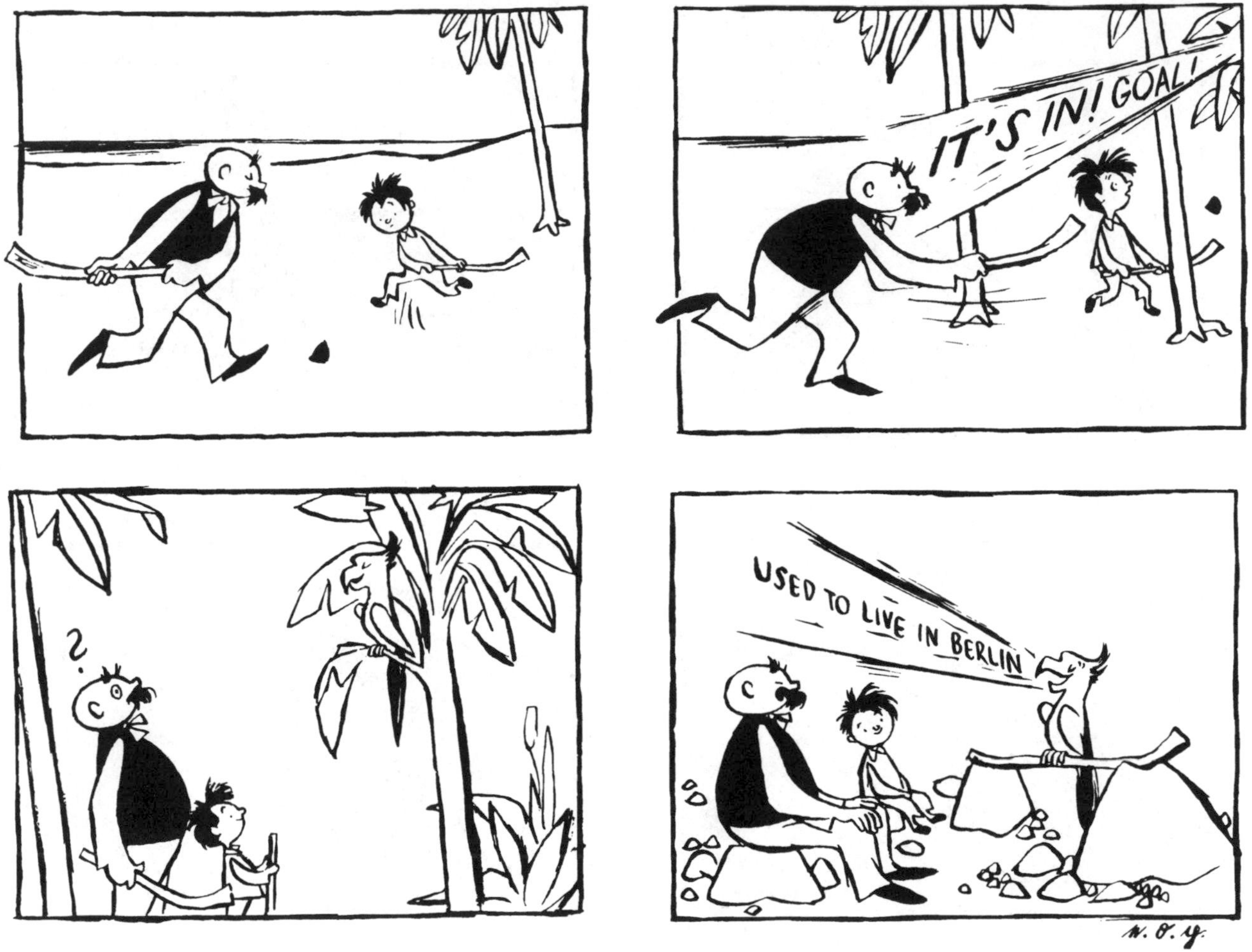
IT'S IN! GOAL!
?
USED TO LIVE IN BERLIN

The peanut gallery

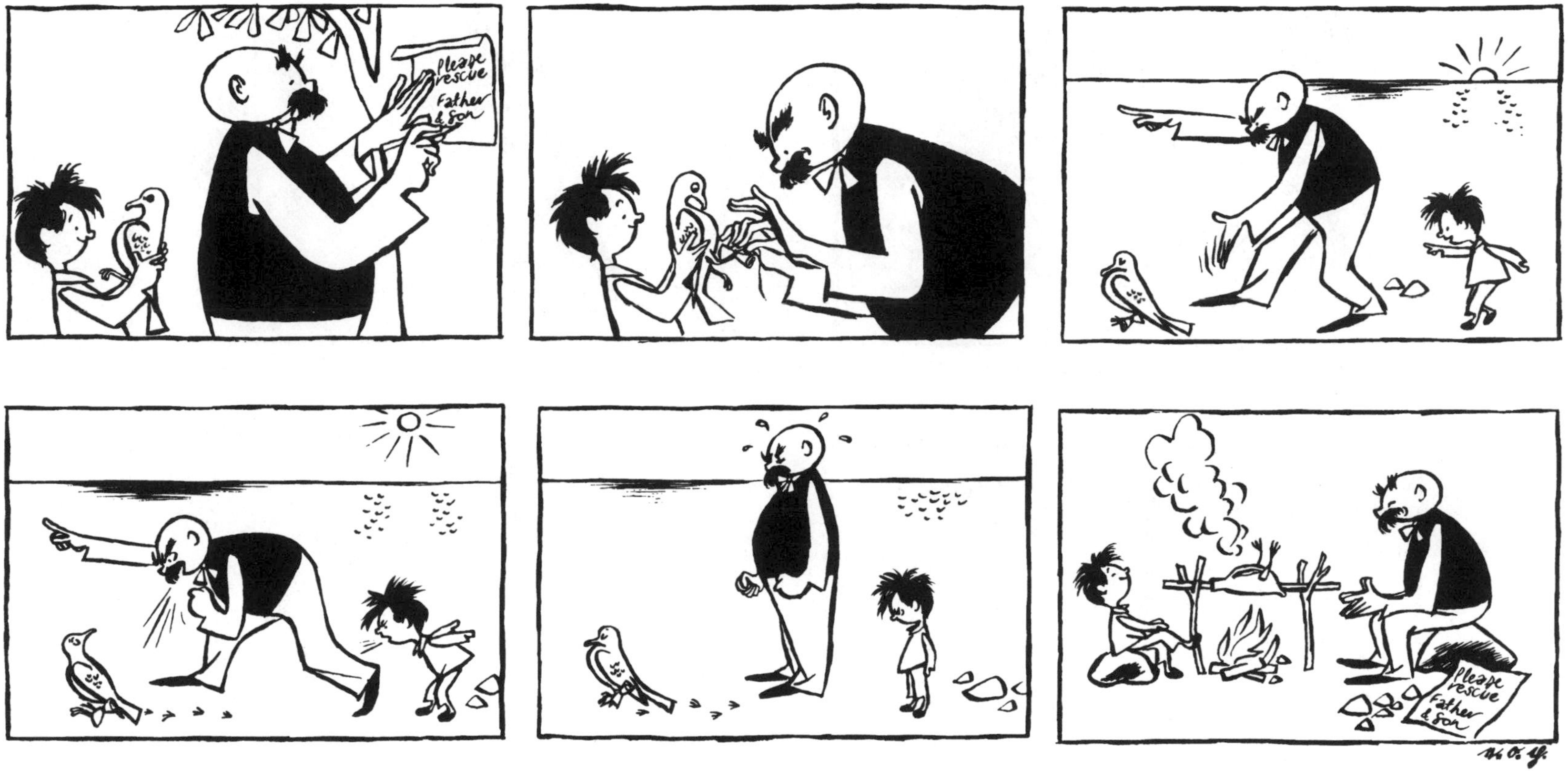
Please rescue Father & Son
Please rescue Father & Son

The reluctant carrier pigeon

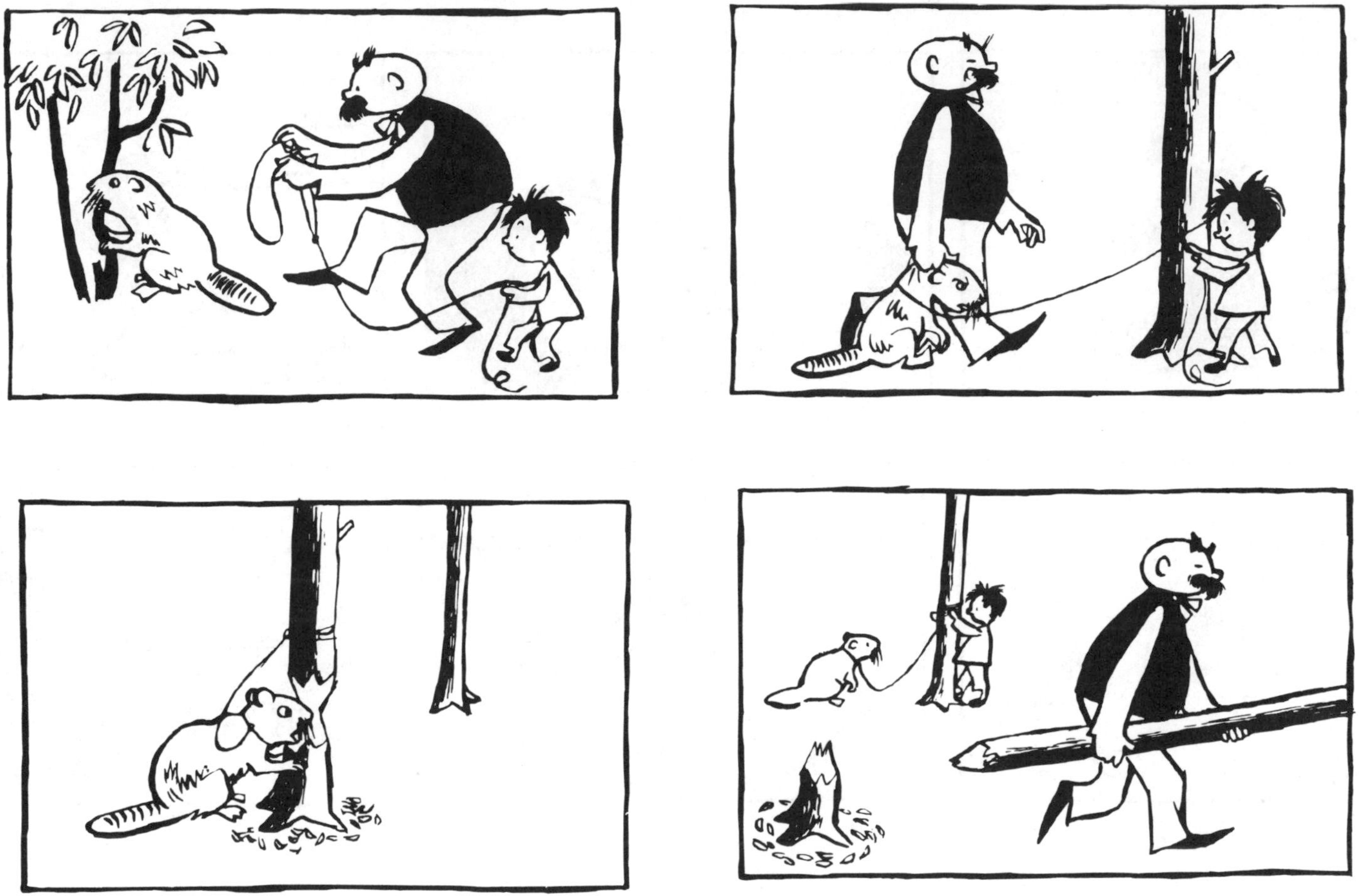

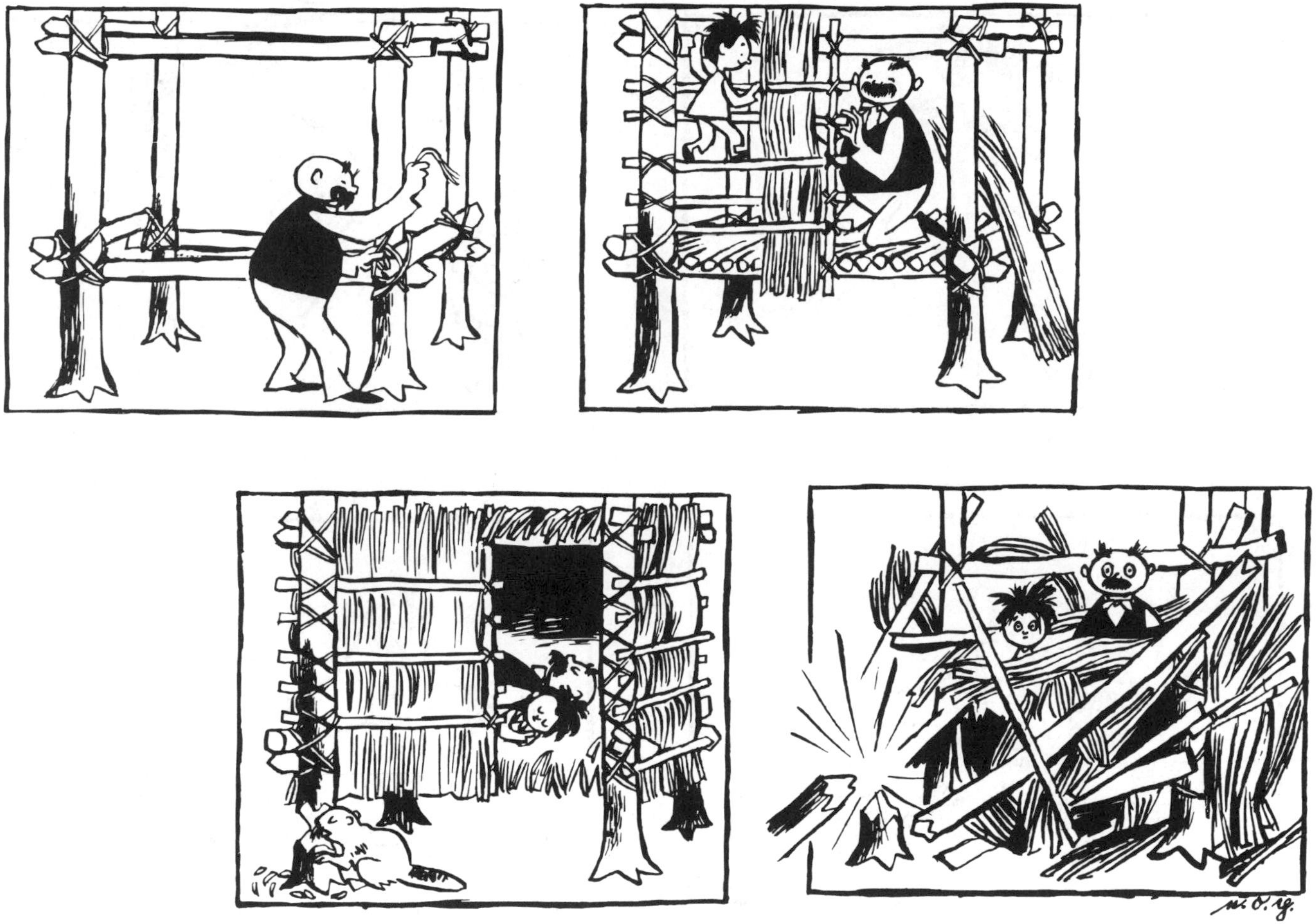

Beaver's revenge

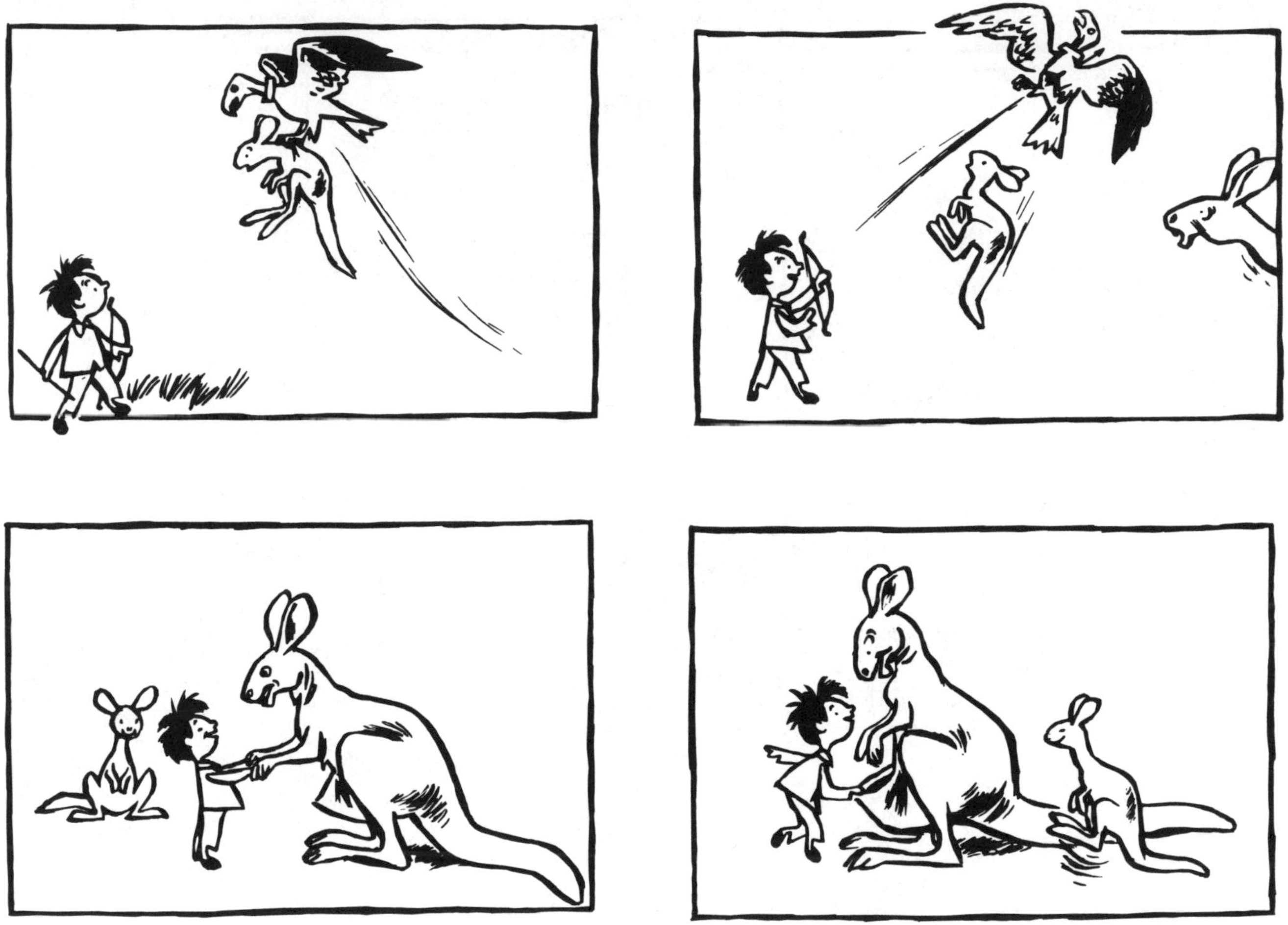

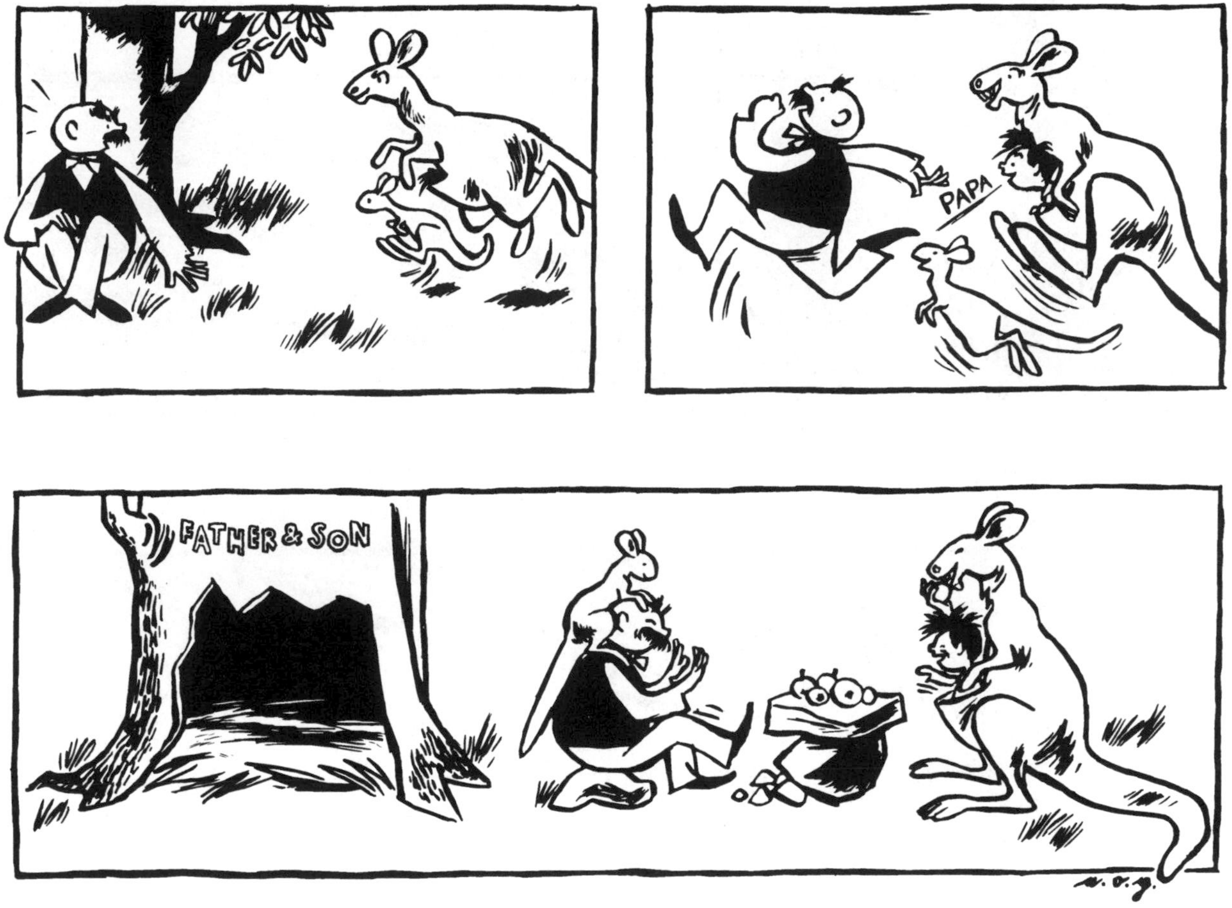
PAPA
FATHER & SON

Making friends with kangaroos

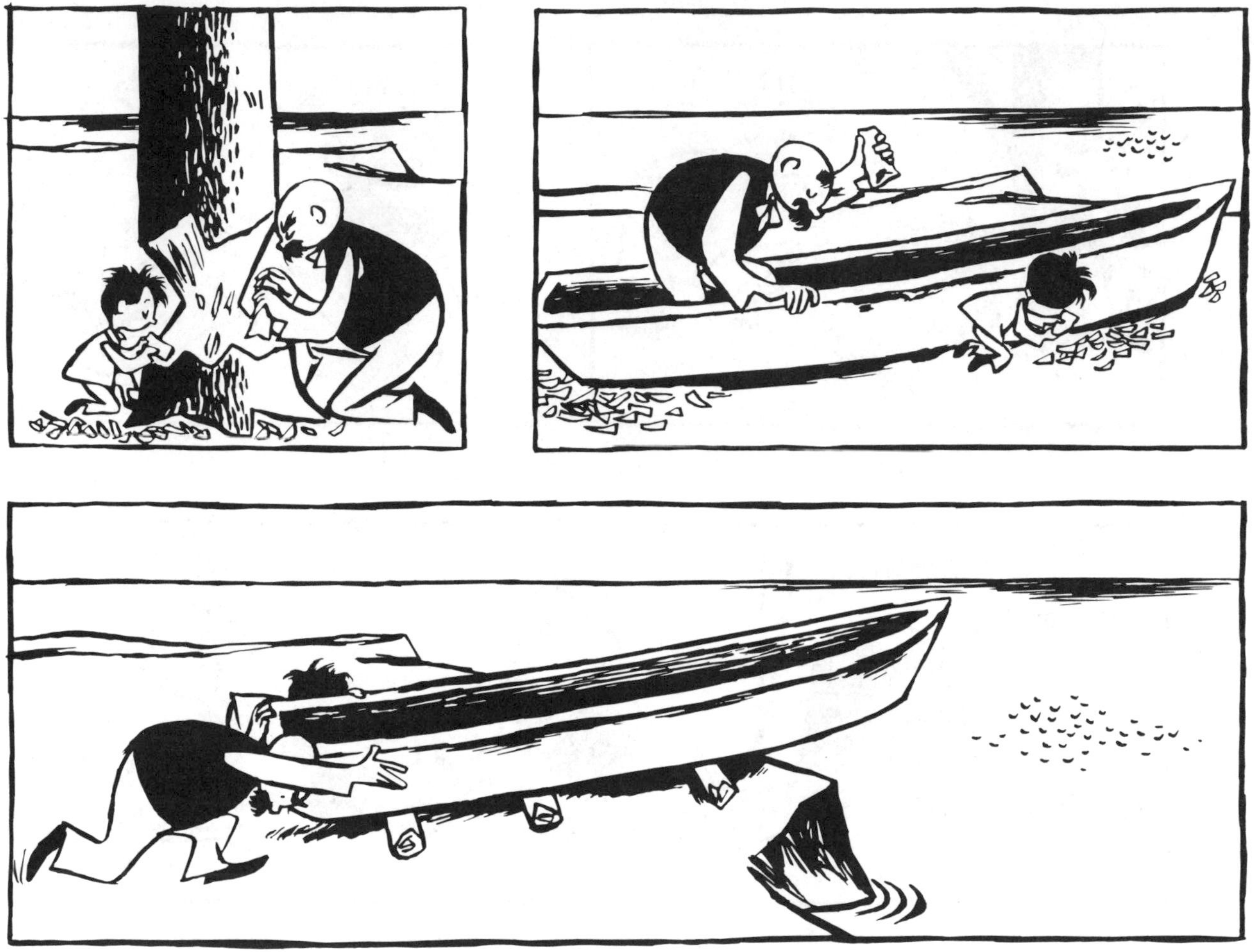

The launch

FATHER & SON

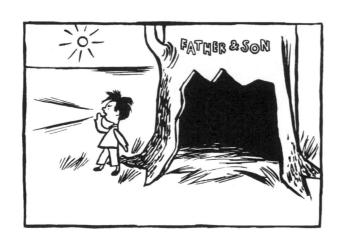

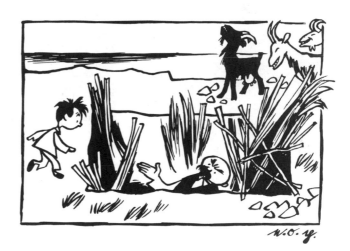

The goat trap

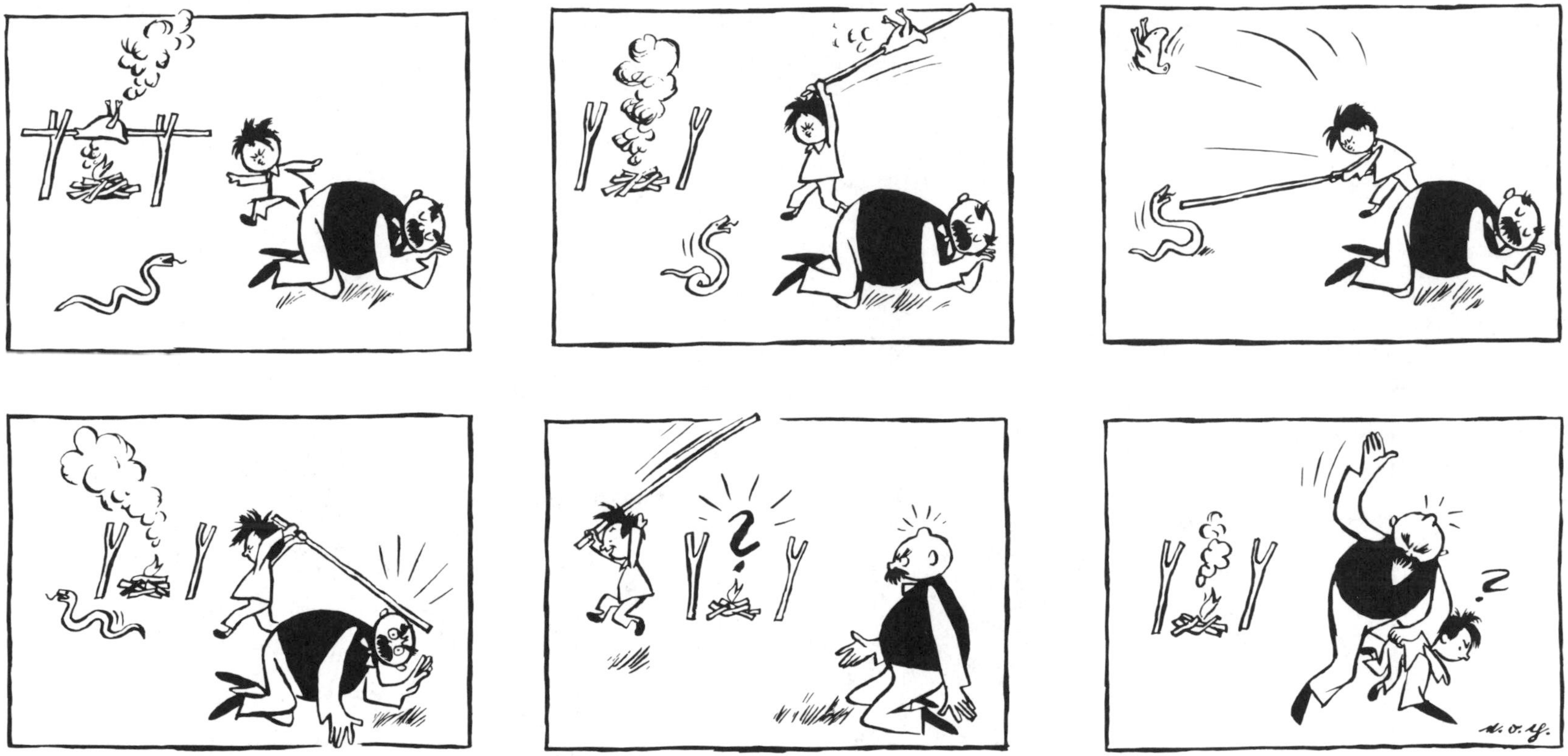

That's the thanks he gets

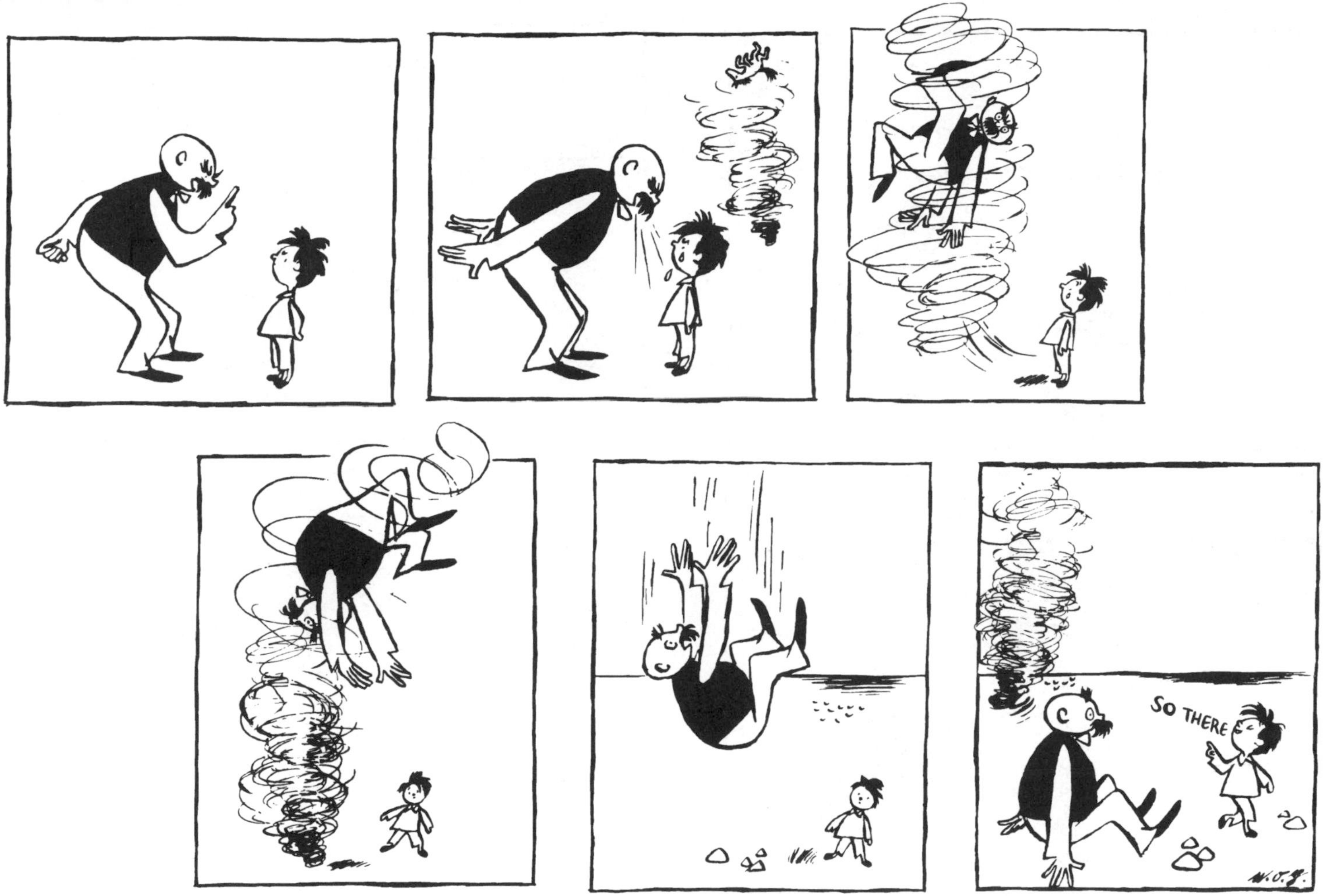
SO THERE

A perfect storm

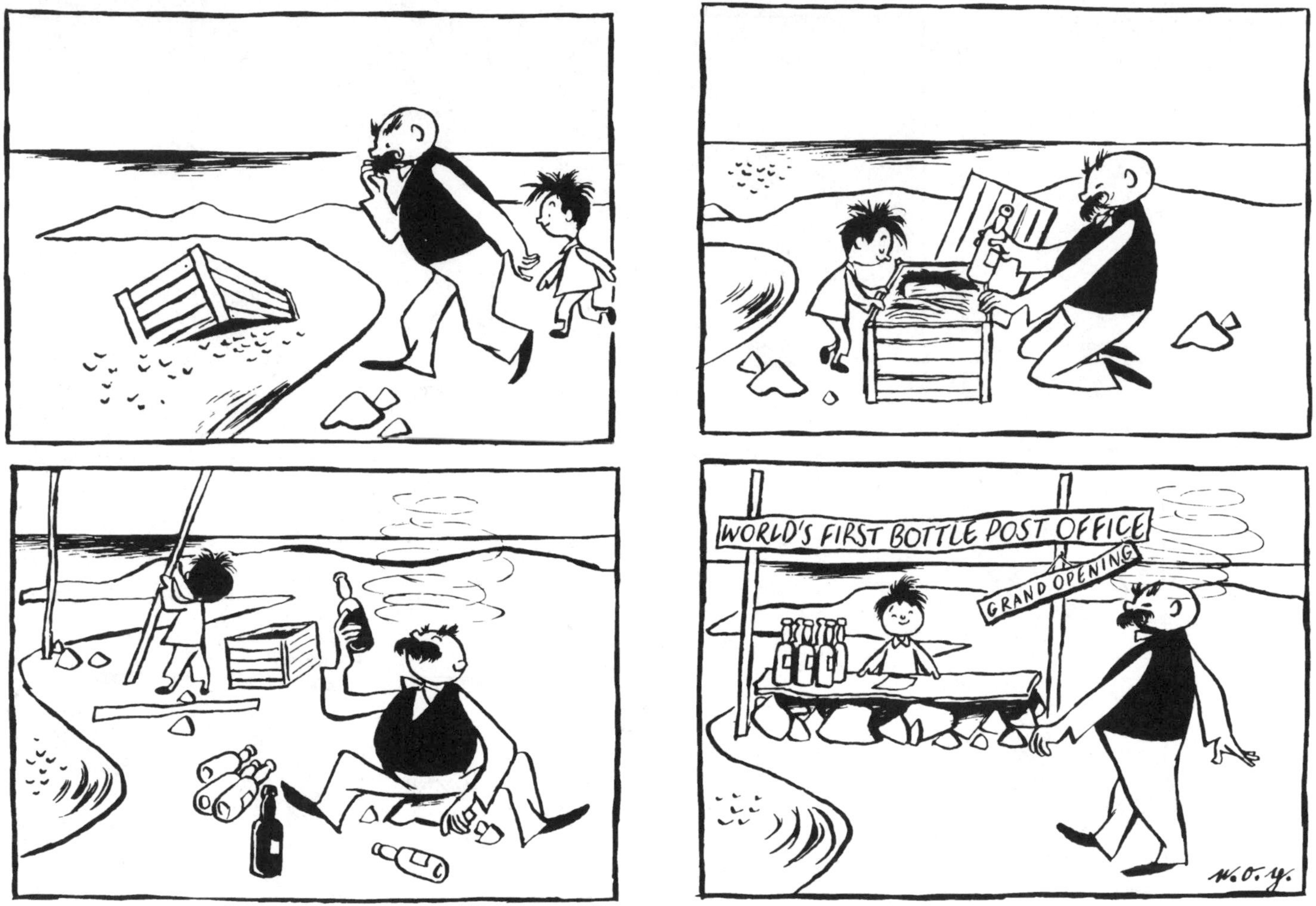
WORLD'S FIRST BOTTLE POST OFFICE
GRAND OPENING

Everything in its right place

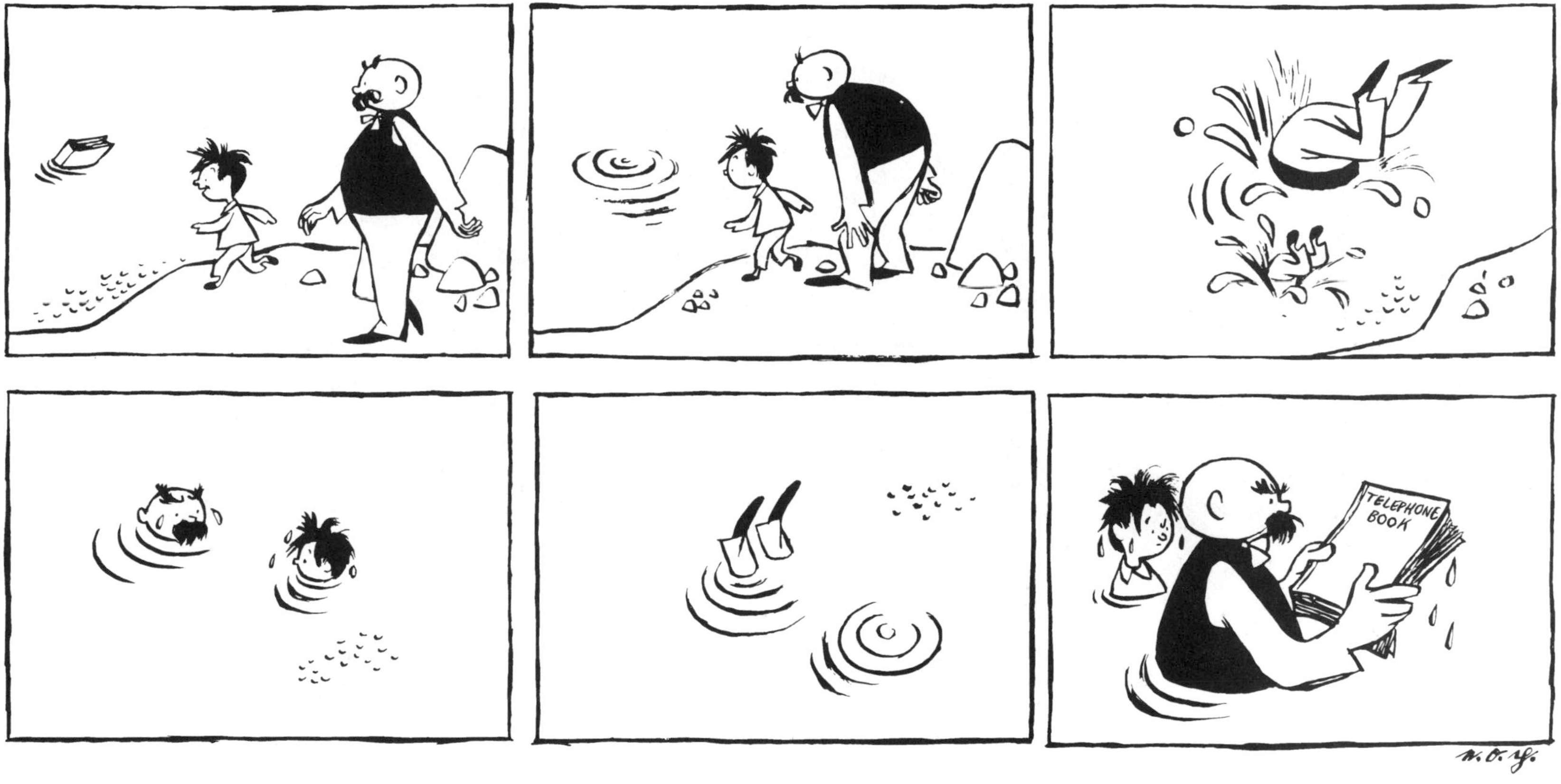
TELEPHONE BOOK

Spiritual nourishment at last

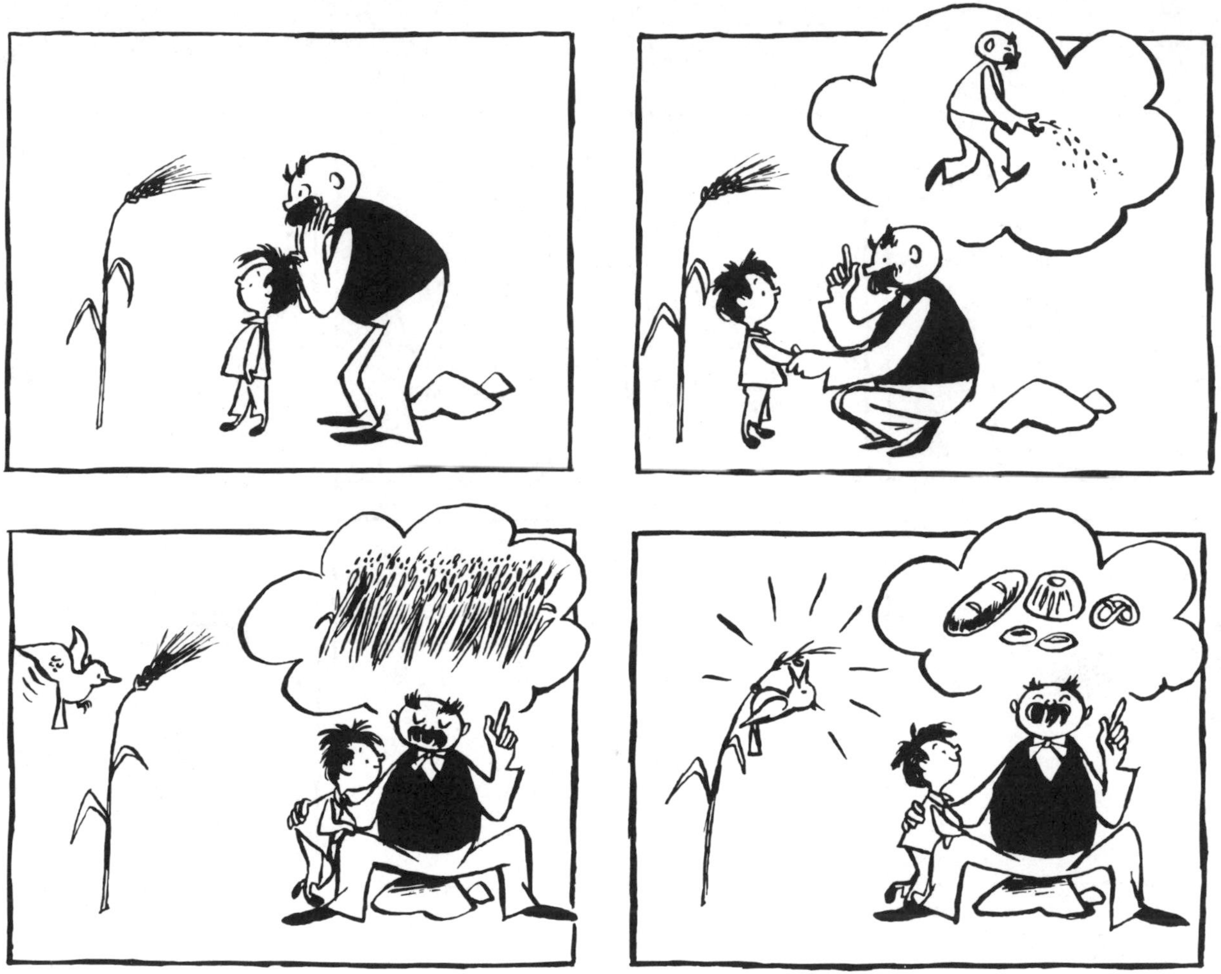

Dream over

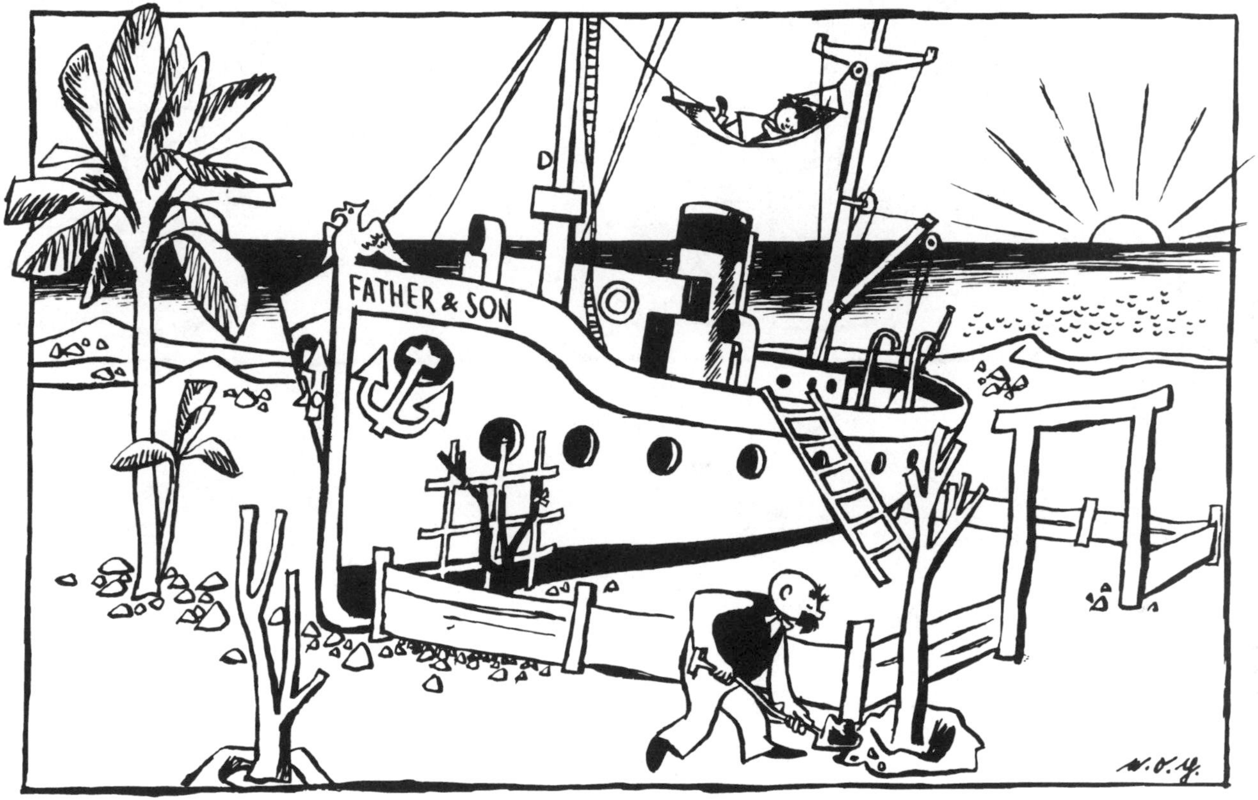
FATHER & SON
W.O.Y.

Crusoe redux

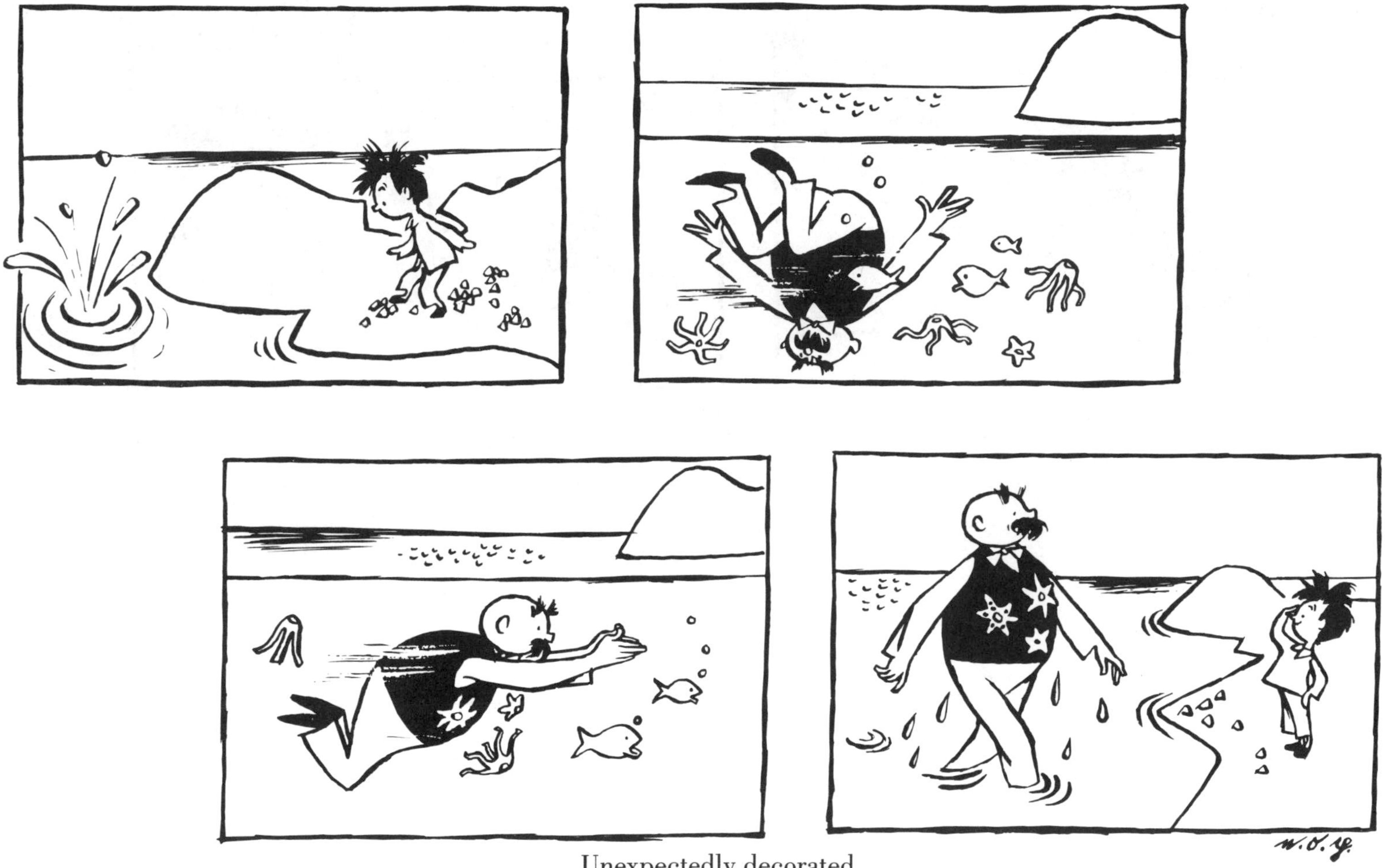

Unexpectedly decorated

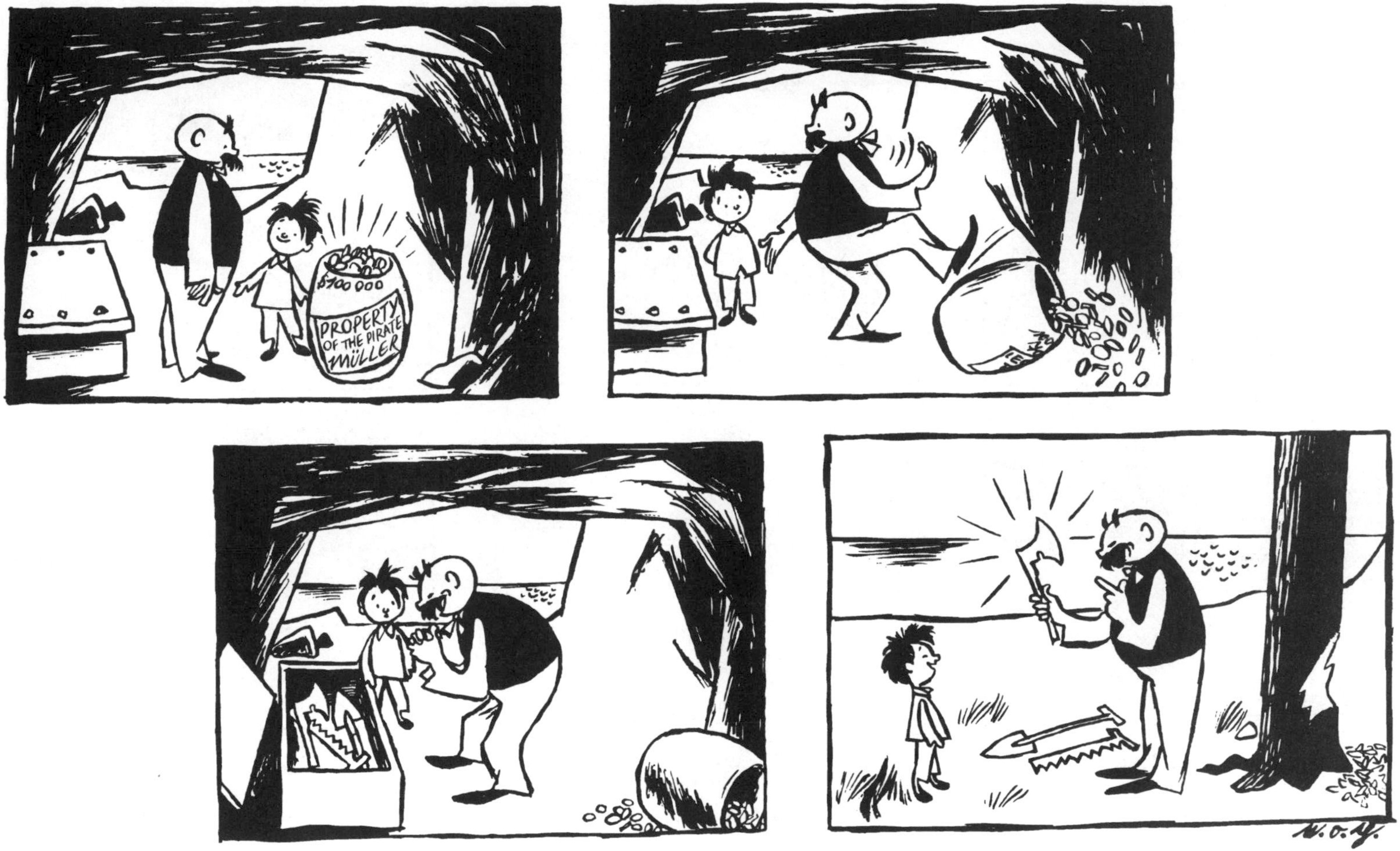
$100 000
PROPERTY OF THE PIRATE MÜLLER

“This here — this is gold!”

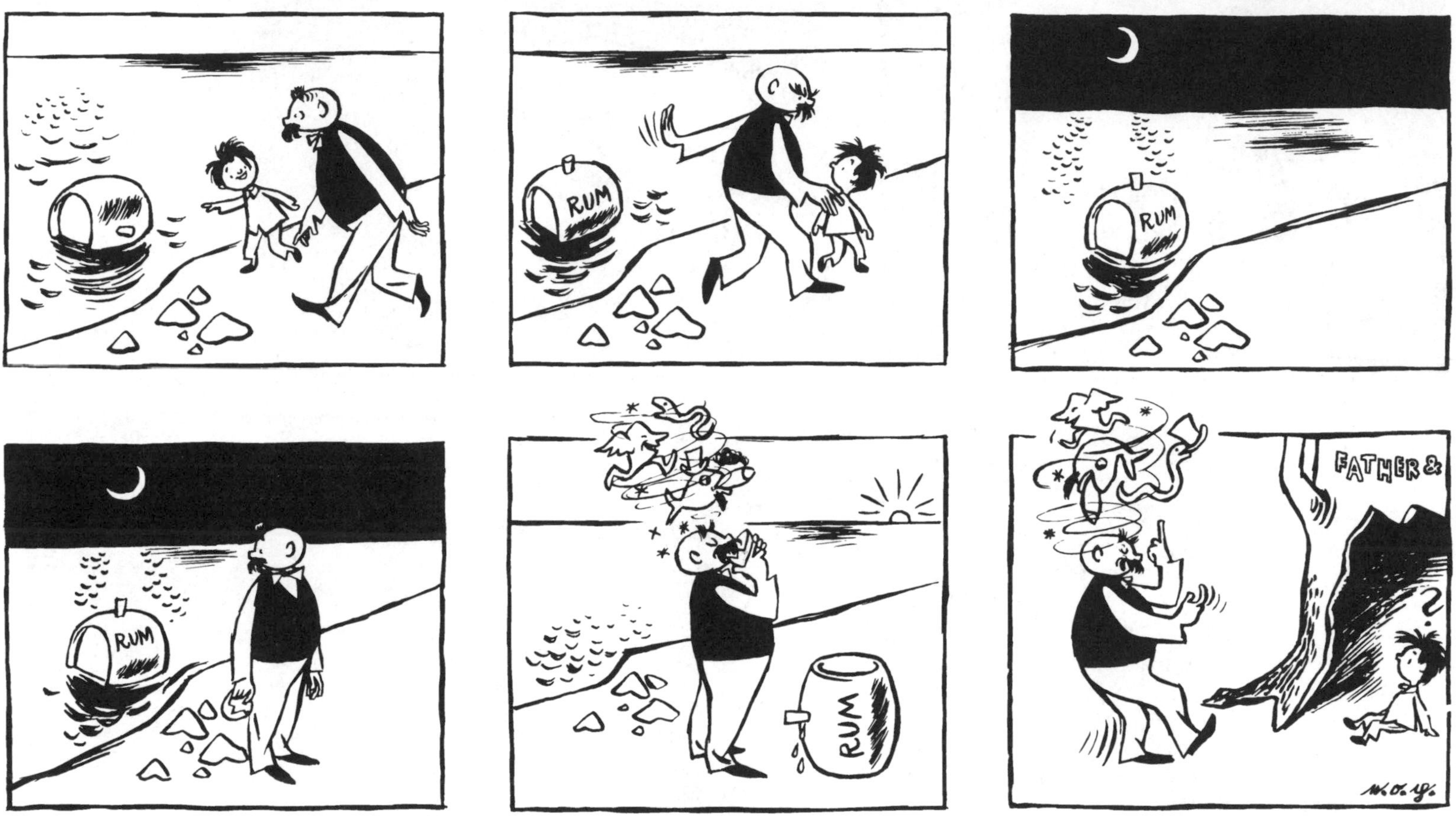
RUM
RUM
RUM
RUM
FATHER &
?

"Look what I — hic — brought you"

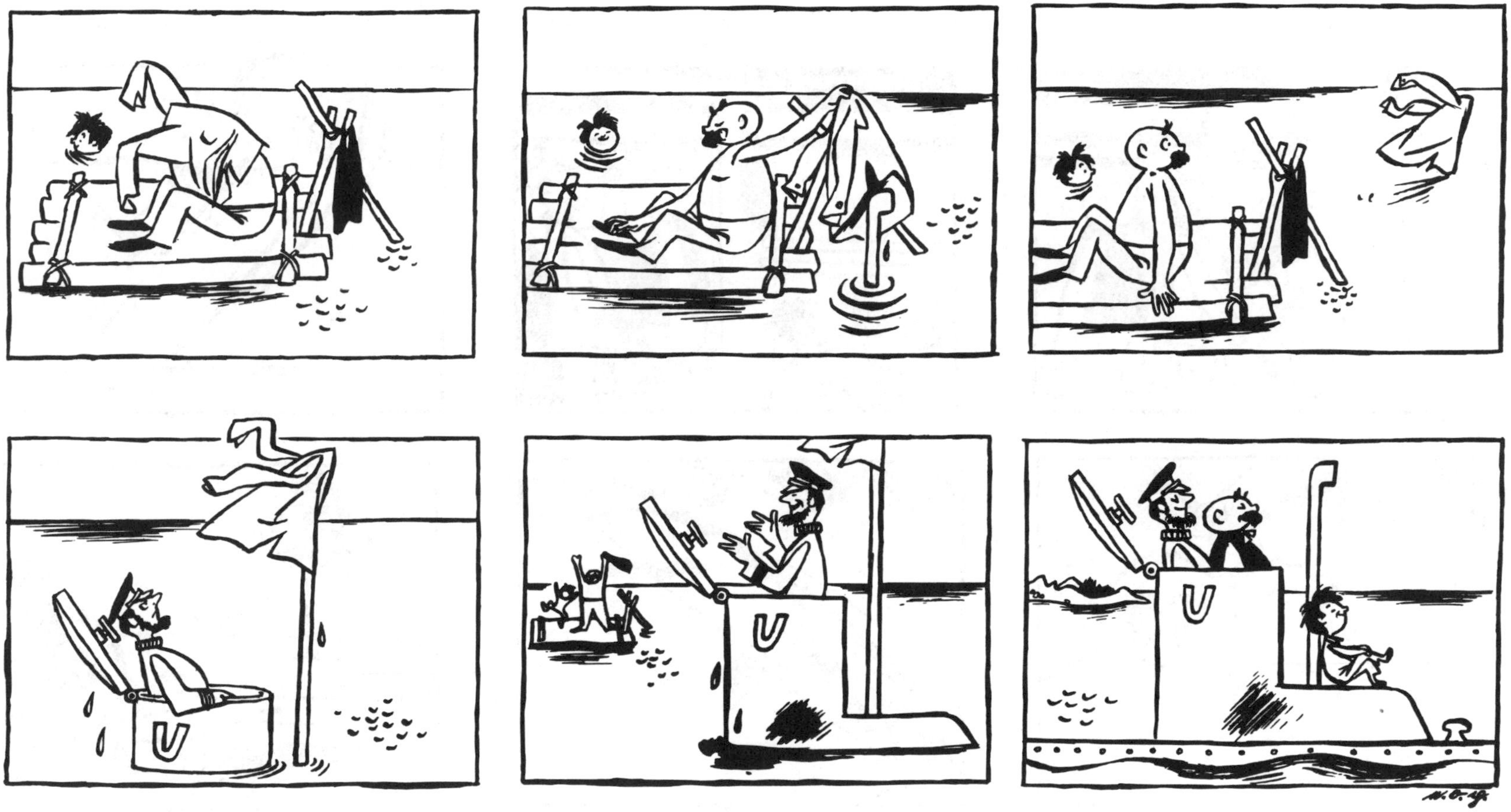

Unexpectedly rescued from the island

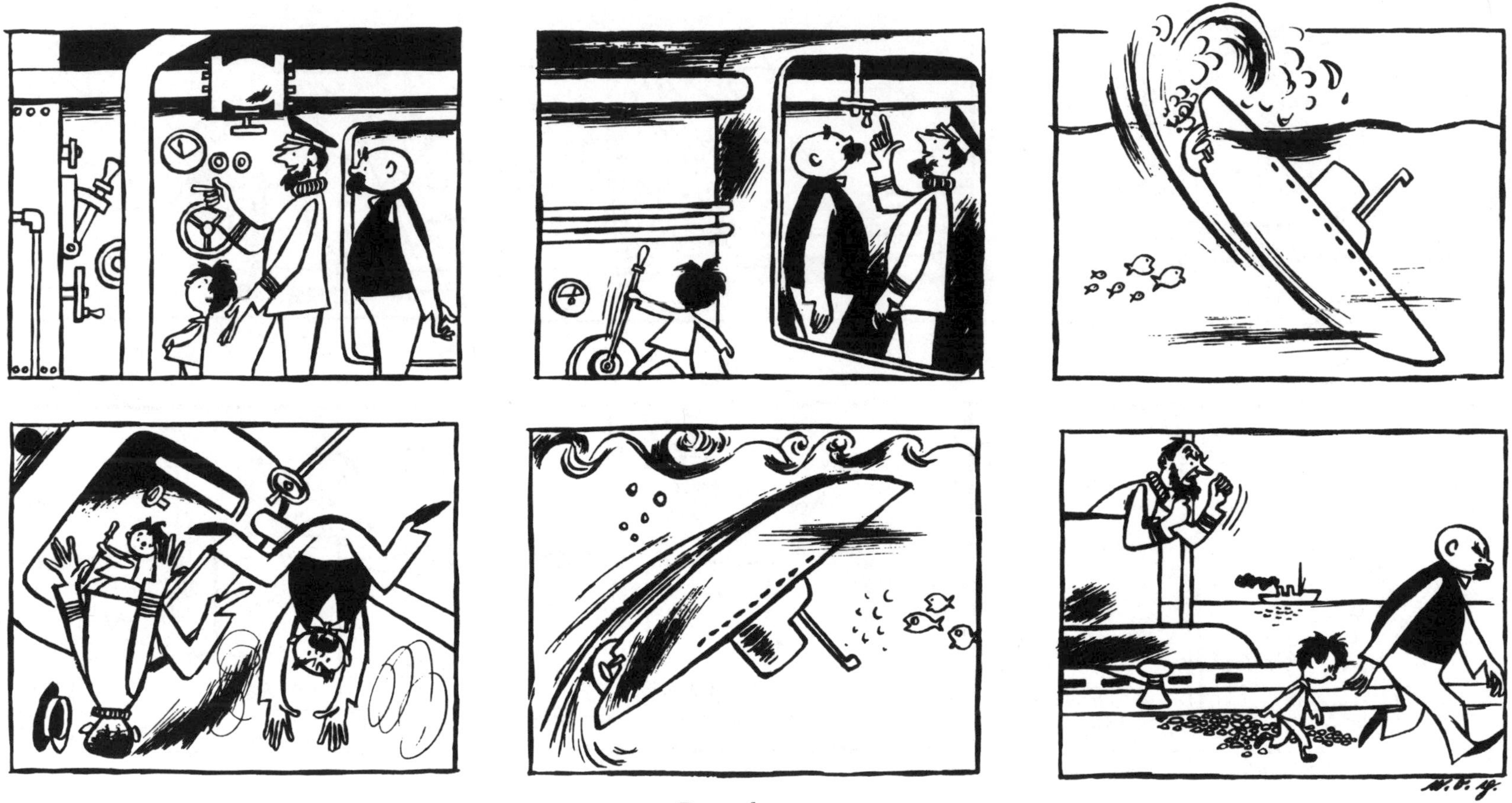

Put ashore

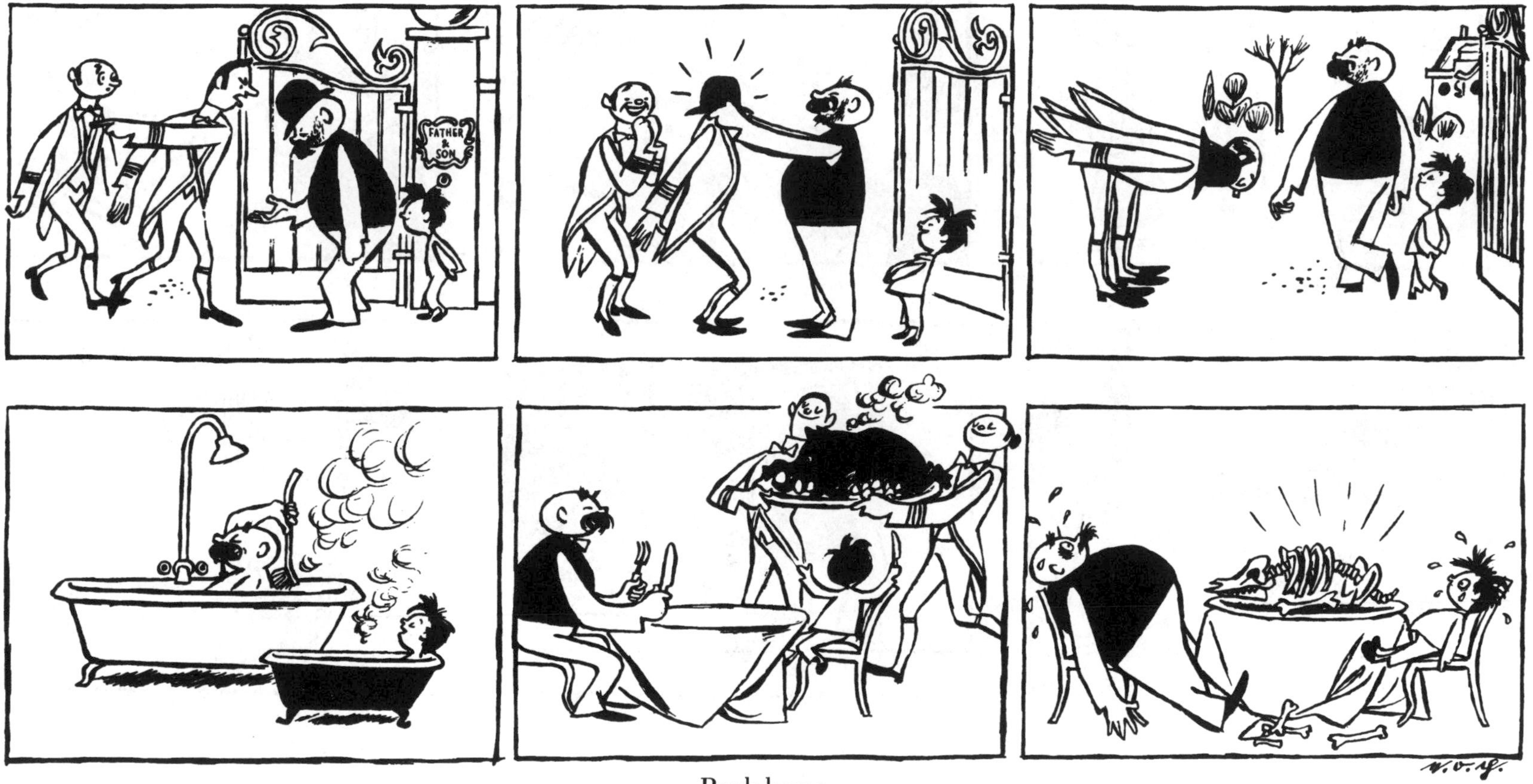
FATHER & SON

Back home

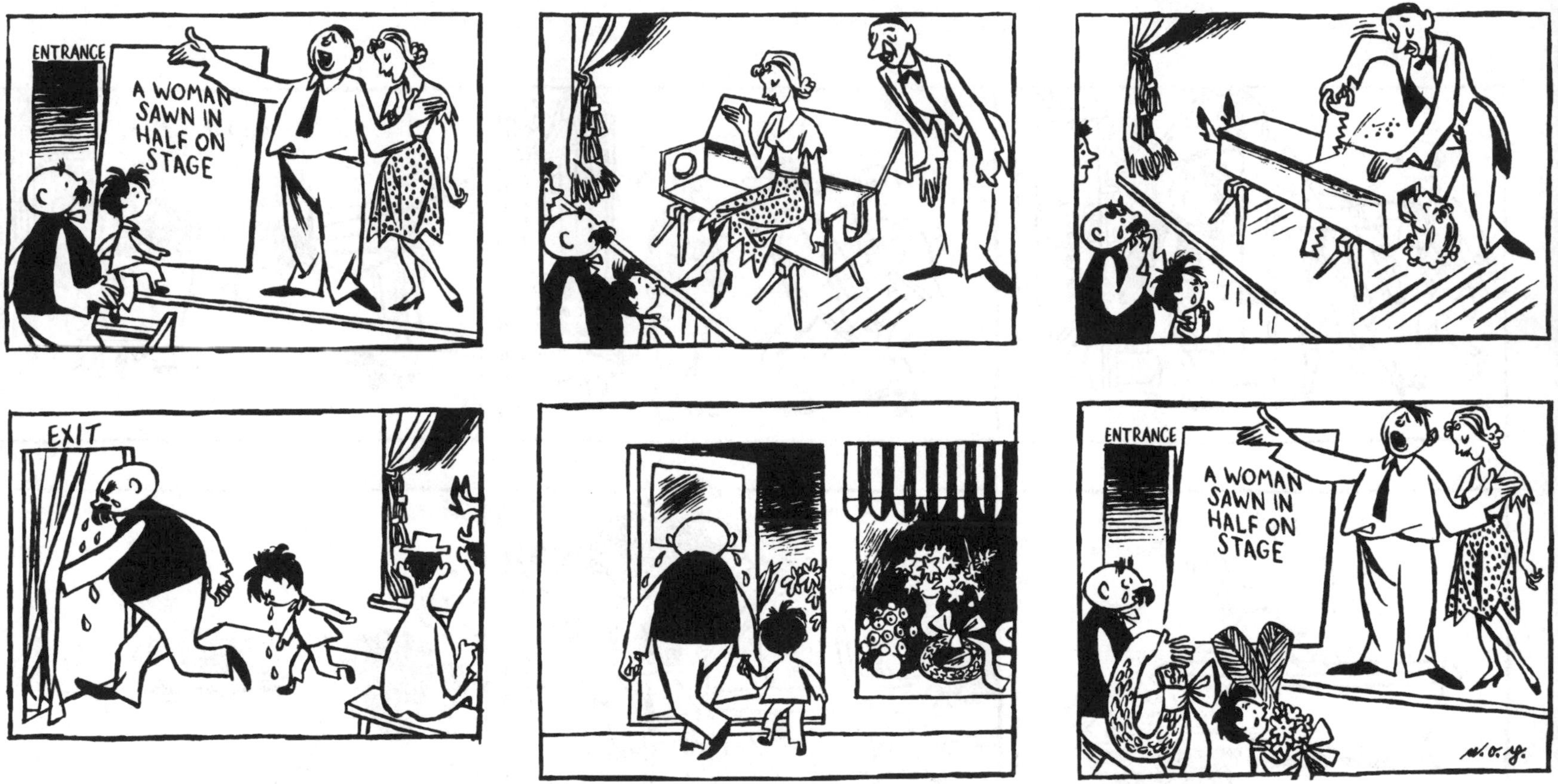
ENTRANCE
A WOMAN SAWN IN HALF ON STAGE
EXIT
ENTRANCE
A WOMAN SAWN IN HALF ON STAGE

Mourning the woman sawn in half

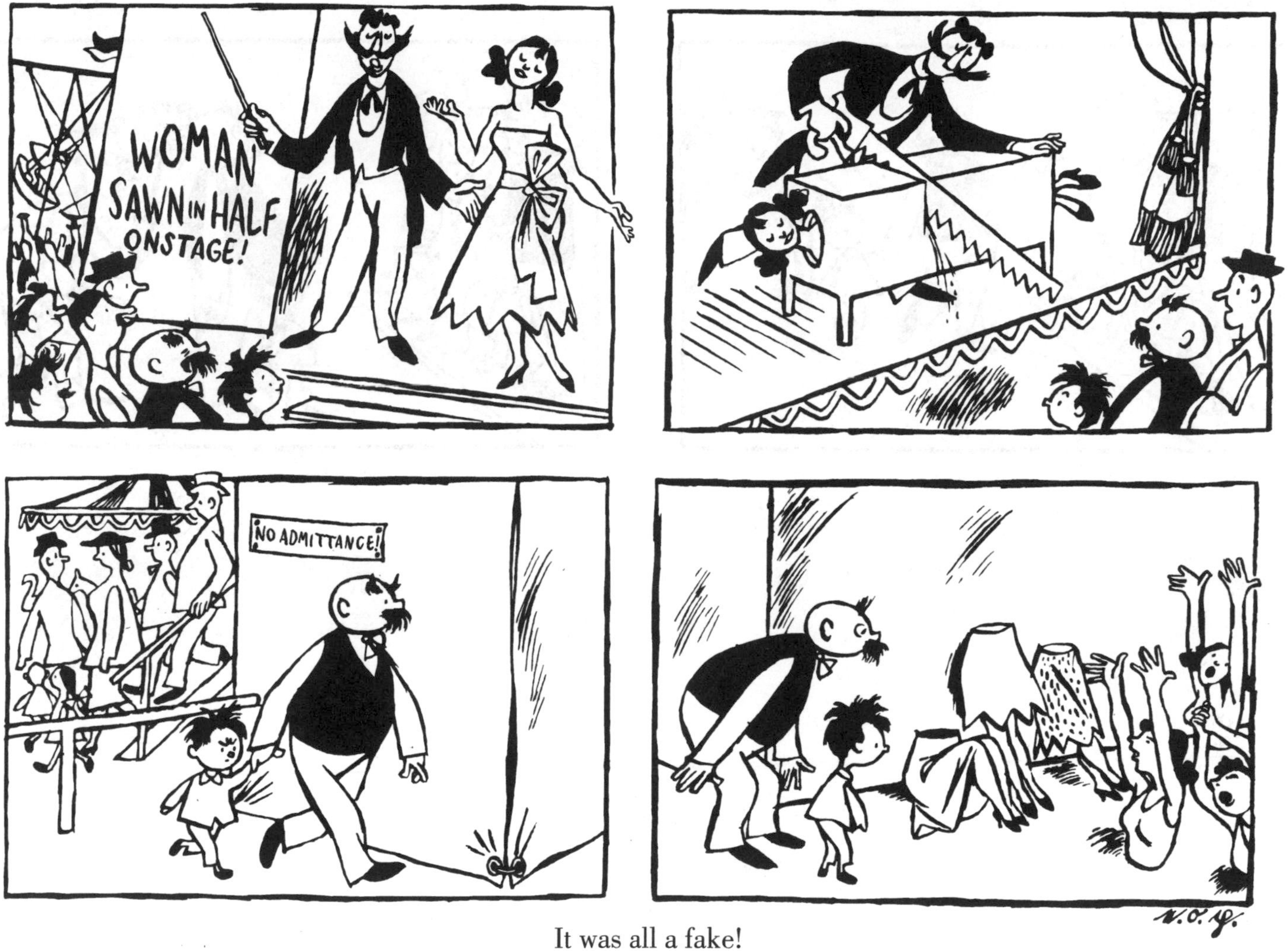
WOMAN SAWN IN HALF ONSTAGE!
NO ADMITTANCE!
N.O.Y.

It was all a fake!

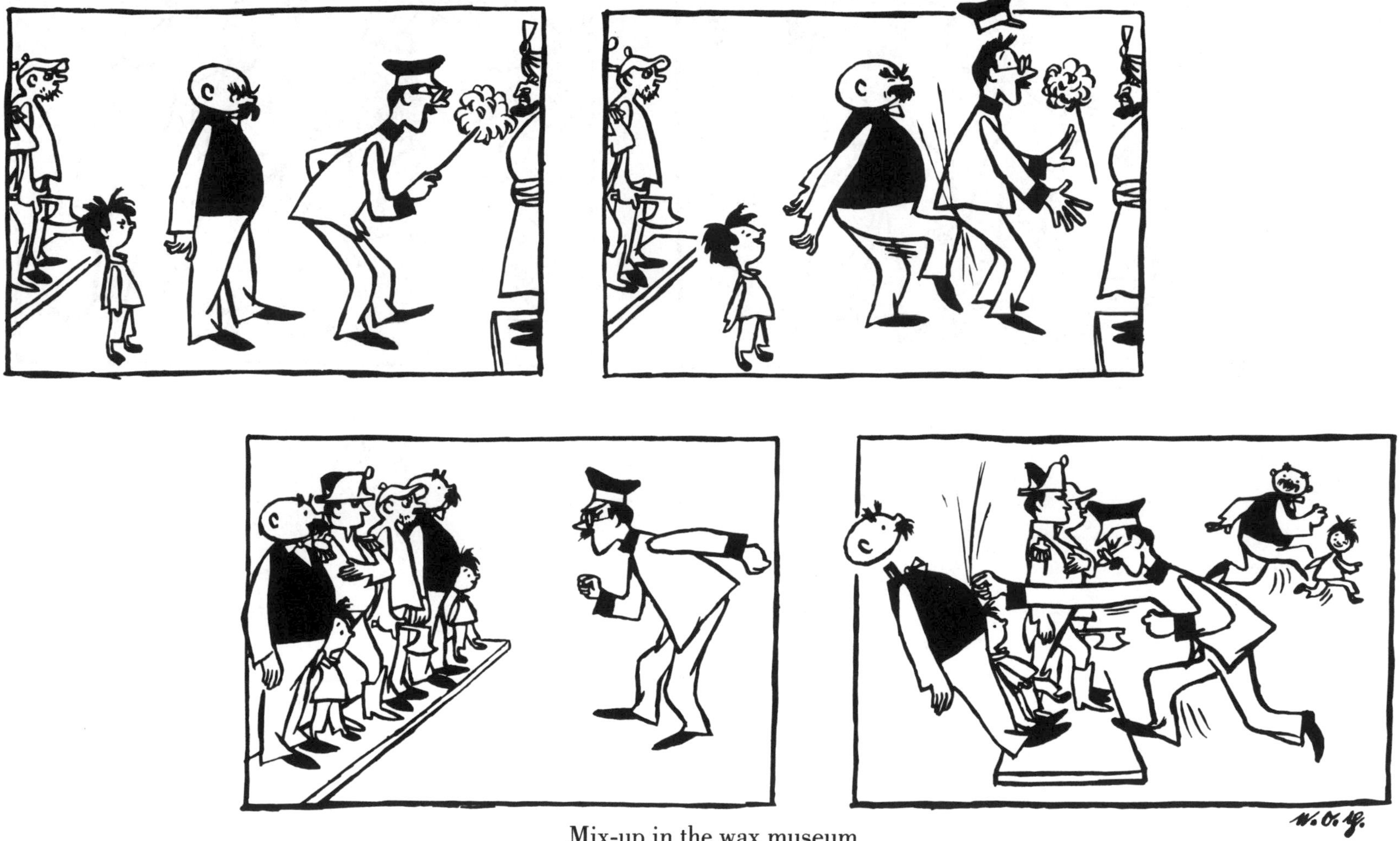

Mix-up in the wax museum

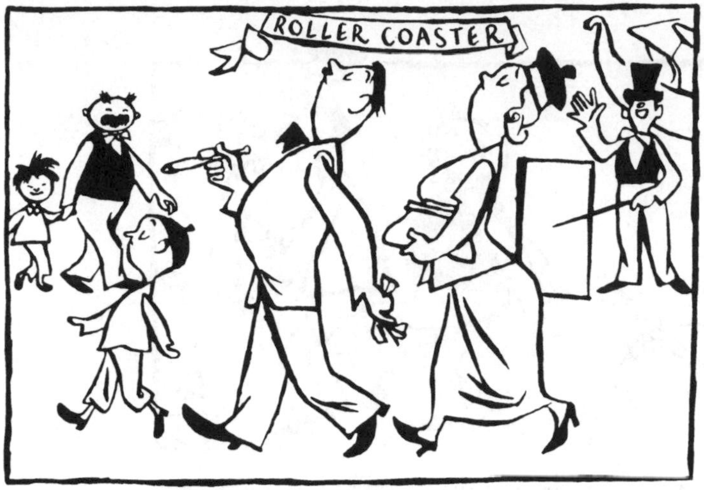
ROLLER COASTER

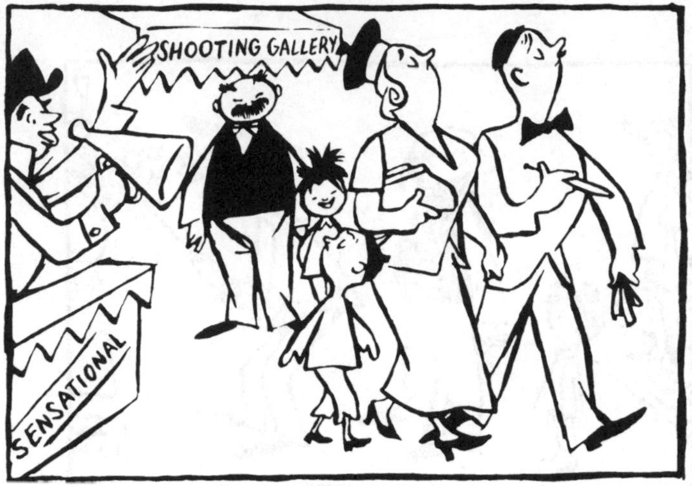
SHOOTING GALLERY
SENSATIONAL

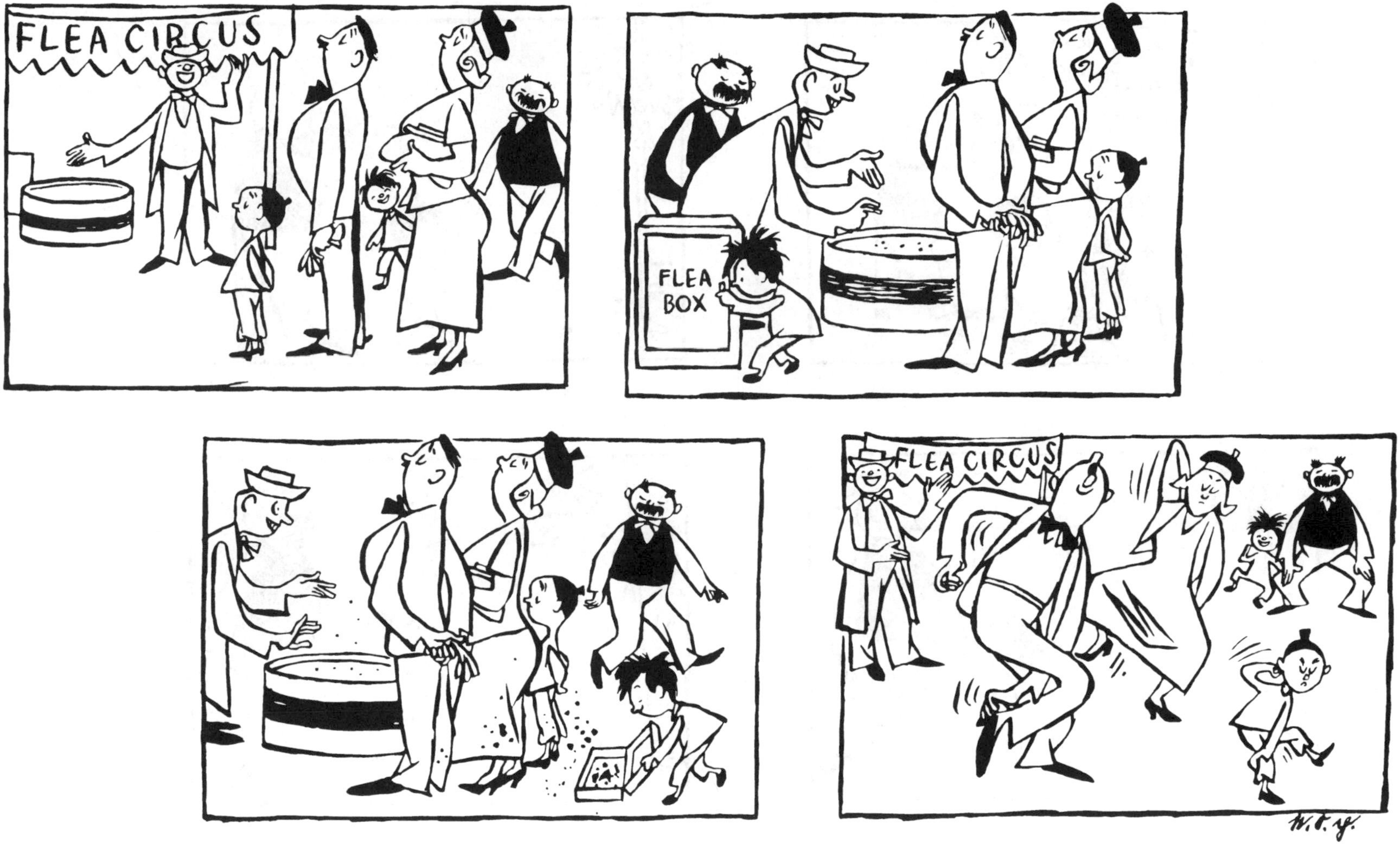
FLEA CIRCUS
FLEA BOX
FLEA CIRCUS

A very, very genteel family

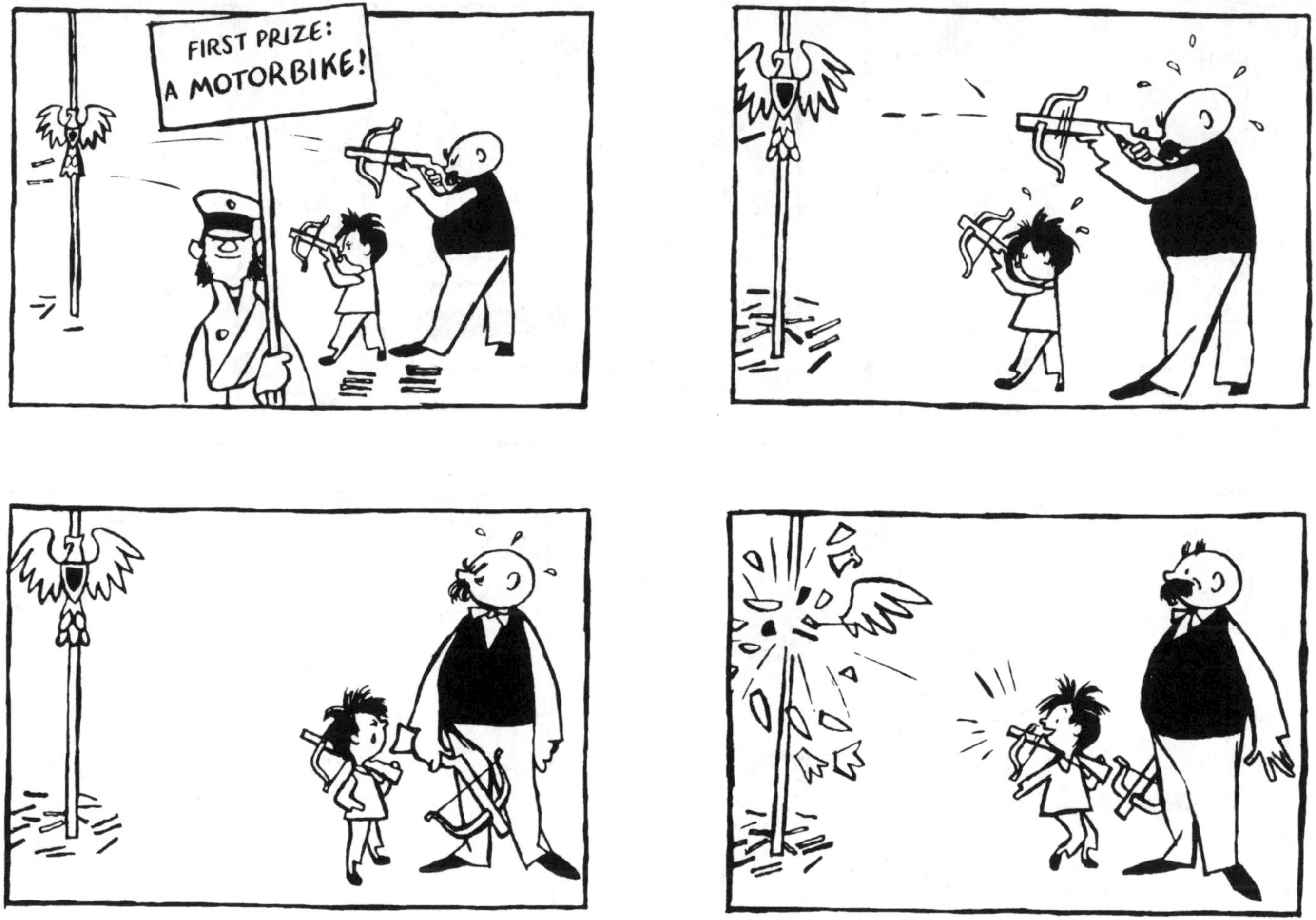
FIRST PRIZE:
A MOTORBIKE!

Bull's-eye by accident

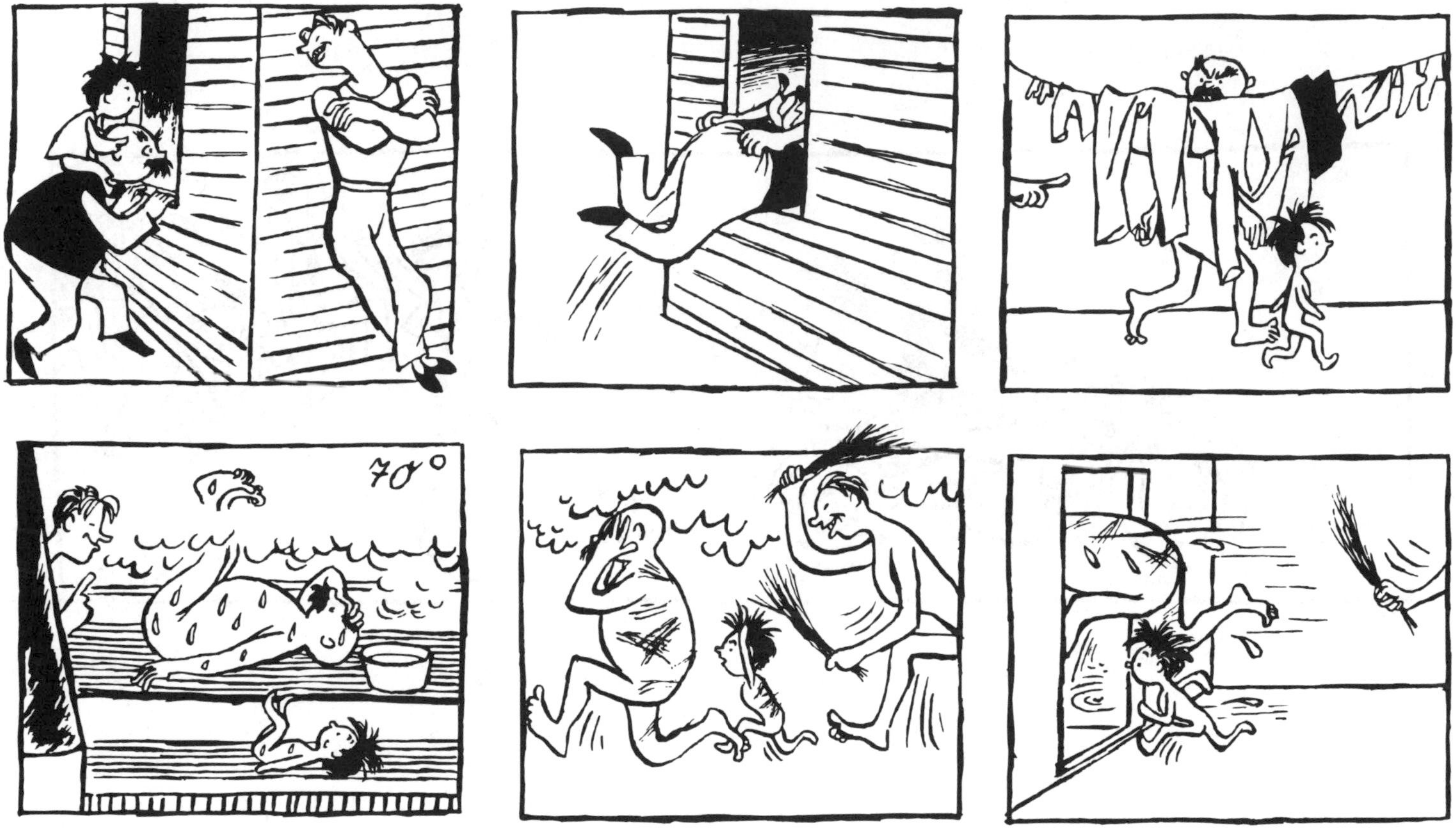
70°

In the sauna

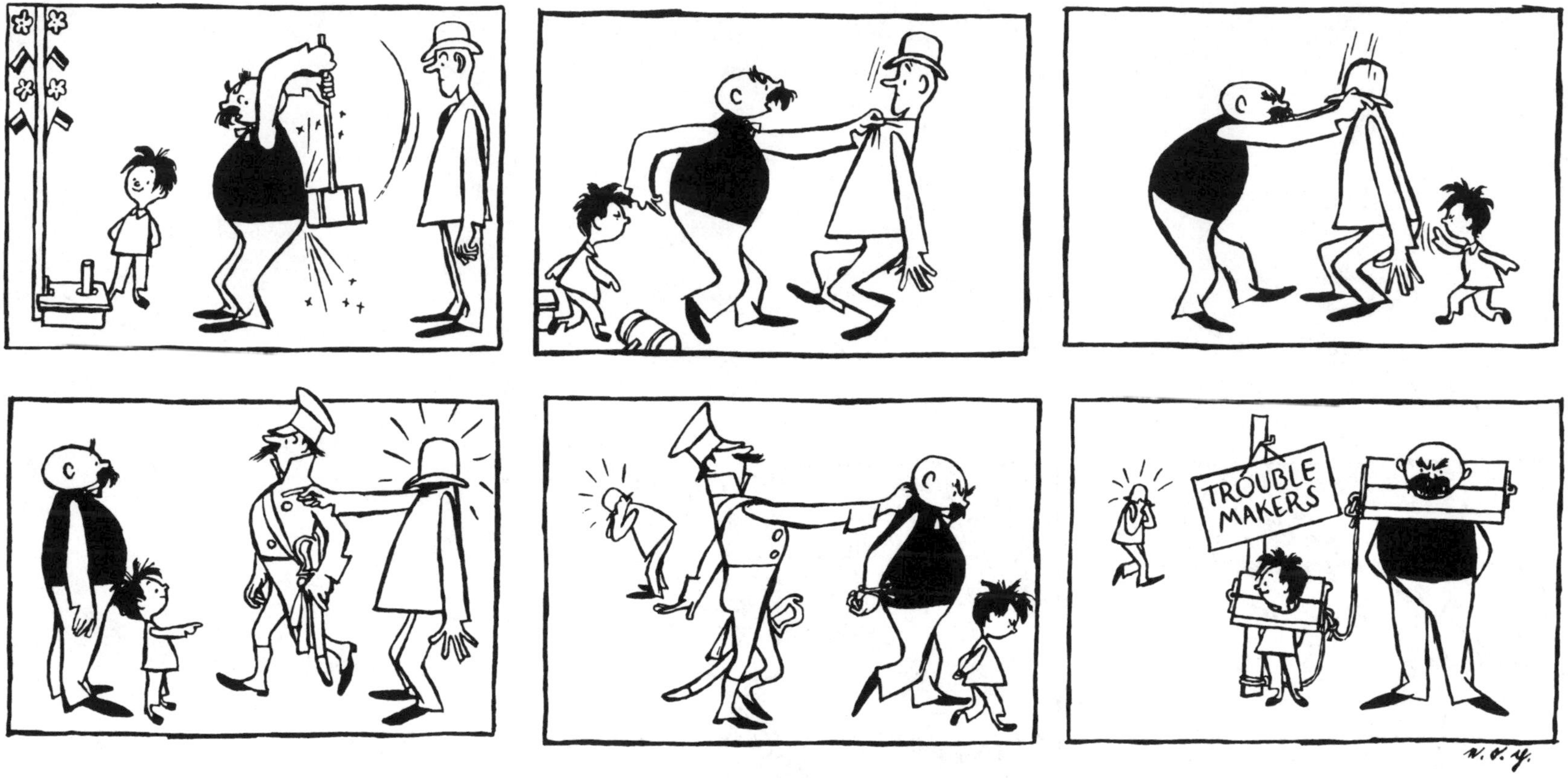
TROUBLE MAKERS

Pilloried

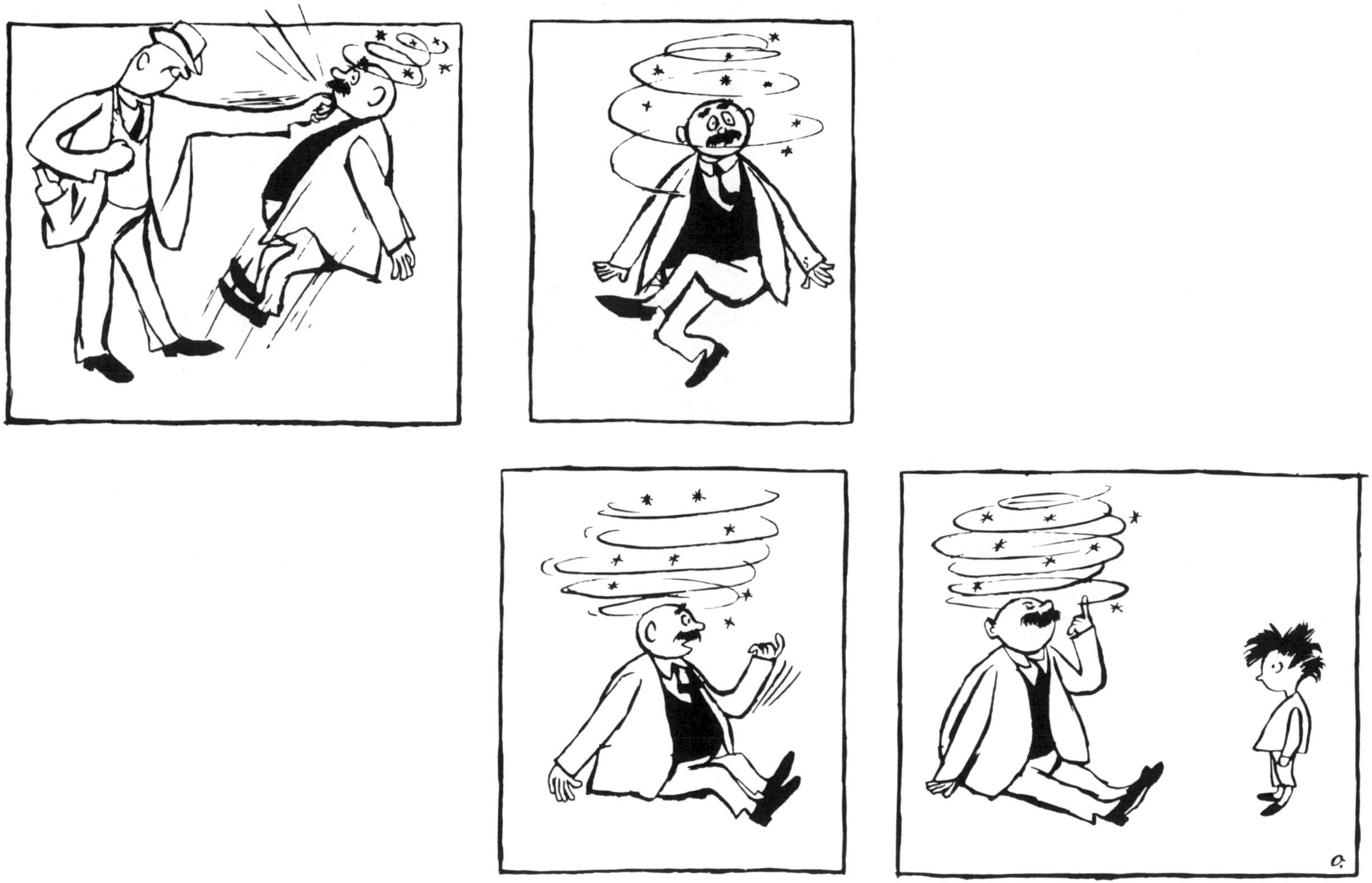

A mean left hook

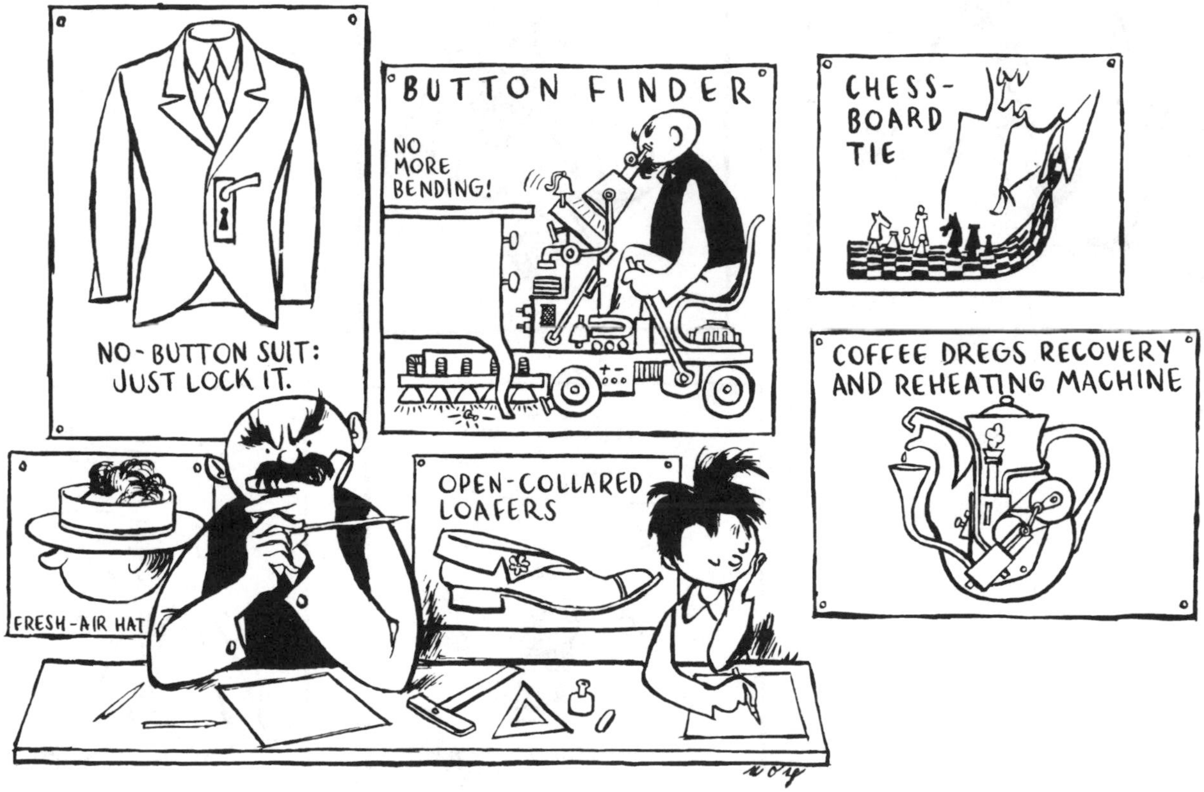
NO-BUTTON SUIT: JUST LOCK IT.
BUTTON FINDER
NO MORE BENDING!
CHESS-BOARD TIE
COFFEE DREGS RECOVERY AND REHEATING MACHINE
FRESH-AIR HAT
OPEN-COLLARED LOAFERS

Occupation: inventor

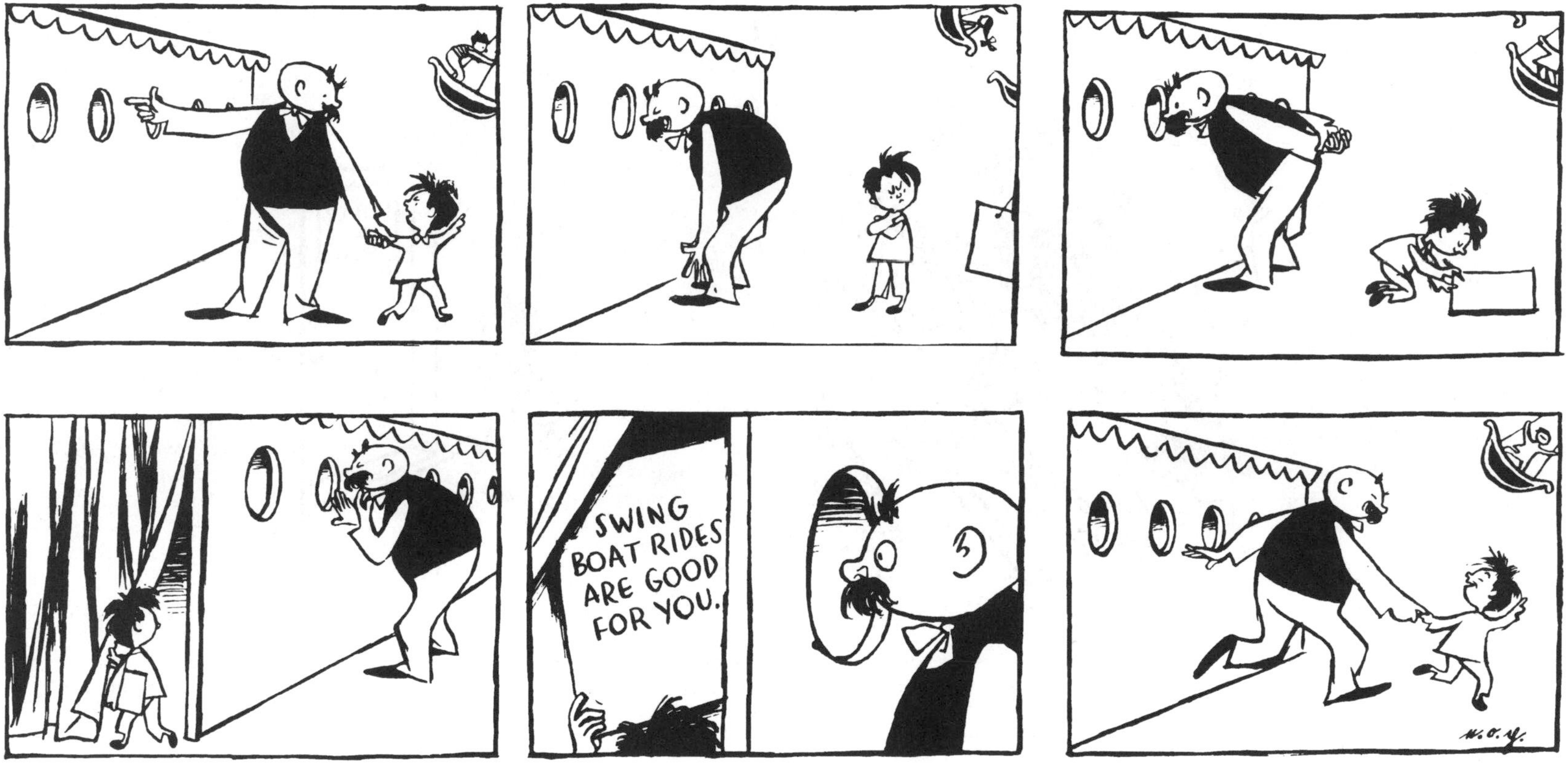
SWING BOAT RIDES ARE GOOD FOR YOU.

A little peephole trick

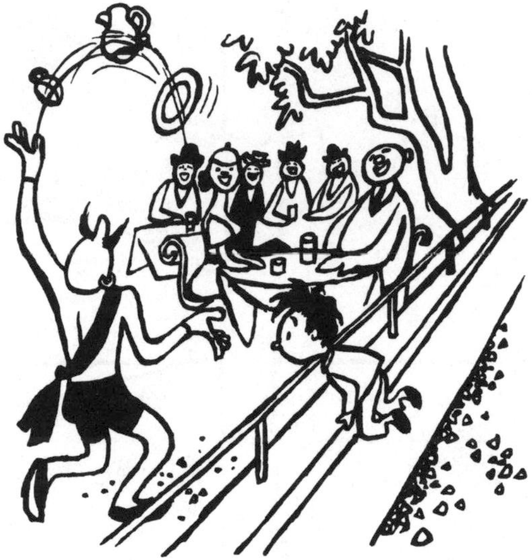

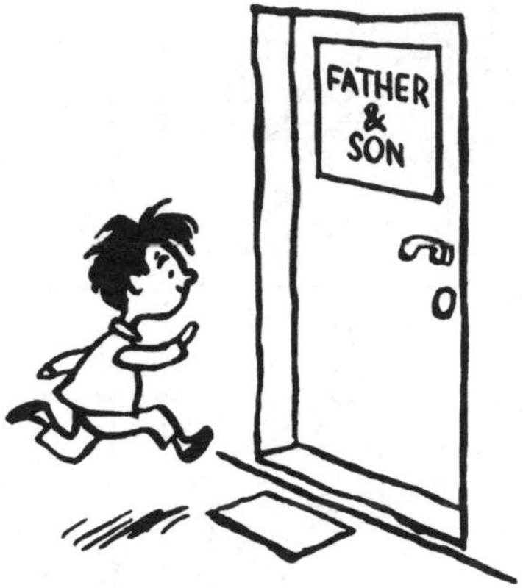
FATHER
&
SON

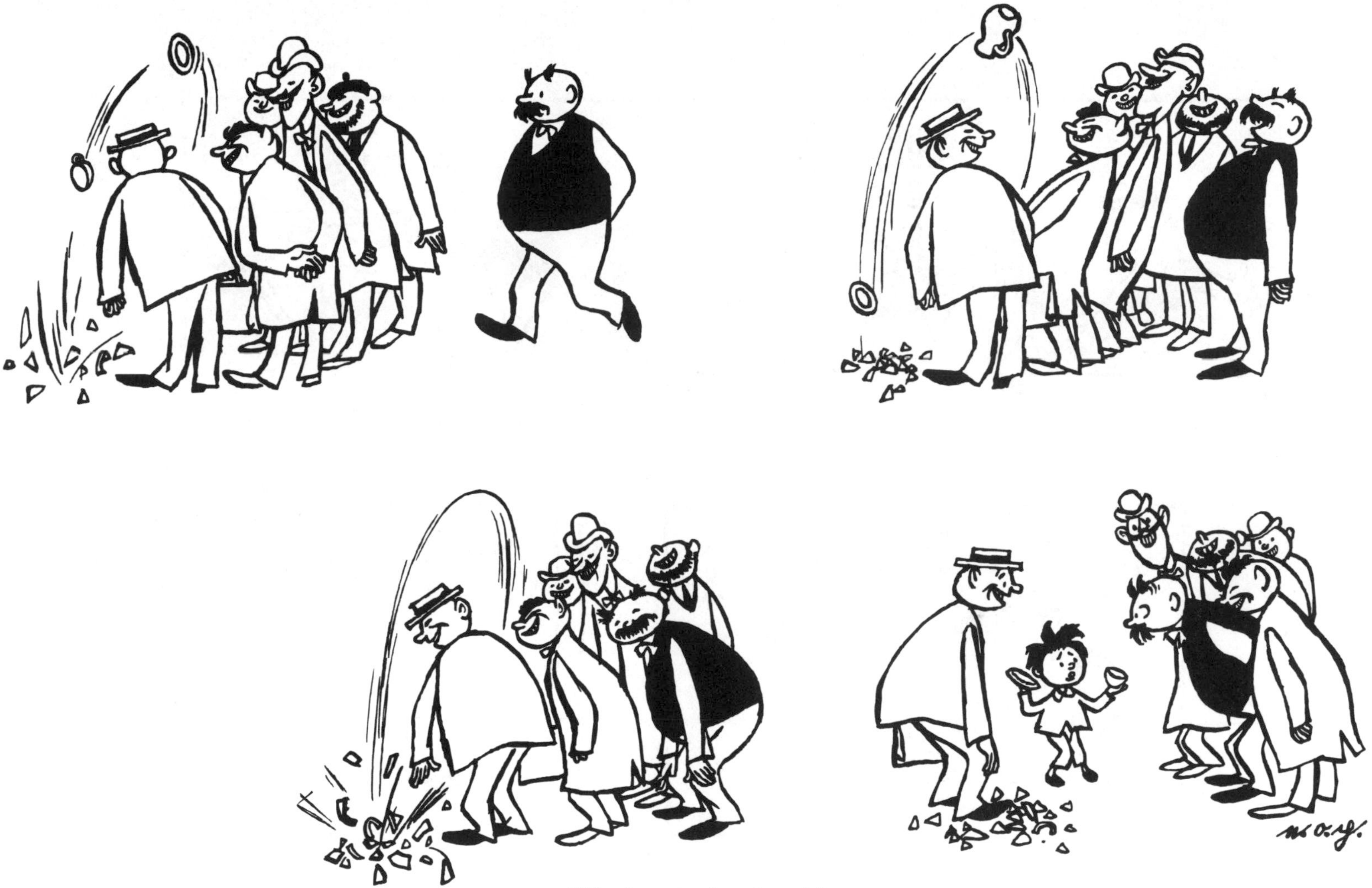

Who has the last laugh?

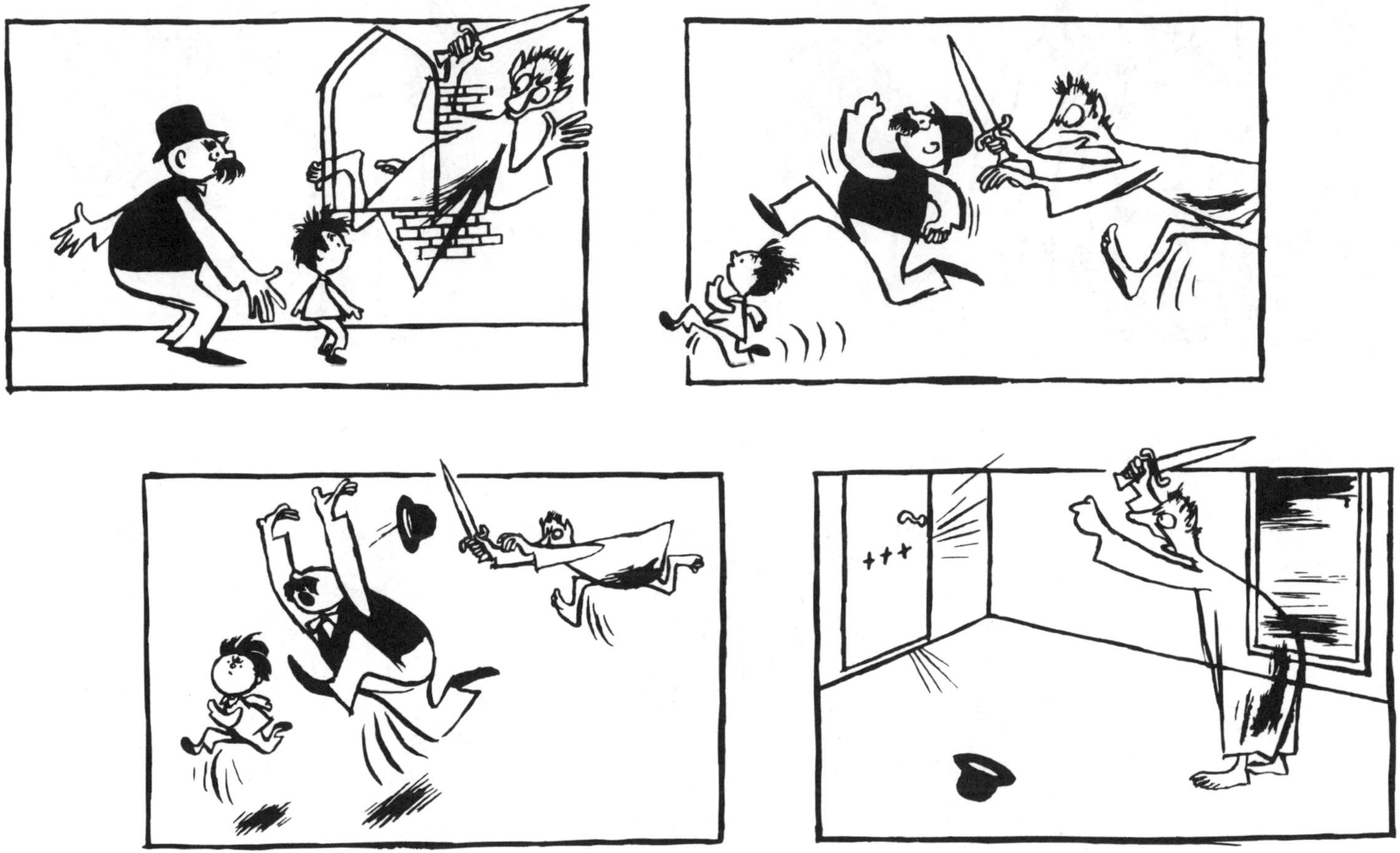

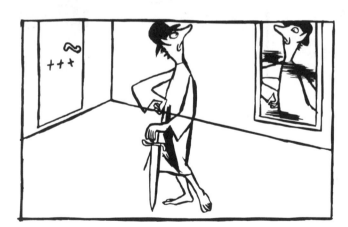

The vain ghost

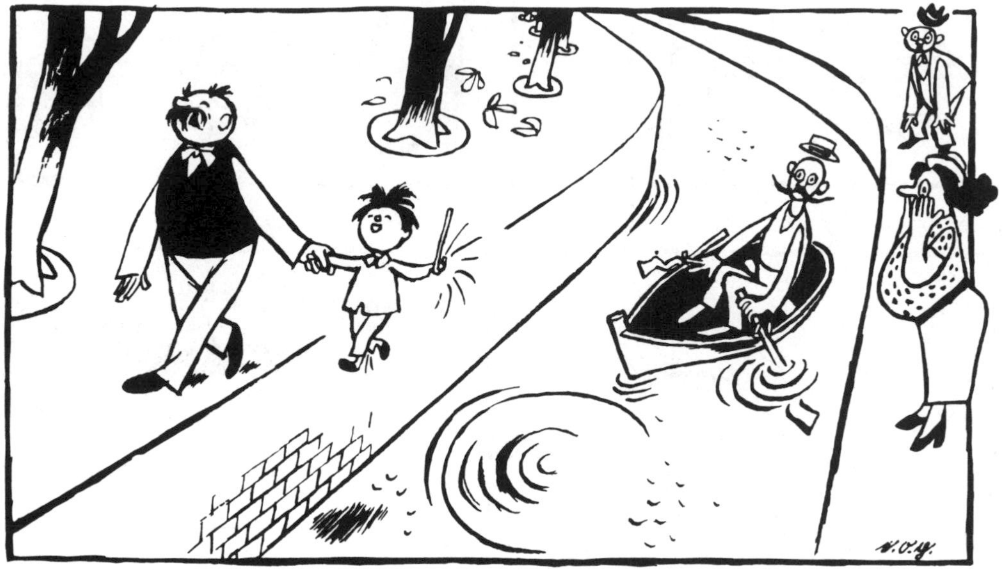

H.O.Y.

The first dreams remembered, or, Back then I thought you were the strongest man in the world

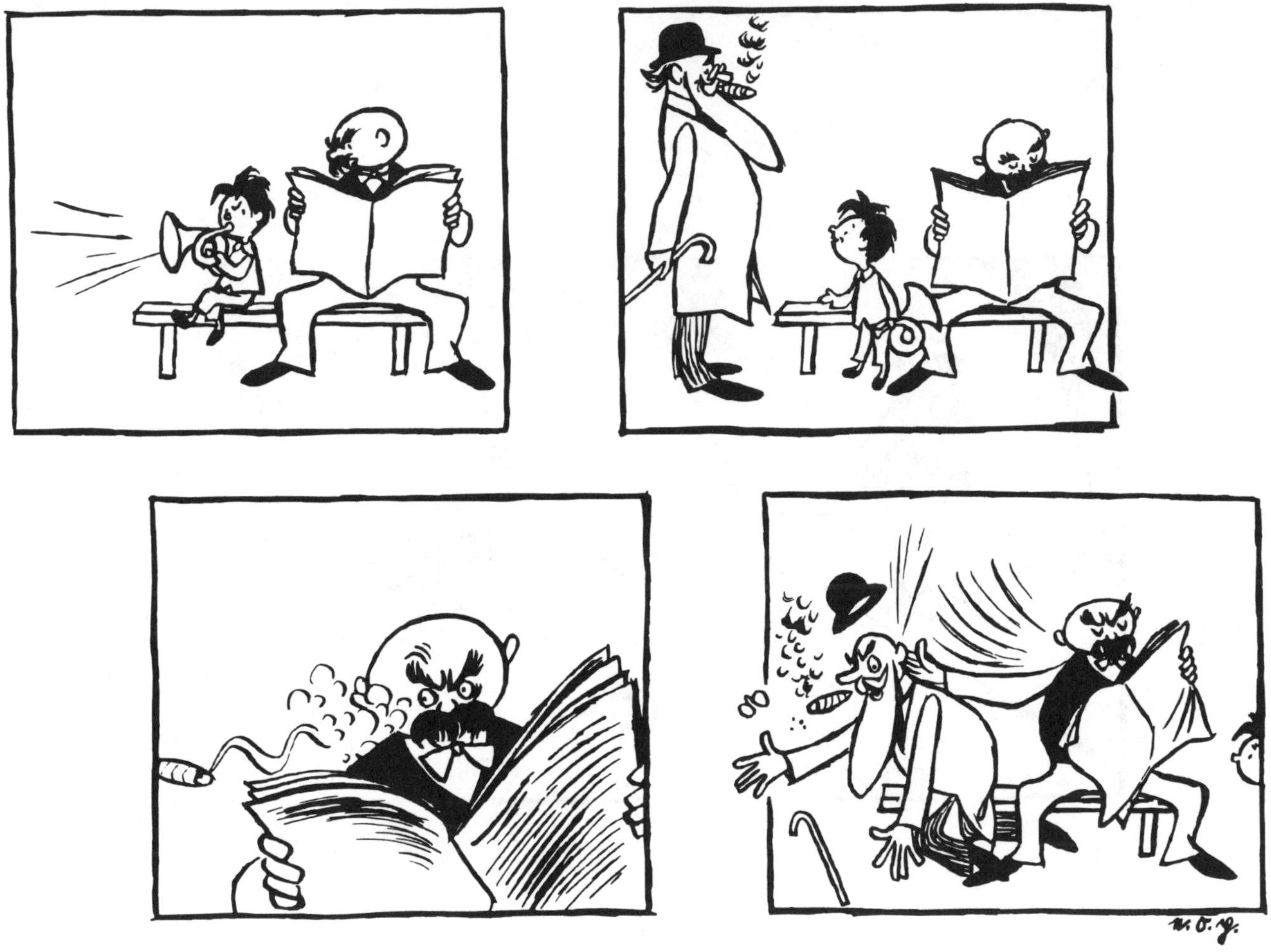

The wrong place to sit

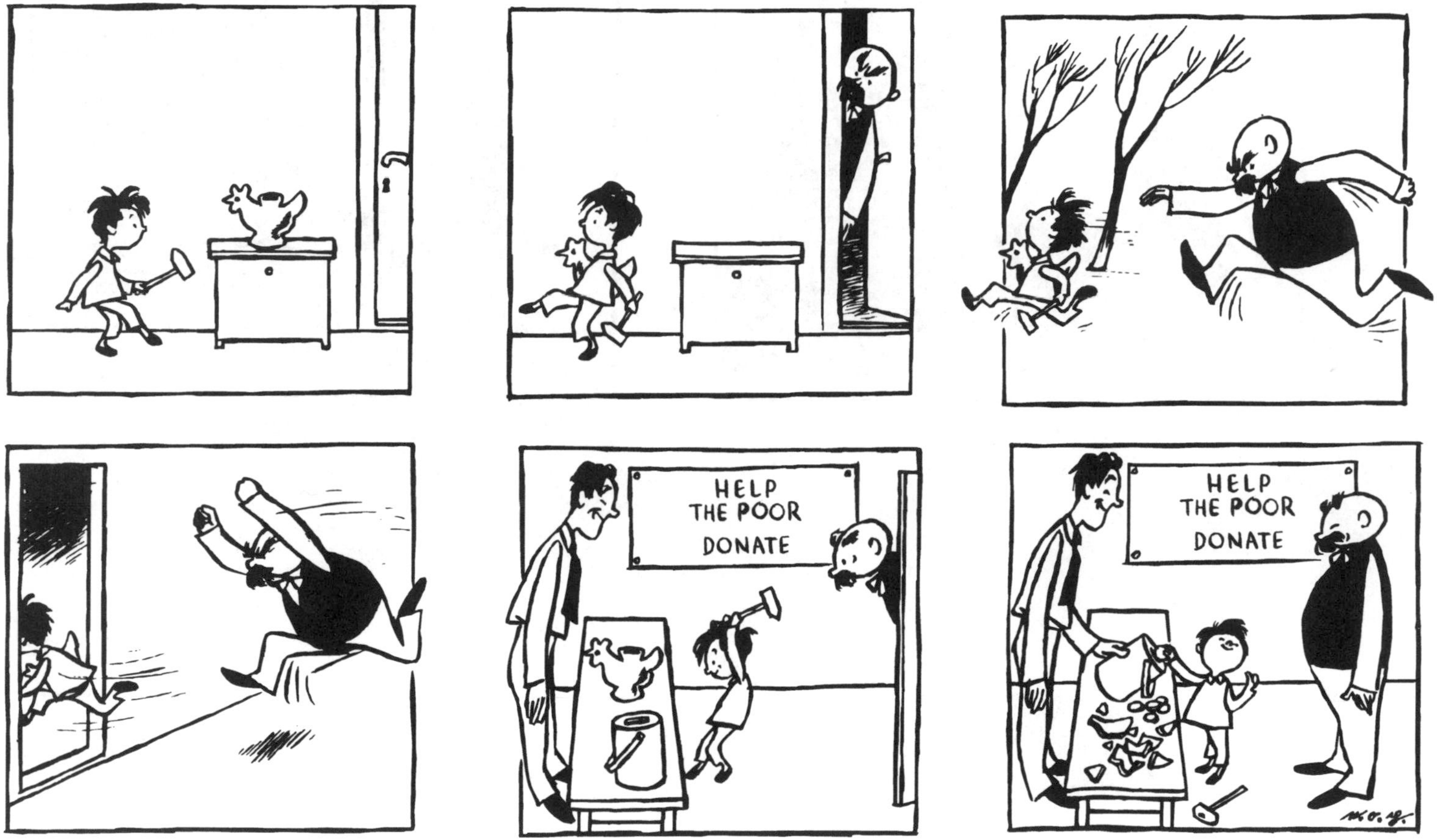
HELP THE POOR DONATE
HELP THE POOR DONATE

Donation

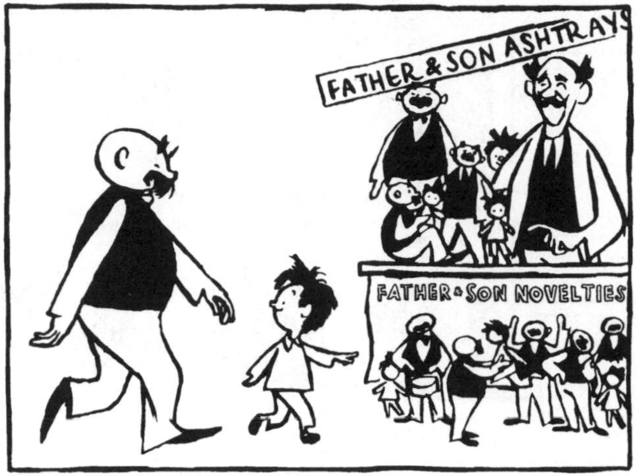
FATHER & SON ASHTRAYS
FATHER & SON NOVELTIES
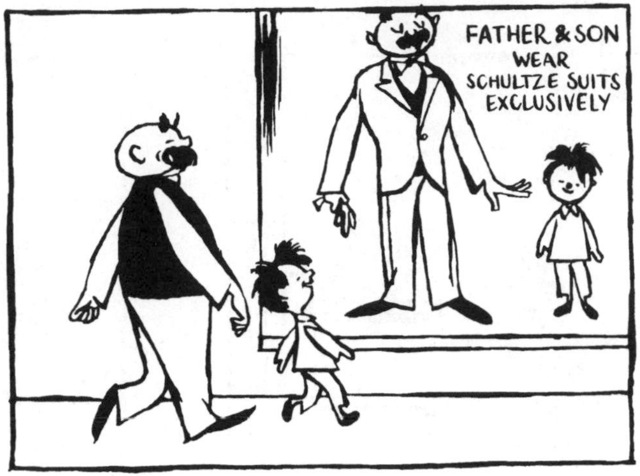
FATHER & SON
WEAR
SCHULTZE SUITS
EXCLUSIVELY

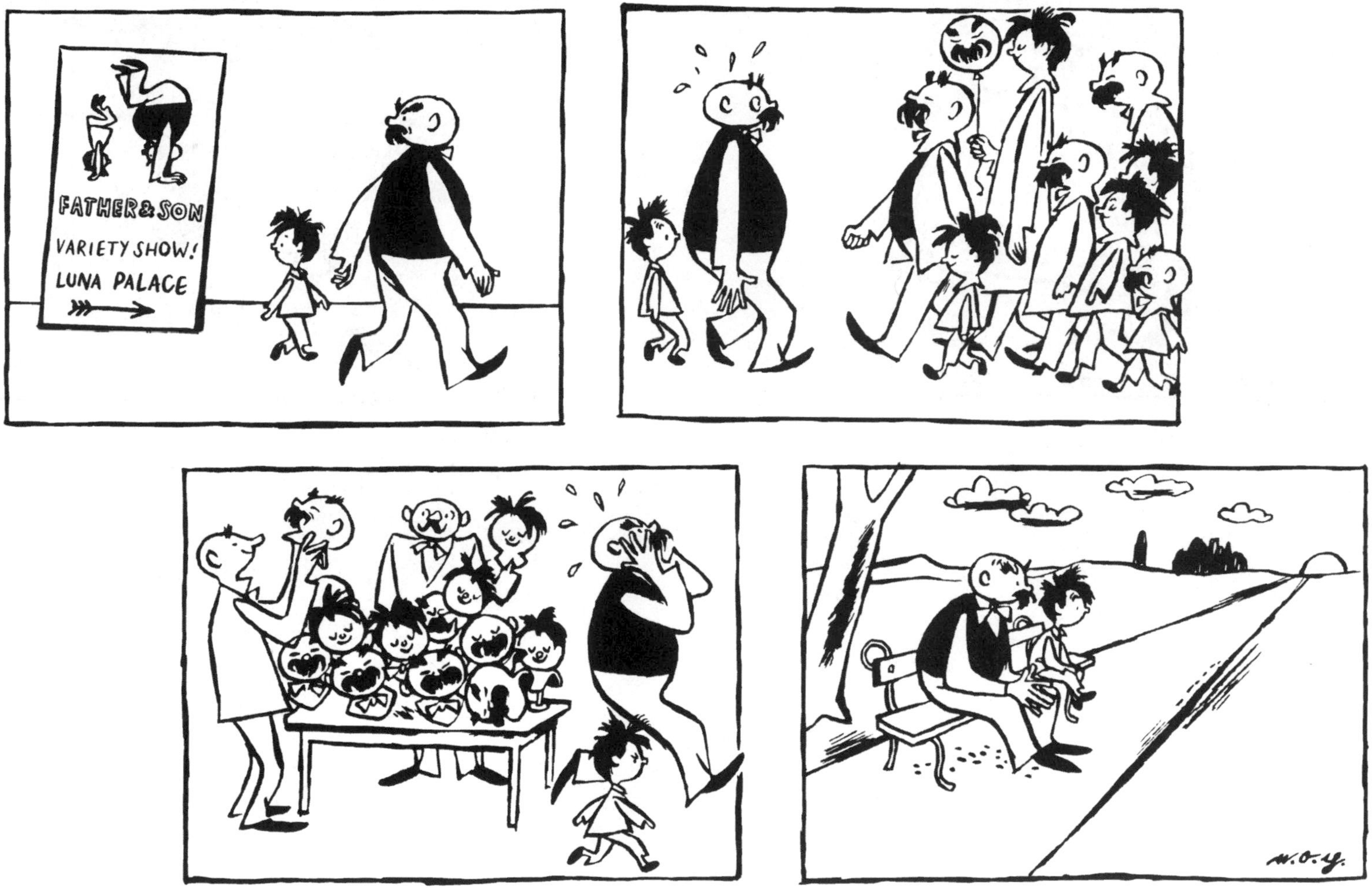
FATHER & SON
VARIETY SHOW!
LUNA PALACE

The other side of fame

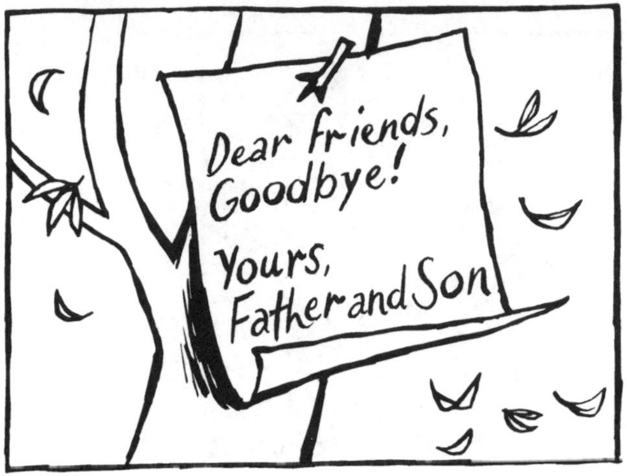
Dear friends,
Goodbye!
Yours,
Father and Son

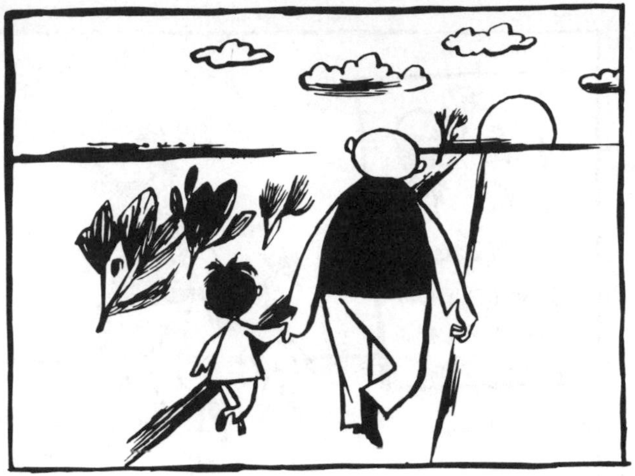

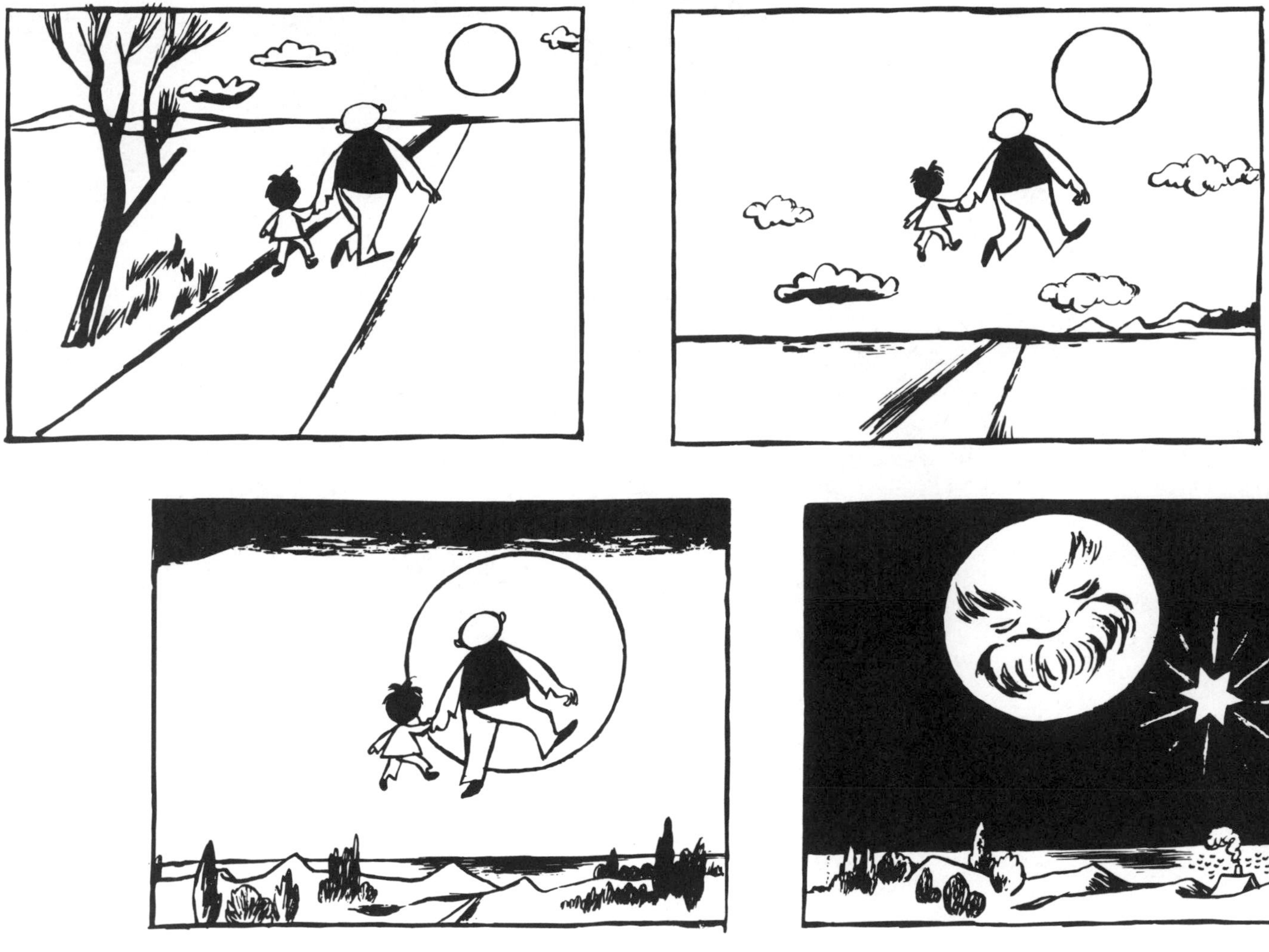

Farewell

About E. O. Plauen

Adapted from the afterword by Elke Schulze to Vater und Sohn *(Stuttgart: Reclam, 2015)*

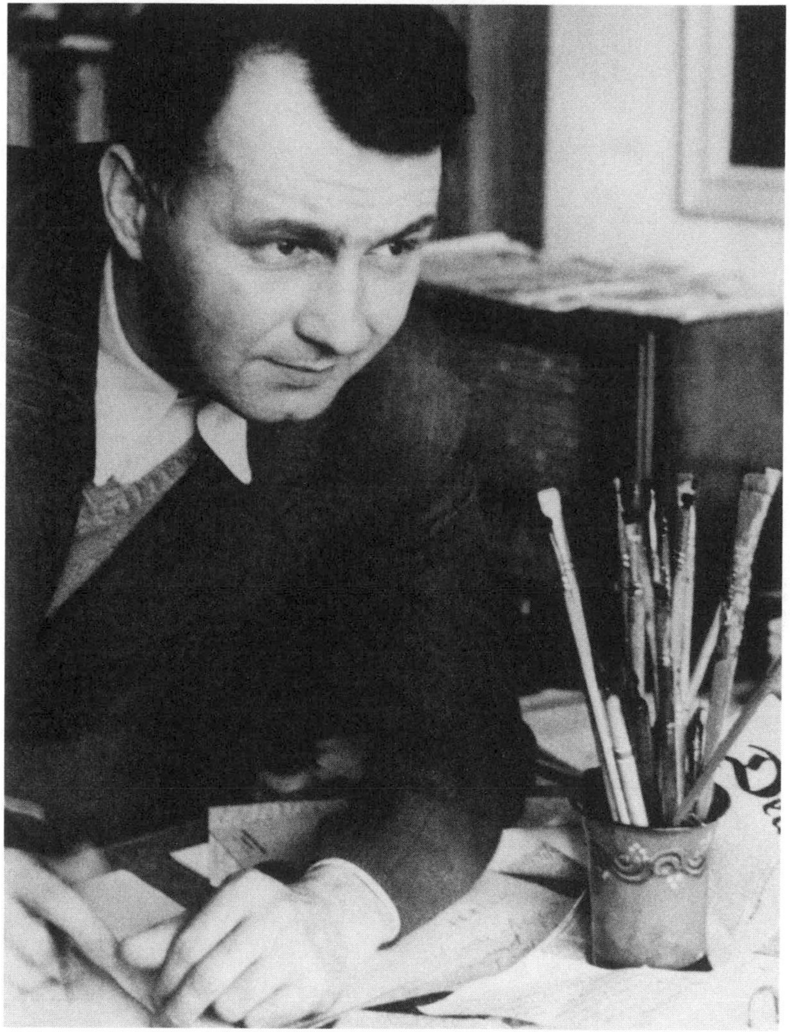

The carefree world of *Father and Son* gives little hint of the fate that would be suffered by its creator. After Erich Ohser, who, as E. O. Plauen, had become world-famous for his comic strips, was driven to take his own life, his friend Erich Kästner wrote: "We're going to mourn him by celebrating his drawings." Ohser was a passionate graphic artist whose versatile talent spanned many techniques: pencil, India ink, writing ink, watercolor, and colored pencil. Along with his journalistic cartoons and illustrations is a large body of work ranging from freehand portraits and landscapes to nudes and studies of people observed in cafés.

Born in Vogtland in 1903, he spent his childhood and youth in the newly prosperous industrial town of Plauen. Here, following his father's wishes, he studied to be a locksmith; for the

rest of his life he would recall this period as drudgery. The town paid particular attention to the cultivation and advancement of drawing—this specialty was related to the international success of "Plauen lace," a brand name covering a range of openwork textiles. Ohser's talent was recognized early; encouraged by his teachers, he made the move to Leipzig in 1920, and soon became a confident and successful student. He was awarded a scholarship and had his first one-man show in Plauen.

He was tall, heavy-set, and hard of hearing. Those close to him described him as humorous, awkward, curmudgeonly. The author Hans Fallada speaks of "an elephant who could walk a tightrope."

In Leipzig Ohser met the writer Erich Kästner, and a productive friendship and collaboration developed between them. While Ohser studied at the well-respected Akademie für graphische Künste und Buchgewerbe, and Kästner established himself as a newspaper wit, they achieved their first joint success. Even as a student Ohser gained recognition as a book illustrator and newspaper cartoonist. He contributed drawings to Kästner's articles and books: three of Kästner's early poetry collections appeared with illustrations and cover designs by Ohser.

Ohser also met the newspaper editor Erich Knauf, who published both Kästner's writings and Ohser's drawings. As an influential journalist and poet, Knauf became a formative voice in the Weimar Republic. Erich Ohser, Erich Kästner, and Erich Knauf were united in their world view and in their aesthetic convictions. All three preferred economy of form and brevity of wit. Their eye was radically modern and unsentimental, with a severely analytical perspective on the contemporary—expressed graphically in Ohser's case. At the Leipziger Akademie, Ohser had experimented with all the genres and techniques of drawing. He soon developed a signature style, which varied with the subject: from the emphatically artless, scratchy line of his caricatures and illustrations to his more ingratiating cartoons and comics, from the color of a few exploratory drawings to the rigorous black-and-white of his unbound sheets.

Following their initial successes, the "three Erichs" relocated to Berlin at the end of the 1920s. If Leipzig was a literary town, Berlin was a newspaper town, and

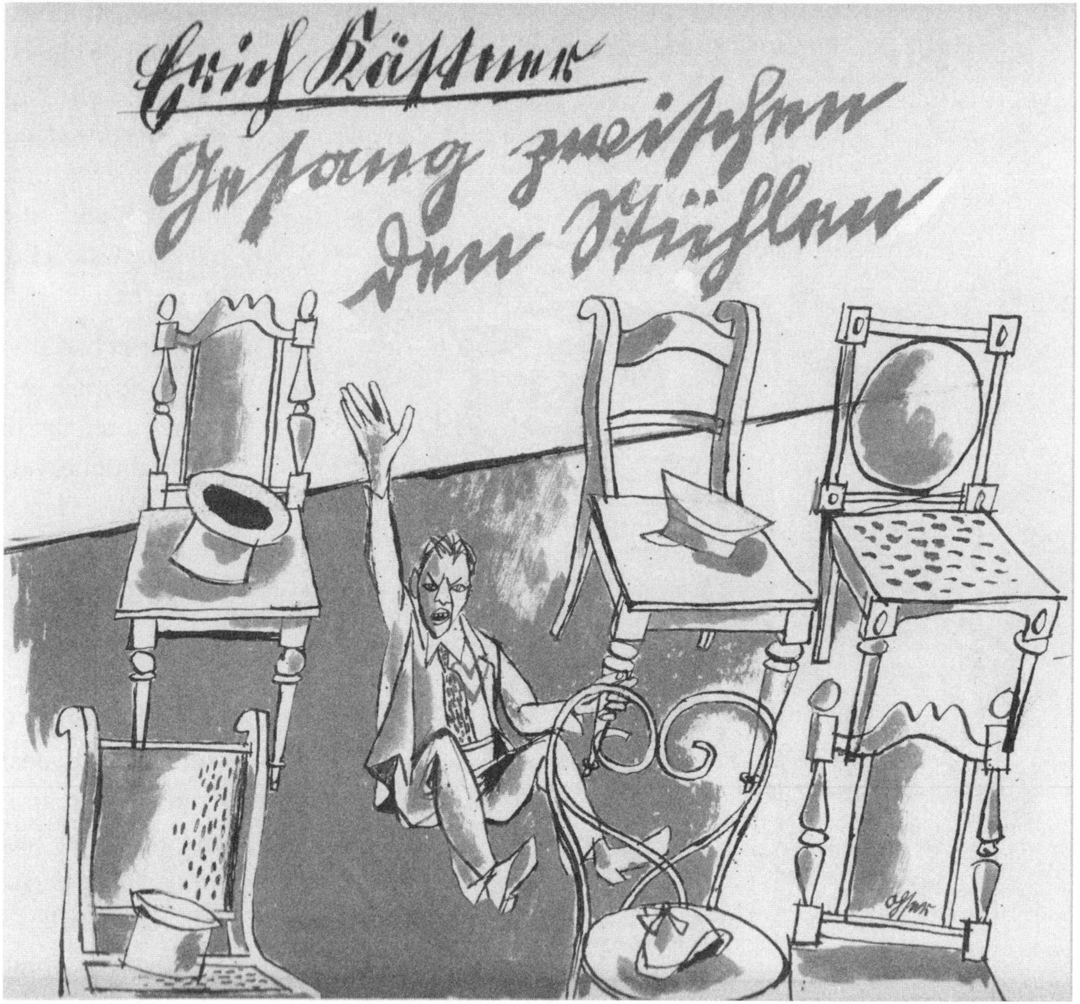
Erich Kästner
Gesang zwischen den Stühlen
Ohser
Illustration for *Gesang zwischen den Stühlen* (Song Between Two Stools), circa 1932

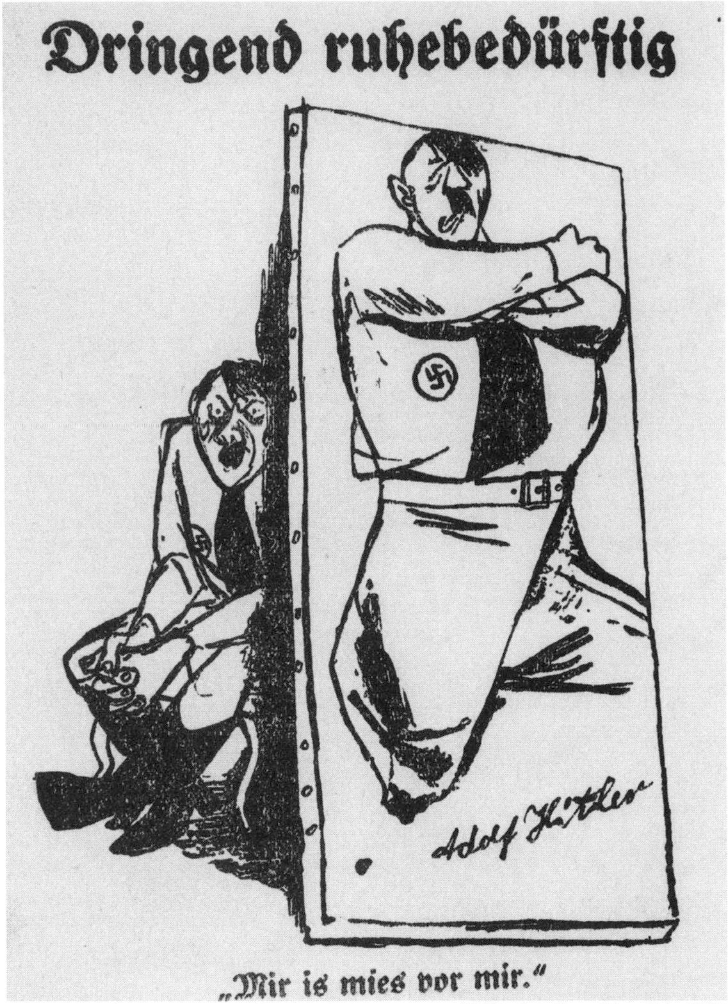
Dringend ruhebedürftig
Adolf Hitler
„Mir is mies vor mir."
Caricature from *Vorwärts*, 1932

it became their stage and artistic home—for Knauf and Ohser it would be the last. Knauf's great panache and fresh ideas as the new editor of the publishing house Büchergilde Gutenberg led to its flowering; Ohser became an important cartoonist and illustrator for him. Ohser's illustrations for the popular Russian humorist and satirist Mikhail Zoshchenko's *Die Stiefel des Zaren* (The Czar's Boots) in 1930 were received with particular enthusiasm.

Ohser had studied the great traditions of European graphics and caricature. Adapting these inspirations to his own style, he earned a reputation as a caricaturist long before the artistic and political upheavals of his time created the necessity for his pen name, E. O. Plauen. An alert observer, he was bitingly critical of the excesses of political extremism in the Weimar Republic.

Kästner's fourth volume of poetry, *Gesang zwischen den Stühlen* (Song Between Two Stools), appeared in 1932 with Ohser's design, and caused a nationwide sensation, as the previous books had done. On the cover, a Biblical figure "crying in the wilderness" appears as a tragicomic hero. The artist sits between empty chairs, an anti-hero literally caught between affiliations, and addresses his warning "song" directly to his public. This sorry singer personifies skepticism about the effect and the effectiveness of art—as well as the defiant stance, both artistic and personal, that Kästner and Ohser adopted toward the Nazis, one year before they took power.

Ohser was particularly aggressive in using his skills as an artist against the emerging National Socialists. In his drawings he exposed the megalomania of Hitler and Goebbels and depicted their cohorts as gangs of dull-witted thugs, employing all the weapons of caricature: exaggeration and distortion, one-sided emphasis and intentional grotesquerie. The blunt visual language he developed for this purpose is parsimonious but effective. The originals of these caricatures, many of them published in *Vorwärts*, do not survive; Knauf and Ohser are said to have burned them in the spring of 1933 for fear of persecution.

Their concern was not unjustified. With the rise of the Nazis, the "three Erichs" all had to make compromises in order to stay in Germany and survive. By this time Ohser had a family: he married his one-time fellow student, Marigard Bantzer (herself an artist and children's book illustrator), in December 1931. Their marriage was soon followed by the birth of their son, Christian.

After Hitler took power 1933, Ohser's ridicule of the Nazis made it almost impossible for him to find work. Thus it was a stroke of luck when the editor of the *Berliner Illustrirte Zeitung* asked him for ideas for a comic strip. Ohser's proposal, a strip about the day-to-day adventures of a good-natured father and his imaginative and unruly son, won him over. Ohser's well-known and canny new editor was able to pull strings at the Propaganda

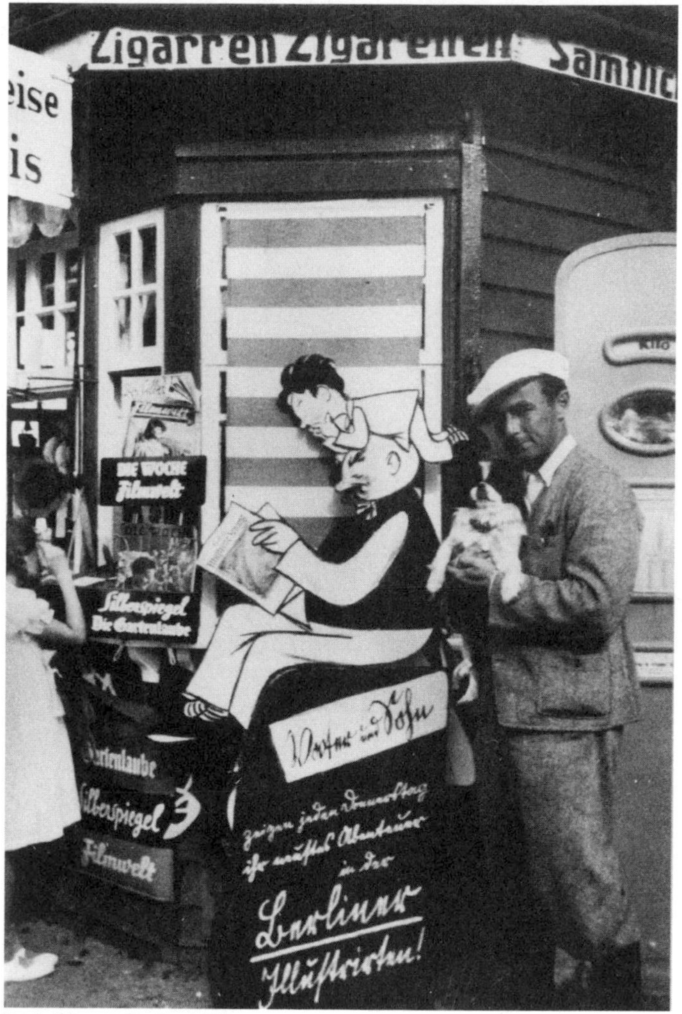
Zigarren
DIE WOCHE
Silberspiegel
Die Gartenlaube
Filmwelt
Vater und Sohn
Berliner
Illustrirten!

Erich Kästner, Berlin, 1930s

Self-portrait, circa 1925

Ministry allowing him to work—as long as he used a pseudonym, and worked only on nonpolitical newspaper comics. Ohser, who was not only a great inventor of gags and funny stories but also liked to play with language and dialect, remembered his Vogtland beginnings: Erich Ohser from Plauen became "E. O. Plauen." Though this pen name was originally intended simply as a safety measure, it became so popular that the artist's real name was practically forgotten.

The strips that Ohser delivered every week between 1934 and 1937 quickly won him an audience of millions and brought him financial success and prominence. Father and Son were not superheroes, but rather, as a contemporary critic remarked, "circus acrobats of life," inhabiting a humane utopia. *Father and Son* made its creator famous during his time, but he was unable to avoid official appropriation: *Father and Son* was used to advertise the Nazis' annual *Winterhilfswerk* charity drive. Similarly, the marketing of Ohser's characters was sometimes a frustration to him, a situation he referenced in the strip as it wound down. Ohser's creations were duplicated, imitated, took on an uncontrollable life of their own. Father and Son, like their creator, could not escape the evils that beset them.

He ended the strip in 1937, but kept the pseudonym and continued to work on cartoons, caricatures, and illustration. With his subtle humor and lighthearted pen he addressed the entire range of issues covered in the illustrated magazines—

sports, new technology, sex roles, celebrities—striking his own idiosyncratic note.

In 1940 he was given the opportunity to work for Joseph Goebbels's newly launched newspaper *Das Reich*. Ohser eventually accepted—in part because, with the outbreak of World War II, employment at Goebbels's paper ensured he would not be drafted. So Ohser drew political caricatures of the enemies of the Reich, while still trying to differentiate between the Nazi regime and his beloved Germany. Privately steadfast in detesting National Socialism and increasingly disillusioned about the war, Ohser was walking a fraying tightrope.

From Christian, we know that he and his father were regular visitors to the nearby Berlin Zoo. An exquisite group of animal studies bears witness to these excursions. Ohser usually drew from nature, concentrating entirely on each animal's form and characteristic way of moving; the surroundings are mostly ignored. He was more interested in an animal's particularity than in the details of its physical appearance. These drawings demonstrate an affection for animals, which sometimes become veritable characters. In the world of *Father and Son*, too, animals are always treated as friends and playmates. But, even more than animal forms, it was specifically the human figure that concerned Ohser.

Ohser felt that characterizations like "pretty" or "ugly"

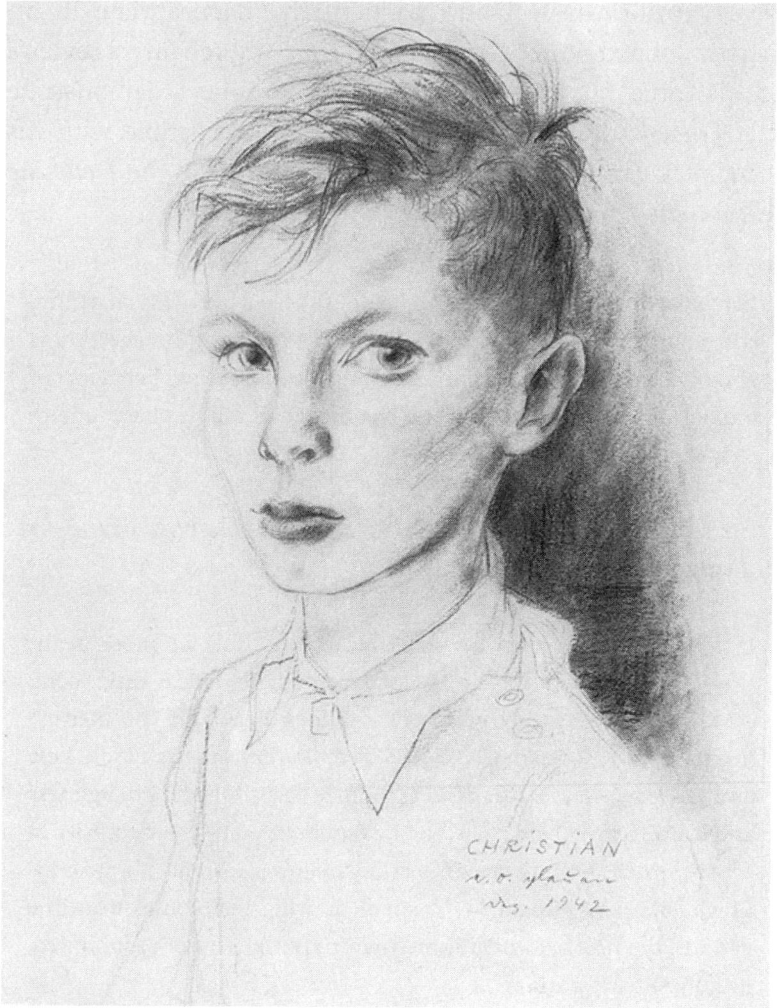
CHRISTIAN

Portrait of Christian, 1942

were a priori suspect and particularly inappropriate in an artistic context, if not plain wrong. The comprehensive reviews of his large one-man show in Berlin in 1942 demonstrate that Ohser's drawing found recognition compatible with his principles. For example, Werner Fiedler wrote in the *Deutsche Allgemeine Zeitung*:

Plauen's gift is to look as though he doesn't have one. This charming con man convinces us he has forgotten everything he ever knew about composition, anatomy, and the load-bearing behavior of biological structures, because he has moved to a new phase, one of innocence.

Ohser himself spoke out in 1943 in his *In Defense of the Art of Drawing*:

If you draw, the world becomes more beautiful, far more beautiful. Trees that used to be just scrub suddenly reveal their form. Animals that were ugly make you see their beauty. If you then go for a walk, you'll be amazed how different everything can look. Less and less is ugly if every day you recognize beautiful forms in ugliness and learn to love them.... Don't be bamboozled by the virtuosity of artists, which in many cases is terribly hollow.... Vanity always trips us up—it's very human.... A small drawing that comes from the eye and the heart is worth more than sixty square feet of inhibited, dishonest hack work.

Like the other two Erichs, Ohser considered himself a patriot and hoped the nightmare would soon end. Knauf and Kästner had found refuge working in film, also believing the era could be weathered. But the war was coming home to Germany's civilians—all three men lost their homes to bombings. Ohser and Knauf found shelter in a building on the edge of devastated Berlin. There, imagining they were safe, they aired their resentment and desperation in jokes about Hitler, Goebbels, and the hopeless war—and were denounced by their neighbors. They were arrested in the spring of 1944, and quickly sentenced to death. Ohser eluded his executioners and committed suicide the night before the hearing. He was just forty-one years old. His friend Erich Knauf was executed a month later. Kästner was the only one of the "three Erichs" to survive the Third Reich.

With pencil in hand had Erich Ohser explored his world, again and again finding the comic and grotesque aspects of any situation. Even after his tragic end, his art endures, as does the encouragement he gave us to rediscover his world and ours.

Details of original publication

7.	*Berliner Illustrirte*, 50, 1934	24–25.	*Berliner Illustrirte*, 12, 1935	40.	*Berliner Illustrirte*, 26, 1935
8.	*Berliner Illustrirte*, 51, 1934	26.	*Berliner Illustrirte*, 13, 1935	41.	*Berliner Illustrirte*, 28, 1935
9.	*Berliner Illustrirte*, 52, 1934	27.	*Berliner Illustrirte*, 14, 1935	42–43.	*Berliner Illustrirte*, 27, 1935
10.	*Berliner Illustrirte*, 1, 1935	28.	*Berliner Illustrirte*, 17, 1935	44.	*Berliner Illustrirte*, 29, 1935
11.	*Berliner Illustrirte*, 3, 1935	29.	*Berliner Illustrirte*, 16, 1935	45.	*Berliner Illustrirte*, 35, 1935
12.	*Berliner Illustrirte*, 2, 1935	30–31.	*Berliner Illustrirte*, 15, 1935	46–47.	*Berliner Illustrirte*, 30, 1935
13.	*Berliner Illustrirte*, 5, 1935	32.	*Berliner Illustrirte*, 18, 1935	48.	*Berliner Illustrirte*, 31, 1935
14–15.	*Berliner Illustrirte*, 4, 1935	33.	*Berliner Illustrirte*, 20, 1935	49.	*Berliner Illustrirte*, 33, 1935
16.	*Berliner Illustrirte*, 6, 1935	34.	*Berliner Illustrirte*, 22, 1935	50–51.	*Berliner Illustrirte*, 32, 1935
17.	*Berliner Illustrirte*, 7, 1935	35.	*Berliner Illustrirte*, 19, 1935	52–53.	*Berliner Illustrirte*, 36, 1935
18–19.	*Berliner Illustrirte*, 9, 1935	36.	*Berliner Illustrirte*, 21, 1935	54–55.	*Berliner Illustrirte*, 37, 1935
20.	*Berliner Illustrirte*, 8, 1935	37.	*Berliner Illustrirte*, 23, 1935	56.	*Berliner Illustrirte*, 34, 1935
21.	*Berliner Illustrirte*, 10, 1935	38.	*Berliner Illustrirte*, 24, 1935	57.	*Berliner Illustrirte*, 38, 1935
22–23.	*Berliner Illustrirte*, 11, 1935	39.	*Berliner Illustrirte*, 25, 1935	58.	*Berliner Illustrirte*, 42, 1935

59.	*Berliner Illustrirte*, 40, 1935	88.	Ùllstein vol. 1, p. 49	112–113.	*Berliner Illustrirte*, 19, 1936
60–61.	*Berliner Illustrirte*, 39, 1935	89.	*Berliner Illustrirte*, 51, 1935	114–115.	*Berliner Illustrirte*, 21, 1936
62–63.	*Berliner Illustrirte*, 41, 1935	90.	*Berliner Illustrirte*, 52, 1935	116.	*Berliner Illustrirte*, 22, 1936
64.	*Berliner Illustrirte*, 43, 1935	91.	*Berliner Illustrirte*, 1, 1936	117.	*Berliner Illustrirte*, 27, 1936
65.	*Berliner Illustrirte*, 46, 1935	92.	*Berliner Illustrirte*, 2, 1936	118–119.	*Berliner Illustrirte*, 23, 1936
66–67.	*Berliner Illustrirte*, 44, 1935	93.	*Berliner Illustrirte*, 3, 1936	120–121.	*Berliner Illustrirte*, 24, 1936
68–69.	*Berliner Illustrirte*, 47, 1935	94–95.	*Berliner Illustrirte*, 4, 1936	122.	*Berliner Illustrirte*, 25, 1936
70.	*Berliner Illustrirte*, 48, 1935	96.	*Berliner Illustrirte*, 5, 1936	123.	*Berliner Illustrirte*, 26, 1936
71.	*Berliner Illustrirte*, 49, 1935	97.	*Berliner Illustrirte*, 6, 1936	124.	*Berliner Illustrirte*, 28, 1936
72–73.	*Berliner Illustrirte*, 50, 1935	98–99.	*Berliner Illustrirte*, 7, 1936	125.	*Berliner Illustrirte*, 29, 1936
74–75.	*Vater und Sohn* vol. 1 (Ullstein, 1935), p. 1	100.	*Berliner Illustrirte*, 8, 1936	126–127.	*Berliner Illustrirte*, 31, 1936
76.	Ullstein vol. 1, p. 3	101.	*Berliner Illustrirte*, 11, 1936	128–129.	*Berliner Illustrirte*, 30, 1936
77.	Ullstein vol. 1, p. 10	102.	*Berliner Illustrirte*, 10, 1936	130–131.	*Berliner Illustrirte*, 34, 1936
78–79.	Ullstein vol. 1, p. 17	103.	*Berliner Illustrirte*, 12, 1936	132.	*Berliner Illustrirte*, 32, 1936
80–81.	Ullstein vol. 1, p. 19	104–105.	*Berliner Illustrirte*, 15, 1936	133.	*Berliner Illustrirte*, 35, 1936
82.	Ullstein vol. 1, p. 20	106–107.	*Berliner Illustrirte*, 16, 1936	134–135.	*Berliner Illustrirte*, 36, 1936
83.	Ullstein vol. 1, p. 26	108.	*Berliner Illustrirte*, 14, 1936	136–137.	*Berliner Illustrirte*, 38, 1936
84–85.	Ullstein vol. 1, p. 40	109.	*Berliner Illustrirte*, 17, 1936	138–139.	*Berliner Illustrirte*, 39, 1936
86–87.	Ullstein vol. 1, p. 46	110.	*Berliner Illustrirte*, 18, 1936	140–141.	*Berliner Illustrirte*, 40, 1936
		111.	*Berliner Illustrirte*, 20, 1936	142.	*Berliner Illustrirte*, 37, 1936

143. *Berliner Illustrirte*, 42, 1936

144–145. *Berliner Illustrirte*, 43, 1936

146. *Berliner Illustrirte*, 44, 1936

147. *Berliner Illustrirte*, 46, 1936

148–149. *Vater und Sohn* vol. 2 (Ullstein, 1936), p. 13

150. Ullstein vol. 2, p. 15

151. Ullstein vol. 2, p. 19

152–153. Ullstein vol. 2, p. 16

154–155. Ullstein vol. 2, p. 18

156. Ullstein vol. 2, p. 14

157. Ullstein vol. 2, p. 20

158–159. Ullstein vol. 2, p. 21

160–161. Ullstein vol. 2, p. 33

162. Ullstein vol. 2, p. 39

163. Ullstein vol. 2, p. 23

164–165. *Berliner Illustrirte*, 47, 1936

166–167. *Berliner Illustrirte*, 48, 1936

168–169. *Berliner Illustrirte*, 51, 1936

170–171. *Berliner Illustrirte*, 52, 1936

172–173. *Berliner Illustrirte*, 49, 1936

174–175. *Berliner Illustrirte*, 53, 1936

176–177. *Berliner Illustrirte*, 1, 1937

178. *Berliner Illustrirte*, 50, 1936

179. *Berliner Illustrirte*, 6, 1937

180. *Berliner Illustrirte*, 2, 1937

181. *Berliner Illustrirte*, 3, 1937

182–183. *Berliner Illustrirte*, 4, 1937

184–185. *Berliner Illustrirte*, 5, 1937

186–187. *Berliner Illustrirte*, 7, 1937

188–189. *Berliner Illustrirte*, 8, 1937

190–191. *Berliner Illustrirte*, 9, 1937

192–193. *Berliner Illustrirte*, 10, 1937

194. *Berliner Illustrirte*, 11, 1937

195. *Berliner Illustrirte*, 13, 1937

196–197. *Berliner Illustrirte*, 12, 1937

198–199. *Berliner Illustrirte*, 14, 1937

200–201. *Berliner Illustrirte*, 16, 1937

202. *Berliner Illustrirte*, 15, 1937

203. *Berliner Illustrirte*, 17, 1937

204–205. *Berliner Illustrirte*, 19, 1937

206. *Berliner Illustrirte*, 18, 1937

207. *Berliner Illustrirte*, 20, 1937

208–209. *Berliner Illustrirte*, 21, 1937

210. *Berliner Illustrirte*, 22, 1937

211. *Vater und Sohn* vol. 3 (Ullstein, 1938), p. 19

212–213. *Berliner Illustrirte*, 23, 1937

214–215. Ullstein vol. 3, p. 20

216-217. *Berliner Illustrirte*, 24, 1937

218. *Berliner Illustrirte*, 25, 1937

219. *Berliner Illustrirte*, 26, 1937

220. *Berliner Illustrirte*, 27, 1937

221. *Berliner Illustrirte*, 30, 1937

222–223. *Berliner Illustrirte*, 28, 1937

224–225. *Berliner Illustrirte*, 29, 1937

226–227. *Berliner Illustrirte*, 31, 1937

228–229. *Berliner Illustrirte*, 32, 1937

230. *Berliner Illustrirte*, 33, 1937

231. *Berliner Illustrirte*, 34, 1937

232–233.   *Berliner Illustrirte*, 35, 1937

234.   *Berliner Illustrirte*, 36, 1937

235.   *Berliner Illustrirte*, 41, 1937

236–237.   *Berliner Illustrirte*, 37, 1937

238–239.   *Berliner Illustrirte*, 38, 1937

240–241.   *Berliner Illustrirte*, 39, 1937

242–243.   *Berliner Illustrirte*, 40, 1937

244.   *Berliner Illustrirte*, 42, 1937

245.   *Berliner Illustrirte*, 43, 1937

246.   *Berliner Illustrirte*, 44, 1937

247.   Ullstein vol. 3, p. 42

248–249.   *Berliner Illustrirte*, 45, 1937

250–251.   *Vater und Sohn* (Südverlag, 1982), p. 166

252–253.   Ullstein vol. 3, p. 39

254–255.   *Vater und Sohn* (Südverlag, 1952), p. 167

256.   Ullstein vol. 3, p. 36

257.   *Berliner Illustrirte*, 46, 1938

258.   *Berliner Illustrirte*, 47, 1937

259.   Ullstein vol. 3, p. 48

260.   *700 Years of Berlin*, postcard, 1937

261.   *Südkurier*, 1953

262–263.   *700 Years of Berlin*, postcard, 1937

264–265.   *700 Years of Berlin*, postcard, 1937

266–267.   *700 Years of Berlin*, postcard, 1937

268–269.   Südverlag (1982), p. 201

270.   *700 Years of Berlin*, postcard, 1937

271.   Südverlag (1982), p. 201

272.   Ullstein vol. 3, p. 12

273.   *700 Years of Berlin*, postcard, 1937

274–275.   *Südkurier*, 1953

276–277.   *Südkurier*, 1953

278–279.   *Südkurier*, 1952

280.   *Südkurier*, 1952

281.   Unknown

282–283.   Ullstein vol. 3, p. 49

284–285.   *Berliner Illustrirte*, 49, 1937

ALSO AVAILABLE
FROM NEW YORK REVIEW COMICS

AGONY
Mark Beyer

PEPLUM
Blutch

ALMOST COMPLETELY BAXTER
Glen Baxter

WHAT AM I DOING HERE?
Abner Dean

SOFT CITY
Pushwagner

PRETENDING IS LYING
Dominique Goblet